The Russian Far East
and
Pacific Asia

The Russian Far East
and
Pacific Asia

UNFULFILLED POTENTIAL

Edited by
Michael J. Bradshaw

LONDON AND NEW YORK

First Published in 2001
by Curzon Press

This edition published 2012 by Routledge
2 Park Square, Milton Park, Abingdon, Oxfordshire OX14 4RN
711 Third Avenue, New York, NY 10017
Routledge is an imprint of the Taylor & Francis Group, an informa business

Editorial Matter © 2001 Michael J. Bradshaw

Typeset in Baskerville by LaserScript Ltd, Mitcham, Surrey

British Library Cataloguing in Publication Data
A catalogue record of this book is available from the British Library

Library of Congress Cataloguing in Publication Data
A catalogue record for this book has been requested

ISBN 0–7007–1417–0

Contents

List of Tables

List of Figures

Preface

This book, and the project on which it is based, have been a number of years in the making. The UK's Economic and Social Research Council's Research Programme on Pacific Asia provided the research grant that underlies the project. The programme ran from 1995 to 1999. The programme's coordinator was the late Gerry Segal and it is down to his interest and enthusiasm that a project on the Russian Far East was included in the programme. The initial intent of the project was to assess whether or not the Russian Far East had the potential to develop as a resource-supplying region for the economically vibrant, but resource-poor, economies of Pacific-Asia, but more particularly Northeast Asia. The method employed involved detailed research on the regional economic development of the Russian Far East and patterns of foreign trade and investment. It also involved research visits to key potential markets in the form of Japan, Korea and China (the latter being conducted by David Kerr). Finally, the projects assessed the attitudes of possible competitors, principally the Pacific Northwest of the US and Australia. Much of the research 'from the outside looking in' benefited from cooperation with scholars and institutions in those countries. Some of those people have contributed to this book. The project also benefited from a team of post-doctoral research fellows based at the School of Geography at the University of Birmingham. Nick Lynn worked on the initial assessment of the prospects for resource-based development in the Russian Far East. Rahul Moogdal continued this work, focusing on the mining industry and Russian Far East-Japan economic relations. Finally, Warwick Murray conducted an analysis of patterns of production and trade in the resource industries of the Asia-Pacific Region. I thank them for their contributions. I would also like to thank all of my colleagues from the project team who have written chapters for this book. We worked together through difficult times, the Asian Financial Crisis, then the Russian Financial Crisis. A project seminar took place in September 1998 at the Royal Institute of International Affairs in London. Thanks are due to our host Dr Roy Allison of the Russia and Eurasia Programme at Chatham house. This seminar proved an invaluable opportunity to take stock of the situation.

Various chapters underwent constant revision as the economic and political landscape changed. Many of the authors faced the additional challenge of writing in a language that was not their native tongue. I thank them for that endeavour and hope that they are not too alarmed with the editorial changes that I have made. Because of the geographical spread of the contributors, I chose to exercise a rather dictatorial and highly centralised approach to the production process. Any errors and oversights that remain are the responsibility of the Editor. The complexity of the manuscript and the fact that the book's topic has been a moving target proved a challenge when finding a publisher. I am indebted to Malcom Campell and Peter Sowden at Curzon Press Ltd for taking on the project. I would also like to thank David McCarthy and his colleagues at Laserscript for handling the manuscript. I hope that all involved in the project will agree that the book has been worth the wait. Much has been published on political aspects of the Russian Far East and its relationships with its neighbours, but very little has been said about the economic dimensions of this relationship. After ten years of economic transition, this book serves as a benchmark of the situation in the Russian Far East and the problems that have left its potential unfulfilled. Lastly, but by no means least, I would like to thank Sally for her constant support.

Mike Bradshaw
Leicester
January 2001

Contributors

Professor Michael Bradshaw, Department of Geography, University of Leicester, UK.

Timothy Heleniak, The World Bank, Washington D.C., US.

Dr Vladimir Ivanov, Economic Research Institute for Northeast Asia, Niigata, Japan.

David Kerr, Institute of Central and East European Studies, University of Glasgow, Scotland, UK.

Dr Chung-Bae Lee, Department of Foreign Trade, Chung-Ang University, Seoul, South Korea.

Dr Nicholas Lynn, Department of Geography, University of Edinburgh, UK.

David Lockwood, Flinders University of South Australia, Australia.

Dr Elisa Miller, President, Russian Far East Advisory Group LLC, Seattle, US.

Professor Pavel Minakir, Director, Institute of Economics, Khabarovsk, Russia.

Professor Robert North, Department of Geography, University of British Columbia, Vancouver, Canada.

Professor Kazuo Ogawa, Director General, Japan Association for Trade with Russia and Central-Eastern Europe, Tokyo, Japan.

Dr Keun-Wook Paik, The Royal Institute of International Affairs, London, UK.

Professor Judith Thornton, Department of Economics, University of Washington, Seattle, US.

Dr Vladimir Tikomirov, Contemporary European Research Centre, University of Melbourne, Victoria, Australia.

Dr Tamara Troyakova, Institute of History, Vladivostok, Russia.

Chapter 1

The Russian Far East: An Introduction

Michael J. Bradshaw

This book has its origins in a research project entitled 'The Russian Far East: Resource Frontier for the Pacific Century?' The project was funded by the UK's Economic and Social Research Council as part of a major research programme on Pacific Asia.[1] The aim of the Far East project was twofold:

- To present a rigorous appraisal of the present and potential future role of the Russian Far East as a resource-supplying region for the core economies of Pacific Asia; and
- To provide a comprehensive and critical assessment of the role of export activity and foreign investment in promoting the regional economic development of the Russian Far East.

That question mark remains of relevance, but the whole notion of the 21st Century being the 'Pacific Century' has been cast in doubt by the Asian financial crisis of 1997. In fact, this research project has been crisis ridden, no sooner had the crisis in Asia dampened demand for resources and quashed any desire to invest in high-risk locations like the RFE; then the Russian financial crisis struck in August 1998. The associated rouble devaluation made imports from Asia-Pacific too costly for the impoverished consumer in the RFE. Thus, in the space of a year or so the RFE was been dealt a 'double whammy'. This book would have been published sooner had it not been the need to re-evaluate the prospects for the RFE in light of these events. The original intention had been to name the book after the project. As the project proceeded it became clear that the notion of the RFE as a resource frontier for the Pacific Century was both premature and problematic. The intention had always been to present a *critical* assessment of the simplistic argument that there was a 'natural fit' between the RFE and Pacific Asia (hereafter APR); the former had natural resources, but lacked the capital

1

and technology to develop them; while the latter lacked natural resource, but had a surplus of capital and access to the necessary technology. This book explains why this expectation has not been realised. It is the case that the RFE has substantial *potential* natural resource wealth, but for the reasons explained in the following chapters, that potential remains largely unfulfilled.

For a region that is of limited economic significance, the RFE and its relations with APR have attracted a great deal of interest from foreign scholars. During the 1990s geographers, economists, historians and political scientists have published a host of books on the region. It is not my intent to provide a comprehensive review, but some of the more recent contributions include Akha (1997), Blank and Rubinstein (1997), Chung and Chung (1994), Harada (1997), Ivanov and Smith (1999), Kotkin and Wolff (1995), Rogers (1990), Rozman et al (1999) and Valencia (1995). Like the current book, with one exception, these are all edited collections that bring together scholars from the region elsewhere. A casual review their contents reveals the 'usual suspects', some of whom are included in this volume. A closer inspection of the literature shows a concentration on the external perceptions and relations of the RFE and Russia's place in Asia-Pacific and, more specially Northeast Asia. At the same time the emphasis is primarily on international relations. The internal situation in the RFE is relatively neglected and there is a primacy of politics over economics. It is that research gap that this book seeks to fill by offering both an analysis of the internal situation in the RFE and an assessment of its foreign economic relations with its key trading partners. The two are combined to provide a critical evaluation of why the RFE has failed to make the most of its resource wealth and proximity to export markets to promote an export-oriented and resource-based trajectory out of the transitional recession that followed the liberalisation of the Russian economy.

STRUCTURE OF THE BOOK

The book is comprised four sections. The first section examines the internal situation in the RFE. The sections start by considering the supposed advantages and disadvantages of the pursuit of resource-based economic development. This is then followed by an assessment of the political and economic situation in the RFE by scholars from the region itself. The next chapter then looks at the state of the region's transportation infrastructure, essential for enabling resource development and delivering goods to export markets. There then follows an assessment of the legal and management systems related to resource development in the Russian Federation and in the key resource sectors of the Far East. The section concludes with an analysis of the demographic situation, the region's declining population is a clear signal of the economic stress that it has suffered.

The second section places the RFE in multilateral perspective. The first chapter considers the problems and prospects for greater economic integration in

Northeast Asia. Then plans for energy development and cooperation are examined. The third section of the book examines trade relations with the countries of greatest significance to he RFE. China represents the largest potential markets, while Japan and South Korea are both markets and potential sources of capital investment. The United States is both a source of capital and technology and also a competitor. Finally, Australia is both a trading partner and a major competitor. All of these country case studies illustrate the complex interplay between politics and economics in shaping relations between the RFE and APR. They also reveal a common set of barriers that have hindered foreign investment and reduced the level of cooperation.

The final section assesses the prospects for the new millennium through the presentation of three possible scenarios for the future development of the RFE and its relations with the APR.

THE RUSSIAN FAR EAST DEFINED[2]

The subject of this book is the Russian Far East (RFE). The RFE has no legal administrative status in the Russian Federation. The region of the RFE, as defined in *Table 1.1* and illustrated in *Figure 1.1*, has its origins in a system of

Table 1.1 Characteristics of the Administrative Regions of the Russian Far East

	Territory '000 Sq. Km	Total Population ('000s) 1st Jan 1997	Population Density Persons Per Sq. Km	Regional Capital	Per cent of population living in urban areas
Russia	107075.4	14750	8.6		73.1
RFE	6215.9	7421	1.2		75.7
Sakha (Yakutia)	3103.2	1016	0.3	Yakutsk	64.3
Jewish aut. oblast	36.0	207	5.7	Birobidzhan	67.5
Chukotka aut. okrug	737.7	85	0.1	Anadyr	69.8
Primorskii krai	165.9	2236	13.5	Vladivostok	78.1
Khabarovsk krai	788.6	1557	2.0	Khabarovsk	80.5
Amur oblast	363.7	1031	2.8	Blagoveshchensk	64.5
Kamchatka oblast	472.3	404	0.9	Petropavlovsk-Kamchatskii	80.8
Inc. Koryak aut. Okrug	301.5	32	0.1	Palana	24.9
Magadan oblast	461.4	251	0.6	Magadan	90.0
Sakhalin oblast	87.1	634	7.3	Yuzhno-Sakhalinsk	86.1

Source: Goskomstat Rossii (1997), *Demographic Yearbook of Russia, 1997*, Moscow: Goskomstat, pp. 15–29.

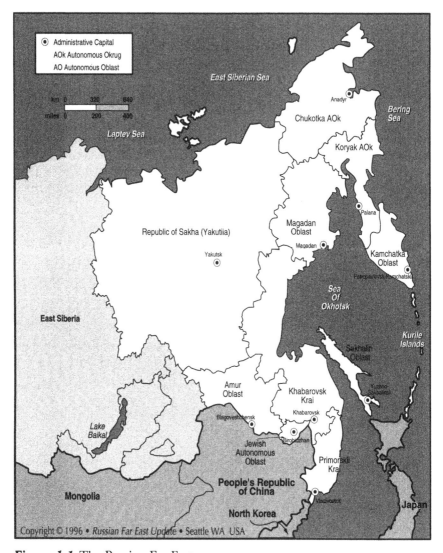

Figure 1.1 The Russian Far East

economic planning regions devised by Gosplan USSR. These regions were used for strategic long-term planning during the Soviet period. Nonetheless, these regions have come to take on an identity of their own. Politicians, planners and the population of Russia also recognise these regions and they have served as the focus for the development of inter-regional economic associations, such as the Inter-regional Association for Economic Cooperation of Subjects of the Federation of the Far East and Transbaikal (previously the Far Eastern Economic

Association). The RFE is composed of ten separate administrative units, or federal subjects, that are recognised by the Federal Constitution; however, those ten units occupy varying positions within Russia's Federal structure. These ten regions account for 36.4 per cent of the territory of the Russian Federation, 5.1 per cent of its population and, in 1995, and 5.8 per cent of Russia's gross regional product.

Although the Russian Constitution deems all of federal subjects to be equal, the reality is somewhat different. The republics within the federation, whose name reflects the existence of particular ethnic groups, have seized greater autonomy. Thus, the Republic of Sakha (Yakutia) has negotiated a special relationship with the Federal Government and has greater autonomy than the other regions within the RFE. The asymmetrical nature of Russian federalism also helps to explain the relative weakness of inter-regional alliances in Russia. For most regions, so far at least, the most important political and economic relationship is their relationship with Moscow. This explains why some of the lower order administrative units, which were previously sub-ordinate to an oblast or krai, have declared themselves to be independent units in their own right. Thus, the Chukotka autonomous okrug has separated from Magadan oblast and the Jewish autonomous oblast has separated from Khabarovsk krai. As autonomous units, which again relates to the presence of distinct ethnic groups, these regions are granted certain privileges not bestowed upon 'ordinary' oblasts and krais. For the purpose of the current analysis it is sufficient to recognise that the RFE is comprised of 10 administrative units, one of which is a republic. The real nature of any individual regions relationship with Moscow, and thus place in the federal hierarchy, is determined by bargaining between the centre and the regions. Numerous regions have signed 'power-sharing agreements' with Moscow that divide rights and responsibilities between the Federal Government and the regional administration. This makes it impossible to generalise about the true nature of centre-region relations in the RFE, or anywhere else in Russia for that matter.

If the internal structure of the RFE where not confusing enough, matters are further complicated by the fact that the Federal Government's Programme for the 'Economic and Social Development of the Far East and Transbaykal 1996–2005' refers to a region that is bigger than the conventional definition of the RFE. Three regions which are normally considered part of the East Siberian Economic Region, the Republic of Buryatia, Chita oblast and the Aga-Buryat autonomous okrug (which is subordinate to Chita) are included as the 'Transbaykal'. These larger region accounts 40.9 per cent of Russia's territory, but only 6.7 per cent of its population and 7 per cent of its gross regional product. This area, which is basically all of Russia east of Lake Baykal is sometimes referred to as Pacific Russia. Although it is a significant share of Russian territory and of considerable strategic significance, it is not at present a vital component of the Russian economy and is some considerable distance for the political and economic core of the country in European Russia. The current analysis focuses upon the administrative units of the RFE; however, the larger region of Pacific Russia, which may even include Irkutsk oblast, needs to considered in relation to federal policy. As we shall see, this is rather academic, the Federal Government cannot afford to implement its development programme anyway![3]

THE SOVIET LEGACY

Many of the economic problems that now face the RFE are a direct result of the priorities of Moscow during the Soviet period and the role that the region played in the centrally planned economy. To understand the current socio-economic situation it is therefore necessary to assess the impact of the Soviet legacy as this constrains what is possible today and in the near term.

The making of a resource periphery

The Soviet system produced a very 'narrow' economic structure in the RFE. The emphasis was upon resource development, principally for the needs of the national economy (*Table 1.2* compares the branch structure of industrial production in the RFE with that of Russia). The degree of economic specialisation was even more extreme in the northern regions, for example in Sakha and Magadan the mining industry has accounted for over 60 per cent of industrial production and this degree of specialisation has actually increased

Table 1.2 Branch Structure of Industrial Production in 1995

Branch	Russia	RFE	LQ
Electric Power Generation	13.5	19.3	1.4
Fuel	16.4	10.5	0.6
Ferrous Metals	9.1	0.5	0.1
Non-ferrous Metals	6.5	20.7	3.2
Chemical & Petrochemicals	7.5	0.7	0.1
Machine-building and Metal-working	17.9	8.5	0.5
Wood, Cellulose and Paper	5.1	5.4	1.1
Building Materials	4.8	4.0	0.8
Glass and Ceramic	0.3	0.2	0.7
Light	2.5	0.6	0.2
Food*	12.1	25.3	2.1
Flour grinding and mixed fodder	2.1	2.0	0.9

*Includes the fishing industry.
LQ = Location Quotient, a figure a greater than 1 indicates a level of specialisation above the national average.
Source: Goskomstat Rossii (1995) *Rossiyskiy Statisticheskiy Ezhegodnik*, Moscow: Goskomstat.

since the break up of the Soviet Union (Miller and Stephanopolous 1997: 122–23).

Because of the region's remoteness from the European core region, a great deal of economic effort was expended on transportation. Most of the machinery and equipment needed by the region's industries and the food and consumer goods required by the population were imported from the western regions of the Soviet Union. In the late Soviet period inshipments into the RFE exceed outshipments 1.8 times by value and 2.5 times by volume. The region imported 95 per cent of products of ferrous metallurgy, 80 per cent of those of the chemical industry, 70–80 per cent of light industry and over 50 per cent of machine-building products from elsewhere in the Soviet Union (Dienes 1990). Equally, the market for the region's industrial goods and food products (fish) was the western region of the country. This 'shuttle' of goods too and forth was possible because the Soviet system did not account for the cost of transportation

The geostrategic role of the RFE further aggravated the attitude of 'development regardless of cost'. The ports of Vladivostok and Petropavlovsk-Kamchatka, for example, were key to the Pacific Fleet and the Soviet Union's power projection into north-east Asia and the Pacific Ocean; the border regions with China was highly militarised as were the Kurile Islands (Northern Territories); the mining activities in the region (particularly in the far North) were crucial to maintaining self-sufficiency in strategic minerals and metals; and finally, the expansion of the Northern-Sea Route was seen as a key component of the effective occupation of the Arctic. All of these activities required the development of a substantial socio-economic infrastructure, which was way beyond the means of the region's economy to sustain. As Leslie Dienes noted (1982)

> This subordinate, dependent relationship with the rest of the country is shown even more clearly by the huge volume of interregional subsidy flowing into the Far East and Transbaykalia. Through the vast area east of Lake Baykal, a full third of the regional income utilized during the mid-1070s was subsidy from other regions of the country

Export-oriented development

Despite it geostrategic role, according to official statements, the RFE was just about the only region in the Soviet Union where the promotion of an export-based development strategy was pursued. Thus, during the 1970s and 80s the region was supposed to have benefited from expanded trade with the APR. The reality was somewhat different. In fact, most of Moscow's trade with the APR was economic support for client states such as Vietnam, Cambodia and Laos and involved commodities that were not produced in the RFE (Bradshaw 1988a). Thus, the RFE contributed less than a third of the Soviet Union's trade with the APR and most of that trade was with Japan. Added to which, Moscow continued to exercise central control over foreign trade. Only a small amount of local trade was permitted through *Dal'intorg.* The creation of a number of large-scale, long-term compensation agreements between Japan and the Soviet Union formed the centrepiece of this export-base strategy (Bradshaw 1988b). The resources of the RFE were mortgaged to finance the purchase of machinery and equipment for resource development. These agreements were important in developing the South Yakutian Coal Complex and in delineating the oil and gas deposits offshore of Sakhalin. They also financed the development of the Vostochnyy port at Nakhodka. In the forestry sector they resulted in exports of logs and woodchips, but did not promote the expansion of the forest products industry. Thus, these agreements helped establish the RFE's role as a potential supplier of natural resources to the Asia-Pacific. They also created the expectation that foreign governments (principally Japan) would finance large-scale, long-term resource development projects.

A dependent periphery

At the end of the Soviet period the RFE exhibited all the characteristics of a resource-periphery locked into a colonial relationship with the economic core of European Russia. It had a 'truncated' economic structure, heavily biased towards resource production and dependent upon the core for manufactured and consumer goods and required substantial financial assistance to maintain its socio-economic infrastructure. The region's manufacturing industry was oriented to the needs of the military-industrial complex and not the resource sector (Minakir and Freeze 1996: 13). Furthermore, that military activity demanded a level of infrastructure provision which the region could not support. Moscow provided substantial economic assistance because of the region's geostrategic significance and paid little attention to the long-term economic viability of the region's economy.

A recent study by the Australian Government's East Asian Analytical Unit (1996: 1) aptly describes the current plight of the RFE.

> For decades, Pacific Russia's economic growth was based largely on Moscow's desire to develop the region for defence and strategic reasons. A wide range of subsidies and other forms of economic support were provided by Moscow to develop industries and attract personnel to the region. When these supports were removed by reforms and the collapse of the USSR, Pacific Russia's economy was virtually cut adrift.

This book examines how the RFE has fared during the 1990s and identifies the problems that have hindered its desire to become a major resource-exporting to the APR as a means for dealing with the loss of economic support from Moscow.

NOTES

1 Professor Bradshaw would like to acknowledge funding provide by the UK Economic and Social Research Council, grant number: L324253005.
2 The remainder of this chapter is based on Bradshaw 1999: 1–8.
3 According to V.I. Ivanov et. al., in 1996 4.7 trillion roubles, about 13 per cent of the funds required by the programme, were allocated to its projects. In 1997 the Federal Government allocated a mere 1.034 trillion of the 40.5 trillion requested by the region *ERINA Report* (1997), 23, 39–40.

REFERENCES

Akha, T. (1997), *Politics and Economics in the Russian Far East: Changing Ties with Asia-Pacific*, London: Routledge. Blank, S.J. and Rubinstein, A.Z. (eds) (1997) *Imperial Decline: Russia's Changing Role in Asia*, Durham, North Caroline: Duke University Press.

Bradshaw, M.J. (1999) *The Russian Far East: Prospects for the New Millennium*, London: Russia and Eurasia Programme, The Royal Institute of International Affairs, Discussion Paper 80.

Bradshaw, M.J. (1988a) 'Soviet Asian-Pacific Trade and the Regional Development of the Soviet Far East', *Soviet Geography*, 29 (4), 367–393.

Bradshaw, M.J. (1988b), 'Trade and High Technology'. In R. Swearingen, (ed.) Siberia and the Far East: strategic dimensions in international perspective, Stanford: Hoover Institution Press, pp. 100–13.

Chung, I. Y. and Ching, E. (eds.) (1994), *Russian in the Far East and Pacific Region*, Seoul: The Sejong Institute.

Dienes, L (1990) 'Economic and Strategic Position of the Soviet Far East: development and prospect', in A. Rodgers, A. (ed.) *The Soviet Far East: Geographical Perspectives on Development*, London: Routledge, pp. 269–301.

Dienes, L. (1982) 'The Development of Siberian Regions: Economic Profiles, Income Flows and Strategies for Growth', *Soviet Geography*, 23 (4), 205–244.

East Asian Analytical Unit (1996) *Pacific Russia: Risks and Rewards*, Canberra: EAAU: Canberra.

Harada, C. (1997), *Russia and North-east Asia*, International Institute for Strategic Studies, London: Adelphi Paper 310.

Ivanov, V.I. and Smith, K.S. (eds) (1999) *Japan and Russia in Northeast Asia: Partners in the 21st Century*, New York: Praeger.

Kotkin, S. and Wolff, D. (eds.) (1995) *Rediscovering Russia in Asia*, Armonk, New York: M.E. Sharpe.

Miller, E. and Stefanopoulos, S. (eds.) (1997) *The Russian Far East: A Business Reference Guide* Seattle: Russian Far East Update.

Minakir, P.A. and Freeze, G.L. (1996) *The Russian Far East: An Economic Survey* (2nd Edition) Khabarovsk: RIOTP.

A. Rodgers, A. (ed.) (1990) *The Soviet Far East: Geographical Perspectives on Development*, London: Routledge.

Rozman, G., Nosov, M.G. and Watanabe, K. (eds) (1999) *Russia and East Asia: The 21st Century Security Environment*, Armonk, New York: M.E. Sharpe.

Valencia, M.J. (1995) *The Russian Far East in Transition: Opportunities for Regional Economic Cooperation*, Boulder, Colorado: Westview Press.

Chapter 2

Resource-based Development: What Chance for the Russian Far East?

Nicholas J. Lynn

INTRODUCTION

It has become common-place in economics and economic geography to emphasise the difficulties that 'developing' countries face if they are well-endowed in natural resources. The argument largely stems from the many studies which have shown the poor economic achievements of mineral economies (see Gelb 1988; Roemer 1985; Wheeler 1983). Richard Auty (1985, 1988, 1990, 1993), the greatest advocate of the 'resource-curse thesis', argues that inefficiencies are bred by the extraction of rents and their wasteful re-application, by the volatility of mineral prices in the world economy, and by the effects of 'Dutch disease' (the shrinkage of the agricultural sector and underdevelopment of the manufacturing sector in mineral economies).

At the same time, several recent analyses of Russia's economic collapse have also highlighted the important role played by resource industries. Gaddy and Ickes (1998), for example, argue that the key problem in the Russian economy is that it remains driven by resource industries. The bulk of value added continues to be produced in energy and other resource sectors. Large resource enterprises like Gazprom remain the most important producers of value in the economy, and in exchange for the rights to keep what they earn from exports Gazprom and others: 'pump value into the system by supplying gas without being paid for it. Arrears to Gazprom, which then lead to arrears for the government, are the primary way in which unprofitable activity is subsidised today in Russia' (Gaddy and Ickes 1998: 6).

The resource-curse approach has a number of important implications for understanding the economic development of the Russian Far East (RFE). Economists in the Far East and elsewhere have claimed that the natural resources of the region could fuel tremendous economic growth, especially as the RFE could potentially supply the mineral and energy requirements of the Asia-Pacific economies. In the USSR the natural resource wealth of Siberia and the Far East was largely mortgaged by the centre in exchange for foreign capital and technology (Bradshaw 1992; North 1978). With the regionalisation of foreign trade activity that has accompanied Soviet collapse and post-Soviet restructuring, the Far East is able to trade directly with the Asia-Pacific region and can benefit from its comparative advantage in natural resources (especially energy resources). However, the resource-curse thesis suggests that the development of the region's natural resource base might actually harm the prospects for 'sustainable' economic development in the region. Indeed, rather than seeing natural resource production as an engine for economic growth Auty, (1993: 10) argues that: 'the mineral sector should only be regarded as a bonus with which to promote competitive economic diversification rather than as the backbone of the economy.'

This chapter has three main aims. Firstly, it re-assesses the potential for sustainable economic development in the RFE in the light of the work that is critical of resource based development. Secondly, it assesses how well the resource-curse thesis fits the post-Socialist world; a region whose development experience differs from the usual examples of mineral economies studied by economists and economic geographers. Finally, it examines the particular problems that the RFE faces in developing its economic relations with the rest of Russia, the former Soviet Union and the Asia-Pacific Region. The chapter concludes by considering how the problems highlighted by the resource-curse thesis can inform debates on the economic development of the RFE.

THE RUSSIAN FAR EAST REGION

The economy of the RFE is dependent on natural resource extraction, producing significant quantities of oil, coal, natural gas, timber, gold, diamonds and other precious stones. During the Soviet period, the Far East acted as a resource colony for the USSR, accounting for 16.4 per cent of the USSR's total extraction industry in 1990, for example (*Goskomstat RSFSR* 1991). Soviet era development of the Far East emphasised resource extraction rather than processing and industrial production was largely limited to defence related projects. The economy of the Soviet Far East was truncated and specialised and economic activity was concentrated in the urban settlements in the southern parts of the region. Dienes (1987) characterised the economic relationship between the Far East and the rest of the Soviet economy as 'parasitic' because the region was so heavily dependent on external supplies and central subsidies. Since 1991, however, there has been a reorientation of Far East trade and a greater emphasis on trade relations with the Pacific Rim economies. Associated with this, there has also been an attempt at restructuring resource production in the Far East. There has been an attempt to increase the level of processing in important resource industries, an attempt at regional resource based industrialisation.

The most important aspects of this restructuring have taken place at the regional level, both the level of the Far East as a whole and at the level of the individual territories. This reflects the fact that, despite the claims of the Russian President Boris Yeltsin (and before him, the Soviet president Mikhail Gorbachev) that Russia wants to become a major Pacific power, attempts at greater integration with the Asia-Pacific economies have taken place on a regional level (between regions within states) as much as on a national level (see Kin and Savateev 1995; Kovaleva 1995). As such, although the Russian Federation does not qualify as a mineral economy in the sense that most economists mean – that natural resource production accounts for around 10 per cent of GDP and 40 per cent of export earnings – the RFE (as a region) does meet many of the criteria necessary for mineral economy classification. Fuels and minerals account for one-third of all foreign exports and on top of this, raw material products, including cellulose and forestry products, contribute another 20 per cent of export earnings (Minakir and Freeze 1996). And in terms of the contribution of natural resource production to the total volume of industrial production in the RFE, natural resources accounted for 55 per cent of industrial production in 1996 (*Goskomstat Rossii* 1997). However, there are great differences in natural resource production between the individual territories of the RFE. In Sakha-Yakutia for example, mineral extraction accounted for almost 90 per cent of industrial production in 1996, while in Kamchatka mineral resources only accounted for around 20 per cent of total industrial production.

The concern of this chapter, then, with regard to the prospects for resource based development in the RFE, is focused on the regional level; the level of the regions of the RFE, within the Russian Federation, within the Asia-Pacific region, within the world economy. This clearly raises a number of difficulties in terms of applying the resource-curse thesis to the RFE. In particular, Dutch disease is a problem that affects national rather than regional economies, or to be more specific, it is a problem that affects areas which share a single currency. The effects of Dutch disease, then, would be expected to be felt throughout the Rouble zone; in other parts of the Russian economy from the Far East. Despite the regionalisation of foreign economic activity that has taken place since 1991, the most important issues affecting the Far East economy remain outside of the region's control. The Far East continues to rely on investment decisions made by the federal treasury and it does not have its own central bank or its own currency: it continues to operate under constraints imposed by monetary and exchange rate policies constructed in Moscow to meet national economic goals (Campbell 1995).

At the same time, though, the extent to which the RFE can be identified as a distinctive regional economy is increasing (Andriyanov 1995). In more than one sense the RFE is increasingly isolated from the rest of the Russia. For example, economic linkages with Western Russia are increasingly under strain as transport tariffs rise, and the end of the Cold War has reduced the military importance of the Pacific Fleet, whose home port is Vladivostok. The RFE is also increasingly reliant upon trade with its regional partners in Northeast Asia, rather than with the rest of the Russian economy. The RFE also inherited an economy from the Soviet period that was quite distinctive: highly truncated and specialised (see Bradshaw 1988). *Table 2.1* shows the branch structure of the economy in greater detail, but it can be seen that Far East industries specialise in a limited number of branches: natural resource extraction, food production and military-defence related production. At the same time there is a clear economic geography to this pattern of development, and a sharp contrast between the remote northern periphery which is dependent on capital intensive extractive industries and the relatively developed and accessible southern core, which has a greater degree of industrial diversification (see Bradshaw and Lynn 1998).

This chapter focuses on the implications of the resource-curse thesis for two sets of debates surrounding the economic development of the RFE. Firstly, the problems highlighted by the resource-curse thesis have implications for the long-running debate in Russia (and the former USSR) on the economic relationship between the Far East and European Russia. The RFE has long been a resource periphery of the national economy and in the post-Soviet Russian Federation the economic development of the Far East remains dependent on decisions made outside the region, not only in Moscow but also increasingly in multinational

Table 2.1 Branch structure of RFE regions in 1996

Region	Electro-Energy	Fuels	Non-Ferrous Metals	Machine-Building and Metal working	Wood Products	Food Stuffs
Russia	12.5	16.6	6.6	18.2	5.2	12.1
RFE	19.3	10.5	20.7	8.5	5.4	25.3
Sakha (Yakutia)	10.2	15.3	59.9	1.9	1.3	5.5
Jewish	16.5	–	2.7	19.6	7.7	15.2
Chukotka	31.6	16.1	45.6	0.5	0.4	4.3
Primorskii	16.9	5.3	2.7	9.8	5.1	45.6
Khabarovsk	25.4	11.7	8.7	20.0	10.4	10.8
Amur	35.5	8.5	13.7	6.0	8.3	13.2
Kamchatka	19.8	0.3	0.5	8.3	1.3	63.0
Magadan	34.9	3.1	43.1	3.9	0.8	10.8
Sakhalin	13.2	24.9	0.3	4.3	11.7	39.6
RFE	19.3	10.5	20.7	8.5	5.4	25.3

Source: Goskomstat Rossii 1997.

company boardrooms in global financial centres. Decisions made outside the region will determine whether the Far East will maintain its historical role as a provider of raw materials.

Secondly, the resource-curse thesis highlights the problems that the Far East would face in pursuing sustainable economic development if it was allowed a greater degree of economic autonomy. Ideas about economic self-sufficiency in the regions of the former USSR have been an important element of economic debates since the mid-1980s, although there has only been limited practical realisation. However, if the federal government in Russia decided to allow a greater devolution of economic decision making, the resource-curse thesis would have important implications for both the ecological sustainability of resource production in the Far East and its long term economic prospects. In particular, it would highlight the importance of using resource rents for regional economic diversification – for promoting regional resource based industrialisation.

However, before examining these two broad sets of implications, it is first necessary to consider in more detail the conceptual framework within which these debates are located. In this chapter four different frameworks are examined, all of which reveal the geo-economic and geopolitical complexity of resource based development in the post-Soviet RFE.

Regionalisation and globalisation

Regional development in the RFE has to be seen within the context of the increasing role of regional (both sub-state and supra-national) actors more generally in the world economy, and also within the context of the increasing globalisation of economic activity (characterised by the increasing role of multinational companies and technological changes in communications which have had a significant impact on the structure of global economic relations). The idea of globalisation is much disputed, but as a concept it describes a change to a new phase of capitalist relations: an increased internationalisation of economic activity, and a restructuring (deregulation) of state activity (van der Knapp and Le Heron, 1995). McGrew (1992) highlights how globalisation involves a number of contradictory and dialectical tendencies: integration and fragmentation, universalisation and particularisation, homogenisation and differentiation, centralisation and decentralisation, and juxtaposition and syncretisation.

A key point for the transformation of the RFE is the growth of regional trading and political blocs, which some writers have claimed challenge the raison d'tre of the nation-state (see Horsman and Marshall 1994). A key factor in the RFE's development within the Asia-Pacific region, then, will be Russia's, and the region's, involvement with APEC (Asia Pacific Economic Co-operation), ASEAN (the Association of South East Asian Nations) and other supra-national and regional (including non-governmental) organisations. However, thus far, the Russian Federation has only been allowed a minimal role in Asia-Pacific regional institutions. Although a member of the Pacific Economic Co-operation

Conference since 1992, Russia has had very little contact with the Asian Development Bank, it has only been an observer at ASEAN ministerial conferences (since 1992) and it has only had a limited connection with APEC. As Ziegler (1994: 541) pointed out: 'it is an implicit commentary on Russia's economic status that Malaysia, tiny Brunei, and the anaemic Philippines are included in APEC and Russia is not.' Russia has since joined APEC.

The collapse of the USSR's administrative-command system, to some extent at least, meant the collapse of the distinctive socialist system in the world economy (Bradshaw and Lynn 1994). The period of the Cold War was one of anti-systemic conflict between two politically opposed economic systems and the collapse of the Soviet Union has meant not only the construction of new economic relations within the former USSR, but also the post-Soviet countries' wider incorporation into a single global economy. At the macro-level, the Commonwealth of Independent States has, so far, largely failed to promote regional reintegration, except between a few core states (Russia, Belorussia and Kazakhstan) and has been unable to re-establish a single post-Soviet economic space. Instead, the process of economic disintegration and fragmentation has continued, and with the collapse of the Soviet command economy there has been an increasing regionalisation of economic activity in the post-Soviet countries: with regional actors and the local state playing a more important role in economic and other decision making, and with regions and enterprises establishing more direct links with other regions and enterprises in foreign states.

One aspect of this regionalisation has been the growth of regional economic associations such as the Siberian Agreement and the Far East Economic Association. However, thus far, these organisations have only played a minimal role in effective economic management. They have instead tended to act as fora for the promotion of certain elite interests (see Hughes 1994). The increasing role of regional actors in the economy of the Russian Federation, however, has important implications for the regions of the RFE. In particular, the regions of the RFE have tried to build new links with neighbouring states (and regions within states): to locate new markets for their products, and to attract foreign investment into their industries. However, their attempts at encouraging inward investment and initiating more cross-border ties have come at a time of increasing economic pressure (recession) in the East Asian region as a whole. The new geo-economic context of the development of the RFE (globalisation, internationalisation and regionalisation) is one within which any attempt at resource based development must be seen to take place.

Van der Knapp and Le Heron (1995: 237) suggest a new research agenda for economic-geographers in the 1990s, that focuses attention on inter-organisational relations (networks) that operate at a variety of different scales and that takes into account the dynamics of globalisation and regionalisation in the world economy. It can also be seen to provide a framework within which the development of the RFE may be studied (see *Table 2.2*), one that is sensitive to

Table 2.2 A research agenda for studying resource-based development in the Russian Far East (after Le Heron and van der Knapp 1995)

Point of Entry	Regional (local-state)	National (nation-state)	International (supra-state)
Resource based development in the Russian Far East: - Resource-base? - Resource-demand? - Resource-wealth as the basis for sustainable development?	Inventory of the resource-base of the RFE and analysis of the demand for RFE natural resources in APR. Role of RFE enterprises in resource-production. Structure of ownership of RFE enterprises involved in resource-production. RFE local government policies towards resource-development: restructuring and new markets.	Role of federal state in RFE resource-production (enterprise ownership, legal, tax, and regulatory framework). Federal development strategies for RFE (role in Russian national economy: energy requirements and export revenue). Role of centre-region political relationships in determining RFE resource-production (centre-region-republic relations in the Russian Federation and RFE). Influence of federal economic restructuring on RFE resource-producing enterprises.	Role of TNCs in RFE resource-production (attitudes of TNCs to RFE natural resources). Role of RFE natural resource production in FSU (especially in terms of Russia's commitment to the CIS). Geopolitical context of RFE development (in Russian Federation, in Asia-Pacific and relations with China especially). RFE regions in supra-national NGO and governmental political structures (eg APEC, Regional Associations, ASEAN. etc.)

the geo-economic context of post-Soviet 'transformation' in the RFE. This conceptual frame allows the identification of key questions about the nature of resource based development during this period of geo-economic change: about the role of transnational corporations in Far East resource production; about the role of supranational economic associations in facilitating access to markets for Far East resource products; about the role of the federal state in Far East resource production (licensing, ownership, taxation, etc.); about the role of the Far East in federal development strategies; about the role of Far East enterprises in resource production; about the role of the local state in the organisation of the regional resource industry, etc. This frame identifies key questions at a variety of different scales (local state through nation-state to supra-state) in terms of the prospects for resource based development in the Russia Far East at a time when economic activity is facing increasing globalisation and regionalisation.

Models and stages of growth

More traditionally, geographical perspectives on economic development have been informed by neo-classical regional models that were mostly developed in the 1950s: growth pole models (Myrdal 1957), export based models (North 1955) centre-periphery models (Friedmann 1956), etc. An essential feature of these liberal models was the concept of 'stages of growth'. In particular, Rostow (1960) described a process of industrial 'take-off' for developing countries that had a long-lasting popularity among policy makers. The idea of stages of growth has also been applied to mineral-based development. Spooner (1981) for example, described a three-stage process of economic development in mineral economies (largely based on the experience of the UK coal mining industry). First, he identified an early stage of development (the 'minerals dominant phase') in which mineral extraction plays an important role in 'transitional' societies (those approaching take off). Second, he identified a middle stage of development, when mining regions are depressed areas in an industrial society approaching economic maturity (and that requires diversification and conversion to a new and more sustainable economic base). Third, he identified a late stage, where mining undergoes something of a revival in 'post-industrial' societies, acting as a resource frontier within an increasingly interdependent economy.

In the light of more recent changes in the UK coal mining industry the model clearly needs revising, and it provides an example of the problems that are inherent in this kind of developmentalism. But Spooner's model reflects the common opinion that natural resource production is only important in the early stages of economic development (in later stages natural resource production is never as important as in the early phase of economic development). Although, this does not contradict Auty's resource-curse thesis, together they portray a gloomy prospect for resource dependent economies: one of 'immaturity' and 'unsustainablity'.

A more optimistic scenario is provided by another 1960s model of economic growth. Gerschenkron (1962) argued that regions can actually benefit from their economic 'backwardness' because they are able to import the most modern industrial technologies and are able to benefit from the largest economies of scale. Gerschenkron's model clearly has positive implications for the RFE during transformation. In particular, there are significant energy resources in the RFE (oil and gas) that were largely untapped by Soviet industry and which, it could be argued, have benefits for foreign investors precisely because of their lack of Soviet era investment. However, once again the advantages of resource based development are unclear because Gerschenkron's model looked to industrialisation (rather than resource based development) as the key to economic growth.

In the late 1960s and 1970s structuralist critiques provided alternative models of regional economic development. Frank (1967) rejected the idea of stages of growth and described a process by which peripheral regions were systematically underdeveloped by a metropolitan core (which depended on the exploitative relationship for its own growth). Dependency theorists described a neo-colonial pattern of economic development (of core and periphery, and of dominance and dependence) in which satellite economies might be characterised by high levels of raw material extraction and very little resource processing. In other, words, a pattern of development that might seem to describe the RFE resource periphery of the European economic core of the former USSR.

The question which arises is how different the economic relationship will be between the European core of the post-Soviet Russian Federation and the Far East. Certainly there will be a different mechanism of economic control with the demise of the Soviet administrative-command system. Moreover, the regions of the Far East have begun to construct new political relations with the rest of the Russian Federation (characterised by greater political assertiveness and greater local state power) as well as new economic relations with foreign states (and regions within foreign states). It is also possible to identify the beginnings of a 'retreat from colonialism' in the Far East as there has been a steady out-flow of Russian and other industrial workers from the region since the late 1980s (Helgeson 1990; Minakir 1994, 1995). However, it is equally clear (especially from recent debates on post-colonialism in social science that stress the political, economic and cultural inheritance of former European colonies) that the post-Soviet development of the RFE will be a long, protracted and difficult process of transformation and change: development prospects need to be seen in the long-term.

The nature of resources

In its most general sense, the term 'resource' refers to something that is valued by someone, or by some group, and that can be used for some end. Something is not a resource because it physically exists, but because it has a value; there is both the ability to use it and a demand to be satisfied. It is the nature of resources that they are functional and dynamic, therefore. Their definition varies over time and space, responding to changes in technology and knowledge, although it always depends upon the existence of appropriate knowledge and technical skill *and* a demand for the material or service (see Chapman 1989; Rees 1990). There are various systems for measuring and categorising different types of resources, but the best kinds of classification take into account the dynamism that is inherent in resource definition.

Chapman (1989) and Rees (1990), for example, both describe a four-fold typology of resource classification. First, there are the proven/current reserves: deposits already discovered and known to be economically extractable under current levels of demand, price and technological conditions. Second, there are the conditional/probable reserves: deposits already discovered but not economic-ally viable to extract under current levels of demand and price and with available extraction technology. Third, there are hypothetical reserves: deposits that have not yet been discovered but can be expected to be found in the future in areas that have only been partially explored. Finally, there are speculative reserves: deposits that may be found in previously unexplored areas with favourable geological conditions. The development of resources not only depends on cost (and its relation to the price at which it can be sold) but on a range of variables including: the level of information that is attained by exploration, the level of technological development as well as social and political objectives. This means that as well as distinguishing between undiscovered resources and explored reserves, and between proven and conditional reserves, categories of resources can change over time. That is, conditional reserves may become proven/current reserves with 'favourable' changes in certain variables, and also proven/current reserves may revert to being conditional/probable with 'unfavourable' changes in circumstances (see Bradshaw and Lynn 1998).

There are fundamental problems with resource exploitation in the Far East and many of these problems have intensified with the economic recession that has hit the region following the collapse of the USSR. Resource production in the Far East faces problems because of ageing production and processing plants, a chronic shortage of capital, poor transport, inadequate infrastructure, poor management techniques and labour disputes. On top of this, Soviet collapse has also changed the conditions (social, political and economic) that surround resource development in Russia. This means that reserves that were seen as proven/current under the Soviet planning system are now no longer 'profitable' to extract. With a change in economic mechanism (some kind of market replacing central planning), with a change in political aspect (international co-operation to some extent replacing isolationism) and with a change in social policy (the end of large scale state subsidised social provision) some of the reserves that were exploitable in the Soviet period will revert to conditional status in the new system.

Sustainable development

The phrase 'sustainable development' has definite environmental connotations, in terms of the degree of environmental degradation that industrialising societies are prepared to tolerate. However, a more general definition of the phrase (and one that is common in much economic literature) is one where sustainable development simply refers to long-term and stable economic growth. It is the claim of the resource-curse thesis that natural resource abundance actually undermines a country's ability to sustain a prolonged period of stable economic growth. Countries that have an abundance of minerals and natural resources may appear to have advantages over less well-endowed countries: not only as a potential source of foreign exchange, but also as an alternative strategy for industrialisation (raw material processing rather than import substitution or competitive exports). However, the resource-curse thesis highlights the disadvantages that these countries face in their attempts to achieve long-term economic growth, rather than their advantages. In particular, natural resource dependent countries face two potential (and interrelated) problems: the volatility of raw material prices, and Dutch disease (the underdevelopment of other key industrial sectors).

A fundamental problem for resource based development arises from the volatility of raw material prices in the world economy. Studies have shown that economies have great difficulty is coping with booms and down-swings in mineral prices (see Wheeler 1984; Gelb 1988; Sachs and Warner 1995). In times of high prices (and so higher rents) governments misallocate wind-fall profits, and during price down-swings governments are late readjusting to new patterns of expenditure. In a study of oil producing economies, Gelb (1988) highlighted four critical management problems: a lack of saving during booms; the establishment of unsustainable patterns of consumption and investment during booms; the neglect of the competitiveness of other industrial sectors (especially agriculture and manufacturing) during booms; and late adjustment to down-swings.

The phrase 'Dutch disease' originally referred to the experience of Holland in the 1950s after its discovery of large natural gas reserves, and it describes the process by which investment in natural resource production leads to a shrinkage of an economy's agricultural and manufacturing sectors. Problems arise because investment in natural resource production is often very costly (and leads to a diversion of capital away from productive investment), and also because a rise in resource exports (or a cut in resource imports) leads to an exchange-rate appreciation that undermines the competitiveness of traded goods. According to Auty (1993: 15) this can also lead to an over-subsidising of agriculture and manufacturing sectors during periods of price booms, which causes particular difficulties during periods of price down-swings: 'the resulting insulation of a large segment of the non-mining tradable from import competition then makes it difficult to generate the foreign exchange and tax revenues needed to substitute for those lost from mining during a mineral down-swing.'

The resource-curse thesis, then, paints a gloomy picture of the prospects for successful long-term economic growth in natural resource dependent economies. Perhaps it even overplays the difficulties that mineral and other resource economies face (at the neglect of these countries' 'natural' advantages). For example, the effects of Dutch disease on a developing economy can be overstated. Exchange-rate appreciation does not necessarily lead to manufacturing uncompetitiveness, and it can also increase domestic consumer spending and make possible greater investment. At the same time, careful economic management can also reduce the problems caused by the booms and down-swings in raw material prices. There have been some notable attempts to create mechanisms to cope with the volatility of mineral prices in developing countries. Perhaps the best example is provided by the Chilean copper stabilisation fund.

The stabilisation fund was established in 1987, after pressure from the IMF, and it sets a reference price each year for copper that is equal to that used in the annual budget of the non-financial public sector (Auty 1993: 120). It acts to balance-out some of the risks investors face in undertaking resource development projects.

For the RFE, and other resource-rich regions of the former USSR, the disadvantages of natural resource production are also far outweighed by the greater problems caused by post-Soviet economic collapse. So far, resource-rich regions have fared better than many other 'types' of regional economies during systemic transformation (see Bradshaw and Lynn 1996). In fact, resource based development may even provide a survival strategy for those regions that are able to develop their natural resource base during transition. During this period, those regions that have significant natural resource production (like the RFE) are more able to 'develop' their economies than regions which lack the same natural resource wealth, although, whether this will be a short, medium or long-term benefit can only be a matter for speculation at the present time.

RESOURCE PRODUCTION DURING SYSTEMIC TRANSFORMATION

This discussion of the more general and conceptual framework within which the regional development of the RFE has to be placed highlights the fact that post-Soviet transition is a complex process that involves both the dismantling of the former administrative-command system and the establishment of new political-economic structures in its place. In other words, it is a comprehensive process of change – a 'systemic transformation' (see Lynn 1999). The scale and scope of this transformation distorts the impact that resource based development might have on regional economies. Transformation both reduces and amplifies the difficulties that might be faced by mineral economies. In particular, systemic transformation establishes both opportunities and constraints for resource based development in the RFE. The most important of these are considered in turn below:

On the plus side

A simple standard of living index for all the regions of the Russian Federation (see *Figure 2.1*) reveals that some of the regions that have the highest 'quality of life' in post-Soviet Russia have significant levels of natural resource production (the index was based on 1997 Goskomstat data for infant mortality, natural increase, unemployment and production decline since 1991). Although *Figure 2.1* shows that resource-rich regions are not universally 'blessed' with a higher standard of living, two of the best placed regions in the index are the Republic of Sakha (Yakutia) and Tyumen oblast where mineral production (diamonds and gold, oil and gas) accounted for 91 and 98 per cent of all export earnings in 1996

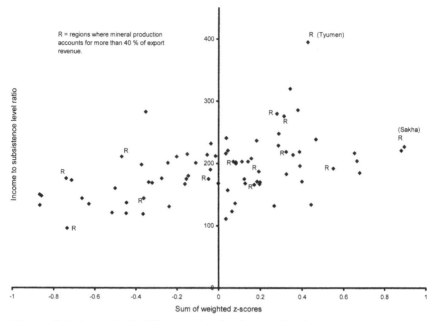

Figure 2.1 A standard of living index for Russian Regions

respectively. Bradshaw and Hanson (1994) identify two different types of regional economies that are likely to cope best during transformation: gateway regions and natural resource-rich regions, and parts of the RFE can be seen to fulfil both of these criteria – resource-rich regions which border the industrialising Pacific Rim economies.

Another benefit accrued to resource producing regions during transformation is the fact that some of them have been allowed greater local autonomy than many other regions of the Russian Federation. Autonomy in this sense is quite narrowly defined, since key industrial enterprises in so-called 'strategic industries' in Russia remain under the tight control of the federal government, but it can be taken to include local governments' ability to take decisions on regional social infrastructure and on regional economic diversification. Autonomy in this sense, is especially great in natural resource regions that also have the political-territorial status of republics within the Russian Federation, like Sakha-Yakutia in the Far East (Lynn 1997).

More generally, though, resource-rich regions have been able to pursue more independent development programmes than other (more industrial) regions because the foreign exchange that their resources earn is desperately needed by the Russian federal treasury during the period of transformation. Resource production is a valuable tool, therefore, in negotiations between regional and central governments over local economic decision making powers and intergovernmental budgetary arrangements in the Russian Federation. By way of illustration, a number of resource-rich regions have signed bilateral agreements with the federal government since the establishment of a constitutional system of federal relations in 1993 (see Lynn and Novikov, 1997), and in 1996 the Russian President Boris Yeltsin established a special federal programme for the development of the RFE (although perhaps a more critical factor in the programme's establishment was the approaching Russian presidential election).

Another plus for the RFE, in terms of the opportunities provided by resource based development, lies in the fact that the region actually has a very diverse natural resource base. As well as diamonds, Sakha-Yakutia produces large amounts of gold, other precious stones and metals, and also coal (and there is some foreign interest in exploiting its projected natural gas reserves). Other regions in the Far East also produce gold and other precious metals, and there are also considerable coal, oil and natural gas reserves (an international consortium has begun exploring the natural gas reserves off Sakhalin, for example – see Bradshaw 1997). The Far East also produces significant amounts of timber and fish products. Of course, some of the individual administrative units within the RFE have more specialised economies than others (as with diamond production in Sakha-Yakutia), but generally the regions of the Far East actually have quite diverse natural resource bases, and as such, the RFE is able to avoid some of the problems anticipated in the resource-curse thesis, which assumes a high degree of dependence on a single mineral or resource commodity (and so a vulnerability to price volatility). Diversification in the RFE would involve increasing the level of processing in a wide range of different resource industries.

However, perhaps the most cited reason for the good prospects of resource based development in the RFE is its strategic location. This argument rests on two interrelated assumptions. First, that the RFE is fortunate because of its proximity to the expanding Asia-Pacific economic region: it has a ready market for its raw materials. And second, that because of the fact that its economy has remained largely undeveloped (and taking into account Gerschenkron's model of the advantages of relative backwardness) the region is able to avoid the problems other regions face in inheriting Soviet era industries. The RFE could either try and industrialise on the lines of a model based on the recent experience of the NICs (Newly Industrialising Countries) in the Asia-Pacific region, or follow a resource based model on the lines of the experience of British Columbia in the Pacific Northwest.

However, all of these hypotheses remain untested. The extent to which there is a demand for the RFE's raw materials in the Asia-Pacific region is unclear. The economic crisis in East Asia has serious implications for the development of RFE resources, especially since there is already tremendous resource competition in the region and raw material and energy prices are highly competitive (see Sheales and Smith 1993). The greatest uncertainty is provided by China.

Although potentially a great source of demand for Russian natural resources, the extent to which Russia and China can actually establish a complementary trading relationship in Northeast Asia remains to be seen (see Mozias 1994). On top of this, many of the RFE's most valuable mineral reserves (diamonds, gold, oil and gas) are located in extremely inaccessible and environmentally difficult sites, and the costs involved in their exploration, exploitation and transportation are considerable. The costs of transportation (by pipeline) of interior-located oil and gas deposits are even more considerable when the likely markets for these resources are taken into account: China, Korea and even Japan (see Paik 1995). At the same time, political problems in Russia act to both deter foreign interest in Russian economic production (including investment in the production process) and also to limit the likelihood that the Russian government would be able to follow a model of state-initiated industrialisation (and export-oriented growth) that characterises NIC development in the Asia-Pacific region.

On the minus side

Some of the positive aspects of resource based development in the RFE have to be highly qualified, therefore, and this includes the standard of living index highlighted above. The standard of living index shown in *Figure 2.1*, which looked at administrative units within Russia, hides tremendous intra-regional variation. Especially in the northern units (such as Sakha-Yakutia and Magadan), there is a great divide in the standard of living between urban and rural communities, and also between ethnic groups (with many of the small indigenous nationalities marginalised in poor rural communities and most social provisions concentrated in a few urban-industrial enclaves that are dominated by Russian and other Slav immigrants). In fact, there has been a crisis in the Russian North since the late 1980s and a steady out-migration of Russian and other industrial workers since 1991 as working bonuses have been cut (see Bradshaw et al. 1995). The standard of living index above (*Figure 2.1*) masks deep intra-regional divides in the RFE and exaggerates the scale of the benefits that regions have accrued from resource exploitation. As in other parts of the world (and as the resource-curse thesis also highlights) it is mainly an elite group in the RFE that has benefited from resource production and inequalities are likely to intensify with continued marketization in post-socialist Russia.

This last point, is one of the most serious deterrents to successful resource development in the RFE. The scale of corruption in the Russian economy during transformation has been great. There have been a number of studies that have highlighted the problems caused by spontaneous privatisation in Russia and elsewhere and only a few bold observers believe that the foundations of a capitalist and liberal-democratic society (that is, one akin to the economies of the West) have been successfully established in Russia. Economic studies of transformation have highlighted how political and economic power has remained concentrated in the hands of a technocratic and corporatist (and often corrupt) elite in Russia (see, for example Aslund and Layard 1993; and also Lane 1996); albeit one that has been somewhat reconfigured since the collapse of the Soviet command economy. In the RFE (and especially in the Primorskii region which includes the city of Vladivostok) the scale of corruption is reported to have been especially high (Troyakova, 1995).

This is in part a consequence of the distance that lies between Russia's Pacific coast and Moscow, which causes problems for the centre's control mechanisms. It is also a consequence of the fact that business people and enterprise managers (and others) have easier access to foreign capital in the Far East than in other parts of Russia because of its proximity to the Asia-Pacific economies (as a gateway region criminal groups are keen to exercise their own control over imports and exports). In part, corruption has also been caused by the scale of the military presence in the Far East Military District, and by the continued role of the Russian Pacific Fleet, which is in a state of considerable crisis (see Blank 1994). Corruption is also a consequence of the fact that the resource industry of the Far East already generates significant amounts of foreign capital; a proportion of which furnishes enterprise managers' and others' own private interests. Put together, then, the scale of corruption in the RFE does not augur well for successful resource based development. In fact, it suggests a scenario more akin to the political and criminal problems that have been identified in Nigeria and elsewhere (countries where people can truly be said to be cursed by the exploitation of natural resources).

The scale of corruption, though, is only a symptom of the political and economic chaos in Russia more generally. The Far East cannot be separated from the political problems of Russia more generally. Political and economic instability has been one of the greatest deterrents to foreign investment and continued instability in Russia looks inevitable. Successful resource based development in the RFE requires a period of stability in Russia and the region so that foreign investment can be attracted and so that a working mechanism for reinvesting rents and protecting resource production from price falls and down-swings can be established. Thus far, the activities of multinational companies (which are key institutions in the world economy) have been limited and cautious in Russia and the Far East. The RFE lacks the business, service and transport infrastructure that is vital for creating a favourable investment climate.

There are also a number of political problems between the Russian Federation and its neighbouring Asia-Pacific states. The clearest example of Russia's geopolitical problems in the Asia-Pacific region can be seen in its territorial conflict with Japan over the Kurile islands (islands that were annexed by the Soviet Union at the end of World War Two). The dispute over the Kuriles has sparked heated exchanges between the two governments, although a greater reason for the lack of co-operation between the two countries is probably political instability in Moscow. At the same time, long-running border disputes between Russia and China over the Amur and Ussuri rivers have still not been fully resolved (in 1997 the Russian and Chinese governments did manage to set up a border demarcation commission, which caused some local political protest in the RFE). Geopolitical problems are complicated by the strong support that Russian nationalists have received in recent elections, which place a great political value on territorial issues (the prospects of Chinese reunification nationalism raises the geopolitical stakes even further).

CONCLUSIONS: THE RUSSIAN FAR EAST AS RESOURCE PERIPHERY

The problems highlighted by the resource-curse thesis, therefore, need qualifying in order to fit the case of the RFE during systemic transformation. Its resource base provides the RFE with a number of regional opportunities as well as a number of regional problems. During systemic transformation it provides a series of pluses and minuses in terms of the potential for longer-term economic growth in the region. Resource based development in the Far East could also alter the region's economic relationship with European Russia. In both the Tsarist and Soviet empires the Far East acted as a resource periphery for European Russia. The Far East has historically been a supplier of raw materials, although the revenue from that resource exploitation has been controlled by and has largely benefited Moscow ('the centre'). In order to break the economic relationship that the Far East has long been locked into, the region requires a diversification of its economy. But such a diversification is unlikely to come from central government initiatives. With the collapse of the Soviet system much of the rationale for industrial development in the Far East has been lost. Over a long period, different writers have argued over the idea of locating industrial production in Siberia and the Far East (see, for example Aganbegyan 1984; Granberg 1984; and Dienes 1987). However, with the introduction of market reforms, the weakening of Russia's military-defence complex and a greater spirit of political and economic co-operation in Northeast Asia, much of the logic behind Far East industrialisation has been lost. It is inevitable that there will be a downsizing of the RFE industrial base following the collapse of the Soviet system. The key question for the RFE (and the rest of Russia) will be how that downsizing is managed.

An alternative method of economic diversification could stem from a greater devolution of economic decision-making to the regions of the Far East and from local policies that promote resource based industrialisation. The discussion, above, of the costs and benefits accrued to resource regions during transformation, highlights the necessity of adopting careful (and consistent) management strategies in the development of the Far East's natural resources. In particular, resource development in the region needs to have three different foci: an outward trade orientation, linkages with industrialisation, and an emphasis on diversification. Auty (1990) defined resource based industrialisation (RBI) as the further processing of natural resources, such as minerals into metals and timber into wood products. His 1990 study (and others, see Gelb 1988, for example) highlighted the factors that constrain RBI in developing countries. In particular, there are two different types of constraint, both of which affect the RFE greatly: efficiency constraints and country-size constraints.

The first set of constraints, efficiency constraints, operate at both the macro and micro-levels. According to Auty (1990), there need to be macro-level measures that ensure the sensible investment of resource wind-falls in infrastructural and RBI projects, and that limit the impact of Dutch disease. Macro-level efficiency is closely linked to political, bureaucratic and fiscal regimes in states, and generally political, fiscal and monetary stability facilitates more sustainable RBI (which is clearly a problem in post-Soviet Russia). At the micro-level, both the product strategy and internal organisational structure of firms are vital in setting the scale of investment and risk in RBI projects.

The second constraint on RBI is country-size. Put simply, in large countries there should be a wider choice of RBI projects (and less reliance on individual projects) and there should also be greater economic linkages and a larger domestic market. The RFE, then, should be able to benefit from its position within the Russian Federation, which is one of the largest states in the world. However, the Far East only has limited communication links to the European Russian economic core and as a region, although it covers a large area, it only has a relatively small population of 7.6 million. The RFE also has a peculiar structure of economic linkages (characterised by departmentalism) that it has inherited from the Soviet command system. As such, the benefits of country-size for RBI in the Far East are limited. The problems of achieving sustainable economic growth in the RFE, even if there was a devolution of economic decision-making responsibility to the regions, remain great.

The RFE faces a number of obstacles to achieving stable economic growth. There are infrastructural and social obstacles that will take many years for the Far East to overcome (Linge 1992). The sustainability of a resource based strategy is called into question by both economic and ecological factors. Ecologically, the environment of the north of the RFE is particularly fragile and vulnerable to resource extraction activity. At the same time, permafrost and seismicity limit the economic viability of large resource projects in the Far East (see Mote 1983; Pryde and Mote 1989). Large-scale timber-felling in the south of the Far East by Hyundai in 1991–1993 also acted to galvanise local environmental awareness into local (and global) political action (see Gordon and Scott 1992, Newell and Wilson 1996; and also Osherenko 1995). Economically, the ability of the RFE to achieve long-term growth is also open to question. A key factor in the region's ability to undertake successful RBI will depend on its ability to attract foreign investment, especially into processing industries. Thus far, however, the extent of foreign direct investment into the RFE economy has been limited and cautious.

The resource-curse thesis highlights the problems that can be caused by natural resource production in developing countries. However, even though transformation exacerbates some of the problems highlighted in the resource-curse thesis, natural resource production still provides opportunities for industrialisation and diversification that regions which lack natural resources do not have. It is possible that, given a commitment in both Moscow and the regions of the Far East to create a favourable investment climate, resource production could provide a short-to-medium term survival strategy for some regions of the RFE. In fact, with the collapse of the Far East's industrial base, it is possible to argue that resource development is the only option that the region has. But there are three key problems that a resource based development strategy in the Far East must try to resolve.

Firstly, regions and enterprises in the RFE face a great problem of access to capital. That capital will need to come from abroad, and because the scale of resource development in the Far East is potentially large, investment will involve international consortia and economic co-operation with neighbouring Northeast Asian states. Unfortunately, the second problem facing economic development in the RFE is the attitude towards foreign investment and international co-operation in the region. Some local political leaders have increasingly adopted a programme of economic isolationism and nationalist politicians have been successful in tapping deep-rooted feelings of xenophobia and insecurity in the Far East (see Troyakova 1995). The third question relates to the problems of transporting Far Eastern resources (see North 1996 and Chapter 5). New transport tariffs have significantly raised the costs of importing consumer and other goods from European Russia and have encouraged the reorientation of Far Eastern economic development strategies towards the Asia-Pacific. However, the costs of pipeline construction and other communication projects for supplying these new markets add to the initial capital costs of a resource based development strategy. All of these problems are further compounded, of course, by the economic recession in East Asia and the collapse in the world price of oil.

It is also apparent that one of the most important questions relating to the economic development of the Far East concerns the extent to which it is possible to talk about a 'Far East Region' at all. Politically and economically processes of de-integration and fragmentation have characterised post-Soviet transformation in the Far East. Successful examples of regional political and economic co-operation are hard to find. Moreover, resource based development will inevitably mean that within the Far East, different regions, different groups, and different places, will benefit to different extents. This chapter has highlighted the spatial context for resource based development in the RFE. At each scale of analysis (the local, national and supra-national) resource based development in the RFE incurs different costs and benefits – at each spatial scale the RFE faces different opportunities and constraints in developing its resource wealth, and in pursuing sustainable resource based development. Increasingly the different regions of the Far East face different economic futures.

REFERENCES

Aganbegyan, A. (1984) 'Sibir na rubezhe vekov.' *Sovetskaya Rossiya* 77.

Andiyanov, V. (1995) 'Resursnyy potentsial i struktura ekonomiki Dal'nego Vostoka Rossii', *Problemy Dal'nego Vostoka* 6: 19–27.

Aslund, A., and R. Layard, eds. (1993) *Changing the Economic system in Russia.* New York: St Martins Press.

Auty, R. M. (1985) 'Multinational Resource Corporations, Nationalisation and Diminished Viability: Caribbean plantations, mines and oilfields in the seventies.' In *Multinational Corporations and the Third World*, edited by C. Dixon, D. Drakakis-Smith, and H. D. Watts, London: Croom Helm: 160–87

Auty, R. M. (1988) 'Oil-Exporters' Disappointing Diversification into RBI: the external causes.' *Energy Policy* 16: 230–33.

Auty, R. M. (1990) *Resource based Industrialisation: sowing the oil in eight developing countries.* Oxford: Clarendon.

Auty, R. M. (1993) *Sustaining Development in Mineral Economies: the resource-curse thesis.* London: Routledge.

Blank, S. (1994) 'The New Russia in the New Asia.' *International Journal* XLIX: 74–907.

Bradshaw, M. J. (1997) 'Sakhalin: the right place at the right time. *Russia Euro-Asia Bulletin* 6: 1–7.

Bradshaw, (1992) M. J. *Siberia at a Time of Change: new vistas for Western investment.* London: The Economist intelligence Unit.

Bradshaw, M. J. (1988) 'Soviet Asian-Pacific Trade and the Regional Development of the Soviet Far East.' *Soviet Geography* 29: 367–393.

Bradshaw, M. J., and P. Hanson. (1994) 'Regions, Local Power and Reform in Russia.' In *Issues in the Transformation of Centrally Planned Economies: essays in honour of Gregory Grossman*, edited by R. W. Campbell, Boulder, CO: Westview Press: 133–59.

Bradshaw, M. J., and N. J. Lynn. (1998) 'Resource-Based Development in the Russian Far East: problems and prospects.' *Geoforum* 29: 375–392.

Bradshaw, M. J., and N. J. Lynn. (1996) *Resource Based Development: what chance for the Russian Far East?* School of Geography Working Paper No. ?, The University of Birmingham.

Bradshaw, M. J., and N. J. Lynn. (1994) 'After the Soviet Union: the post-Soviet states in the world- system.' *Professional Geographer* 46: 439–49.

Bradshaw, M. J., et al. 'Special Issue on the Russian North in Transition.' *Post-Soviet Geography* 36: 195–245.

Campbell, B. O. (1995) 'Prospects for Trade and Regional Cooperation.' In *The Russian Far East in Transition: opportunities for regional economic cooperation*, edited by M. J. Valencia, Boulder, CO: Westview: 9–47.

Chapman, J. D. (1989) *Geography and Energy: commercial energy systems and national policies.* New York: Longman.

Dienes, L. (1987) *Soviet Asia: economic development and national policy choices.* Boulder, CO: Westview.

Frank, A. G. (1967) *Capitalism and Underdevelopment.* New York: Monthly Review Press.

Friedmann, J. (1956) 'Locational Aspects of Economic Development.' *Land Economics* 32: 213–27.

Gaddy, C. G., and B. W. Ickes. (1998) 'Russia's Virtual Economy.' *Foreign Affairs* 77: 53–67.

Gelb, A. H. (1988) *Oil Windfalls: blessing or curse?* Oxford: Oxford University Press.

Gerschenkron, A (1962) *Economic Backwardness in Historical Perspective.* Harvard University Press.

Gordon, D., and A. Scott. (1992) 'Russia's Timber Rush.' *The Amicus Journal* 14.

Goskomstat Rossii (1997) *Regiony Rossii.* Moscow.

Goskomstat RSFSR. (1991) *Pokazateli sotsial'nogo razvitiya respublik, kraev i oblastey RSFSR.* Moscow.

Granberg, A. (1988) 'Ekonomika sibir – zadacha strukturnoy politiki' *Kommunist* 2: 31–40.

Helgeson, A. C. (1990) 'Population and Labour Force.' In *The Soviet Far East: geographical perspectives on development,* edited by A. Rodgers, London: Routledge: 58–82

Horsman, M., and A. Marshall. (1994) *After the Nation-State.* London: Harper Collins.

Hughes, J. (1994) 'Regionalism in Siberia: the rise and fall of Siberian Agreement.' *Europe-Asia Studies* 47: 1133–62.

Kin, A. A., and A. V. Savateev. (1995) 'Novye Transportnye Vykhodky Rossiiskoi Azii' *Region* 2: 178–189.

Kovaleva, G. (1995) 'Torgovlya so stranami ATR' *EKO* 2: 16–34.

Lane, D. (1996) 'The Transformation of Russia: the role of the political elite.' *Europe-Asia Studies* 48: 535–50.

Linge, G. J. R. (1992) 'Developments in Russia's Far East and Their Implications for the Pacific Basin.' *Australian Geographical Studies* 30: 125–41.

Lynn, N. J. (1999) 'Reconceptualising Systemic Change in the former USSR.' *Slavic Review:* forthcoming.

Lynn, N. J. (1997) 'The Republics of the Russian Federation: national-territorial change.' In *Geography and Transition in the Post-Soviet Republics,* edited by M. J. Bradshaw, London: Wiley, 1997: 59–72.

Lynn, N. J. (1996) *The Resource-Base of the Russian Far East.* School of Geography Working Paper No. , The University of Birmingham.

Lynn, N. J., and A. V. Novikov (1997) 'Refederalizing Russia: debates over the idea of federalism in Russia.' *Publius* 27: 187–203.

McGrew, A. (1992) 'A Global Society?' In *Modernity and Its Futures,* edited by S. Hall, D. Held, and A. McGrew, Cambridge: Polity Press: 61–102.

Minakir, P. A. (1995) 'Economic Reform in Russia.' In *The Russian Far East in Transition: opportunities for regional economic cooperation,* edited by M. J. Valencia,. Boulder, CO: Westview: 49–64.

Minakir, P. A. (1994) *Ekonomkia dal'nego vostoka: reforma i krizis.* Khabarovsk: Dal'nauka.

Minakir, P. A., and G. L. Freeze. (1996) *The Russian Far East: an economic survey, second edition.* Khabarovsk: RIOTOP.

Mote, V. (1993) 'Environmental Constraints to the Economic Development of Siberia.' In *Soviet Natural Resources in the World Economy,* edited by R. Jensen, T. Shabad, and A. Wright. Chicago: University of Chicago Press: pp?.

Mozias, P. (1994) 'Options of Economic Development in the APR: prospects for Russia and China.' *Far Eastern Affairs*: 9–24.

Myrdal, G. (1957) *Economic Theory and Underdeveloped Regions.* London: Duckworth.

Newell, J., and E. Wilson. (1996) *The Russian Far East.* Tokyo: Friends of the Earth.

North, D. C. (1955) 'Location Theory and Regional Economic Growth.' *Journal of Political Economy* 69: 319–40.

North, R. N. (1996) *Russian Transport: problems and prospects.* London: Royal Institute of International Affairs, 1996.

North, R. N. (1978) 'The Soviet Far East: new centre of attention in the USSR.' *Pacific Affairs* 51: 195–215.

Osherenko, G. (1995) 'Indigenous Political and Property Rights and Economic-Environmental Reform in Northwest Siberia.' *Post Soviet Geography* 36: 225–227.

Paik Keun-Wook. (1995) *Gas and Oil in Northeast Asia: policies, projects and prospects.* London: Royal Institute of International Affairs.

Pryde, P. R., and V. Mote. (1987) 'Environmental Constraints and biosphere protection in the Soviet Far East.' In *The Soviet Far East: geographical perspectives on development,* edited by A. Rodgers, London: Routledge: 36–57.

Rees, J. (1990) *Natural resources: allocation, economics and policy.* London: Routledge.

Roemer, M. (1995) 'Dutch Disease in Developing Countries: swallowing the bitter medicine.' In *The Primary Sector in Economic Development,* edited by M. Lundahl,. London: Croom Helm: 234–52.

Rostow, W. W. (1960) *The Stages of Economic Growth.* Cambridge: Cambridge University Press.

Sachs, J. D., and A. Warner (1995) *Natural Resource Abundance and Economic Growth.* Harvard Institute for International Development.

Sheales, T., and V. Smith (1993) 'Issues Affecting Northeast Asian Minerals and Markets.' In *CIS Energy and Minerals Development,* edited by J. P. Dorian, P. A. Minakir, and V. T. Borisovich, Dordrecht: Kluwer: 191–224.

Spooner, D. (1981) *Mining and Regional development.* Oxford: Oxford University Press.

Troyakova, T. (1995) 'Regional policy in the RFE and the rise of localism in Primorye.' *Journal of East Asian Affairs* 9: 428–61.

van der Knapp, B., and R. Le Heron, eds. (1995) *Human Resources and Industrial Spaces: a perspective on globalisation and localisation.* London: Wiley, pp?

Wheeler, D. (1983) 'Sources of Stagnation in Sub-Saharan Africa.' *World Development* 12: 1–23.

Ziegler, C. E. (1994) 'Russia in the Asia-Pacific: a major or minor power?' *Asian Survey* 34: 529–43.

Chapter 3

The Economic Situation in the Russian Far East: contemporary problems and prospects for the future

Pavel A. Minakir

The beginning of economic reform in the Russian Far East (hereafter RFE) was marked by an improvement in the general economic situation in comparison with Russian economic performance in general. However, this advantageous situation has turned out to be short-lived. The supposed advantages of the region were soon destroyed by a severe financial crisis, provoked, in part, by a policy of stabilization in the money market. The stabilization of the rouble eroded the cost-based comparative advantage of the region. The subsequent fall in production reflected the worsening financial situation in the region, which, in turn, by a principle of feedback, promoted further decline in the industrial sphere (see *Table 3.1*)

Table 3.1 Decline in industrial production 1992–1997 (% of the previous year)

	1992	*1993*	*1994*	*1995*	*1996*	*1997*
Russian Federation	81.2	88.8	79.0	96.0	96.0	101.9
Russian Far East	84.3	83.7	79.2	–	87.7	–
Sakha	79.0	94.9	10.0	100.4	102.4	95.8
Primorskii	90.3	83.4	74.5	99.0	91.2	94.4
Khabarovsk	88.3	78.1	63.1	77.5	86.4	93.5
Amur	84.3	84.4	80.1	81.3	76.7	94.5
Kamchatka	65.0	85.3	73.2	106.1	100.2	93.1
Magadan	92.7	87.3	91.0	79.0	87.2	87.0
Sakhalin	85.7	86.3	77.6	109.0	83.6	88.2

Sources: Data from Goskomstat Rossii and statistical offices in the RFE.

The strength of interregional trade relations is a major parameter describing the condition of a region's economy. Economic reform in the RFE has seen a significant reduction in the volume of interregional trade and a change in its character. At the most general level, reform has reduced foreign trade activity to the export of raw materials and products of primary processing and import of consumer goods. The decline in trade with other regions in Russia has been even more dramatic than the decline in production and the slump in foreign trade. For example, for the period from January to May 1995 of the total volume of production produced in the RFE, 72 per cent was consumed inside region, more than 15 per cent was exported abroad and only about 13 per cent was exported in other regions of country. Thus, transitional recession brought with it a 'distancing' of the economy from the rest of Russia. In fact, analysis of the intraregional and external interactions shows that the RFE is experiencing double autarchy: increasing isolation of the RFE from the Russian market and increasing self-sufficiency of the subregional economies with the RFE.

The relative share of the RFE in total Russian investments in a fixed capital has constantly declined during the period of economic reform: in 1991 the RFE received 7.9 per cent of total investment; in 1992, 7.3 per cent; in 1993, 6.9 per cent; in 1994, 6.1 per cent; in 1995, 5.2 per cent and in 1998, 4.6 per cent. Of course, this was also a declining share of an increasing amount of investment in total – a shrinking slice of a shrinking pie. From 1995–1998, the regional economy experienced a process of restructuring whereby the share services in gross regional product increased, while the share of industrial production declined in all subregions of the RFE (see *Table 3.1*). However, this increase, in main, was not connected with real growth in the volume of services, but with higher growth rates of prices. At the same time, the inflation of costs in the productive sector simply increased the costs of the manufacturing sector and resulted in a higher-than-average reduction of gross regional product.

During the years of reform, there has been an important change in production proportions in the RFE. At the beginning of the reform period, regional supply and demand were about balanced. The system has maintained this relative balance, but each year at a lower level. The size of exogenous demand is relatively insignificant, in comparison with the volume regional product produced for local consumption. As intraregional supply and demand meet one another, and external demand on output disappears, a vicious circle develops whereby: low intraregional demand results in low volumes of production, which depresses incomes, which results in reduced intraregional demand and so on. By 1995, the industrial production index suggested that production in the RFE was only 46 per cent of the 1990 level. The decline in GDP in the RFE since 1991 has been higher than the Russian average. The only way out of this situation is exogenous demand for new production. That is why since the beginning of the reforms producers in the RFE have been trying to reorient production to external markets.

The reaction of the Far East to this new situation was very grave because of the raw material orientation of the economy, underdeveloped industrial, transport and social infrastructure and long distance from the economic core of the domestic economy. By losing home markets for sales of raw materials, the region had only one way out – to use the available comparative advantages. The presence of overland and sea borders with the Asia-Pacific countries, together with rich natural resource potential, allowed for a rather quick reorientation of regional economic ties in the direction of more effective external markets. It is, therefore, quite natural that the expansion of economic cooperation with the external world occurred first by strengthening the region's orientation towards the markets of the Asia-Pacific region (hereafter APR). In 1992, the APR accounted for 85 per cent of RFE exports. At this time, the share of Far East in total Russian trade with the Asia-Pacific was 17 per cent and in the case of Japan 26 per cent, China 27 per cent and the Republic Korea 32 per cent.

The growth of the foreign trade activity in this early period of economic reform was possible due to the influence of a combination of factors (both external and internal). On the one hand, the presence of certain economic complementarity between the region and China; and, on the other hand, the reform of foreign trade activities allowed the rapid expansion of free economic exchange between the region and the northeast provinces of China. The volume of export-import transactions grew due to the rapid expansion of intermediary operations and direct barter trade, where the regulation was imperfect and the most liberal. However, improving terms of trade on the international market soon made producers in the RFE turn to more lucrative 'cash' markets. Under these influences, there was an appreciable change in the geographical structure of foreign trade of the RFE (see *Table 3.2*). First, at the expense of a sharp reduction of trade with China, the share of which in the foreign trade turnover of the Far East was reduced from 36.7 per cent to 11.1 per cent. While the share of Japan and the Republic of Korea in the foreign trade of the region increased in 1994 in comparison with the previous year from 34 per cent to 49 per cent and from 5.8 per cent up to 11.6 per cent, respectively. This apparent 'reorientation' was also due to changes in the border regime and a clampdown on cross border trade. (See Chapter 10.)

Thus, the APR has 'naturally' turned into the major market for the RFE and now accounts for more than 75 per cent of the total foreign trade turnover of the RFE. This foreign trade activity is responsible for more than 15 per cent of the gross domestic regional product of the region. However, despite an increase in the value and importance of exports, its commodity structure has not undergone substantial change; it remains tied to raw material exports. In spite of the fact that the nomenclature of the region's export includes more than 100 commodities, 85.5 per cent of the volume of export deliveries was comprised of four commodities: fuel, metals, wood and fish. As can be seen in *Table 3.3*, the modern commodity structure of regional exports differs little from the structure of exports in the 1960s–80s. Economic reform has preserved, and even enhanced, the raw orientation of exports as a whole.

Table 3.2 Geography of the foreign trade of the Russian Far East
(Million and US$ %)

	1992	*1993*	*1994*	*1995*	*1996*	*1997*
All countries	2728.9	3238.9	2254.0	4180.2	4568.3	5268.5
	100.0	100.0	100.0	100.0	100.0	100.0
Japan	960.6	1100.2	1105.1	1361.3	1196.8	1244.0
	35.2	34.0	49.0	32.6	26.2	23.6
China	984.1	1188.3	250.6	328.0	926.2	619.7
	36.0	36.7	11.1	7.9	20.3	11.8
Republic of Korea	247.6	188.5	261.9	465.7	635.7	815.5
	9.1	5.8	11.6	11.1	13.9	15.5
USA	106.5	104.1	176.0	597.2	541.5	845.1
	3.9	3.2	7.8	14.3	11.9	16.0
Other countries	430.1	657.8	460.4	1428.0	1268.1	1744.2
	15.8	20.3	20.5	34.1	27.7	33.1

Source: The data have been obtained from the statistical offices and Customs Services in the RFE.

Table 3.3 Commodity structure of export of the Russian Far East. (per cent)

	1991	*1992*	*1993*	*1994*	*1995*	*1996*	*1997*
Total export	100.0	100.0	100.0	100.0	100.0	100.0	100.0
Machines. Equipment. Transportation facilities	1.9	13.2	10.4	2.0	7.7	23.4	10.6
Fuel. Minerals. Metals	21.8	20.4	27.3	28.8	22.6	21.1	20.4
coal	13.0	9.2	7.0	9.4	8.9	6.9	4.5
oil and oil products	3.8	4.1	6.1	6.0	5.5	8.7	9.9
Steel	1.5	3.5	12.8	7.4	2.4	1.9	1.9
non-ferrous metals	1.0	1.2	1.4	3.8	4.8	2.4	2.6
Chemical goods	6.9	7.3	2.5	1.2	1.5	1.2	0.9
Fertilizers	5.1	4.9	0.5	0.1	–	–	–
Construction materials	0.1	0.2	0.3	0.3	0.1	–	–
Raw materials and processed goods	21.7	12.4	21.0	19.7	17.2	12.5	13.1
wood products	13.3	11.0	20.6	19.2	16.6	12.3	13.0
Cellulose	0.6	1.1	0.1	0.3	0.4	0.1	0.0
Food products	46.2	40.8	33.6	43.7	46.6	19.3	29.2
fish and sea products	45.2	30.9	33.4	40.3	46.3	18.3	28.4
Consumer goods	0.6	0.5	3.4	0.2	0.1	0.1	0.0
Others. Including services	0.8	3.5	1.5	4.1	4.2	22.4	25.8

Source: based on data from the statistical offices of the RFE.

At the same time, the current structure of exports has developed under the influence of a set of negative factors, among which are the continuing recession in industrial production, absence of a consistent export policy, deteriorating terms of trade, artificial stabilization of the rouble, unstable government policy in the field of tariff regulation, and so on. All of this has done little to promote the modernization of the export structure and to increase its profitability. Nevertheless, in the context of falling internal demand for export production, and further growth of mutual nonpayment, export activity is one of the few ways, if not the only way, of really ensuring maintenance of production and prospects for its stabilization. As *Table 3.4* shows, during the 1990s, exports have accounted for an increasing share of the region's resource production.

If state policy in the field of export has had an inconsistent character, in the field of imports, during the 1990's, it is difficult to determine the presence of any policy whatsoever. Up to the middle of 1991, in relation to imports, there were no barriers. Having rejected import duties, the government deprived itself of a traditional source of income and an important commercial-political tool in foreign economic relations. Customs regulations on imports were applied only from the middle of 1992. In this period, under conditions of shortage in the consumer market and a fall of investment activity in the region, the commodity structure of import underwent significant changes. Alongside the fall in the share of machines and equipment, consumer goods took the leading position in the commodity structure of import of the RFE. In 1992, their share in regional import was about 60 per cent, compared to 40 per cent in 1990. The introduction of the new import tariffs in 1993 favoured the import of raw material, where the rate of duties was 3 times lower than in 1992. Import of

Table 3.4 The Commodity structure of imports into the Russian Far East (per cent)

	1991	*1992*	*1993*	*1994*	*1995*	*1996*	*1997*
Total import	100.0	100.0	100.0	100.0	100.0	100.0	100.0
Machines and Equipment	23.3	30.1	31.2	32.4	29.6	26.3	35.3
Fuel. Minerals. metals	0.7	2.1	1.6	5.6	2.4	7.9	10.4
Chemical products	1.2	0.7	1.6	3.4	1.5	2.8	2.6
Construction materials	1.4	0.8	0.7	1.4	0.7	0.5	0.3
Consumer goods	65.5	58.5	56.2	49.1	46.2	36.5	29.0
Industrial goods	30.3	35.8	30.7	22.2	19.4	11.2	4.2
food	35.2	22.6	25.5	26.9	26.8	25.2	24.7
Others. Including services	7.9	7.8	8.7	8.1	19.6	25.6	21.8

Sources: based on data from the statistical offices of the RFE and materials from the Regional Administrations.

foodstuffs and some industrial consumer goods was duty free. However, despite a favourable regime for the import of consumer goods, in 1993, the volume of Far Eastern import of these goods remained unchanged. The most likely explanation is that the consumer market was already saturated with rather cheap goods of poor quality, corresponding to the incomes of consumers in the region. Since then, the share of consumer goods has appreciably decreased, while the share of machines and equipment in commodity structure of imports has remained stable. The small, and relatively impoverished, nature of the regional market provides little incentive for inward investment.

Attempts by the government, through the reduction of import duties on a wide nomenclature of machine-building production, to increase the buying power of the enterprises and encourage the modernization, have exerted little any influence on the commodity structure of Far Eastern imports. The share of machines and equipment in the structure of imports of the region during the period after 1992 was rather stable (29 per cent on the average), having only a little increased to 35 per cent in 1997. At the same time, the strict measures taken by the state in relation to the import of consumer goods, directed to the protection of domestic manufacturers, have not had any restrictive influence on the growth of their imports into the region. This is for a number of reasons. First, is the continuing recession in the branches responsible for domestic production. In some kinds of food and non-food goods, the share of imports in the retail trade turnover of the registered enterprises of all forms of ownership has reached 70 per cent (oil, meat products, household equipment and others). Second, high transport tariffs and the low competitiveness of domestic production maintains demand for imported goods. Third, stable demand for imported consumer goods, mainly food products, provides a high profits from foreign trade operations, despite high level of customs payments and low consumer purchasing power.

Internal economic factors have also influenced the region's foreign trade activity. In the current economic environment of falling domestic demand, a shortage of investment funds, widespread non-payments, engagement in foreign trade activity maybe the only way to insure survival. Increasing transportation costs have also be a decisive factor in promoting increased exports. In the pre-reform period, the average cost of transportation of one ton of cargo per kilometer was 0.003 rubles, in 1997 the cost as almost 66 rubles. Therefore, the growth of average transportation cost for this period was almost 22,000 times. The rates of growth of transportation costs far outstripped the increase in prices of industrial production in the region, which for similar period increased little more than 8,000 times. For example, the case of Far Eastern coal, the difference in cost in the case of its transportation for export versus to the central regions of Russia is 3.3 times (1992 2.5 times). The share of the transport constituent in the production for export is 25 per cent, for delivery to central regions of the country its share is 77 per cent. A similar situation is found in relation to other goods as well. Therefore, it is quite natural that under conditions of the extreme growth of tariffs on transportation of cargo to the Far East, there was no other way out than to reorient formerly interregional economic connections towards external ones.

The increased importance of foreign economic relations in the RFE has influenced the basic economic parameters of the region, in particular the volume of manufacturing. In the early period of reform, the region's industry experienced decline, but beginning with 1995, there emerged a tendency of growth, primarily in the production of products for export (see *Table 3.5*). It would seem that further expansion of export-related production offers the only hope for economic stabilization in the RFE. The current economic and political situation in Russia does not leave the region any other way out, however, the potential of the present model of Far Eastern foreign trade to stimulate structural transformation and the creation of conditions for self-maintaining economic growth, are rather limited. In other words, raw-material exportation has helped to sustain the region's economy, but it does not provide a basis for economic recovery.

EXPORT-BASED DEVELOPMENT IN HISTORICAL PERSPECTIVE

The stabilization and activation of foreign economic relations with the APR is one of the most important strategic directions of the future economic policy in the RFE. This is not a new proposition in the field of the regional economic policy. The history of large-scale economic utilization and development of the

Table 3.5 Dynamics of the indexes of the physical volume of production and export for selected industrial products in the Russian Far East (in percentage of the previous year)

	1993	1994	1995
1. Timber			
– production	71.4	60.5	106.3
– export	177.9	85.4	114.1
2. Fish & Sea products			
– production	88.0	82.2	122.5
– export	83.0	144.9	151.9
3. Coal			
– production	96.6	82.4	104.7
– export	103.9	116.3	103.4
4. Oil			
– production	93.7	104.4	107.8
– export	179.7	71.6	345.8

Sources: based on data from the statistical offices of the RFE and materials from the Regional Administrations.

RFE is relatively short – it started only at the end of the 19th century with the construction of Trans-siberian railroad. Since then several models of utilization and development have succeeded each other.

Model 1 From the end of the 19th century until 1918 the region was developing mainly thanks to the patronage of the state, which directly and indirectly supplied basic resources (subsidies, reduced transport tariffs, support of migrants, etc.). Economic interaction between the Far East and the rest of Russia was limited to the flow of resources eastwards. The products of the region itself found demand mainly in the regional market and were also exported. Economically the region was fully open, economic barriers in the western direction were lessened by the protectionist policy of the state while there were no barriers to external interaction with the APR. Labour resources were to the large extent formed by legal and illegal immigrants from China. However, at that time an extended export base was absent in the region, the economy was mostly agrarian with a strong defense component. The Far East was seen as a reserve territory for agrarian migrations and a base for the pacific marine fleet and army. No concern about the non-competitiveness of local industry due to high costs was apparent in this model: the state's military orders and shipments were paid for according to their factual cost (the state viewed high costs in the region as inevitable). Private producers focused on those markets and products that were most profitable. This did not allow for fast economic growth but helped maintain equilibrium.

Model 2 During the period 1922–1930, the RFE developed as a relatively autonomous economic area. Resource flows from central Russia practically stopped. Due to civil war and subsequent economic chaos in European Russian, there was effectively an economic barrier on the western boarders of the region. However, the eastern boarders stayed free and external trade contributed up to 30 per cent of all capital forming resources during that period. Chinese immigrants still comprised a considerable part of the labour force. This meant a rapid narrowing of the reproduction resource base, but the equilibrium of the economic system was sustained and production stayed profitable.

Model 3 In 1930, the model of the state patronage of the region was restored. Development resources almost entirely came from the centre. The economic barrier on the western boarders disappeared due to subsidies from the state's budget, which compensated for the transport tariff, high wages and high costs of heat and electricity. The region's economy was transformed into an industrial one with a strong mining sector and defence industry. The region supplied the internal Soviet market with raw materials and played the role of the economic base for the Pacific Navy and the Far Eastern military area (frontier). The goods produced were almost entirely sold on the internal market, external trade freedom disappeared and was substituted by the supply of raw materials and military equipment which was governed by the state's plan and carried out through centralized channels. Therefore, this model was characterized by the existence of a strong barrier on the eastern boarders, together with the full integration of the region into the country's spatial division of labour. The profitability of production and resources use was substituted by the non-economic expediency of production placement and plan-fulfillment. The region started functioning as a war citadel. This model existed up to the end of 1980s, but several modifications of the base model appeared during that long period.

In the period 1946–1965, the defense and political situation in the Far East somewhat softened: non-economic criteria for the supply of the region with resources became less influential, but economic efficiency stayed low. As a result, economic growth rates decreased. At the end of 1950s, there was an attempt (V. Nemchinov) to rationalize the model. The partial restoration of the region's focus on APR markets was proposed in products that were not competitive on the internal market due to economic criteria. Because of this idea, the use of Japanese capital for the development of the raw material resources of the Far East in the form of compensation agreements and boarder trade has started in the 60s. This modification, however, did not change the fundamentals of the base model since compensation agreements and boarder trade were carried out according to the central economic plan and resources from these activities came to the region through the Centre.

From 1967, the intensity of supply of the region's defense industry and mining economic sectors with centralized resources increased again due to restoration of military and political threat (coming from China this time). The rate of centralized investments in the region in 1970s and 80s was not that much less (5 per cent of the entire volume of centralized investments in all of USSR) than that which existed in 1930s (6.3 per cent). However, some interaction with APR was sustained (the export quota was around 4 per cent of regional production).

Overall, then, for sixty years the RFE had been developing according to the 'one market, one supplier' model. This model also supported equilibrium in the region's economy through the state budget, although this was a 'planned variant' of achieving the equilibrium and production profitability was substituted by pseudo profitability.

Model 4 In 1986, an attempt was made to proclaim a new model for the region's development, one that would account for the impossibility of guaranteeing the state's patronage in full. The stress on APR markets – included in the state programme adopted in 1987 – meant a transition to at least partial distribution of resources on the base of competition of suppliers' markets (internal and Pacific) and Far Eastern industries. However, the total destruction of model 3 happened only after the start of the economic liberalization program (including external economic liberalization) at the end of 1991 – beginning of 1992. The initial model of competitive markets (of 1987) had received a solid official base, but this model began to transform very fast.

The state budget's guarantees of compensation for cost increasing factors in the region were practically annulled and only starting from 1994 were partially restored in a very limited form of compensations for long distance transportation of fuel. Development resources (capital investments) from the state budget began rapidly decreasing and now amount to less than 20 per cent of all investments (down from over 90 per cent in the pre-reform period). The ideas of regional self-accounting proposed in 1960s were practically realized – natural increases in prices and infrastructure costs now were to be compensated for in the region itself. A guaranteed (and compulsory) internal market had disappeared together with central orders and funding distribution. Therefore, guaranteed supplies and their guaranteed financing disappeared.

This meant the restoration of an economic barrier on the western boarders of the region. The region on its own could not manage to break this barrier which led to the forcing of the region out of the internal market of Russia and the other CIS countries. Together with this 'forcing out' – because of liberalization of external economic activities there was now the opportunity to expand trade in APR markets. In other words, the idea was to remove the barrier that had existed between the region and APR for 60 years to the boarder between the Far East and Siberia. This would obviously result in the economic and political isolation of the region. This was practically the restoration of the 1920s model under new conditions.

However, only industrial areas of traditional export specialization have managed to increase their export to APR countries. This cannot compensate for the decrease of internal demand or provided support to those areas financially, since the profits from export now go directly to the accounts of the Far Eastern exporters. The proceeds of export activity cannot be channeled to promote other sectors of the economy. Attempts to increase the export of raw materials have met strong competition in APR markets (first of all from Japan) and instability of demand. Diversification of export demands large investments, resources that are absent from the region. After 1994, exports became a means of earning money and not a means of solving a problem of sales. The growth of internal costs has lead to the rapid decrease in the profitability of raw material exports. However, because of the non-payments problem in the processing sectors, a shift to local processing of raw materials would mean giving them to the processing plants for free,. To stop non-profitable export – means stopping production. Therefore, the model that worked satisfactory in 1920s, when the region was almost entirely isolated from the rest of the country, does not work so well in the contemporary situation.

In the RFE natural resources are strongly bound to inefficient users and producers who lack the means and the will to change this situation. At the same time, the restoration of commercial criteria of effectiveness has resulted in the shrinking of production volumes in branches focused on internal regional exchange. Relative equilibrium was established due to the above mentioned redistribution of economic circulation: around 75 per cent of the product is now sold on the internal regional market, 10 per cent on the internal market of Russia and CIS countries and 15 per cent on the external market (mostly APR countries). This shows that the 'boarder' between the region and Russia is very effective. The region's internal market is very limited, both for the raw materials and for the products of processing industries. Consequently, the narrowing internal regional demand created in 1995–1997 an 'inclined corridor of stable degradation' with an average annual rate of decline of 5 per cent. Therefore, the achievement of equilibrium has created a threat of the collapse of regional industry.

THE RUSSIAN FAR EAST IN THE ASIA-PACIFIC REGION

The Far East forms a natural 'Pacific gateway' for Russia, giving direct access to the World's ocean and direct contact with the dynamic Asia-Pacific region. At the same time, however, Russia and its Far East, historically, ethnically, culturally and economically still – in spite of the recent admission to APEC – remain a foreign body in the APR. It is improbable that Russia will be able to eliminate cultural and ethnic barriers. However, without the destruction of economic barriers, specifically the isolation of the region from global economic and financial processes, as well as sharp differences in standards of economic and administrative mechanisms, the real participation of Russia in global economic and financial processes in the Pacific Rim will always remain questionable.

We should also keep in mind the global 'Chinese factor'. After the assimilation of Hong Kong, the joint economic and financial power of the 'Big China' without a doubt has turned it into one of the most important factors of global military, political, economic and financial equilibrium. A triangle of contradictions – USA-Japan-China – has emerged and within its limits it will be necessary to search for ways of stabilization and compromise. The international status of Russia and its financial and economic stability will depend on whether it will be an active participant in this search for compromise or just a helpless witness or even a victim. To activate its participation in the processes starting in APR, Russia must become a true part of the Asian-Pacific economic order. Russia can achieve this only by including its Far East in this world.

We should also take into account the fact that under the contemporary development model, and due to certain economic and geographic factors, the RFE can be viewed as an 'economic island', isolated from Russia in general and the Russian market. This region is a 'no man's land' – Russia is no longer able to bring it up to the level that would satisfy northeast Asian standards and northeast Asia (hereafter NEA) does not recognize it as a 'member of the club' either. Russia probably has only two territories that can be called islands: the Far East and Kaliningrad oblast, but the latter is in a much better position being situated in the middle of Europe. It also has much tighter bonds with inner Russia. Possessing an 'island' in the east Asia, it would seem rational for Russia to try to model the 'Hong Kong phenomena', but on a much larger scale.

Therefore, from the point of view of narrow economic expediency and from the position of national security it is absolutely necessary for Russia to: 1) integrate the RFE into the Asian-Pacific community and 2) support the restoration of commercial profitability in industries focused on the internal markets of the RFE and Russia itself. The main question is how to do it, what is the strategy for solving this problem?

DEVELOPMENT ALTERNATIVES FOR THE RUSSIAN FAR EAST

Proximity to the APR and NEA in itself does not give any decisive economic advantages. The challenge is in finding a way to help the region gain relative advantages in both the international and Russian division of labour.

The general goal of developing a large social-economic system, such as the RFE, is relatively simple and universal. It can be formulated just as the goal laid out in one of the government's programs as a goal of Russian economics: 'a flourishing of economy, building on that base the wealth and freedom of citizens'. This is an inherent goal of any democratic society. More specifically this goal – as applied to the RFE – transforms as: the creation of conditions for the development of a competitive regional economy (one that has areas of comparative advantages), enabling the stable development of the region's economic system within the limits of the international and Russian division of labour, and providing comfortable standards of living for its citizens.

We can propose the following probable scenarios of for future development.

Scenario 1 The return to the above-mentioned model 3, but with elements of integration (as described in the Federal program of social-economic development of the Far East). This assumes considerable state support for the region in the initial stage, creating the basis for the restructuring of the regional economy, which will in turn provide the basis for self-financing in the long run.

Basic premises of this scenario are:

- in the future the RFE becomes a leading natural resource base for Russia, able to satisfy the demands of the country and provide considerable financial resources to the state and regional budgets from export;
- the regional economic system must be *equally open* in the eastern (APR) and western (internal Russian market) directions for effective interaction with both internal and external markets, and;
- external economic relations must be allowed to compensate for the large distance between the region and Russian markets and the associated high transport costs.

This scenario for the Far East's development presents a cautious shift in the role of state regulation from the concept of passive support for regional development to the one of active development promotion. But the regional development model that is implied by the original Federal Programme is based on reforming the region's economic structure through the production of goods with a high level of value added as a potential source of self financing.

Under this type of the regional development model, structural reform of the regional economy (which implies staged shifting of tendencies of the region's development, from economic stabilization and considerable improvement of the situation by the year 2000, through stable development in 2001–2005; and addressing the shortfall in basic macroeconomic indicators relative to the Russian average by 2005) becomes the main task, and can be formulated as follows:

- diversification of the economy by developing complex and infrastructural industries;
- reprofiling existing enterprises and creating new machine building industries, focused on the satisfaction of the regional demand, especially for equipment for the mining, logging and fishing industries;
- in the period following 2005 – the expansion of sectors of industry involved in the deeper processing of mineral raw materials and biological resources.

Therefore, structural policies – which are the central link of this scenario presuppose support to enable the region as a whole, and specific territories, to carry out effective and stable exchange with other regions of the country and the creation of specializations for the region in the national and international division of labour and the development of export-oriented industries.

As the experience of first two years of the Federal Programme has demonstrated, the region's development according to this scenario depends largely on the amount of state support available. Entrepreneurs in the region have high incentives to continue to exploit the existing economic situation and are unlikely to provide the capital to develop the region's economic infrastructure and processing industries. In other words, there are strong vested interests in the private sector that are doing very well out of the current situation. Only the State can provide the necessary capital and direction to create the basis for economic diversification. At the same time, this scenario was formed based on the goal of creating a highly effective and diversified economic complex, which could support the future extension of Russia's influence on the Pacific Ocean. Thus, the State has geopolitical interests in seeing the economy of the RFE recover.

The realization of these tasks may be carried out by the development of modern dynamic industrial branches, which can assure high growth rates in the region. First, this means the diversification of the machine building complex. Also of importance is the development of marine branches, firstly offshore oil and gas extraction, production of physiologically active matter from marine organisms and the mining of solid mineral resources of the ocean. According to this scenario, the Far East will sustain its traditional specialization in supplying the country with valuable mineral raw material resources, *but* the development of extracting branches will be aimed at the complex use of raw materials *and* their processing.

Scenario 2 Maintaining the traditional export (resource) specialization of the region. The creation of a regional economic system, which could effectively function within this scenario, is based on the principal of its interaction with markets within and beyond the country based on *existing comparative advantages*. This scenario presumes that the Far East has a potential comparative advantage only in the area of extraction and exploitation of natural resources and that this advantage can be effectively used for a relatively long period.

This potential advantage – in the case of the RFE – can be turned into a real one, due to the existence of another natural development factor – geographic position, which reduces the economic distance between the place of extraction and processing of raw materials and markets in the APR. The starting point of this scenario is the fact that the share of exports in the Far East's industrial production has grown from 4 percent in the pre-reform period to over 15 per cent today. Accordingly, the central idea of this scenario is to strengthen and further develop the export specialization of the region, promoting the exploitation of natural resources as the basis for socio-economic development in the first quarter of the twenty-first century. This scenario presumes that this route of development is less capital intensive (at least in the initial stages of its realization, when only proven resources will be exploited) compared to the forming of a more diversified industrial structure, and therefore, is more attractive.

In this scenario, there is no guarantee that resource rents will be used wisely (see Chapter 2 on the resource curse thesis and Chapter 6 on rights to resources). The problem is one of creating conditions for effective development of competitive areas in the regional economy that allow for the stable development of the region's economic system within in the limits of the Russian and international divisions of labour.

The development strategy for the Far East according to this scenario is based on the following principle: the advantageous resource provision and geographic position of the region can be used due to the readiness and economic expediency of countries of NEA and the APR to accept this as its natural role. The role of the RFE as a resource appendage of the APR does not threaten the competitive position of others in the region. Therefore, this scenario can be realized within the conception of a globally oriented regional development.

By comparison, scenario 1 is based on a transition from raw material specialization to the development of processing industries and the belief that the products of the processing industries have higher added value and therefore, their production is preferable. Scenario 2 is based on the belief that the competitive advantage of the RFE lies in resource extraction and *not* processing. That is because those resource-processing opportunities are 'already occupied' by other regions in the international division of labour. However, those regions are the natural markets for the resource exports of the RFE.

Therefore, scenario 2 implies that regional development be built on the prevailing openness of the economy, which in its turn is defined by the structure of industry, the limited dimensions of the internal regional market and deep vertical specialization. Also, unlike the scenario based on the premises and goals that correspond to the Federal program of social-economic development of the Far East, the regional economic system must be more open in the eastern direction (APR) than in the western one (Russian market). This implies the creation of privileges for operations connected with the international market. This means not only distancing from the unified customs policy that currently covers the Far East, but also finding special ways and procedures for stimulating economic interaction with the APR.

Under this scenario, it is necessary to create the conditions for the free circulation of capital, labour and technology between the RFE and its potential foreign partners, which in turn will stimulate the inflow of Russian investments into the region. In the conditions of certain competition with other APR countries in raw material markets, the Far Eastern region can achieve stable development only if the countries buying the raw materials participate in the production process. This means that, along with domestic companies, they have to gain access to the exploitation of land and biological resources. Internationalization of property, then, is an essential element for the realization of this scenario in face of competition for APR resource markets. Moreover, it is also possible that including foreign partners in the process of development and exploitation of raw materials may give real impetus to the diversification of economic activity in the future.

The formal ability to purchase objects of governmental property and other forms of property must be considerably strengthened. First, a network of companies working with stocks and real estate and focused on foreign investors and customers, must be created in the subregions of the Far East.

The actual situation in the raw materials sector of the Far Eastern economy is such that the existing raw materials are the subject of fierce competition between the traditional and new financial-economic structures. However, there still exist considerable new potential and many opportunities that are either undiscovered or are inaccessible now due to the financial limitations of Russian entrepreneurs and the state. They must become the object of fast and rational development as concession projects. The following conditions for concessions must be created:

• the supply of a certain part of produce to the internal market;
• reinvestment in the maintenance of the territory and social development;
• guarantees on the utilization of modern technologies, assuring rational use of resources and ecological safety.

It is obvious that the strategy of export orientation, which is key to this scenario, implies a more cautious approach to the import substitution policy that exists in the RFE today. For the Far Eastern region, an import substitution policy might result in a return to the full integration of the region into the internal Russian market. This might bring with it increases in production costs for export-oriented industries and the restoration of budget-oriented support and financing of the region's development.

One of the main conditions of the region's development, according to this scenario, is the improvement of the investment environment. General improvements in the investment climate in Russia will positively effect the prospects for the RFE, but will not solve the region's problems in the long run. Comparative advantages for investors must be created in the region. One of the methods for the creation of such advantages is the formation of free economic zones, or analogous conditions, on large territories of the region.

In sum, this scenario implies that the regional economy and the external environment will be such that conditions of competitiveness in the international vertical labour division will appear and the region's 'niche' as a supplier of raw materials will assure stable economic development.

Scenario 3 The 'Chinese card' (integration into the APR through the involvement of China in the Far Eastern economy).

The 'Chinese' option of cooperation of the RFE and the APR is attractive for a number of reasons.

1   The Chinese economy is one of the most dynamic in the world and even in the future – after the decrease of average annual growth rate to 5–6 per cent – will likely sustain its advantage over the rest of the region. Potentially, the Chinese market is almost inexhaustible.
2   The existence of a large land border between Russia and CPR, including the territory of the Far East. Development of relations with China might not only support traditional branches of the Far East, but also create new industries (processing of mineral raw materials, paper and furniture production, etc.) New impulses for the development of agriculture (cultivation and processing of soybeans and other agricultural products) as well as some sub-branches of machine building.
3   More active and administratively unrestrained use of Chinese labour in the RFE would help develop agricultural production and light industry in the region and could solve a series of social problems (apartment building, social objects, etc.) which in the long run could create the conditions for attracting and settling people from other areas of RF in the region.
4   Favourable international political factors. Both the USA and Japan are interested in keeping the forces in APR balanced, which means that destructive scenarios for the development in the Russian Federation or China are unwelcome. Therefore, large scale trilateral economic projects are possible on the territory of the RFE, where goods are produced with the use of Japanese (American, Japanese or South Korean) technology and capital, natural resources and territory of the Far East, and Chinese labour will be sold on the APR markets.

We should also account for the fact that one of the worst problems for China is the growing gap between the level of economic development and people's income in the different provinces. Therefore, in its wish to sustain the legitimacy of its power and prevent the country from civil collapse, the Chinese government will be ever more interested in the expansion of economic cooperation with neighboring countries, including the Russian Federation.

The possibility of a certain level of independence of the Far Eastern region is based on the experience of the gradual opening of the Chinese economy during economic reforms in that country, which, as is well known, started from littoral provinces. In addition, the relatively small population of the RFE and its modest share of the production of the Russian Federation should enable the region to become a territory that enjoys a special economic status, without causing problems elsewhere in the national economy.

This scenario is based on equal openness of the RFE to economic interaction with all APR countries without discrimination. Along with that, the stress would be made placed on wider integration with the Chinese economy to acquire greater access to the APR.

The end goal is to form a single economic (but not political) space covering the RFE and the northeastern China.

Under such a scenario, it seems reasonable to propose the introduction of a simplified border and customs regime in certain zones (cities) along the Russian-Chinese boarder. The purpose being to create a free trade zone there as a specific step towards realizing this long-term scenario. Later this regime could be extended to the entire or considerable part, of the RFE. The creation of an advantageous customs and investment climate on the territory of the RFE would also attract Russian capital and private investment.

The key factors promoting the creation a single economic space between the RFE and China are therefore: the gradual loosening and future destruction of limitations on the free transportation of capital, services, technology and labour between the Far East and China, gradual integration of transport and energy systems, and so on.

Scenario 4 An open model of the region's development. This scenario assigns the primary role to economic cooperation with the countries of APR and NEA. However, here the entrance into international cooperation occurs without bonding with any specific country, but through internal institutional resources. Social-economic development of the region is based on the raw material sector of the economy, and the tertiary sector (tourism, services, etc.) is used to promote further growth. Access to international markets is still of primary importance; but relations with the internal market are maintained as a stabilization mechanism.

Creation of the open mixed economy includes:

- accepting the APR's rules of regulation and guarantees on the territory of the RFE;
- internationalization of property as a basis for integrating markets for capital and technology;
- accepting effective and sensitive export-import regulations;
- the creation of functioning free economic zones with possibilities for effective development of local territorial knots on that base.

This scenario is aimed at the creation of a self-regulating system in the region, which would provide effective ways of solving the problems facing the region's development. However, strong federal influence through the foundations of regional development must ensure the desirable regulation and orientation of the regional system.

CONCLUSIONS

If the conditions necessary for the creation of an 'open model' (scenario 3 or 4) are not created, the only option left for the region's development will be to focus on internal sources of development. In this case the region will be forced to rely on development through, first of all reproduction resources formed in the region, which will then be used not only for extended material reproduction but also to support the living standards of the region's population. The solution in this case will be to build a regional economy based on industries that could supply the region with the necessary financial resources. These resources can be used for raising in the long term the population's level of life under the condition of strict environmental limitations. Maximization of the population's incomes and ensuring the ability of their use will then be the criteria for the region's development. Therefore, the strategy of the region's development must be built upon the analysis of comparative costs of different industries, meaning their comparison on internal and external markets. The strategy of using the natural resources of the region must also comply with that goal. These resources must be included in economic circulation (excluding national programs that are supplied with all the necessary resources, including the costs of creating non-industrial infrastructure adequate for the proposed tasks) only to the extent to which the profits from their use are adequate for ensuring normal reproduction in the region.

Since the creation of a set of highly effective industries in the region under such conditions is practically impossible, two types of structural shifts were evaluated: 1) creation of the industrial structure that includes an increased processing component in the extracting industry in the region; 2) sustenance of the traditional resource extracting type of development focused on the internal Russian market. Analysis demonstrates that the differences in the development of separate groups of industry branches in the first and second cases are insignificant, since the development itself is directed first of all on the elimination of disproportions existing in the regional economies. Only the resource sector and supporting industries receive development priority. This cannot provide the change of industrial structure in the nearest future, since the region doesn't posses the necessary level of development in neither social, nor industrial infrastructure. In its turn, the creation of infrastructural objects demands considerable investment resources, which are unlikely to be profitable in the near future. Therefore, it is necessary to break from tradition for the future stage of the Far Eastern region's development.

Another option is the formation of economic structures focused on the tertiary sector of the economy. Development of services is not necessarily connected with large industrial centers, it is carried out on the base of small companies, and is characterized by low investment consumption, high added value, and short pay back period of investments. Such branches include transport and habitat services, finances, insurance, business consulting, and tourism. Development of transport services in ports and transit transportation system of the Baikal-Amur railroad, seems most rational due to the geographic position of the region. These development trends can be focused on the international market and present a serious source of foreign currency inflow for the region. This also applies to the development of domestic and international tourism.

Chapter 4

The Political Situation in the Russian Far East

Tamara Troyakova

INTRODUCTION

This chapter describes the mosaic of political moods that have shaped the regions within the Russian Far East (hereafter RFE) during the 1990s. The colour scale includes various hues of black, white and red, with the predominance of this or that shade being determined to large degree by the nature of relationships between federal and local authorities. The RFE cannot be considered a unified political space, not only because of the immense distances between regional capitals, but also because, for the moment at least, there is no unifying power to pull it together.

During the 1990s, the federal government's inability to guarantee even the basic economic and social rights to the population, forced the regional authorities to expand their functions and powers. Polishchiuk (1998: 83) maintains that a model of 'negotiated federalism' has appeared in Russia, which results in 'the relationships between central and regional authorities taking a cyclic shape'. In the RFE, these cyclic relationships have revealed themselves a struggle between the local authorities and the federal government over the conclusion of bilateral agreements demarcating powers and competence. These so-called power-sharing agreements have normalised relations between individual federal subjects and the federal governments. The provisions within the agreements are designed to meet the specific needs of that region. These agreements have supported a tactic of 'divide and rule'; however, in the RFE the notion of Far Eastern Republic still finds currency. On the subject of the republic, the Governor of Khabarovsk krai Viktor Ishayev (1998a: 49–50) writes:

> While until recently there have been only a few ambitious local politicians among its adherents, now one can say that it penetrates the masses.

> Everywhere, among entrepreneurs, in factories, at logging-lumbering enterprises, or in mines, protests are being raised against Moscow functionaries who pump virtually all the money and resources out of the territories and never offer anything in return. Under such circumstances, the idea of 'our own' republic does not seem that absurd.

Thus, despite the attempts of Moscow to defuse the situation, separatist tendencies remain in the Far East, in large part because the Federal Government has failed to deliver on its promises.

In an attempt to address the growing fractures in Russia's federal system, several new laws on the character of federal system of were introduced in 1999, including the law 'On the principles and order of demarcation of powers and competence between organs of state power of the Russian Federation and organs of state power of subjects of the Russian Federation' and the law 'On the general principles of organisation of legislative organs (representative) and executive organs of state power of subjects of the Russian Federation' clarifies several regulations of the Russian Constitution. There are also legal guaranties of the rights and interests of subjects of the Russian Federation in the law 'On the coordination of international and foreign economic relations of subjects of the Russian Federation' (on the foreign relations of Russia's federal subjects). The resignation of Boris Yeltsin in December 1999 and presidential elections in March 2000, are also symptoms of a desire to stabilise the institutional structure of power in Russia. There seems every possibility that President Putin will try and reign in the privileges gained by the regions during the 1990, thus we may see renewed centre-region conflict.

The nature of the regional political space in the RFE can best be described as a confrontation between the adherents of the old and the new elite, those in favour of or against the existing regime, whatever it might be. Analysis of the 1993,1995 and 1999 parliamentary election results identifies a spectrum of political preferences among the electorate in the Far East. The political creed within the Russian Federation is described in detail in a series of publications on the results of parliamentary elections in 1993 and 1995 (see Chugrov 1998; Chugrov et al 1994).

According to Chugrov (1999: 63), 'a certain type of mentality and electoral behaviour, i.e. non-conformist, has developed in the Far East.' One could add to this that a greater degree of adventurism and authoritarianism on the part of the region's political elites is a 'special Far East characteristic'. The election of heads administration and the lack of a clear-cut procedure for their dismissal have strengthened the position of the regional leaders, in particular, in the Republic of Sakha, and in Primorskii and Khabarovsk krais. In other Far Eastern regions, the ruling groups are still in a state of consolidation. So far, there is no leader in any of the Far East's constituent regions who would be able to consolidate local political movements in order to confront Moscow. In fact, the behaviour of many of the regions with regard to the formation of Yedinstvo (Unity) suggests that many are all too willing to change their political affiliations as suits Moscow.

ALL TOGETHER OR ONE BY ONE?

In Russia today, a simultaneous combination of processes of decentralisation and centralisation are typical of relations between the central and regional authorities. The RFE has been forced by economic necessity to decrease the volume of its economic ties with the central territories of Russia and has sought orient itself toward the Asia-Pacific region (see Chapter 3). Despite this distancing of the RFE from the European core of the country, in the early 1990s, the federal government declared its intentions to support the region through a long-term state programme of economic and social development of the Far East economic region and Transbaikal district for the period up to 2000 and the Federal target programme for the economic and social development of the Far East and Lake Baikal district for 1996–2005. However, economic crisis and the erosion of state control over the economy, plus strong competition between local leaders for financial resources, have impeded the promotion of internal integration within the region. As Minakir and Ishaev (1998: 153) note, 'It is clear, that this programme became obsolete just in time for its signing, however it is obvious that programme as a formal document is the only source for working out real plans and means of regional development and of itself has to be a system of continuously adjustable strategies and mechanisms of implementation.'

The aim of the 'Association of Soviets of People's Deputies of the Far East Districts and Provinces' and its successor the 'Far East and Lake Baikal Inter-regional Association for Economic Co-operation' (IAEC) was to consolidate the efforts of the region and promote unity. The enlargement of the association to include the Republic of Buryatia and Aga-Buryat autonomous okrug, which are also members of association of 'Siberian Accord', was not very helpful. The 'Far East and Lake Baikal' Association has the largest territory of the eight regional associations in Russia, but its economic significance is very low. Recently, the issue of revising the territorial administrative structure of the Russian Federation has been raised. It has been suggested that eight administrative territorial units or regions could be created based on the existing regional associations for economic co-operation. The political strength of each region would be directly dependent on its level of economic development, the strength of inter-regional integration. Such a development would do little to strengthen the position of the Far East within the Federation.

Co-ordination of the activities within the State Duma and the Federation Council is done through IAEC. The idea of a Far East Republic has been transformed into the creation of a Far East Group of Deputies headed by S. Goriacheva, the second State Duma deputy Chairperson, and through the introduction of a draft law 'On the Special Status of the Far East and Lake Baikal Region'. According to E. Galichanin (1997: 9), IAEC Deputy Director General, 'Its main contents are the creation of a system of conditions and measures which would help us cope by our own efforts with priority needs and tasks incorporated in the Programme, rather than a set of privileges.' However, the desire to seek solution through individual, rather than collection action, has prevailed. A case in point is he Republic of Sakha (Yakutia), which managed to obtain a new status in 1990 and its own Constitution in April 1992 along with special agreement on retaining 20 per cent of the revenue from diamond production. These privileges tempted other regions to follow the same route. In February of 1991, the Chukotka autonomous okrug declared itself the Chukotka Soviet Autonomous Republic. In June of 1992, the Supreme Soviet of the Russian Federation issued a law 'On the new status of Chukotka as a member of the Russian Federation'. In 1992, the Jewish autonomous oblast divorced itself from Khabarovsk krai. In 1993, the Koryak autonomous okrug withdrew from Kamchatka oblast. According to Tsuriupa (1998: 84–85), assistant professor at Kamchatka State Teacher Training College, the 'Mining Company of Koryakiya', successor of the North-Kamchatka Prospecting Company, initiated the separation. The breakdown of the structure of national property and the process of privatisation had made it possible for local elites to control industrial enterprises in the region.

The percentage of the ethnic 'Russians' in the population of the RFE fluctuates from 45.5 per cent in the Republic of Sakha to 90.1 per cent in Khabarovsk krai. The indigenous or aboriginal population does not predominate anywhere in the region. As a rule, small groups of Koryaks, Chukchis, Evens, and Nanays are represented in national districts, on Sakhalin and in Khabarovsk krai, but take no active part in political life. Only in the Republic of Sakha, where Yakuts constitute 39.6 per cent of the electorate, is the President, Mikhail Nikolayev, a representative of the titular nationality. In the Koryak autonomous okrug, where 10.7 thousand out 31.9 thousand people are Koryaks, Evens, Chukchis, and Itelmens, the elected governor is Valentina Bronevich, an Itelmen. There are several thousand Koreans in Primorskii krai and on Sakhalin, but their activity is limited to national-cultural unions. The one exception is a businessman from Khabarovsk Valentin Tsoy, who was a deputy of the State Duma and a candidate in the gubernatorial elections.

According to General Menovshchikov, head of the Far East regional board on fighting organised crime, certain national criminal groups operate within the region, such as a Chechen group in Primorskii krai, and Azerbaijani and Chinese groups in Khabarovsk krai. The Chechen group buys restaurants and cafes; for instance in Nakhodka the Chechens own most of the real estate. Azerbaijani groups produce and distribute alcohol. The Chinese criminal association has established links with local drug dealers in the delivery of ephedrine.[1] Thanks to the economic political and cultural diversity of the RFE, there would appear to be very limited potential to create a unified political platform. Even attempts to use anti-Chinese slogans to consolidate residents of border territories in opposition to Moscow failed.

In 1995–1996, the centre actively pursued a strategy of divide and rule and sought to establish contractual relations with individual administrative territorial units. An agreement on the demarcation of powers with the Republic of Sakha was signed in June 1995 as a ploy to improve relations with president Nikolayev. In the spring of 1996 Boris Yeltsin had need of support from regional leaders and signed a treaty with Khabarovsk krai. The signing ceremony was organised in Khabarovsk in April 1996, all the heads of Far Eastern administrations were present because at Yeltsin's visit. Viktor Ishayev (1998b: 126), Khabarovsk krai governor, writes:

> On the one hand, the concluded treaty and agreements are characterised by their large scale and a lot of problems are typical for the province, which we tried to emphasise in the course of the analysis, on the other hand, the economic-geographical position of the territory, the presence here of unique water and mineral resources, and an extensive shelf zone served as quite a good ground for the demarcation of powers in the sphere of possession, utilisation, reproduction and protection of water and biological resources, mining and rational use of mineral resources on the continental shelf, and on the issue of the northern territories' development.

As part of the tactics of combining punishment and reward by the federal government, in May 1996 Sakhalin oblast received a power-sharing treaty. At the same time, Governors who failed to provide support to Boris Yeltsin's election campaign were dismissed. The head of Amur oblast V. Dyachenko was fired following allegations of the 'improper use of the oblast budget'. However, this action failed to win support for Yeltsin, who received only 40.7 per cent of votes, while his opponent Zyuganov received 53.1 per cent. A power-sharing treaty with Amur oblast was signed only in May 1998. The Governor of Magadan oblast V. Tsvetkov, who was elected in November 1996, was rewarded with a treaty in July 1997. The signing of the treaty was a result of the mutual efforts of former Duma deputy V. Tsvetkov and the next Duma deputy from Magadan V. Butkeev, who had influence in Moscow as the deputy chair of the Committee on the North and Far East issues. The conclusion of a similar treaty between the Russian Federation and Koryak autonomous okrug was planned for the end of 1998, but has yet to be signed. In fact, no new power-sharing agreements have been signed since the installation of the short-lived Primakov government in late 1998. An indication, perhaps, of the Kremlin's desire to reassess centre-region relations.

Evgeny Nazdratenko, governor of Primorskii krai, was supportive of Yeltsin in the presidential election, but he was not rewarded. What is more, his long-term rival Viktor Cherepkov was re-established as mayor by presidential decree and a Supreme Court decision nearly resulted in government's dismissal. It may be assumed that the lack of an agreement on the demarcation of powers with Primorskii krai is connected with the Nazdratenko's position with regard to the demarcation of the Russian-Chinese border. The governor has been waging a battle with the RF Ministry for Foreign Affairs in favour of reviewing the 1991 Agreement between the USSR and the People's Republic of China on the eastern part of the Soviet-Chinese border. The use of the 'Chinese factor' in the struggle for reviewing the powers between Moscow and Primorskii krai also promoted the growth of Nazdratenko's popularity at the national scale. For instance, in the September 1998 'Best National Lobbyists' a rating published in the 'Nezavisimaya Gazeta' Nazdratenko occupied 24th place, amongst all the Far East leaders Nikolayev alone was in the first group of 25 persons and occupied 14th place.[2]

Thus, half of the administrative regions in the RFE, Primorskii krai, Kamchatka oblast, the Jewish Autonomous oblast, Koryak autonomous okrug and Chukotka autonomous okrug, so far, have yet to reach power-sharing agreements with the federal centre (for a full list of power-sharing agreements see OECD 2000: 122). This asymmetrical relationship between individual regions and the centre results in an uneven distribution of financial resources from federal budget. The amount of financial aid depends not only on the economic situation, but also on political contact and the success of lobbying strategies. In the RFE, in this fight for privileges, the main rivals are Governor Nazdratenko of Primorskii krai and Governor Ishayev of Khabarovsk krai.

Ishayev (1998b) promotes the interests of the country and his territory, but unlike Nazdratenko, he states: 'we are trying not to trouble the population, to come forward with chauvinist mottoes or to ring warning bells, but we advocate our opinion and our stand firmly, persistently and continuously.' He is also the author of several publications on regional economics and holds a doctoral decree in economics. Ishayev's obvious striving for leadership in the region is noteworthy. His work 'Special Region of Russia' was published in the *Tikhookeanskaya Zvezda* newspaper, the *Dalniy Vostok* magazine, and as a separate publication. The local journalist B. Reznik, who helped to edit the book, got support from a nominating group, which included Governor Ishayev, Chair of the Khabarovsk krai Duma V. Ozerov and commander of the Far East military district Y. Yakubov. In December 1999 he was elected as a deputy of State Duma. By comparison, Governor Nazdratenko seems content with a collection of newspaper articles and speeches and colour pictures, which were published in a book with the symbolic title 'The whole of Russia behind us....' Sakhalin's governor, Igor Farkhutdinov, appears to have little or no influence in the RFE; however he was re-elected with an increased majority in October 2000.

Economic differences are essential in the struggle for leadership in the region. President Nikolayev of the Republic of Sakha (Yakutia) is sharing with the federal government Sakha's diamonds and the diamond mining company ALROSA. However, this diamonds wealth does not tie Sakha into close economic relations with neighbouring regions. The republic remains rich, but isolated. In contrast, an agreement between the administrations of Sakhalin oblast, Khabarovsk and Primorskii krais 'On the Development of Economic Co-operation up to 2005' was signed in Yuzhno-Sakhalinsk in the summer of 1997. It was planned within the framework of an agreement to pool efforts in the development of the fuel and energy production complex of the region in relation to oil and gas exploration offshore of Sakhalin. However, political unity alone has proved to be insufficient for implementing these plans.

A WAVE OF POPULAR PATRIOTIC FORCES

The deterioration of the economic situation has prompted a negative reaction among the local population. Meetings, picketing of administration buildings, strikes, hunger strikes, and the blocking of transport routes are becoming normal events in the life of people in the Far East. The region is experiencing problems with energy and fuel infrastructure that result in frequent power disruptions. The local authorities and the energy producers are blaming each other. Under such conditions, the popularity of the existing regime has declined and the influence of leftist forces has grown.

In recent years, political preferences in the region have been undergoing change because of a number of factors. However, economic factors have played the decisive role. The growth rate of the gross regional product (GRP) continues to decline (see Chapter 2 for a detailed analysis of the economic situation in the region). Over the past three years, the first place in terms of volume of gross regional product (GRP) has been occupied by the Republic of Sakha followed by Primorskii and Khabarovsk krais, then Sakhalin, Magadan and Kamchatka oblasts.

Against the background of a deteriorating economic situation, the population in the region has decreased by approximately 10 per cent in 1990s (further details in Chapter 7). The largest population declines have been seen in the Chukotka and Koryak autonomous okrugs, Kamchatka and Magadan oblasts, and the Jewish autonomous oblast. The most economically prosperous groups of the population have left to live in the European part of the country. Among those that remain, the conviction that the existing regime must be replaced dominates public opinion.

The heads of republics, krais and oblasts are now 'elected', but the procedure for their dismissal or re-election, so far, has no clear-cut legislative foundation. It has become possible to form ruling elite on the principle of personal loyalty to president or governor. In the 1999 elections, the governors and speakers of local legislative assemblies participated in electoral associations and blocs to a much higher degree those in previous elections. As a rule, a governor supports those who are useful to him or her personally; they can exploit different political flags or operate without any party affiliation. For example, A Nazarov, head of Chukotka autonomous okrug, in May 1998 supported V. Babichev, the former head of government apparatus and R. Abramovich in 1999. Abramovich got 58, 9 per cent of the vote and it was predictable that a man from Sibneft could warm the hearts of the Chukotka natives to his Duma campaign simply by paying to deliver several ships of coal to the region, where heat is severely rationed. In Koryak autonomous okrug G. Oivind from the NDR fraction lost his position. A candidate sponsored by a financial company, R Gimalov won with 35 per cent of the votes.

In Primorskii krai, Governor Nazdratenko supported A. Romanchuk from the krai administration, she is from the Dalnegorsk team and was elected via the party list. Despite of her popularity S. Goriacheva (Communist) did not participate in the gubernatorial election in 1999, but preferred the status of deputy. In the opposite direction, in 1998 S. Orlova, State Duma deputy, announced her plans to run for governor's elections in the Primorskii krai in 1999. However, she failed to overcome Nazdratenko. She lost her status in 1999 because of her participation in the gubernatorial election. She was on the OVR party list but was not elected.

In the single-mandate district No. 50, which covers the city and nearby settlements, 19.2 per cent of votes were marked 'against all'. This was a protest vote against the treatment of Viktor Cherepkov. The previous year, when a court struck Cherepkov's name from the ballot in the mayoral election, the proportion of 'none of the above' was high and the election was declared invalid. The Primorskii krai regional court excluded Cherepkov from running in the State Duma election for financial violations. According to the Vladivostok District Electoral Commission for the Election of State Duma Deputies, Cherepkov was late in submitting a report on how he spent money from his election bank account. The results in the Vladivostok single mandate district were declared invalid because of strong opposition to Nazdratenko.

The evidence presented in the tables below on the State Duma elections in 1993,1995 and 1999 indicate a growth of leftist parties' influence among the Far East electorate.[3] Because neither OVR (Fatherland-All Russia) nor Unity and SPS (Union of Right Wing Forces) participated in the 1993, 1995 election; it is only possible to compare the vote for DVR (Democratic Choice of Russia) and NDR (Our home is Russia) against the vote for the CPRF. The LDPR complicates the situation because a vote for Zhirinovskiy's right wing nationalist party was a vote against the Yeltsin administration, but not necessarily a vote for a communist alternative. The following section examines the patterns of voting in the State Duma elections during the 1990s.

Sakha: In 1993, the single mandate district was held by independent E. Zhirkov (NPR-Duma-96), in 1995 by deputy Z. Kornilova from the fraction 'Narodovlastie' (People's Power); and in 1999 V. Basygysov, head of administration of Mirniy, won the election. He was subsequently elected as deputy Chair of Committee on natural resources and nature development. No representatives from Sakha have been elected via the party lists.

Primorskii krai: The party list vote has delivered a number of representatives from the region: in 1993, Y. Yakovlev (DPR), E. Bolschakov (LDPR), and S. Orlova, (Zhenschiny Rossii); in 1995, V. Grischukov (CPRF), E. Bolschakov (LDPR), and M. Glubokovskiy, Yabloko; in 1999, A. Romanchuk, (Unity). Romanchuk worked in the Primorskii Krai Administration and is now a member of Duma Committee on budget and taxes. The three single mandate districts returned the following results: in 1993, V. Nesterenko (fraction 'Stabilizatsiya'), I. Ustinov (fraction 'the 12 December'), M. Glubokovskiy, (Yabloko); in 1995, S. Orlova and V. Shakhov (both 'Russian regions'), S. Goryacheva, (CPRF); in 1999

Table 4.1 Voting patterns in the Republic of Sakha (Yakutia)

Party or bloc	1993	1995	1999
CPRF	10.2	17.6	22.4
LDPR	15.4	6.8	6.2
NDR	–	13.8	1.9
OVR	–	–	10.0
SPS	–	–	8.0
DVR	13.4	2.4	–
Unity	–	–	26.0
Yabloko	7.0	3.6	3.4

Table 4.2 Voting patterns in Primorskii krai

Party or bloc	1993	1995	1999
CPRF	8.7	18.5	22.5
LDPR	23.3	18.5	10.1
NDR	–	3.4	0.6
OVR	–	–	5.9
SPS	–	–	6.2
DVR	14.1	1.3	–
Unity	–	–	27.1
Yabloko	8.6	9.6	6.8

Table 4.3 Voting patterns in Khabarovsk krai

Party and bloc	1993	1995	1999
CPRF	12.1	16.4	20.8
LDPR	19.9	12.3	9.2
NDR	–	4.0	0.8
OVR	–	–	5.3
SPS	–	–	8.9
DVR	19.1	2.2	–
Unity	–	–	27.1
Yabloko	7.3	7.5	8.8

she was re-elected to the same Ussuriysk district. V. Grischukov was elected in Arsenyev district (CPRF), but in Vladivostok district the highest vote (18.8 per cent) was 'against all' and the result was declared void. A new election was held in March 2000. S. Goryacheva is chair of the Committee on women, family, and young people's issues; while V. Grischukov is deputy chair of the Committee on the North and Far East affairs.

Khabarovsk krai: In 1995 and in 1999, V. Knysch was elected to the State Duma from the CPRF party list. In the 1995 Duma, he was elected as a deputy chair of the Committee on the North and Far East affairs, but his current position is as a member of Committee on international affairs. In 1999, E. Galichanin was elected via the Unity party list. The only deputy elected via the SPS party list in the region is M. Barzhanova, director of Khabarovsk meat factory. Both deputies are members of Committee on energy, transportation and communication. The single mandate districts have returned the following results: in 1993 V. Baryschev and V. Podmasko (both in fraction 'Stabilizatsya'); in the 1995 election N. Kamyschinskiy, (CPRF) ceded to his co-worker from Komsomolsk-on-Amur aircraft plant V. Shport (independent). As a deputy Chair of the Committee on industry, building and scientific technologies V. Shport was considered more effective and was re-elected in 1999. In 1999, V. Tsoy, (Russian Regions) lost his seat to B. Reznik (independent) who was elected as a deputy Chair of Committee on information policy in the 1999 Duma.

Amur oblast: In 1993 A. Zakharov (independent) was elected and remained an independent. In 1995 and 1999 G. Gamza was elected from the CPRF party list and remains a member of the Committee on international affairs. In the single mandate district, L. Korotkov (independent) was elected in 1995 (CPRF) and 1999 (People's Deputy fraction). He is currently a member of the Committee on labour, social policy and veteran issues.

Kamchatka oblast: The single mandate district returned the following results: in 1993, A. Lezdinsch (independent) was elected and in 1995 M. Zadornov (Yabloko). However, in 1997, Zadornov was appointed as Minister of Finance. In April 1998 the former Minister on Agricultural A. Zaveryukha was elected with only 20.2 per cent votes, and 'against all' were 20.1 per cent. In 1999, Y. Golenischev, secretary of Oblast Committee of the CPRF, and former Deputy of Soviet Peoples Deputies, stood for election but was not elected because of the high percentage of votes 'against all candidates'.

Magadan oblast: In the 1999, V. Pekhtin, speaker of local Duma, was elected on the Unity party list. He now holds the influential post of chair of the Committee on property. The single mandate district has returned the following results: in 1993 E. Kokorev ('NRP-Duma-96'), in 1995 independent deputy V. Tsvetkov (Russian Regions). In 1996 he was elected as governor and V. Butkeev was elected (Russian Regions) and served as deputy chair of the Committee on

Table 4.4 Voting patterns in Amur oblast

Party and bloc	1993	1995	1999
CPRF	16.2	34.9	33.0
LDPR	24.9	12.9	11.3
NDR	–	3.5	0.6
OVR	–	–	3.5
SPS	–	–	4.5
DVR	12.5	1.4	–
Unity	–	–	36.2
Yabloko	4.7	3.4	3.3

Table 4.5 Voting patterns in Kamchatka oblast

Party and bloc	1993	1995	1999
CPRF	5.0	11.3	17.9
LDPR	27.2	16.0	10.9
NDR	–	7.0	0.8
OVR	–	–	6.0
SPS	–	–	9.6
DVR	15.5	2.1	–
Unity	–	–	29.9
Yabloko	17.6	20.4	6.2

Table 4.6 Voting patterns in Magadan oblast

Party and bloc	1993	1995	1999
CPRF	6.0	12.6	18.6
LDPR	29.2	22.3	11.5
NDR	–	8.2	0.7
OVR	–	–	2.2
SPS	–	–	6.6
DVR	14.4	1.9	–
Unity	–	–	42.9
Yabloko	16.5	7.6	3.9

the North and Far East affairs. In 1999, V. Butkeev was re-elected, and has been appointed as deputy chair of the Committee on legislation.

Sakhalin Oblast: The single mandate district has returned the following results: in 1993 B. Tretyak was elected ('NRP-Duma-96'), but in 1995 he lost to I. Zhdakaev (CPRF). In 1999, the Sakhalin election commission denied registration to I. Zhdakaev for financial reasons. He contested the decision in the Moscow courts and was eventually reinstated as a candidate. He was subsequently re-elected with 24.6 per cent of the votes, B. Tretyak, now chair of local Duma, was second with 20.9 per cent (for more details see: Zimine and Bradshaw 2000). Zhdakayev is a member of Agropromyschlennaya group. He was elected as a deputy chair of the Committee on energy, transportation and communications. An influential position given Sakhalin's island location and the importance of its offshore oil and gas projects (see Chapter 9).

Jewish Autonomous oblast: The single mandate district has returned the following results: in 1993 A. Birukov (APR), fraction APR, in 1995, S. Schtogrin, (CPRF) was elected in 1995 and again in 1999. He was appointed as deputy Chair of Committee on budget and taxes in the third Duma.

Chukotka autonomous okrug: The single mandate district has returned the following results: in 1993 and again in 1995, T. Nesterenko (Russian Regions). She subsequently joined the Government as deputy of Minister of Finance and in May of 1998 V. Babichev, former head of machinery of government was elected. In 1999 R. Abramovich (independent) was elected with 59 per cent of votes. However, in February of 2000 a new union was formed in the State Duma 'Energia Rossii' with V. Chernomyrdin as its head and it is possible that R. Abramovich, as head of the company 'Sibneft', will be a member of this group. R. Abramovish is a member of Committee on North and Far East affairs. He has promised to organise a free economic zone in Chukotka. Chukotka is highly dependent on the federal government and its loyalty is guaranteed. In the 1996 presidential election 74.3 per cent voted for Yeltsin, which was the highest ratio in the region and only 19.1 per cent for Zyuganov.

Koryak autonomous okrug: The single mandate district has returned the following results: in 1993 M. Popov (independent), fraction 'Stabilizatsiya', in 1995 G. Oivind, presidential representative from 1991, (independent and later NDR). In 1999, R. Gimalov, director of the financial company 'Rus' from Kazan, was elected and is now a member of the Committee on credit organisations and financial markets. This region has the smallest number of voters among Russia's electoral constituencies.

The relationships between deputies and regional elites are changing because the local leaders have come to dominate the regional political space. *Table 4.11* provides a summary of the 1999 single mandate vote in the region. It also shows the governor's party affiliation. In some regions, the governor was able to influence the result, such as Khabarovsk krai, in others not, for example Sakhalin.

Table 4.7 Voting patterns in Sakhalin oblast

Party and bloc	1993	1995	1999
CPRF	8.9	24.6	27.0
LDPR	36.9	15.3	10.6
NDR	–	4.1	0.7
OVR	–	–	4.9
SPS	–	–	9.0
DVR	9.6	1.8	–
Unity	–	–	23.0
Yabloko	7.6	6.8	8.1

Table 4.8 Voting patterns in the Jewish autonomous oblast

Party and bloc	1993	1995	1999
CPRF	12.3	23.4	34.0
LDPR	25.0	11.6	8.7
NDR	–	5.1	1.9
OVR	–	–	6.4
SPS	–	–	6.9
DVR	15.4	1.7	–
Unity	–	–	21.1
Yabloko	4.9	4.6	5.1

Table 4.9 Voting patterns in the Chukotka autonomous okrug

Party and bloc	1993	1995	1999
CPRF	6.6	11.0	11.1
LDPR	23.3	13.3	8.1
NDR	–	17.4	1.0
OVR	–	–	3.2
SPS	–	–	7.6
DVR	14.4	1.8	–
Unity	–	–	43.4
Yabloko	12.2	6.5	7.0

Table 4.10 Voting patterns in the Koryak autonomous okrug

Party and bloc	1993	1995	1999
CPRF	7.3	10.0	11.7
LDPR	24.1	13.1	8.3
NDR	–	17.4	1.0
OVR	–	–	4.2
SPS	–	–	5.2
DVR	14.9	2.5	–
Unity	–	–	42.5
Yabloko	11.9	9.4	6.3

Table 4.11 The 1999 State Duma party list vote in the Russia Far East

Region	Turn-out	CPRF	OVR	Unity	Yabloko	SPS	LDPR	None of Above	Others
RUSSIA	61.85	24.29	13.33	23.32	5.93	8.52	5.98	3.30	15.32
Sakha	64.00	22.40	10.03	26.07	3.38	8.02	6.12	3.38	20.59
Jewish	59.99	34.01	6.35	21.14	5.09	6.85	8.72	3.72	14.12
Chukotka	69.04	11.13	3.24	43.44	7.00	7.60	8.06	3.82	15.70
Primorskii	59.69	22.45	5.89	27.19	6.78	6.23	10.09	3.51	17.87
Khabarovsk	64.49	20.88	5.33	27.10	8.81	8.99	9.22	4.28	15.39
Amur	62.49	24.33	3.47	36.21	3.32	4.48	11.29	3.25	13.65
Kamchatka	59.69	17.84	6.04	29.87	6.15	9.59	10.92	5.16	14.43
Koryak	69.20	11.67	4.16	42.49	6.32	5.27	8.29	3.77	18.01
Magadan	57.56	18.86	2.24	42.95	3.92	6.60	11.51	2.55	11.36
Sakhalin	53.16	24.27	4.98	23.06	8.12	9.07	10.60	4.46	15.53

In two regions, heads of regional Duma ran for a place in the State Duma; B. Tretyak from Sakhalin failed, but V. Pekhtin from Magadan was elected via the Unity party list. Sergey Dudnik from Primorskii krai is running for State Duma in March 2000. Deputies in Jewish autonomous oblast, Amurskaya and Sakhalin oblasts preferred to rely on party sponsorship, in both these cases the CPRF, rather than on their local bases of support. Deputies in the Jewish autonomous oblast and Amur oblast preferred to rely on CPRF sponsorship, rather than on their local bases of support. In Kamchatka and Sakhalin the governors do not have a strong control over the local political process. In Kamchatka candidate V. Boltenko, the presidential representative, who was supported by governor Birukov, came second after the Communist candidate Golenishev.

The results of the 1999 party list vote are shown in *Table 4.12*. The disappointing results for OVR and SPS demonstrate their poorly defined identities within the regional electorate. It is no surprise that the northern territories supported the Unity bloc. Electors of Amur oblast are supporting CPRF and Unity. The success of the CPRF in the Jewish autonomous oblast was

Table 4.12 Results in the Single-seat constituencies in the 1999 State Duma elections in the Russian Far East

Region	Governor's Candidate	Winner	Governor's Party affiliation
Sakha	V Basygysov (Independent)	V Basygysov People's Deputy fraction	OVR
Jewish	A. Tikhomirov OVR	S. Shtogrin CPRF fraction	NDR
Chukotka	R Abramovich (Independent)	R Abramovich	Unity
Primorskii	1. G. Dubovik Unity 2. S Goryacheva (Incumbent: Communist)	1. Declared invalid 2. S. Goryacheva CPRF	Unity
Khabarovsk	V Shport (Independent) B Reznik (Independent)	V Shport People's Deputy B Reznik People's Deputy	OVR
Amur	G. Gamza (Communist)	L Korotkov (Incumbent: People's Deputy)	Communist
Kamchatka	V Boltenko (Independent)	Declared Invalid	Unity
Koryak	R. Gimalov (Independent)	R Gimalov (People's Deputy)	Unity
Magadan	V. Pekhtin Unity	V. Butkeev (Incumbent: Russian Regional fraction	Unity
Sakhalin	B. Tretyak (Independent)	I. Zhdakaev (Incumbent: APR fraction)	NDR from September-Unity

Note: There would seem to be a correlation between strong opposition to the governor and high percentage 'against all' votes. In the Vladivostok single mandate district – 18.08 per cent against all, G. Dubovik – 11.01 per cent. In Kamchatka – 15.81 per cent against all, Y. Golenischev, CPRF – 14.41 per cent, V. Boltenko – 14.37 per cent. In Sakhalin – 14.82 per cent against all, I. Zhdakaev – 24.43 per cent, B. Tretyak – 20.55. In the Jewish autonomous oblast – 14.89 per cent against all, A. Tikhomirov (NDR) – 14.33 per cent.
Source: Institute of East–West Studies website (www.iews.org).

because of the personal popularity of S. Shotgrin who was re-elected with about 50 per cent of the vote. The LDPR lost popularity throughout the region. In 1999, in terms of LDPR support, Magadan occupied first place in the region, but the level of support was twice less compared with 1995. Yabloko has a stable 3 per cent of supporters in Amur oblast, but in Kamchatka Yabloko lost one third of its supporters, maybe because the voters preferred the SPS, which had the highest support in that region. The group 'Narodniy deputat' (People's deputy) was created by a Government initiative to unify all loyal deputies from single mandate districts who were not aligned to the major political parties. There are five regional deputies in this group: V. Basygysov from Republic of Sakha, V. Schport from Komsomolsk-on-Amur (Khabarovsk krai) B. Reznik from Khabarovsk, L. Korotkov from Amur oblast and R. Gimalov from the Koryak autonomous okrug. Five regional deputies are members of CPRF fraction. All three deputies elected via the party lists are in Unity: E. Galichanin, A. Romanchuk, and V. Pekhtin.

GUBERNATORIAL ELECTIONS

Elections of administration heads took place in the majority of units in the RFE in 1996. These election campaigns demonstrated that ideological concerns have been replaced by pragmatism and an ability to manage and resolve local social and economic problems has become paramount. In other words, in the gubernatorial elections, local concerns, and not national party politics, were the most important factors. The heads of administration in the Primorskii and Khabarovsk krais, the Republic of Sakha, Kamchatka and Sakhalin oblasts, the Jewish autonomous oblast and Chukotka autonomous district were all re-elected for the second term. Governor Nazdratenko was re-elected in December 1999.

The early election in the Jewish autonomous oblast will be in March 2000. In 1991 Nikolay Volkov was supported by local deputies and then was appointed as the head of the oblast. In October of 1996 he was elected by 70 per cent of voters.

In Amur oblast, Anatoly Belonogov, candidate of leftist forces, Chair of the Oblast's Soviet of People's Deputies, won, 41.77 per cent voted for him. The turnout in the September 1996 elections was 41.69 per cent. In Amur oblast, the legislative body is still called the Soviet of People's Deputies and Viktor Martsenko, its chair, was re-elected in 1997. In the Koryak autonomous okrug, in November 1996, a bitter struggle resulted in the victory of Valentina Bronevich, chairperson of the Kamchatka oblast election commission. She gained 47.1 per cent of votes, while S. Leushkin, head of administration, received 25.6 per cent of the votes cast. The turnout was 57.2 per cent. The losing incumbent, S. Leuschkin, former chair of the District Executive Committee, who was appointed in November 1991, tried to cancel the election results. In Magadan oblast, Valentin Tsvetkov, State Duma deputy and member of the Russian Regions faction, won in 1996.

Since the early 1990s the local political elites have been consolidating their control over regional politics. They now exert a significant influence on the processes of socio-economic transformation and to a large degree determine the character and orientation of reforms. In the current situation, the regional ruling elites are an important link in the system of 'centre-periphery' relationships.

Leaders in the RFE fall into three groups, which determine the political orientation of a republic, krai, oblast, or okrug.

The most numerous group consists of 'economic managers' with an engineering education, who have extensive experience of managing some enterprises and working in Soviet Communist party structures; their average age is about 50. This group includes Viktor Ishayev, governor of Khabarovsk krai, Nikolay Volkov, head of administration of the Jewish autonomous oblast, Vladimir Biriukov, governor of Kamchatka, and Igor Farkhutdinov, governor of Sakhalin oblast. It is obvious that a combination of economic and organisational management has allowed them to keep their posts from the early 1990s to the present time. Moreover, Ishayev is a doctor of sciences in economics and Farkhutdinov in sociology.

Within several years, Ishayev had managed to concentrate all the political power in Khabarovsk krai in his hands. In an article devoted to the 50th birthday of the Governor a journalist wrote:

> There is no opposition to Ishayev in the territory. The local communist leaders are strong in their claims but weak in concepts, especially in economics. The democrats have discredited themselves by the fire and fury of speeches. The local intellectuals are much too clever, too dependent on the budget and power, too scattered to become an opposition force. Entrepreneurs on the whole have not realised the advantage of unification. The Duma as an opposition does not count. The pet phrase of Ishayev is: 'I can do without the Duma'. The governor's meetings with the Duma are rare while misunderstanding is frequent.[4]

Valentin Tsvetkov, Governor of Magadan oblast and Vladimir Pekhtin, Magadan Duma Chair, represent the group of 'directors'. They had a career in production, the peak of which was as the director of a major enterprise. To some extent, they have been forced to go into public political activity. It should be noted that Tsvetkov is the only person in the region who has traded his State Duma seat for the office of head of a Federation unit.

Magadan oblast is looking for the advantages of a free economic zone and benefits in the exploitation of mineral resources. It is also striving for more central assistance. In January 2000, Ilya Rozenblum, a businessman from gold mining industry, (chair of the board directors of the 'Omolon gold mining company', member of the board of the Russian-Canada joint venture 'Serebro Dukat', general director of 'Geometall plus) was elected as the Chair of Magadan Oblast Duma.

The group of 'administrators' consists of Anatoly Belonogov, governor of Amur oblast, Alexander Nazarov, head of administration of the Chukotka autonomous okrug, Valentina Bronevich, governor of Koryak autonomous okrug, and Vitaliy Ozerov, Khabarovsk Krai Duma Chair.

Bronevich is a lawyer by education; she practised in court, headed a district executive committee within Kamchatka oblast, and headed the section of Nations of the Extreme North of the Kamchatka oblast Executive Committee. In 1991, the Bronevich family became a member of the national joint-stock company 'Iyanin Kuthe' (in translation from the Itelmen language – black raven). By 1998 the 'Iyanin Kuthe' limited membership stock company had become one of the leaders in the Koryak's fishing business, and was also engaged in hunting fur with plans to commission a shop for bottling mineral water.[5] The director of the company is Ivan Mikhnov, who simultaneously acts as an adviser on economics and industry to the governor of the Koryak autonomous okrug.

Ozerov graduated from the Novosibirsk higher military-political school and the military-political academy; he also has a philosophical and legal background. He is comparatively young (in January 1998 he was 40). Before being elected deputy of the Khabarovsky Duma, he had held the office of Viazma District Soviet Chair. In 1998 he was re-elected Chair of Khabarovsk krai Duma for a second term.

Mikhail Nikolayev represents the 'Pragmatists', who are characterised by a balanced of economic and administrative experience and a continuous career during the period of reform. He graduated from Omsk Veterinary College and Communist Party Higher School, then for several years were a Young Communist League and Communist Party functionary, from District Committee Secretary to Province Committee Secretary. In 1975, he was Chair of the Council of Ministers of the Yakut Autonomous SSR and Minister of Agriculture, in 1989 Chair of the Supreme Soviet of Yakutia. In 1991 and 1996 he was elected President. This type of career is typical of the present-day leaders of national republics within the Russian Federation.

Evgeny Nazdratenko, Governor of the Primorskii krai, belongs to the group of 'foremen'. He made a career from worker to team taskmaster to director of a mining company. When the privatisation process began, Nazdratenko became actively engaged in business activities. Becoming Governor was a crucial step in his career. However, attempts to become leader for the Far East have not me with success, such a leadership role belongs to Ishayev who from 1993 has been head of the Far East Association for Economic Co-operation and later was Chair of the Council of IAEC. At the national scale, however, because of his conflict with the former mayor of Vladivostok and his outspoken criticism of the Moscow, Nazdratenko is probably better known than Ishayev.

Sergey Dudnik, the present Chair of the Primorskii krai Duma, belongs to the new generation of leaders. He graduated from the Ussuriysk Railway Technical School, worked as a builder, received a higher education diploma at the Far East Polytechnic College, and attended refresher courses in Moscow and in Germany. At the top of his career, he held the office of Chair of the Administrative Council of the 'Nakhodka' company. His ability to reach compromises gained him the support of half the deputies during the election of the Duma Chair. Dudnik responded to the question regarding his political views as follows: 'My party is Primorskii krai. As Chair of the Duma I must be impartial, therefore my attitude towards all political parties is neutral. Of course, I am not enthusiastic about extremist movements of fascist orientation or sects. Democracy is undoubtedly what we need, but it must be built without going from one extreme to the other.'[6] Dudnik's activity shows a strong personality able to compete with governor in Primorskii krai's political arena. However, his political activity has been limited. The deputies of the faction 'Revival of Primorye' managed to oust the speaker from his position in January 2000. Dudnik was on the party list of OVR, but was not nominated and is now running for the State Duma in the March 2000 by-election for the Vladivostok district.

To a certain degree, the opinion poll ratings of Far Eastern leaders depends on the political preferences of the institution conducting the polling. The Centre of Russia's Political Culture Studies conducted polling in spring 1998. The rating of 76 governors was evaluated. Ishayev took third place, and was nominated 'the most honest governor', 'takes the best care of economics' and 'the social sphere'. The other leaders occupied the following places: Belonogov – 25, Nikolayev – 27, Volkov – 38, Farkhutdinov – 45, Biriukov – 50, Tsvetkov – 55, Nazdratenko shared 73rd and 74th places with Geniatullin (Chita oblast).[7] In the list of leading Russian politicians published monthly by *Nezavisimaya Gazeta*, the Far East politicians in 1993–1994 were only represented by Nikolayev. However in 1995–1996, Nazdratenko, who in 1995 occupied 132nd–133rd places, rose to 37th place in 1996, fell to 44th place in 1997, and in April–May 1998 occupied 11th place.[8] In the ratings conducted by *Expert* magazine, using a different method, Nazdratenko occupied 32nd place in September 1997, while in January 1998, he shared 35th and 36th place.[9]

POLITICS AT THE LOCAL SCALE: KHABAROVSK AND PRIMORSKII KRAIS

An analysis of campaigns for election to legislative bodies held late in 1997 in the Primorskii and Khabarovsk krais reveals the nature of the activity of CPRF and LDPR representatives. The low influence of other parties and public organisations is demonstrated by the fact that the majority of candidates preferred to be nominated by groups of voters. The results of the Khabarovsk elections show a strengthening of conservative mood among the voters. It was decided to reduce the number of deputies from 50 to 25. In total, 194 candidates ran for election. Of the candidates elected, 13 of them represented regional branches of the CPRF, 7 – LDPR, 3 each for the Russian popular Republican Party, 2 for the Agrarian party and the Peasants' party, one for the Socialist party of labourers. Also, there were two candidates from the trade union movement 'Union of Labour', four from the city Club of Afghan War Soldiers, and two from the Khabarovsk krai Association of Entrepreneurs, and one each from

Khabarovsk city Union of Women, Khabarovsk Popular Home, and the Public organisation of military service Veterans of Khabarovsk krai, and the inter-regional public association 'Vozrozhdeniye'.

For the first time the 'People's Democracy' group of deputies was created consisting of seven communist party deputies, two deputies' who were journalists and one 'popular advocate'. The group started to act as an active opposition. In October 1998, when the issue of granting a 20 per cent tax privilege to the companies taking part in the reconstruction of the central square in Khabarovsk arose, nine deputies of the 'People's Democracy' group put forward a vote of no-confidence to the Duma Chair. At the same time, Deputy E. Isakov came forward with a proposal to terminate the Duma's term before time 'on the grounds of repeated violations by the "People's Democracy" People's group of the standing order'; according to him, '. . . the Duma, which must work in the interests of the territory, has turned into a place of political showdown, a rostrum for the political debates of a group of deputies'.[10] The attempts of the Deputies to attract attention to their activity are obvious, however the criticism of the territory administration so far remains at the level of discussions in the Duma.

A total of 292 candidates were registered to run in elections to the Primorskii krai Duma with 39 seats to be filled, four seats more compared with the first convocation. Included among the candidates were: 10 candidates from the CPRF, 9 from the LDPR, three from the Primorskii branch of 'Honour and Motherland', five from the NDR, and one each from All-Russia Women's Union, the People's Patriotic Union, the Congress of Russian Communities, and the Russian People's Republican Party. There were also two candidates from the krai foundation 'Resurgence' of Primorskii Koreans and one from the 'Protection' block. The great majority of the candidates preferred not to bind themselves to parties or organisations and declared their own programmes. The candidates from the People's Patriotic Union were especially active.

Among the elected Deputies, there were three CPRF representatives, who, together with other representatives, formed a faction of 12 deputies. Eight out of 10 representatives of the 'Our City' election block were elected. The campaign of the block was conducted under the motto of support for the policies of Viktor Cherepkov, Mayor of Vladivostok. Four deputies from the Duma's previous convocation gained the support of the voters, including Sergey Dudnik, who was re-elected as its Chair. Political opposition in the Primorskii territory has acquired a personal character. The struggle is waged as Nazdratenko versus Cherepkov, rather than as a programme for raising living standards and getting out of crisis. The governor strives to gain personal control over the situation within the territory.

The struggle for active participation in public life is a common feature of the legislative bodies in Primorskii and Khabarovsk krais. Many deputies were re-elected for the second term and have become professional lobbyists for financial and entrepreneurs' circles, as well as for the administration's interests.

In the course of establishing a constitutional order in the RF, the restructuring of governmental bodies has shifted to the regional level and the organisation and development of a legislative basis for the 'local' state authorities has started. In such conditions, when civil associations and political parties remain weak and the powers of the local leaders are strong and extensive, there is a danger that more authoritarian methods of management will become increasingly widespread.

CONCLUSIONS

Market transformations in the RFE have fostered the growth of administrative control over the region's economy. The development of the market and the election of administration leaders of the federation units have served to increase their independence from the federal centre, but at the same time, it has failed to ensure democratisation. Authoritarian and personal power has expanded the popularity of 'leftist' parties at national and local elections in the region. Given the lack of significant national orientations, political preferences within a given region may change depending on the specific situations as created by the local authorities. The overall process of shaping an open civil society in the RFE has slowed. Rather, the consolidation of the ruling groups and the establishment of totalitarian control over political and ideological processes are taking place. Partial democratisation and incomplete federalisation of Russia has fostered the establishment of authoritarian political regimes in the Far East of the country.

NOTES

1 *Tikhookeanskaya Zvezda* (Khabarovsk). August 29, 1998, p. 2.
2 *Nezavisimaya Gazeta* (1998) October 28, p. 8.
3 Tables were compiled from the Central Election Committee: http://www.izbircom.ru and *Rossiyskie regiony posle vyborov-96* (1997).
4 *Tikhookeanskaya Zvezda I* (1998) (Khabarovsk), April 16, p. 2.
5 *Vostok Rossii* (1998) (Khabarovsk), 2–3 (4): 30.
6 *Zavtra Rossii* (1998) (Vladivostok), January 29–February 5, p. 5.
7 *Zavtra Rossii* (1998) (Vladivostok), January 29–February 5, p. 5.
8 *Nezavisimaya Gazeta. Supplement 'NG-regiony'*. (1998) No 8, May, p. 11.
9 http://www.expert.ru/expert/politiki/01/data/reiting.htm.
10 *Tikhookeanskaya Zvezda* (1998) (Khabarovsk), October 10, p. 1.

REFERENCES

Chugrov, S (1998) 'O regionalnoi fragmentatsii rossijskogo politicheskogo soznaniya' *Mirovaya economica i mezhdunarodnyie otnosheniya*, 1, pp. 29–41.
Chugrov, S. (1999) 'Ob osobennosyah politicheskogo soznania rossiskogo Dalnego Vostoka' *Mirovaya economica i mezhdunarodnyie otnosheniya*, 10, 57–65.
Chugrov, S., D. Slyder, and Gimpelson, V. (1994) 'Political Tendencies in Russian Regions: Evidence from the 1993 Parliamentary Elections'. *Slavic Review*, 53 (3), 711–732.
Galichanin. (1997) 'Ekonomicheskaya model Vostoka Rossii', *Vostok Rossii*, 1, 5–9.
Ishayev, V.I. (1998a) 'Osobyi raion Rossii', *Dalniy Vostok*, 10, 49–50.
Ishayev, V.I. (1998b) *Ekonomicheskaya reforma v regione: tendentsii razvitiya i regulirovaniye*, Vladivostok: Dalnauka.

Ishaev, V. and Minakir, P. (1998) *Dalniy Vostok Rossii: realonosti i vozmozhnosti ekonomicheskogo*, Vladivostok: Dalnauka.

OECD (2000) *OECD Economic Surveys 1999–2000: Russian Federation*, Paris: OECD.

Polishchiuk, L. (1998) 'Rossijskaya model 'peregovornogo federalisma', *Voprosy economiki*, 6, 68–86.

Rossiyskie regiony posle vyborov-96 (1997) Moscow: Yuridicheskaya literatura.

Troyakova, T. (1998) 'A Primorskii Republic: Myth or Reality?' *Communist Economies & Economic Transformation*, 10 (3), 391–404.

Tsuriupa, I. (1998) 'Alaska, Kamchatka i Siberia v geopoliticheskom areale', *Polis*, 2, 84–85.

Zimine D A and Bradshaw M J (2000) *Economic Restructuring, Regional Equality and Local Politics in Sakhalin*, Birmingham: Russian Regional Research Group Working Paper 19, School of Geography and Environmental Sciences and Centre for Russian and East European Studies.

Chapter 5

The Transport System in the Russian Far East

Robert North

INTRODUCTION

This chapter examines the transport system of the Russian Far East (RFE) and how it has changed since the late 1980s. The state of the system at that time has already been described by the present author (North 1990). Here we begin with a summary of that paper, then examine in turn changes in institutional and traffic-generating conditions; the impact of change on specific transport modes and sub-regions; and the prospects for transport in the RFE.

TRANSPORT IN THE RUSSIAN FAR EAST IN THE LATE 1980S

The nature of the demand for transport changed little between 1945 and 1990. The only major exceptions were initiatives relating to foreign trade and sea transport in the 1970s and the emergence of new governmental attitudes to the region in the mid-1980s. The primary links of the region throughout the period were with European Russia. There were two bases for those links: economic and military. Economic interest focussed on natural resources unavailable or scarce farther west, from diamonds and gold to fish. Military interest arose from the region's Pacific location and proximity to China and Japan. The most heavily-used sea route in the RFE linked the two naval ports of Vladivostok and Petropavlovsk-Kamchatskiy, while army and air-force bases guarded the Chinese frontier (see *Figure 5.1*).

Neither resource extraction nor military activity led to multi-faceted regional development. Most activities were located in single-purpose nodes that received the bulk of their manufactured supplies from European USSR and, in the case of primary activities, sent their output in the reverse direction. Raw materials with a

73

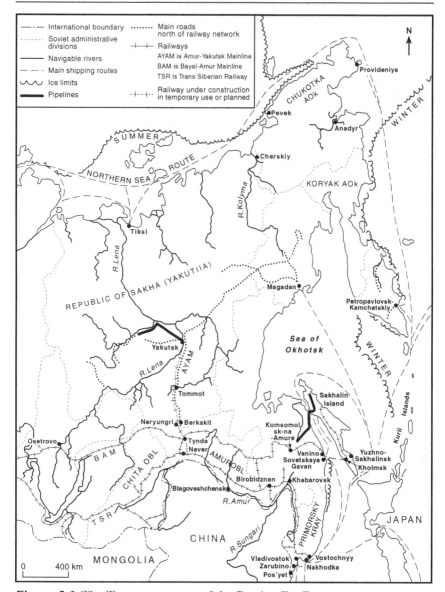

Figure 5.1 The Transport system of the Russian Far East

low value-to-weight ratio, like coal and construction supplies, were produced locally for local use, but even for food the region depended heavily on Siberia and European USSR. In other words the RFE, though to all appearances well located to trade with Pacific Asia, was for most purposes at the end of a very long railway line from Moscow.

The spatial distribution of demand for transport was, through most of the region, nodal or linear and very scattered. More than a third of Russia was occupied by one twentieth of the population, and most of that was concentrated in the extreme southeast. For the rest, non-military settlement was focussed primarily on timber stands and mineral deposits, several of the latter in the extreme north and northeast. The surface routes to them might make other resources accessible enough to be exploitable and, if the primary resources were sufficiently remote, building stone, coal for fuel, and timber might be sought locally. But there was little other concomitant development requiring modern transport.

In such circumstances, as might be expected, the RFE was served by a spine-and-branch transport system. The backbone, and the lifeline to European Russia, was the Trans-Siberian Railway (TSR), and most other components of the system – rivers, roads, and coastal shipping – fed into or distributed from it. The Northern Sea Route (NSR) could in part be seen as a separate spine for Arctic sub-regions, its branches being the rivers draining to the Arctic and the winter roads that supplemented them. But the eastern part of the NSR was itself accessed by way of the railway and the ports it served in the southeast. The R. Lena also joined the two spines, and places along it and the adjacent north coast were served from both. A major task of the combined system was to supply northern settlements, using the short sea and river navigation seasons to the utmost. Surface movements to the remotest places could take up to eighteen months by rail, river, sea, river again, and winter road transport, spanning two navigation seasons and a final winter. Far Eastern resource exploitation was labour-intensive by North American or Scandinavian standards, and permanent family settlement was favoured over flying in shift workers from the south. The demand for supplies was therefore far greater than in Western experience, relative to the scale of resource output. Supplies rather than products determined surface transport needs: indeed such products as gold, diamonds and tin could often be flown out.

Few components of the freight transport system operated independently of the two spines. River transport along the Amur supplied coal to the southern Far East, independently of the Trans-Siberian, and linked settlements along the river directly with the Sea of Okhotsk. One or two northern roads gave independent access to Pacific ports, but they handled very little direct foreign trade. And pipeline transport was used only within sub-regions. Gas and oil lines from Sakhalin reached Komsomol'sk-na-Amure, and a pipeline from a local natural-gas field served Yakutsk.

Long-distance passenger transport outside the southern Far East had two main components: coastal shipping along the Pacific coast and, for all other areas, air transport. The tendency of RFE sub-regions to be linked directly to European USSR rather than to each other was particularly exemplified by air transport. Yakutsk and Khabarovsk, for example, were better linked to Moscow than to each other.

This pattern of activity changed somewhat in the 1970s, for two and possibly three reasons. The first was Moscow's growing interest in foreign trade, including the sale of services. The second was military concern over the perceived vulnerability of the TSR to Chinese attack, at a time of tension between the two countries. The third possible reason was Leonid Brezhnev's desire for a personal monument.

All three reasons have been adduced to explain the building of the Baykal-Amur Mainline (BAM). It was expected to give access to exportable minerals and timber, and to facilitate West Siberian oil exports to Pacific Rim markets. It was located farther from the Chinese border than the TSR, though not particularly far in an era of long-range ballistic missiles. And after dominating government publicity during Brezhnev's leadership, it vanished from public attention thereafter. In the event, the line was not completed before the fall of the USSR and attracted far less traffic than had been planned. Its impact on the RFE economy and transport demand had more to do with the effort of building it than the result of building it. It generated a huge temporary demand for supplies. Hitherto unused rivers became transport arteries, and new roads were built. The only major resource export attributable to the BAM investment was that of coal, which in fact moved along a branch line, the Little BAM, to the TSR rather than to the BAM itself.

Of more immediate importance was investment in maritime transport. That sector had been neglected while Soviet planning constructed a largely internalised economy. Port facilities had fallen well below world standards, and the average Soviet cargo ship was about a third of the world average in size. The new interest in foreign trade brought investment in both ports and the fleet. In the RFE the effects were felt mainly in the south, in the ports and shipping companies engaged directly in foreign trade. In addition the Northern Sea Route received new icebreakers, including more powerful nuclear vessels than the pioneering *Lenin* of the 1950s, and icebreaking freighters.

Interest in the sale of services produced the Trans-Siberian Container Landbridge, set up in 1971 to compete with maritime carriers linking the Far East with Europe. Initially it was successful, capturing about 10 per cent of total traffic and a quarter of that between Japan and northwestern Europe. Later its share fell. Its competitors introduced faster vessels, and the TSR's customers became disillusioned with failure to meet delivery schedules, damage and losses en route, and an inability to keep constant track of the containers.

At the end of Soviet times traffic was still growing, apart from container traffic on the TSR, and growth was expected to continue. Congestion on supply routes to the north was a frequent concern. But when Mikhail Gorbachev came to power in Moscow, questions were raised about the costs of resource exploitation in remote areas. Improving industrial efficiency west of the Urals was seen as more rational than continuing to expand resource exploitation in regions requiring ever more investment per unit of output. The RFE was a prime candidate for re-assessment, not least because of transport costs. They were a very high proportion of total production and delivery costs, partly because freight underwent more transhipments per delivered ton than anywhere else in the country. Transport was heavily subsidised, as indeed were many sectors of the regional economy.

We can thus see transport development to the end of Soviet times as the product of two sets of forces: geography and government policies. Pre-eminent in the former category were a wealth of natural resources and a location on the Pacific Rim, close to China and Japan. Significant policies included the maintenance of rigid central control, leaving little scope for independent regional initiative; the projection of Soviet military power into the Pacific region; changing foreign trade policies; and a willingness to subsidise development and settlement in a relatively empty region close to densely-populated nations. Both tsarist and Soviet governments were sensitive to the need to demonstrate effective occupancy.

THE POST-SOVIET ENVIRONMENT FOR TRANSPORT

During the 1990s Russian transport has been affected by changes in institutional conditions and the conditions for traffic generation. The present author has already surveyed the topic for Russian transport in general (North 1996). Here, a brief summary of major changes will precede a more detailed examination of the RFE.

Institutional changes: ownership, control, and finances

The ownership situation is complex. The central government still owns the railways, but most other ex-Soviet transport organisations have been privatised. Privatization, however, can mean many things. The federal or regional governments may hold large, even controlling blocks of shares. In other cases former managers and employees have become owners. Some companies have acquired foreign partners or major shareholders. Others, mostly in maritime shipping, have transferred assets to foreign subsidiaries to avoid Russian taxes.

Perhaps of more immediate importance than ownership is the changed decision-making environment. In the past major decisions were made in Moscow. Now companies must run their own affairs, and official interference when it does occur is more likely to originate with regional governments. Even the regional railway divisions have more responsibility now. Decision-making criteria have changed too. Formerly the prime objective was to reach physical targets set by the government, expressed mainly in terms of tons carried and ton-kilometres. Now it is profit, and operating in the new mode has been a traumatic experience for many. Firstly, government subsidies, on which both remote-area and urban passenger transport depended, have disappeared or are no longer paid reliably. Secondly, customers frequently default on their debts. Enforcing payment is hampered by the uncertain legal position of creditors – one of many gaps in the Russian legal system. Thirdly, unpredictable tax regimes and uncoordinated taxation by the various levels of government have hindered financial planning. Fourthly, in the early 1990s many transport tariffs were controlled, while the price of fuel was not controlled to the same extent. This put companies into financial straits from which it has been difficult to recover. Finally, in August 1998, following a period of emerging stability, all financial planning was disrupted by devaluation of the rouble. In particular, many foreign investors lost heavily, which made it hard to attract further investment.

New transport companies have appeared. Their success in competing with the ex-Soviet companies has varied. They lack the inherited infrastructure and connections of the latter, but they also lack their inherited social obligations, excessively large labour forces, and equipment designed for state-run monopolies. An example is the icebreaking freighter fleet, designed for reliability in gruelling northern conditions but with little regard for operating economy.

Changes in traffic-generating conditions

Traffic generation is affected by changes both outside and within the transport industry. Pre-eminent among the former are economic decline and the switch from a command to a market system. Traffic on many routes is below half what it used to be. Also, decline has been sectorally and spatially uneven. For example, the armed forces and heavy industries have declined as customers, while importers and exporters have become more important – except for those trading with other ex-Communist countries. Northern regions have lost population (see Chapter 7) and are hard pressed to pay for the supplies they still need. Buyers and sellers in general have formed links differing from those assigned under the command system. Traffic is less predictable now: planning when shippers are responding to rapid market shifts is very different from following a five-year plan.

Within the transport industry there have been two major changes. The first is an increase in domestic competition. There was always intermodal competition during Soviet times, despite the rhetoric of cooperation. The maritime and river shipping companies, for example, competed fiercely to supply Arctic settlements. But the scale of competition, especially intramodal competition, has grown enormously. The second change is a loss of protection against foreign competition, especially in ocean shipping. Most foreign trade through Soviet ports was reserved for Soviet ships, but now Russian ships carry ten per cent or less.

In sum, Russian transport is still adjusting to a new environment. Economic initiatives tend to reflect the possibilities for foreign trade more than the needs of European Russia. Many initiatives now originate locally or abroad rather than in Moscow. The inherited transport infrastructure has proven to be an imperfect fit with the post-Soviet demand for transport. On the one hand there is unusable capacity, on the other a need for new investment. A Russian transport organisation of the present day is likely to be very different from its Soviet predecessor in terms of ownership, control, financial structure, and objectives.

And it faces an environment of uncertainty, depression, and intense competition. For the industry as a whole, it is probably fair to say that long-term strategic planning has been pushed into the background by the imperative of short-term survival.

POST-SOVIET TRANSPORT IN THE RUSSIAN FAR EAST

Transport in the RFE has followed most national trends, sometimes in extreme form. Decline in domestic traffic has been exacerbated by the loss of subsidies, on which the RFE depended more than other regions, and the shift to foreign trade has been especially marked. Exceptions to the national trends have related mostly to foreign trade and the activities of foreign competitors on Russian soil. There is no equivalent to the Finnish and Baltic-State competition faced by European Russian ports, for example, and Chinese motor transport does not compete within the RFE to the extent that foreign firms compete in European Russia. We shall firstly examine changes by transport mode, then focus on sub-regions of the RFE.

Railways

The Far Eastern Railway (FER) serves most of the RFE. The BAM was a separate entity until 1997, when the line was divided between the East Siberian Railway and the FER, and the Sakhalin Island system remains separate. Since the peak years of the late 1980s, traffic in the whole RFE has fallen by two-thirds. The decline has been less than for truck and river transport, however, because rail traffic has been buoyed up by the relative health of foreign trade. This boost has principally affected the FER. In 1988, its peak year for traffic, the line carried 72.5 million tons. In 1997 and 1998 it carried a little less than half that amount. But foreign trade has become distributed among more ports than before, so the FER has been under pressure to improve service to several growing ports at a time of declining traffic and revenues. At the same time it has had to seek new opportunities in order to avoid further decline and find uses for its considerable infrastructure.

One possible source of new revenues is to provide outlets to Russian ports for exports from northeastern China. That region has several potential alternatives for reaching world markets, but those through Russia are the most direct. Recent efforts have focussed on the small ports of Zarubino and Pos'yet, closer to the Chinese border than Vladivostok, and a rail link across the border was completed early in 1999. Traffic of up to 3.0 million tons a year is anticipated (Ivanov 1997: 67–69; *PRN*, 8 February 1999).

Another potential source of revenue is to revive the Trans-Siberian Container Landbridge. In its peak year of 1981 it carried 140,000 TEUs, but the number fell to about 55,000 by the end of Soviet times and 6,000 in 1996 (Pashkova 1998: 40; Wadhams 1997). The earlier decline, as described above, reflected poor service. The more recent collapse reflected high port charges (as traffic declined the ports raised their charges, trying to maintain their income) and even worse service. Containers disappeared en route. Despite a distance of 13,000 km, compared to at least 20,000 by sea, delivery times ranged from 35 to 45 days, compared to 26–35 by sea. As traffic declined, the organisations involved lost interest in cooperating. In 1996, for example, the Ministry of Railways cancelled its container-sharing agreement with its maritime partners (Zil'bershekht and Podol'skaya 1998: 3).

The Russian transport organisations were finally moved to action in 1997. By that time traffic was even being lost to the much worse-equipped Chinese railways. Also, plans were being made to upgrade either a route through China to Kazakhstan, which would join the Russian railways in Siberia, or one farther south through Central Asia that would avoid Russia altogether. The two routes would be 2,000 and 4,000 km shorter than the TSR (Radnayev 1996: 79; Chernogayeva 1997: 19). The Russians obviously needed to demonstrate the advantages of their route before the alternatives received investment.

In 1997 fast container trains were introduced, linking Vostochnyy port to the Finnish border in eleven days and the Polish border in twelve. Armed guards accompany each train, and there is constant tracking of containers. None were lost in 1997. In 1998 demonstration trains using new equipment reduced the time to 8.5 days, four times faster than by sea. More new fast services, between Moscow and Vladivostok, were introduced in July 1999 (*PRN,* 26 July 1999).

Organisational and tariff changes have also been made. An international committee now oversees operations. Customs procedures have been simplified. The railways have a new agreement with the Far Eastern Shipping Company (FESCO), which is expanding its container-ship fleet. Vostochnyy port has introduced three-shift working to accommodate the major maritime container carriers. Finally, tariff and tax discounts, the former up to 50 per cent, have made the route more competitive. The container volume in mid-1998, before the financial crisis, was double that of the previous year, and Vostochnyy port saw a 50 per cent increase in throughput after devaluation (Transsib 1998; Paskova 1998: 40; Krinitskiy 1998: 14; *PRN,* 5 April 1999).

If the present rate of improvement can be maintained, the Landbridge may be able to reestablish its reputation. International opinion is that it might capture up to 30 per cent of the traffic between east Asia and Europe. In 1997 that traffic included 360,000 movements between Europe and Japan alone (Transsib 1998: 12).

Even at its peak the Landbridge accounted for only 2 per cent of TSR traffic. Reduced traffic in the RFE has been due mainly to the collapse of intraregional traffic and that with western Russia. The collapse reflects in part general economic decline and in part a reduced eastward flow of supplies in the absence of subsidies. But it also reflects problems of capacity, in the early 1990s, and tariff policy. The disintegration of the USSR left most Soviet European ports outside Russia. Bad relations with the Baltic States, and high transit and port-use charges, led to the redirection of exports through Pacific ports. Neither they nor the railways could cope. There were protracted delays, and some goods were returned to the shippers. Now European Russian shippers prefer to send their exports through Baltic ports, even if the ultimate destination is East Asia. To recapture that traffic will require as much effort as reviving the Landbridge. Several measures are being undertaken. Electrification of the last diesel section of the TSR, south of Khabarovsk, is to be finished by 2002 (*PRN*, 11 January 1999). The railway bridge over the Amur at Khabarovsk is being enlarged. And tariffs are being reduced. Reductions of 38 per cent for logs and lumber in March 1999 were followed by a 20 per cent increase in shipments to the ports (Moshenko 1999: 5; *PRN*, 29 March 1999).

While there are some positive signs for the future of the FER, the same cannot be said of the BAM. By mid-1997 freight traffic was below half the 1990 level, which itself was far below the forecasts of the 1970s. Unemployment in the BAM zone was 25 per cent, and the population was a third of what it had been at the height of construction. The last major construction project, the Severomuysk tunnel, is still unfinished. By late 1998, after 20 years of construction, 15.1 km had been completed and there were 215 metres to go. In May 1999, 300 metres were wiped out by a cave-in, the latest in a series of disasters. According to some Russian specialists the tunnel location was chosen for directness, ignoring engineering common sense. A bypass route exists but has extreme grades. Much of the completed line suffers from high maintenance costs. It was built through seismically active and permafrost regions, and several station settlements were designed by architects from other parts of the USSR with little experience of northern construction. Coal is still the only mineral resource exploited. Though the BAM provides a shorter route from Siberia to the Pacific coast than the TSR, there is little incentive to complete it when the TSR is operating so far below capacity (Bushin and Merinov 1997; Zhuravel' 1997: 61; *CDPSP*, 2 June 99, p. 13).

There have recently been tentative efforts to rescue the BAM. The Russian railways have formed a joint-stock company, which is trying to promote some 50 projects to foreign and Russian investors. Their initiative has been incorporated into the 1996 – 2005 Federal Program for the Social and Economic Development of the Far East and Transbaykalia (Baliyev 1997: 13–4). But there have been few results so far.

The Sakhalin railways also face big problems. The system is plagued with three different gauges and ton-kilometre costs that in late Soviet times were nearly eight times the national average. Plans for improving the system are associated with firstly, the anticipated need to service an expanded natural-resource sector, based on hydrocarbons and timber, and secondly, schemes for linking the RFE with Japan by a tunnel or bridge from the mainland to Sakhalin and from there to Hokkaido. A tunnel to Sakhalin would take five years to build. Once construction begins, the Japanese are expected to start building twenty two-km bridges, linking Sakhalin to Hokkaido via the Kurile Islands (*PRN*, 2 August 1999). For the present, however, the railway is heavily indebted to the

Sakhalin Steamship Company. In consequence the ferry across the Tatar Strait has been operating irregularly.

There is one other major railway project in the region. The Amur-Yakutsk Mainline (AYAM) had reached the coalfield town of Neryungri, en route from the Trans-Siberian and BAM to Yakutsk, by the end of Soviet times. Since then construction has stalled for want of funds. The line is in temporary operation as far as Tommot, but there are no immediate prospects for completing the last 350 km. Two articles written in 1998 illustrate how the same situation can be portrayed in different ways. The first emphasises the utility of the partially completed stretch, now operated by the company Railways of Yakutia. In 1997 it carried 700,000 tons of freight, mostly in containers. The railway tariff was a fifth that of transport on the road that runs alongside, and using the railway to Tommot, with road transport from there to Yakutsk, was 40 per cent cheaper than by river from Osetrovo, the railway port on the R. Lena. The line, it was claimed, could carry 1.5 million tons in its present state, and more than double that if it could be completed as far as the Lena (Yefremova 1998). The second article described a visit by inspectors of the Ministry of Railways. They found the track, communications and rolling stock in terrible condition. The company appeared to have spent nothing on maintenance in its year of operation, and safety standards were appalling. Several bridges were in imminent danger of collapsing. Train speeds, already no greater than walking pace, should be reduced further, and permissible train weights would allow for barely a dozen freight cars per train. Finally, though tariffs were low, staff had not been paid for a year (Morozov 1998).

Motor Transport

Motor freight transport in the RFE falls into two broad categories. In the south it can handle door-to-door shipments over a reasonable network of surfaced roads, much as in European Russia. Elsewhere it is more an accessory to rail, river and sea transport, and it may depend heavily on winter roads. There is no continuous road linking the RFE with the rest of Russia, though tracks through parts of Amur and Chita oblasts are usable in dry weather. In 1996, to celebrate 100 years of motor transport in Russia, a convoy of vehicles drove from Moscow to Vladivostok attended by great publicity. No such official, non-military expedition, including vehicles that lacked four-wheel drive, had been undertaken before. Even then it was achieved only with expert drivers and teams of mechanics.

The role of motor transport in the north has not changed much since Soviet times. A lack of money to replace equipment that wears out rapidly has been offset to some extent by a decreased demand for transport. Bigger changes have taken place in the south. Official statistics show a 79 per cent drop between 1990 and 1994 in tons carried, a figure exceeded only by river transport, though motor transport statistics are notoriously unreliable. Business probably shifted from the established common carriers to new independent carriers and companies transporting their own goods, and procedures for recording such transport were in their infancy. In particular, there was a considerable growth of import-export traffic with China, nearly four-fifths of it carried in Russian vehicles and without doubt grossly underreported. That trade has fluctuated during the 1990s. The regular opening of new border crossings and road improvement on both sides of the border aided initial growth. This was followed by Russian disillusionment with low-quality Chinese goods, as well as discouragement by regional authorities alarmed by the scale of Chinese immigration. But in 1997 there were an estimated 40,000 truck trips and 3,000 bus trips across the border, and new crossings were still being opened. The truck trips accounted for only 8.5 per cent of all tons moved – sea and rail transport both accounted for over 40 per cent – but much more by value. The main barrier to further expansion appears to be Chinese refusal to allow Russian trucks further than 100–120 km into China (Kurshin 1998).

Rivers

River transport in one respect resembles motor transport. Its functions have remained much the same in the north, but foreign trade has become prominent in the south.

The north has seen changes in organisation and the use of equipment. The Lena United Steamship Company (LORP), covering that river and others draining to the Arctic, still exists, but in 1996 the port of Osetrovo, together with others along the upper Lena, established the Upper Lena Steamship Company. In 1997 it handled about 1.5 million tons, including 1.0 million for the Far North. The quantities seem small but must be seen in the light of a decline in total Lena traffic from 13.6 million tons in 1988 to 3.3 million in 1997. In 1986, the peak year for northern supply through Osetrovo, it alone accounted for 4.8 million tons (Galkin 1998: 21). Even the traffic still offered frequently reaches Osetrovo too late in the season to be carried. Declining traffic and the disappearance of subsidies have decimated the steamship companies' revenues. As many river-sea vessels as possible have been moved to the southern Far East or the Black Sea, where they can earn money year-round in maritime trade. Vessels expensive to operate, like hydrofoils, are now little used.

In the south, traffic on the Amur has declined more than that by any other transport mode. From 32.6 million tons in 1988 it fell to 4.9 million in 1995 – a rate of decline twice that of the Lena. The Amur River Steamship Company owned 150 vessels in 1996 compared with 1,200 in Soviet times. The Company responded by switching river-sea ships to maritime trade. For foreign operations it formed a joint-venture company with a Korean firm, using ships reflagged in Honduras. In common with other owners of river vessels, it is also participating in river trade with China. Like that by road, the trade has fluctuated but generally grown. By 1993 some half dozen Russian and a similar number of Chinese river ports were open to international trade. Freight reached 0.7 million tons in that year, most of it carried in Russian vessels (*RFEU*, November 1993, pp. 3, 4).

Maritime Shipping

The RFE cargo turnover halved from 1990 to 1995, to 37.5 million tons, and has continued to fall (*Table 5.1*). The percentage decline has been less than for other forms of transport, however, thanks to foreign trade: in contrast to European Russia there are few alternatives to using Russian seaports. Cabotage traffic, mainly concerned with supplying northern coastal settlements, has declined

Table 5.1 Russian Far East Ports: Cargo Turnover (million metric tons)

	1991	1994	1995	1997
Total	58.4		37.5	33.8
Including Exports	18.2		23.0	23.2
Imports	4.8		1.4	1.3
Domestic	35.4		13.1	9.3
Types of cargo				
General	12.1		12.0	10.6
Breakbulk	19.5		10.6	9.8
Ferry railcar	10.6		4.3	3.5
Timber	6.5		2.5	2.1
Oil products	6.8		5.8	6.0
From fishing ports	3.9		2.2	1.8
Other	1.0		0.1	0.0
Major ports				
Vladivostok ports*	6.1	4.2	4.4	3.9
Nakhodka ports**	12.3	10.6	10.2	9.5
Including oil	5.1	4.0	4.1	4.0
Vostochnyy	8.8	8.1	8.5	8.1
Including coal	6.0	5.3	6.8	7.2
Vanino	9.8	6.7	6.8	6.4
Sakhalin ports	9.5		3.2	2.5
Including Kholmsk		2.7		2.0
Northern ports	7.6	2.6	2.0	1.8
Including Magadan	0.9	0.9		0.7
Petropavlovsk-Kamchatskiy		0.7		0.5

Notes:
*Commercial and fishing.
**Commercial, fishing and oil.
Source: Data from *The Russian Far East: A Business Reference Guide* (1999) *Seattle*: Russian Far East Update, pp. 91, 93, 97.

catastrophically, while exports have even risen over the past few years. Passenger traffic has declined even more than domestic freight traffic. FESCO used to carry 20,000 passengers a year within Primorskiy kray alone. Now passenger services have virtually ceased along the whole Pacific coast, apart from ferry traffic (*Ports* 1997: 3; 'Itogi goda' 1999: 3).

While import-export traffic has held up relatively well, it is far less reliable than in Soviet times, when the government favoured long-term contracts. In recent years the vagaries of the rouble and of Russian taxes and tariffs, together with erratic world commodity markets, have brought great fluctuations. In 1997, for example, movements through RFE ports fell by 15–20 per cent, mainly because of high railway tariffs, and in 1998 the August financial crisis brought an immediate drop of 20–25 per cent compared to the same period in 1997.

Russian-flagged ships carry a much smaller share of import-export traffic than in Soviet times. In Russia as a whole in the early 1990s, foreign vessels carried no more than 30 per cent, but recent estimates range up to 94 per cent (Mavrichenko and Zholobnyuk 1999: 10). The shift began earlier in the RFE: foreign vessels were already carrying over 70 per cent in 1990 (Radnayev 1996: 77). There are two components in this shift. Firstly, Russian companies entered the 1990s with an elderly fleet. Half their ships have since been scrapped and not replaced for lack of money. Secondly, they have transferred many ships – well over 40 per cent of deadweight tonnage nationally by1998 – to flags of convenience. Some of the 'lost' traffic, therefore, is being carried in Russian-owned but foreign-flagged vessels.

Foreign competition for the carriage of imports and exports, and decline in cabotage, have caused RFE shipping companies to seek business entirely outside the country. Some ships are chartered to foreign customers, others are now owned and operated by Russian-controlled foreign companies. FESCO owns both an Australian cruise line that uses ex-Russian ships, and a container-ship company based in Seattle. The Primorskoye Steamship Company (PRISCO), the major operator of tankers in the RFE and now an entirely private company, works all over the world (*PRN*, 12 July 1999). The Arctic Maritime Steamship Line (AMSL: formerly the Northeast Maritime Directorate of the Ministry of the Merchant Marine, and still government-owned), has seen its Arctic business decline from 28,000 tons in 1991 to 3,300 in 1997. Though still based in Tiksi it now earns 90 per cent of its income outside the Arctic, mostly in the non-Russian Far East but also in the Mediterranean. Similarly, most ships belonging to the Sakhalin Steamship Company have departed to other parts of the world, and the company hires in smaller vessels from the AMSL to fulfil local obligations (*Yakutia*, 6 August 1998). Thus the focus of the RFE companies has changed radically since Soviet times. Then, their primary functions were to service Soviet foreign trade and supply northern settlements. Now, they try to make money wherever they can, and at present the best opportunities are largely outside Russia.

Despite their manoeuvring, virtually all RFE steamship companies have financial problems. The Kamchatka Steamship Company went bankrupt, and the Sakhalin Steamship Company has been operating at a loss. In July 1999, 28 of 38 ships belonging to Vostoktransflot, Russia's largest refrigerated shipping line, were arrested abroad for non-payment of debts (*PRN*, 12 July 1999). PRISCO and FESCO had incurred debts of US$200 millions and US$145 millions by 1998, though they are considered relatively successful, having used the money to rejuvenate their fleets. PRISCO, which owned 45 tankers in 1997, has bought 14 new ones since then. It now has one of the most modern tanker fleets in the world, with an average age of 11.2 years (*PRN*, 12 July 1999). FESCO's fleet will average 12 years by 2005, after it has sold 65 old ships and bought 45 new ones (*PRN*, 24 May 1999).

Changing focus may give the better-run companies reasonable prospects, but what about the services they have abandoned, especially northern supply? Russian maritime writers argue that they simply cannot be maintained on a commercial basis. In particular, it is not commercially feasible to replace the Arctic supply vessels that are approaching retirement. They are uneconomical for use elsewhere, and non-specialised vessels cannot safely replace them. Most are small, so that they can use primitive northern harbours, but the smaller they are, the more uneconomical. It is claimed that an Arctic tanker of 20,000 tons dwt needs a subsidy of 20–30 per cent, a supply vessel of 5,000 to 7,000 tons a 50–60 per cent subsidy, and a 2,500-tonner a full subsidy (Kuzovkin 1997, pp. 21–22). Ships of similar size are needed also for the northern Pacific coast. Unfortunately the government has little money to offer. Under the 1993–2000 'Program for the Restoration of the Russian Merchant Fleet', the RFE was allocated 200 ships out of a national total of 589. But the Program has produced little, apart from the ordering of six 16,000-ton Arctic tankers from a German shipyard. Almost all the remaining government money made available to the merchant marine has gone on the last nuclear icebreaker, *50 let pobedy*, which in 1998 was two-thirds finished and needed another 34 months and US$126 millions for completion. The choice of priorities seems questionable. The existing nuclear icebreakers spend most of their time laid up for lack of money to pay for fuel or repairs. And the entire NSR carries only 2 million tons a year – only 20–25 per cent of what moves north by river ('Ledokol'nyy' 1998: 21).

Seaports

During Soviet times the main RFE ports belonged to the steamship companies. Others were owned by the fishing, mining, and lumber industries. Most ports are now independent, though the consortia that own them may well include their former owners. Also, new ports have been created on the basis of shipyards. What appears to be one port to the outside observer may in fact consist of several. Vladivostok, for example, contains commercial, fishing, shipyard-based, and former naval ports, with separate but partly overlapping ownership (*Ports*, 1997: 8).

In Soviet times almost all foreign trade went through Nakhodka, Vostochnyy, Vladivostok, and Vanino, accounting for 74, 96, 49, and 20 per cent respectively of their cargo turnover in 1985 (*RFEU*, April 1995, p. 4). Economic collapse left foreign trade as one of the few opportunities for ports to make money, so many others requested permission to participate. In consequence a smaller volume of trade is now divided among far more ports than before. The established ports are underused: recent estimates suggest up to 40 per cent spare capacity. This does not mean they have adequate facilities. On the contrary, competition has forced them to invest heavily. The present situation may be transitory: the world trend is for major traffic flows to be channelled through fewer and fewer huge ports. No RFE port handles heavy traffic by world standards: turnover at the four major ones together in 1997 was under 28 million tons (*Table 5.1*).

Nakhodka and Vostochnyy are the most modern large ports in the region, and as the principal conduits for exports they have managed relatively well in post-Soviet times. Exports were 4.6 and 9.4 million tons respectively in 1990, and 4.9 and 7.8 million in 1997. Imports and coastal trade both fell heavily, however, so total cargo turnover declined by about 30 per cent (*RFEU*, November 1998, p. 9; *Ports* 1997: 7–9). Container traffic almost ceased as the Landbridge lost its reputation. The main freight through Vostochnyy recently has been coal, brought by rail from the Kuzbass (2.5 million tons in the mid-1990s) and south Yakutia (4.5 million). The port could handle nearly twice as much, but Australian and Chinese coal is cheaper. New terminals for fertiliser and clinker exports may attract more traffic, but there is much spare capacity ('Vostochnyy port' 1997: 16–17). The same is true of Nakhodka, which handles mainly oil, metals, and timber. Oil exports have expanded since duties were removed in 1996.

Vladivostok's cargo profile and trends resemble those of Nakhodka, on a smaller scale and without the oil. Between 1990 and 1997 exports rose from 0.3 to 2.9 million tons, with a sharp rise in 1991 when the port was first opened to foreign ships. Total cargo turnover fell about 40 per cent. The port is served mainly by rail, though some Chinese exports are trucked from Harbin for shipment to Seattle by FESCO (*PRN*, 26 April 1999).

Vanino, the fourth major port, shows similar trends again. Exports comprise coal, timber – partly from the nearby ex-naval port of Sovetskaya Gavan' – and, recently, fertilisers and aluminium. They rose from 1.9 to 2.1 million tons, while total cargo fell from 9.8 to 6.4 million, between 1990 and 1997. Coastal trade slumped from 7.8 to 2.7 million tons. The future of Vanino largely depends on the BAM. If it were in good order, offering a route into Siberia 1,000 km shorter than from Nakhodka, Vanino as the terminal port could prosper. It is normally ice-free and offers deep-water berths comparable to those of Nakhodka. But at present, to take one example, 75 per cent of fertilizer exports from Siberia and the Urals to eastern Asia leave Russia through Baltic ports (*RFEU*, November 1998, p. 10; *Ports 1997*: 12–13).

The section on railways referred to prospective Chinese trade through Pos'yet and Zarubino, two small ports near the Chinese and Korean borders. They have made little progress so far. Cargo turnover was 1.4 and 0.2 million tons respectively in 1990, 0.3 and 0.07 million in 1997. Immediate prospects seem brightest for Pos'yet. The port, controlled by Nakhodka, is being developed with Chinese partners to handle cargo en route to and from Pusan, in South Korea. The first container ship on the route arrived in July 1999, and its containers were then trucked into China (*RFEU*, November 1998, p. 8; *PRN*, 19 July 1999). As for Zarubino, Japanese private and state interests intend to develop the port to handle goods in transit between China and Japan, if the Russian government will give certain guarantees. The government, however, is reluctant, since it thinks most benefits will accrue to China (*Vladivostok News*, 2 October 1998; *PRN*, 17 May 1999).

The remaining RFE ports were built mainly to handle supplies for their local regions, arriving from the main ports, and to send back timber, minerals or fish. A few had naval functions. Now, several participate in foreign trade to a small extent, whether exporting directly or importing fuel and supplies. But their main function remains the same. As might be expected, turnover has fallen and financial problems are severe. The major ports outside the Arctic used to handle from 2.5 to over 3.0 million tons a year, except that the Sakhalin ferry port of Kholmsk had a turnover of 7.0 million tons. Now they commonly handle a third to a fifth of those amounts. The Arctic ports are in even worse shape, since the supplies that do arrive are rarely enough to meet local needs during the winter. Some, like Cherskiy, have virtually ceased to operate (see *Ports 1997*, pp. 14–18 for more details).

Air Transport

In Soviet times the RFE was served by the Yakut and Far Eastern Air Transport Directorates. Air transport carried twice the share of passenger traffic that it did in the rest of the country, reflecting great distances and poor surface transport, but it was almost all domestic. Khabarovsk was the only international airport. After the fall of the USSR the Yakut Directorate became Sakhaavia, thirteen companies were formed out of the regional detachments of the Far Eastern Directorate, and several new companies emerged (Radnayev 1996: 86). But without subsidies it proved impossible to maintain regional services at the Soviet level, especially in the north. By 1993, those out of Khabarovsk had declined to a quarter of what they were. Northern airports are unlikely to close down unless the local population leaves, since they constitute a vital link with the outside world, but the small ones have been handed over to local communities or industries. Closure is more feasible farther south: out of 29 airports in Primorskii krai, 26 had closed by 1993.

Like their maritime and river counterparts, air transport companies have tried to compensate by opening international routes or seeking business entirely abroad. Another half-dozen airports joined Khabarovsk in acquiring international status by 1993. With the country in almost permanent economic crisis, however, the market for international flights has fluctuated, and providing them has not proved to be a universal solution.

Several companies have failed or remain in business only because of support from or ownership by regional administrations. Mavial, the airline serving Magadan oblast', is assisted by the provincial administration, which owns 51 per cent. Orient Avia went bankrupt in 1997. It was one of the top four Russian airlines, founded by Aeroflot and RFE interests including FESCO and the ports of Vladivostok and Nakhodka, but failed partly because the Ministry of Defence and Federal Border Service did not pay their bills, incurred for flying servicemen on leave (*Vladivostok News*, 24 July 1997). In 1998 Sakhaavia also went bankrupt, its staff unpaid and its aircraft arrested abroad for non-payment of fuel bills and airport fees. It had apparently failed to adapt to market conditions, remaining overstaffed in the Soviet fashion (*Yakutia*, no. 74, 21 April 1998; no. 110, 19 July 1998; Reshetnikov 1998). And after the August 1998 financial crisis, Alaska Airlines closed all its services between the RFE and western North America, having been an enthusiastic pioneer in providing them.

Not all has been disaster. Some companies have been relatively successful, and the availability of international services has greatly improved. Very large freight-transport aircraft and helicopters, inherited from the Soviet era, have been able to find good markets for their services abroad. Shortcomings in the northern-supply system have enlarged the role of air transport: some settlements now import most of their winter supplies by air from abroad. And facilities have been improved with foreign help, influenced by the potential for routing international flights across the region (Zaytsev 1999: 2; *PRN*, 8 March 1999).

In sum, air transport is adapting slowly and often painfully to new conditions. Further changes can be expected, especially the amalgamation of small companies.

SUB-REGIONS OF THE RUSSIAN FAR EAST

The various transport modes have faced common problems and attempted similar solutions. At the same time, some problems and possible solutions for all modes have varied between regions within the RFE. The greatest differences are between the southeast and the north. In the southeast all transport modes have to restructure to serve a more globally-oriented economy. Traffic volumes and revenues are a fraction of what they once were, but there is some hope that they will eventually recover, as the region becomes integrated into a rebounding Asia-Pacific economy.

In the north the picture is different: in neither the short nor the long term is there cause for optimism. Immediate problems relate to the cessation or non-payment of subsidies. Without them, many northern communities cannot pay in advance for vital supplies. Year after year they face winter with too little fuel and food, because shippers and transport companies have learned not to deliver on promise of payment, and the federal government has to react under crisis conditions – which may mean, for example, flying in supplies because the navigation season has ended. This creates an unsustainable situation for the transport system. Companies are expected to be able to move goods when required, but their equipment may lie idle in any year. Efficient planning becomes impossible.

Even if government help becomes more systematic and timely, a longer-term problem will remain. Much of the northern economy was viable in Soviet times only because it operated within a relatively closed system. Its prospects as part of the world economy are much dimmer. That is not to say that resources cannot be exploited successfully. The problem is that Soviet exploitation supported a far bigger infrastructure than would be considered feasible in the world's other northern regions. The transport system was designed to serve a large, permanent population, much of it in cities of a size inconceivable in the non-Soviet north. It seems unlikely that such a system will be needed in the near future, once the population and economy have stabilised. Parts of the surface transport system may continue in use because they already exist. As they wear out, however, air transport may be adequate to serve a much-reduced population in many areas. This assumes, of course, that future Russian governments do not reverse the present internationalisation and open-market policies.

CONCLUSIONS: RUSSIAN VIEWS OF THE FUTURE

Russian writers on transport have widely varying views of the future. Some simply project present trends, anticipating more foreign participation in RFE transport and more foreign activity by Russian firms. Others clearly believe that the present situation is transitory. Eventually the economy will recover. The government will then restore the merchant fleet, protect the transport industry from foreign competition, and once again subsidise remote-area development, especially in the RFE. Recommendations for transport investment are framed to fit this model.

Another view, already implemented to some extent, is that the RFE must identify and capitalise on the advantages of its geographical position. Recognising the potential to service international air routes is one example. Other schemes relate to surface transport. Some, like the export of goods from northeast China through RFE ports and the opening of ferry links to Japan, are based on local geographical potentials. Others are based on the region's position between Europe and East Asia. They include the revival of the Landbridge and the scheme to link the Japanese and European railway systems by way of Sakhalin Island. Other schemes are based on the region's position between Europe and North America. At the more practicable end of the scale is a protocol, signed by Russian, China and the USA in June 1999, to create a transport corridor from northern China and Mongolia through RFE ports to the west coast of North America (*PRN*, 21 June 1999). At the more grandiose end of the scale is an old but still seductive scheme to build a railway through Yakutsk to

Chukotka and then across or under the Bering Strait. A current version of the scheme would involve a tunnel for both railway and power lines, take 15–17 years to build, and cost US$70 billions (*PRN*, 4 January 1999).

However one may regard some of the more fanciful schemes, the central theme seems valid. In Soviet times, as was pointed out at the beginning of the chapter, the RFE was primarily defined by being at the end of a railway line from Moscow. As long as post-Soviet policies promote participation in the global economy, the RFE transport system must be restructured to take advantage of the region's location.

REFERENCES

Baliyev, A. (1997) 'Second wind for the BAM', *CDPSP*, 49 (26): 13–4 (translated from *Rossiyskaya gazeta*, 1 July).

Bushin, A.V. and Merinov, I.I. (1997) 'Stroitel'stvo tonneley', *Zheleznodorozhnyy transport*, 3, 39–44.

CDPSP: Current Digest of the Post-Soviet Press. Weekly translation journal, pub. Columbus, Ohio, USA.

Chernogayeva, G. (1997) 'Bypassing Russia', *CDPSP*, 49 (19), 19–20 (translated from *Kommersant-Daily*, 29 April).

Galkin, V. (1998) 'Zavoz gruzov v rayony Kraynego Severa', *Rechnoy transport*, 1, 19–22.

'Itogi goda' (1999) *Morskoy flot*, 3, 3–4.

Ivanov, A.P. (1997) 'Dal'nevostochnoy doroge – 100 let', *Zheleznodorozhnyy transport*, 10, 61–9.

Krinitskiy, Ye. (1998) 'Transportnyye problemy Rossii na rubezhe tysyacheletiya', *Zheleznodorozhnyy transport*, 6,13–6.

Kurshin, A.B. (1998) 'ASMAP – dvizheniye na vostok' (Interview), *Avtomobil'nyy transport*, 10, 17–20.

Kuzovkin, V.V. (1997) 'Kakiye suda my stroim' (Interview), *Morskoy flot*, 3, 20–2.

'Ledokol'nyy flot Rossii' (1998) *Morskoy flot*, 11–2, 21–2.

Mavrichenko, V. and Zholobnyuk, M. (1999) 'Valyutnyye poteri transportnoy sostavlyayushchey', *Morskoy flot*, 3, 9–10.

Morozov, M. (1998) 'Nam lyubyye dorogi dorogi?', *Yakutia*, 188, 8 October.

Moshenko, O.A. (1999) 'Zheleznodorozhnyy transport i regiony: razvivat' partnerskiye otnosheniya', *Zheleznodorozhnyy transport*, 3, 2–5.

North, R. N. (1990) 'The Far Eastern transport system' in A. Rodgers (ed.), *The Soviet Far East: Geographical Perspectives on Development*, London: Routledge pp. 185–224.

North, R. N. (1996) *Russian Transport: Problems and Prospects*. London: Royal Institute of International Affairs. Post-Soviet Business Forum Series.

Pashkova, T. (1998) 'Transsib – osnovnoy transit Rossii', *Zheleznodorozhnyy transport*, 8: 40–3.

Ports of the Russian Far East (1997) Second edition. Seattle: Russian Far East Update.

PRN: Pacific Russia News. Weekly newsletter, pub. Vancouver, Canada.

Radnayev, B.L. (1996) *Transport vostoka Rossii v novoy sotsial'no-ekonomicheskoy i geopoliticheskoy situatsii*, Novosibirsk, SO RAN.

Reshetnikov, N. (1998) 'Kak nam obystroit' aviatsiyu respubliki', *Yakutia*, 203, 29 October.

RFEU: Russian Far East Update. Monthly newsletter, pub. Seattle, USA

Transsib (1998). Special issue of *Okeanskiye vesti*, June.

'Vostochnyy port – chetvert' let raboty' (1997), *Morskoy flot*, 9, 16–7.

Wadhams, N. (1997) 'Japan still hesitant about krai', *Vladivostok News*, 18 September.

Yefremova, L. (1998) '"Severnyy ekspress"'nabirayet khod', *Yakutia*, 118, 2 July.

Zaytsev, G.N. (1999) 'Sud'ba otrasli reshayetsya v regionakh', *Grazhdanskaya aviatsiya*, 1, 1–3.

Zhuravel', A.I. (1997) 'Povysit' otdachu ot BAMa', *Zheleznodorozhnyy transport*, 9, 61–2.

Zil'bershekht, B. and Podol'skaya, V. (1998) 'Transit za valyutu', *Morskoy flot*, 5–6, 3–4.

Chapter 6

The Exercise of Rights to Resources in the Russian Far East

Judith Thornton

INTRODUCTION

In 1989, on the eve of economic reform, the city of Khabarovsk was a backward, colonial outpost, one of the most distant points in the Moscow-centered allocation networks controlling access to resources in the former Soviet Union. A Western visitor, strolling wide, tree-lined Karl Marx Street, could imagine that he or she had been time-warped back to the 1940s. There were a few autos on the streets, most of them military jeeps. Shelves in the government gastronome were empty except for Bulgarian pickles and stale bread. The local bookstore stocked rows of handbooks on repair of diesel engines and rail car maintenance. In the local market, ethnic Korean farmers sold sunflower seeds, cabbage, and small, pock-marked pears.

Ten years later, in October of 1999, when Prime Minister Vladimir Putin visited the same city to open a new bridge linking Khabarovsk and neighboring Jewish Autonomous Republic, what was now Muraviev-Amurskiy Street had changed. The avenue was crowded with Japanese cars. Shoppers wore Chinese leather coats. Their shopping bags were heavy with local fruits and vegetables, chicken from Heilongjiang, and black caviar from the Amur river. In the freshly-painted private shops, the shoppers could buy cameras from Japan, plumbing supplies from Taiwan, and umbrellas from Hong Kong, although, since the fall in the value of the ruble in 1998, foreign products were often underpriced by new domestic products. New apartments were under construction all over the city. Although the territory had suffered a drastic fall in official employment – industrial employment had dropped from 235,700 in 1992 to 127,100 in 1998 – the city appeared prosperous.[1]

A DECADE OF DECLINE

During the years of reform, residents of Khabarovsk and other regions of the Russian Far East (RFE), lived through a decade of declining production and growing inequality of income. Twice, the value of their savings was wiped out – first, in 1992–93, through hyperinflation, and, next, in the financial crisis and bank collapse of August 1998. A declining military presence in the region and decreased demand for military hardware reduced regional employment. A partial opening to the world market and adjustment of domestic prices to world market levels, revealed that many domestic firms produced negative value added; at world prices, their costs of raw materials, energy, and transport exceeded the value of final output.

The region's problems mirrored those of other regions. Many people were in the wrong places, doing the wrong things. Yet, without land, housing, and labor markets, unemployed workers often had nowhere to go where they could re-employ themselves productively.

In the wake of Russia's financial crisis and the subsequent collapse in the rouble exchange rate, the region's situation is difficult. Households can no longer afford their earlier imports of food and consumer goods, while domestic ability to supply import substitutes remains limited. With reduced federal tax collection, federal obligations for pensions and infrastructure accumulate as arrears. Firms that are unable to collect payment for their products transact through a chain of supplier credits and barter, accumulating rising backlogs of payments and tax arrears. Physical and institutional infrastructure is deteriorating, with frequent interruptions in municipal supplies of heat, electricity, and water. Significant groups of the population survive below the poverty line. A large informal economy offsets some of the decline, but it leaves citizens vulnerable to private enforcement mechanisms and corruption.

The long anticipated inflow of foreign investment that was to turn the RFE into a bustling transport node and exporter to the Pacific has never appeared. Foreign investors, confronting an uncertain political environment and obstructive regulation, postponed investment, while domestic managers transferred their marketing and sales to offshore affiliates and left their revenues offshore.

RUSSIA'S MANY FUTURES

What lies ahead for this resource-rich region? Can Russia stem its decline? Economic decline in the RFE faces Moscow with political risk. Contraction of the regional economy, out-migration of its population, and a reduction of Russian military presence all raise fears in Moscow of an influx of foreign population and eventual loss of control of the region. Yet, a fragmented central government is unlikely to be able to assure regional stability either through direct subsidy or by providing the infrastructure for investment.

The future of the RFE region is hostage to policies determined at the federation level. A new administration headed by Vladimir Putin might pursue three different policies. First, if the legal infrastructure of resource ownership remains ambiguous and the short-run interests of Russia's exporters prevail, then raw material exports will continue to fund capital flight, generating little income for the government budget or investment in the domestic economy.

Alternatively, if a stronger federal government captures a larger share of resource rents, allocating these rents to heavy industry and manufacturing, then Russia's resources might be used, as they were used in the Soviet era, to subsidize a large, inefficient manufacturing sector. In this second case, the government would increase funding for science, engineering, and technology, but technological development would be directed toward industries that strengthened military capacity, such as communications, aerospace, and electronics. In a protectionist Russia, the standard of living is likely to remain depressed and export of skilled labor and capital is likely to be restricted administratively.

A third direction of policy would require major legislative, administrative, and judicial reorganization. It would replace the current intertwining of political power and property with transparent governance institutions and rule of law. A transparent, market-oriented legal framework for natural resources would guarantee private ownership of agricultural land and housing. It would resolve the current stalemate between federal, regional, and local officials in their competition to exercise control over Russia's resource wealth. It would provide a secure legal and administrative framework within which investors were willing to commit resources to development and communities had the ability and incentive to preserve resource stocks for the future.

THE LEGAL FRAMEWORK FOR ACCESS TO NATURAL RESOURCES

What accounts for the gulf between the legal framework for access to resources and the *de facto* administrative arrangements that have emerged? In fact, the Russian framework for management of resources retains many of the perverse features of the Soviet era, but, today, the administrative control rights are combined with considerable opportunity for private capture of resource rents. In the resource sectors, the value of a nominally private firm depends primarily on its access to underlying resource stocks.

That access remains subject to opaque practices and, sometimes, to corruption.

In the former Soviet Union, the state was the legal owner of capital stock, land, and resource wealth, but the control rights to assets were exercised by ministerial bureaucracies and enterprise managers. Decision-makers who controlled wealth also exercised considerable power to allocate benefits to their own constituencies and impose costs on others, but, except at the top, there was considerable monitoring of open corruption.

In the reform economy, although the majority of large firms are privatized with a hybrid mix of ownership, the mineral reserves, fish stocks, and forest lands remain the property of the state. There is a growing body of parliamentary laws, presidential decrees, administrative regulations, and bureaucratic instructions defining the processes and terms by which users gain access to resources. However, legislation is often inconsistent and contradictory. Regulations contradict the laws they are supposed to implement, and administrative practice follows neither the laws nor the regulations.

Many of the fundamental contradictions arose at the start of reform in the conflict between a pro-reform president, issuing decrees, and an anti-reform parliament, overruling the president with new laws. Inconsistencies of implementation often reflect the unresolved struggle for control of resource wealth between local, territorial, and central government agencies. While the original Federation Treaty provided joint jurisdiction of federal and territorial governments over resources, the subsequent basic legislation passed by the parliament provides federal ownership, with federal subjects having the right to participate in management of resources.

The Federation Treaty

The foundations of Russian resource management were built as the Soviet Union collapsed. The Federation Treaty, signed on 13 March 1992, delimited powers between the Russian Federation and the republics. This treaty reflected the competing claims for control over resources by assigning many of the powers over land and natural resources to the joint jurisdiction of federal and republican authorities.

The Russian Federation is assigned exclusive jurisdiction over the federal energy system, territorial waters, and the continental shelf. Utilization of natural resources and protection of the environment are subject to joint jurisdiction as is protection of original areas of habitation and traditional ways of life of small ethnic communities. Article III says, 'Questions of the possession, use and disposal of land, its mineral, water and other natural resources, are settled on the basis of the legislation of the Russian Federation and the legislation of the republics in the Russian Federation. The status of federal natural resources is defined by mutual accord between the federal bodies of the Russian Federation and the bodies of state power of the republics.' The republics have all remaining state power on their territory, other than those powers under the jurisdiction of the federal bodies.

The Law on Mineral Rights

The Russian mineral rights law, *Zakon O Nedrax*, (literally, 'Law on Subsoil') adopted by the Russian Parliament, 21 February 1992 established a State Minerals Fund, *Gosudarstvennyi Fond Nedr*, and delineated procedures for licensing mining activities, surveying mineral resources, and paying for access to mineral rights. Administration of the State Minerals Fund is under dual control of the central government and territorial officials. But, in fact, the procedures described in the legislation assign most of the rights to regulate resource use to the central authorities. All mineral stocks that were under the control of separate industrial ministries in the former Soviet Union are to be administered by the Committee on Geology and Use of Minerals. The Committee on Geology will then license rights to exploit mineral deposits to firms and organizations.

The rights of separate levels of government are spelled out in considerable detail, with virtually all important property rights assigned to the central government.

Central Government Rights

- develop and update legislation;
- develop procedures for payment, together with other entities;
- develop a strategy for exploitation of mineral stocks;
- develop an integrated information data base;
- enforce legislation regarding mineral resources;
- undertake exploration and valuation of mineral resources.

Territorial and Autonomous Republics Rights

- develop and use the territorial geological data base;
- value local resources;
- articulate the interests of national minority groups.

Municipal and Local Rights

- participate in the process of licensing in so far as it involves rights to lease land;
- develop a raw materials base for local firms in the building materials industry;
- license and monitor the mining of scattered resources.

Under the legislation all enterprises, including those currently engaged in resource extraction, receive licenses, issued jointly by the Russian Committee on Geology and Use of Minerals and by the authorities of the republic or territory of the Russian Federation. Licenses may be issued by auction or competitive bidding. A license grants exclusive rights to the mineral wealth of a land parcel together with the right to manage the leased territory for a specified time period, generally five years for exploration or twenty years for extraction.

In the original legislation, contracts could take the form of a concession, a production sharing agreement, or a service contract. Subsequently, enabling regulations failed to support resource concessions.

The high share of the lease specified for local governments set a unique precedent in Russian practice. Payment could be set in money or as a share of output, with the revenues shared among levels of government according to the following scale:[2]

1 Hydrocarbons: federal 40 per cent, territory 30 per cent, municipal or local 30 per cent;
2 Minerals: federal 25 per cent, territory 25 per cent, municipal or local 50 per cent.

A preference for domestic over foreign firms was reflected in the Russian policy of 'reasonable protection.' The term implies an explicit preference for resource development proposals which 1) involve domestic majority control, 2) commit to substantial purchase of domestically produced equipment, and 3) guarantee high levels of domestic employment. In retrospect, these constraints made it more difficult for both foreign and domestic partners to introduce Western technology and know-how and to operate efficiently in Russia.

The pages that follow provide brief surveys of the government policies and administrative arrangements for exercising ownership to resources in several sectors of the Russian economy – mining, forestry, and fishing, based on the experience of investors in the Russian Far East. I argue that Russia's vast endowment of natural resources diverted much of the government's effort away from the building of a framework of market-supporting institutions to strategies for maintaining control of access to resource wealth. The policies of government decision-makers could serve several goals. Resource rents might provide central or territorial budget revenue, used for public infrastructure, economic growth, or social services. Investment in resources might employ workers moving out of declining economic sectors. Low cost access to resource stocks might be used by government allocators to transfer benefits to cronies or to co-opt the political support of interest groups, and, of course, government allocators might extract private benefits from their control of rights to resources. Since the government, itself, was the legal owner of resources and determined the terms on which some would gain access to them, control of the government became the most valuable asset of all.

PRIVATIZATION

Property rights are an essential part of the institutional infrastructure of an economy. If we mean by property rights the rules of the game defining the forms that competition for resources may take in a society, then property rights are defined by formal laws, administrative practices, taxes, and informal custom. In Western practice, private ownership of an asset is associated with two types of rights, called control rights and cash flow rights by Boycko et al (1995) in their book, Privatizing Russia. Control rights are the rights to allocate property among uses, to exclude others from its use, and to transfer it to another. Cash flow rights are the rights to enjoy income or benefit from its use.

Private property rights provide incentives to create wealth and to use it efficiently because they internalize the benefits and costs of the owner's actions on to the owner.

It is not the formal, legal ownership rights that determine people's behaviour. Rather, it is the *de facto* rights that people face that provide incentives. The *de facto* rights to resources take into account the transactions costs of exercising ownership – costs of gaining information and enforcing agreement – as well as legal rules.

The demand for privatization of assets in Russia reflected the widespread recognition that political control of economic activity provided perverse incentives and distorted information. The absence of markets impeded the movement of resources to higher value uses. Political decision makers who bore none of the financial consequences for their decisions could pursue private agendas without accountability for costs. If their goal was maximization of political power, then this goal might be served by establishing bureaucratic regulations controlling all rights of access – access to entry, access to foreign markets, access to scarce, underpriced supplies, and, ultimately, access to positions in a regulatory hierarchy that allowed the decision-maker to give benefits to some constituencies and to hold other groups hostage. Russia pursued a uniquely ambitious privatization program. Yet, private firms in the resource sectors were dependent on their political relationships so long as the government controlled access to land, resource reserves, electric power, and taxes.

Privatization in the Russian Far East

Privatization in the RFE, as elsewhere, was carried out in accordance with the established program of the Russian Federation. The federal privatization agency, *Gosudarstvennyi komitet Rossiiskoi Federatsii po upravleniiu gosudarstvennym imushchestvom – or Goskomimushchestvo RF*, operated through a network of agencies in each territory and municipality. Privatization committees at each level prepared and submitted privatization projects for approval by their higher-level agency, by territorial officials, and by the legislature. When approval was given, they carried out the formal privatization.

In practice, there was intense political pressure for control of valuable assets and many violations of the formal rules.[3] The determination of whether individual production units would be privatized as separate enterprises or as subsidiaries in a larger structure was also negotiated on political, not economic, grounds. Managers of a plant could sometimes buy their independence by agreeing to assign a share of the commercialized firm's stock to a holding company controlled by higher level officials.

Small scale privatization of firms in retail trade, public food services, consumer services, and light industry proceeded rapidly. By 1995, the services sectors comprised a mixture of units – privatized state enterprises, new private firms, and municipal firms. About three-quarters of these small service firms had been privatized by commercial bidding, a process in which bidders agreed to meet a set of formal requirements. Bidders agreed to continue the same profile of services after privatization, to guarantee jobs for existing workers, commit to improvements and repairs, and agree to acquire new machinery and equipment.

Table 6.1 Extent of Small Scale Privatization in June 1997

	Total Firms Privatized (Number)	*Trade (Number)*	*(% of Total in sector)*	*Food Services (Number)*	*(% of Total in sector)*	*Services (Number)*	*(% of Total in sector)*
Primorskii	1274	530	73.8	95	74.2	164	75.2
Khabarovsk	1394	495	51.6	74	13.1	308	88.3
Amur	832	277	18.5	32	3.2	154	12.3
Kamchatka	502	128	15.2	23	16.1	92	93
Magadan	739	220	41.7	47	37	136	77.7
Sakhalin	1053	481	92.3	102	95.3	152	100
Sakha Republic	415	61	18.8	14	30.4	51	66.2
Jewish	159	40	93	6	66.7	20	95.2
Krasnoyarsk	2051	778	15.8	123	11.8	144	8.7
Novosibirsk	1885	596	3.4	118	22.2	116	40.3
Omsk	1325	385	51.4	73	10.6	166	38.3
Tomsk	823	305	63.3	52	58.4	147	74.6
Chita	1305	432	18.7	65	21.4	202	32
Buryat Republic	1362	411	92.8	56	72.8	163	97.6

Source: Primorskii kraevoi komitet gosudarstennoi statistiki (1997), *Ekonomicheskie I sotsial'nye indikatory po Primorskomu Kraiu*, Vladivostok: Goskomstate Rossii.

In the case of small-scale services privatization provided a basis for genuine competition.

Voucher privatization of large-scale firms proceeded more slowly in the Far East than in other regions because of the large share of firms providing infrastructure services and producing military products. Nevertheless, by 1994, in two-thirds of the firms, employees had opted for the second variant of privatization which allowed employees to acquire 51 per cent of the voting stock of their firms, bidding with vouchers.

The relative roles of the federal and territorial levels of governments may be inferred from a 1995 report of the process in Khabarovsk:

Large blocks of stock (15–51% of authorized capital) were assigned to state ownership during the privatization of 259 enterprises. This stock is being managed by:

- The Russian Federation State Property Management Committee (3,443,910 shares valued at 1,783 million rubles and 1 'golden' share),
- The Khabarovsk Krai State Property Management Committee (1,528,744 shares at 916 million rubles and 10 'golden' shares),

- The Khabarovsk Krai Property Fund (later subordinate to the Property Management Committee) (1,457,180 shares worth 754 million rubles.)[4]

Although enterprise ownership was widely dispersed at the end of the first stage of privatization, it became more concentrated at the second stage when large blocks of the remaining shares were sold for roubles. By 1995, most of the large firms in the region were under hybrid ownership with shares of stocks held by employees, managers, members of the territorial elite, outside owners, and the state. In most cases, ownership was initially exercised by inside owners, consisting of enterprise managers and territorial elite, but, gradually, outside investors began to acquire shares of stock in firms with valuable export products from employees who were selling their shares in the secondary market.

One local observer, Pavel Minakir, (in Minakir and Freeze 1996) of the Institute for Economic Research of the Academy of Sciences in Khabarovsk is critical of the resulting concentration of ownership. He writes:

> The initial redistribution of property for privatization checks has been virtually completed ... In reality, for the majority of the population, the stocks acquired in exchange for vouchers have little value, amounting only to a few shares of stock. The real goal, which was achieved, was to create the formal conditions whereby citizens could independently, without later accusing the government of squandering public property, redistribute ownership of the means of production to the 'new Russians,' who for some reason came to be called the 'new' owners. In fact, these are the old owners. But now there is a process (far more simplified and accelerated than the voucher privatization) of transforming the property of the political elite (nomenklatura) into juridical property.

In sum, then, privatization succeeded in creating conditions for competitive markets in small-scale retail and service industries, but in large-scale industry, privatization created hybrid firms which were nominally owned by several groups of stockholders, but which, in reality, were controlled by insiders who enjoyed access to their underlying raw materials.

THE CREATION OF A TAX-BASED STATE

Economic reform requires a changed role for the state. The state in the planned economy allocated to itself the profits and rents from economic activity, collected as the difference between revenues and variable costs of production. However, once the state is no longer the owner of capital, the supply of public services must be supported by an explicit tax system. The expenditures of the state should change as well. While the central function of the Soviet state was control of economic activity, the central functions of a market-oriented state are the provision of institutional infrastructure, social insurance, and public goods.

The separation of government revenue from ownership of capital provides greater transparency in both the capital market and the public sector. Government taxes and subsidies become explicit in the government budget rather than implicit in government prices and allocations.

It would seem that Russia's vast stock of publicly owned natural resources and land would provide the state with a guaranteed base of revenue. Instead, it has impeded attempts to change the role of the state from control of wealth to provision of a framework for civil society. State regulation serves as the mechanism by which the income from resources is transferred to rent-seeking elites. Since access to resources is valuable, there are incentives for state allocators to create opaque arrangements. Although more than half of Russia's export revenue in 1995 originated from energy and raw materials, natural resource charges accounted for only 2.6 per cent of government budgetary revenue, or 4.9 per cent of tax revenue. In the Russian Far East, natural resources charges provided 5.6 of total budget income, or 8.8 per cent of tax revenue.

In an IMF working paper by Dale F. Gray (1998) evaluates potential and actual tax revenues from oil and gas in Russia and the other countries of the former Soviet Union. Gray finds that government oil and gas revenues are about half the level prevailing in other energy producers in the world. He attributes low oil revenues to constraints on export policy, inappropriate tax structures, and weak tax administration. Law gas revenues are due to low statutory tax rates, a tax structure that fails to capture resource rents, and weak tax administration.

In 1996, total tax revenue from the oil sector equaled 2.32 per cent of total GDP, including several production-based levies. There was a wellhead excise tax on each ton of production, averaging 70,000 old roubles per ton ($14). Royalties of 6–16 per cent and a Geology Fund tax of 10 per cent were levied on the value of wellhead production. There were several other extra-budget fees in addition to profits tax and VAT. Today, there is also an export tax.

Tax revenues from the gas sector are collected mainly from an excise tax of 30 per cent on the wholesale value of delivered gas. In addition, there is a royalty of 6–16 per cent, a Geology Fund levy of 10 per cent (based on the wellhead value of gas) and export duties. There are also property taxes on the net book value of assets and several smaller taxes. Profits tax and VAT tax are also collected. In 1996, the sum of these taxes provided government revenue equal to 2.05 per cent of GDP (Gray 1998: 48).

Actual tax revenues collected on energy, says Gray, are about 50 to 66 per cent of statutory levels because of exemptions, noncompliance, and arrears. Compared with other countries, a large share of the natural resource rents accrues to the transport monopolies, Gazprom and Transneft, relatively little of which is passed on to the government budget.

As I will show later, resource charges in forestry and the fishery are also much below economic value. Thus, in the resource industries, although notional ownership is public, much of the potential rent is transferred to producers who

Table 6.2 Russian Far East Budget Revenue from Resources in 1995

Regional Budget Income and Expenditure 1995 (mn rubles)	TOTAL INCOME	TAX INCOME	Total Resource Payments	Payments for Sub-soil Resources	Charge for Use of Minerals	Land Tax and Rent	Other Pmt Natural Resource	Share of Resources in Total Tax
Russian Federation	347046691	188216863	9251425	4922962	602919	3070581	654963	0.049
Far East	17876283	11333539	994586	530496	247685	179599	36806	0.088
Sakha	3659219	2899101	641194	334875	243684	54110	8525	0.221
Jewish	290557	125537	4536	563	0	3795	178	0.036
Chukotka	810628	249394	18672	14432	0	4175	65	0.075
Primorskii	4126084	2851058	59517	15014	2443	33312	8748	0.021
Khabarovsk	3117554	2016474	75494	32070	721	33621	9082	0.037
Amur	1487410	999292	57252	31757	627	20712	4156	0.057
Kamchatka	1280984	662251	6719	1708	70	4056	885	0.010
Koryak	324146	58837	5471	4955	0	273	243	0.093
Magadan	1215996	557879	75327	59233	0	15743	351	0.135
Sakhalin	1563705	913716	50404	35889	140	9802	4573	0.055

Source: date supplied to the editor by Alexei Lavrov.

gain control rights to resources. Access rights are acquired in a relationship system linking industrial leaders and political authorities. To see how the administrative system works, we now turn to several cases: mineral rights, the forest products industry, the fishing industry, and agricultural land.

TENDERS FOR MINERAL RIGHTS

Regional attempts to place resource stocks up for tender quickly revealed the difficulty the government faced in establishing a secure framework for resource extraction when interest groups battle each other for control.

The gold mining industry provides an example. In the former Soviet Union, gold mining cooperatives were required to deliver their gold to state organizations at a price of 200 roubles a gram. The state, in turn, sold gold on the world market for approximately $12 a gram, or $12 million dollars a ton.

In 1993, the Russian government raised the purchase price of gold to 1,129 roubles, but it retained the right to set production quotas defining the quantity of ore that could be extracted in each territory. Territorial governments, in turn, had the right to form joint venture partnerships and to assign their production quotas to a joint venture partner. The balance of production in the region was licensed by federal authorities for delivery either to a federal processing company or to the commercial market.

As soon as implementing regulations were put in place, territories announced prospective tenders of mineral rights. For example, Khabarovsk quickly announced that it would offer deposits at Khakandzhi and Yu'evskoe, 60 miles south of Okhotsk. The territory estimated gold reserves there at 65 tons with development costs estimated to be $10 to 15 million.

Khabarovsk announced plans to form a joint stock company, contributing the gold reserve as the territory's stake. The foreign investor would have the right to bid for a 49 per cent share in the resulting joint stock company. The territorial government proposed to assign the 51 per cent Russian share to the regional association of prospectors, Khabarovsk Gold.

The Khakandzhi-Yu'evskoe joint stock company would be given a temporary, reduced royalty fee of 4 per cent on the value of production, rising to 10 per cent in the eighth year of production. It would pay an environmental tax of 7.8 per cent on output and a license fee. Federal taxes on the company would normally include a 4 per cent royalty on output and excise tax on exports, but export was illegal in the case of gold. Foreign bidders would compete through offer of a license payment, with the license fee divided between the federal government (25 per cent), the territory, or krai (25 per cent), and the locality (50 per cent). After two years, the Khabarovsk gold mining rights were assigned in December, 1994, to a Khabarovsk company, Nizhneamurzoloto, and its foreign partner, Group Schroeder Finance Holding, Paris, France.

Other mining regions, Magadan, Kamchatka, and Amur began to offer tenders as well, although each attempt to define ownership rights created intense conflict. In Amur, conflict developed when the regional branch of the Russian Federation Committee on Geology granted mining rights, including rights to mines already being worked by the local prospectors association, assigning them to a Moscow firm, Tumanov & Co. With support of the territorial legislature, the prospectors' cooperative, Rudnik Pokrovskii, sued the Geological Commission in Arbitration Court and won.[5]

In Irkutsk, the local state gold mining enterprise responded to the federal enabling legislation by registering itself for licenses to all the gold mines being worked by prospector cooperatives in the territory. Thus, the Irkutsk agency responsible for assigning the licenses became owner of 10 per cent of the stock of the newly-privatized state firm, Lenzoloto.[6]

Today, the permitting process is time consuming and depends on relationships at the federal, regional, and local levels. Under the Russian Federation Law, licenses for the right to use minerals are approved jointly by the territorial administration and the Ministry of Natural Resources, or its territorial branch, the Committee on Natural Resources (CNR).

Table 6.3, below, summarizes an extraordinary document prepared by Dan Berkshire of CARANA Corporation and a team of researchers working in Khabarovsk. In the process of studying barriers to investment in Russia's regions, they consulted with executives of existing firms and administrative officials to prepare a 'Road Map' laying out the steps required to apply for approval and go through the permitting process in Khabarovsk. Licenses to mine are issued by conducting tenders and auctions. An investor seeking a license initially goes through a licensing process that involves five agencies (including the Tax Inspectorate) and requires approximately two years of time.

The next stage, geological exploration and environmental approval, involves, on average, another two years. Two federal agencies – the Committee on Environmental Protection and the Committee on Technical Supervision of Mining – have the final say in granting a license for site development. After granting of a license, the mining company completes a feasibility study and environmental impact assessment. These are needed in order to obtain eventual project financing, and they must be presented to the territorial administration and to the public in public hearings. After geological and administrative review, the territorial branch of the federal Committee for Environmental Protection undertakes an assessment (*expertiza*). Then, with approval of the Environmental Expertiza Committee, the principals can seek project finance and political risk insurance.

Having received the necessary licenses and permits to extract ore, the producer still needs to get the right to export production from the federal government. In the case of gold, private producers are required to sell to domestic purchasers. Goskhran, a department of the Russian Ministry of Finance, has a priority right to purchase gold. If production exceeds the amount that the Treasury wishes to acquire, then gold producers may sell to certain Russian banks that hold licenses to purchase and refine gold. Licensed

Table 6.3 Applying for a Mining License: CARANA Corporation Road Map

	Action	Organization	Time (days)
1	Get information on Krai	Investment Promotion Agency	0.5
2	Apply for information on mineral stocks	Department of Natural Resources and Mineral Extracting Industry	0.5
3	Get information on specific deposits	Committee on Natural Resources (CNR)	5 to 60
4	Choose site		1 to 60
5	Requests for license and tender	CNR	0
6	Submit following documents Prepare for tender – Application for tender – Enterprise charter – Certificate of state registration – Certification of tax inspection – Certificate for tax debt to budget – Information on existing licenses	CNR	1 to 1.5 years
7	Bidding for tender under Reg. on commercial tenders 1993 Reg. on international tenders 1997	CNR	
8	Waiting for results of tender	State Property Management Committee	3–6 months
9	Tender results confirmed	Minerals Committee	1 day
10	Preparation of licensing documentation	CNR	1 month after tender
10	Receive license	CNR	1
11	Geological exploration including:	CNR	
11	Issue geological task	CNR	5 to 10
11	Geological-economic review (Ekspertisa)	CNR	up to 1 month
11	Ecological review	Environmental Committee	1 to 3 months
11	Approval for exploration (land, timber)	Khabarovsk Administration	up to 1 month
12	Conduct exploration		up to 5 years
12	State review, approval of reserves	CNR	1 month
12	Preparation of feasibility study Approval of feasibility study		up to 1 year
13	Head of Administration gets signatures of departments on FS	Forestry Mgmt Committee of Nat Resource Environmental Committee	1 month
14	Head of Administration signs and stamps		1 day
15	Head of Administration requests approval from Governor		1 day
16	Ecological review of feasibility study	Environmental Committee	up to 1 month
17	Receive mining allotment	Mining Technical Inspection	10 to 15 days
18	License for special use of water	CNR	10 to 15 days
19	Land allotment	Reg Branch, Land Committee	up to 1 month
20	Fishery committee review	Amur Fisheries Committee	15 days
21	Governor signs	Krai Administration	1 day
22	Start working		

Source: A Summary of 'Mining Road Map' from CARANA Corp., Dan Berkshire et al. Opportunities for Increasing Investment in the Minerals Sector of Khabarovsk Krai.

commercial banks may sell gold bars to the Russian Central Bank, to domestic customers, and, with permission from the Central Bank and Customs Committee, on the world market.[7]

In mining, the Russian regulatory environment creates so much uncertainty that it is difficult to attract foreign commitment. Mining laws are usually complex and comprehensive; mining investors expect this. In addition, strong support from the territorial administration and all levels of the RF Department of Natural Resources and Mineral Extraction are required. During Yeltsin's term of office, government commitment to a project could rarely be assured.

RIGHTS TO TIMBER RESOURCES

In the forestry industry, too, the government derives scant revenue from cutting rights and stumpage charges. Although privatization initially created a population of potentially competitive firms, territorial government control of state shares in timber harvesters, allocation of cutting rights, and allocation of investment funds led to the emergence of one or two powerful timber enterprises in each RFE territory, formed on the basis of pre-reform ministry branch units.

In the Russian Far East, the management of forest resources was assigned to territorial units in the pre-reform era. Yet, in spite of an initial decentralization, the competition for control of assets has been no less fierce. By 1998, there has been a considerable recentralization of authority in the industry based on control of regulations, of exports, and of access to investment. Behind the appearance of a decentralized privatization, there has actually been the re-establishment of the old elite of the Ministry of Forestry in a quasi-privatized cartel. This group of former officials appears to have enjoyed a considerable share of the rents that accrued to the nominally state-owned forests. For example, in Khabarovsky krai, out of total consolidated taxes paid into the government budget of 4483.1 billion (old) roubles in 1996, only 87.3 million, less than 2 per cent, came from resource payments.[8]

During the Soviet era, activity in the forest sector was coordinated by the Ministry of Forestry. The Ministry, itself, was divided into two branches, the Forest Service, or Minleskhoz, which was responsible for forest protection, and the Forest Products Industry, or Minlesprom, which harvested and processed timber. With cutting and replanting under two separate organizations, Minlesprom had no incentives to alter harvest technique in order to foster re-growth. The Forest Service was also dependent on a portion of Minlesprom's profits for its budget, so it was unlikely to oppose Minlesprom's access to a site. Moreover, the Forest Service was allowed to conduct 'sanitary' harvest of over-mature wood in protected areas to supplement it's own budget, so it undertook logging precisely in protected areas.

Despite the problems, Russian Far East timber exports were a fungible commodity used to pay for imports of equipment in the region's trade with Japan. The exchange of wood for machinery was carried out under bilateral general agreements between the Soviet Union and Japan. In the Soviet era, there were five agreements: four on forest products, and one on the construction of the first phase of the port of Vostochny. In these agreements, the Soviet government received credits from the Export-Import Bank of Japan for the purchase of Japanese equipment. Payment was made in kind with raw materials. Three agreements were still in force at the end of 1991: an agreement on wood chips, one on the development of the Sakha coal fields, and a joint feasibility study of Sakhalin oil and gas. Today, long-term agreements for forest products have lapsed because of continuing problems with quality and delivery, but the RFE continues to send more than 80 per cent of its reported timber export to Japan.

With the start of reform, a new law, the Fundamental Forestry Law of the Russian Federation, was passed in March, 1993.[9] The new law gave territorial and district officials unprecedented authority over forest management (Turner 1994: 7–10). Districts had rights to sell timber, allocate rights to log, and monitor compliance, authority which had been in the hands of federal and territorial officials earlier. Under the law, there was to be a license guaranteeing long term leasing rights, although this right would not relieve the user of the requirement to obtain an annual permit as well. Access to forest sites was to be distributed by bidding, by competition (a non-monetary form of bidding), or through direct negotiations. However, in practice, territorial governors were able to assert authority to control resource stocks and an enlarged, multi-level bureaucracy emerged to allocate timber land assignments.

Earlier, in December, 1992, the Property Committee of the Russian Federation created a hybrid joint stock company, Roslesprom, which was partly state and partly privately owned. It was to allocate federal investment funding among regions, to fund research, and to manage access of firms to the export market. 'In reality,' write scientists, Vladimir Karakin, Alexander Sheingauz, and Vladimir Tyukalov, 'Roslesprom [was] attempting to gain control over the Russian Federation forest industry, including those in the RFE' (Sheingauz et al 1996: 14).[10]

Roslesprom received authority to exercise state-owned shares in all sate and private joint stock companies in the forest industry and the right to manage all state-owned assets. Through the Ministry of Economy, the federal government gave Roslesprom the right to distribute 150 billion rubles in government credit at 10 per cent interest (when inflation was almost 1000 per cent). Credits were, in fact, distributed exclusively to Roslesprom holdings, which were required to export through its export subsidiary.

In 1994–95, Roslesprom established fifty local holding companies (kholdingi), based on the former territorial associations of the Ministry of Forest Industry. It named its own appointees to head these companies, to supervise production, and to collect data on all export contracts (Sheingauz et al 1996: 14). The entire foreign network of the former forest products exporting organization, Exportles, was transferred to Roslesprom. In addition, it established a separate exporting organization, Rosexportles, holding 96 per cent of its stock. It also became co-owner of the National Forest Bank and the Russian Forest Investment Company, incorporated in Boston.[11] Export licenses and access to export were managed through a few large former Ministry units.

During this period when the former ministerial units were attempting to re-establish control of the industry from above, a decentralized private sector was emerging in the regions, in the form of privatized firms, production cooperatives, and other small businesses. However, in many cases, territorial and local officials were able disenfranchise the newly privatized production associations by setting up new, shell organizations and transferring timber stocks and cutting rights away from the existing production association into their own 'enterprises.' Gradually, regional officials gained control over the production associations as well.

In Khabarovsk krai, privatization of the 82 timber harvesters, 14 saw mills, 12 furniture factories, 10 pulp and paper plants, and various repair shops created a population of about 150 private or partly private forest sector firms controlling over 90 per cent of output. However, state shares, and, thus, control rights over these nominally private firms remained in government hands.

After the first phase of privatization, controlling interests in these firms were divided between the territorial administration and a Financial Industrial Group (FIG) led by a regional association and marketing organization, Dallesprom. In an exchange of shares in 1995, Dallesprom gave the territorial administration shares representing a 51 per cent controlling interest in its capital. In turn, Dallesprom received a controlling interest in forest harvesting companies managed by the state (Sheingauz et al 1996: 18). Similar territorial FIGs formed in other regions of the RFE.

In 1995, state shares in privatized firms were to be sold on the stock market for rubles. However, fearing loss of control to outside owners, territorial administrators devised a number of administrative strategies to retain local control. The number of firms was increased and rights to harvest were redistributed to them. In 1996, Dallesprom established a joint venture with US Caterpillar Company to sell and service Caterpillar equipment to the region's firms.[12]

Meanwhile, in Moscow, control of export was weakened when the federal system of export quotas and strategic exporters was abolished in 1994, although government approval of export contracts was still required.[13] But, in 1996, Roslesprom's position was bolstered with the signing of a Memorandum of Understanding with the US Ex-Im Bank at the sixth session of the Gore-Chernomyrdin Commission. According to that document, the Ex-Im Bank provided up to $1 billion in credit guarantees for loans issued by US commercial banks to Russian forest industry firms. Russian loan recipients were required to sell timber to foreign firms which deposited revenues directly into an offshore escrow account.

Although the national organization, Roslesprom, fostered cartelization of the industry, the strength of territorial elites kept Moscow from re-creating a national monopoly.

After President Yeltsin ordered the privatization of Roslesprom in August, 1997, the two Moscow banks which financed timber exports, Mezhkombank and Imperial Bank, split the export contracts and operations of Roslesprom's export subsidiary, Rosexportles. They created two new companies with similar names, leaving Roslesprom with few assets and multibillion-ruble debts.[14]

In the spring of 1997, the Russian parliament signed a new Forest Code into law which provided that state forest land was federal property. In response, the territorial governments claimed that this provision contradicted Article 72 of the Federation Treaty. In the Federation Treaty, ownership, use, and disposal of land, mineral resources, water and other natural resources were subject to joint jurisdiction of the federal government and its subjects (oblast, krai, okrug, and republic). General principals of taxation, legislation on land, water, forestry, mineral resources, and environmental protection were similarly subject to joint jurisdiction.

In 1997, the administrations of Khabarovsk and Karelia took this issue to the Constitutional Court, where they lost. The Constitutional Court declared all forests of the State Forest Fund to be federal property, although it did provide that territorial administrations shared in the management of the forests. In practice, Moscow decides the harvesting volumes – the allowable cut – using aggregated information on annual timber growth from the individual regions. The territories, in turn decide who may harvest the forest. Moscow also sets minimum stumpage fees, which are paid to the federation budget. The territories may share in the tax revenue from competitive tenders which yield higher stumpage fees. Since minimum stumpage fees are the same all over Russia, they discriminate in favour of well-located regions. Further, since stumpage fees are charged only on timber removed from the forest rather than on all timber cut, they generate wasteful use of stock and under-reporting of actual sales.

In sum, then, after privatization, the Russian forestry industry remains in the hands of insider elites who control access to stands of timber, to investment and credit, and access to the export market. Potential foreign partners, such as US Weyerhauser, which explored a joint venture with a timber producer in Khabarovsk krai, backed off when they discovered that basic parameters, such as the rights to a forest site and the right to export could evaporate at the whim of the authorities.

Neither the Soviet Ministry of Forestry nor its quasi-privatized progeny have incentives to re-forest accessible areas or to develop sustainable yield practices. Timber stocks are treated like a free good, for much of the felled timber never appears in official sales. Regional production of timber has been falling steadily, as the prices of fuel and transport have risen toward market levels. The Russian Federal Forestry Service, nominally responsible for re-forestation, has a minuscule budget, now in arrears. As in the Soviet era, it still has the right to conduct 'sanitary' harvests in protected areas.

Unable to serve the European market because of high transport costs, local producers have turned to the Pacific. Here, the dominant regional firms attempt

Table 6.4 Russian Far East Total Timber Production

(Mil M^3)	1985	1989	1990	1991	1992	1993	1994	1995	1996	1997	1998
Total Timber	34.45	33.45	29.60	25.67	21.59	15.67	10.12	10.52	9.06	8.25	
Sakha	3.88	3.72	3.40	2.82	2.19	1.67	1.06	0.87	0.70	0.63	
Primorskii	6.14	5.00	4.79	3.95	3.49	2.43	1.78	1.83	1.46	1.28	
Khabarovsk	13.82	13.77	11.93	10.37	8.16	5.99	3.68	4.56	4.34	4.44	3.33
Amur	5.91	6.46	5.57	4.93	4.20	3.13	1.84	1.54	1.23	0.94	
Kamchatka	0.95	0.83	0.72	0.69	0.56	0.35	0.20	0.18	0.14	0.11	
Magadan	0.37	0.31	0.26	0.20	0.15	0.04	0.02	0.01	0.00	0.01	
Sakhalin	3.39	3.37	2.93	2.71	2.63	1.94	1.44	1.45	1.14	0.86	0.43
Jewish					0.21	0.13	0.09	0.06	0.05	0.02	

Source: Goskomstat Rossii, *Promyshlennost'*, various years.

to regulate, not the amount of timber that is brought to market, but the selling price, by establishing minimum allowable prices. However, the quality of timber, and, thus, its market price, is so variable that effective regulation is next to impossible. In the recent past, the Russian timber industry has flooded the Pacific market with wood, depressing prices. Thus, the RFE forest resource is likely to provide little long-run support for the region's recovery.

RIGHTS TO FISHERY RESOURCES

Management of the Russian ocean fishery presents a paradoxical picture. On the one hand, large modern trawling fleets, built in the shipyards of Norway and Spain and financed through long-term leases, harvest Russia's fish stocks. One the other hand, production has fallen substantially, the proportion of product shipped to foreign markets has risen, and export revenues have moved offshore beyond the reach of Russian taxes. Procedures for access to fishing quotas are opaque; corruption is rampant. While Moscow and the regions have struggled with each other for control of the resource, the most important commercial stocks have been drastically reduced through poor management and overfishing.

Administration of the Soviet fishery was always centralized under the Soviet Ministry of Fisheries. At the top were the Minister and his deputies. At the bottom were the production associations, firms, and collectives in each coastal territory. In between were two levels of administration. Below the top were the regional maritime basin administrative organs, such as Dal'ryba, in the Russian Far East; then, below Dal'ryba were the regional fishing councils of each territory (oblast, krai, okrug) within the region. Thus, the Ministry of Fisheries in Moscow controlled the harvest and processing of marine products.

At the same time, the Ministry controlled another scientific hierarchy which was responsible for overseeing the conservation and sustainable development of resources – the policies that were supposed to preserve the value of Russia's marine resources. This hierarchy was headed by the All Soviet Fisheries Oceanographic Research Institute (VNIRO) in Moscow and included territorial research centers, such as TINRO, in most of the RFE territories. Investment and renewal of the fishing fleet and other capital facilities was managed by still another vertical chain of command in the Ministry.

With the collapse of the former Soviet Union, a much smaller Russian Ministry of Fisheries was, briefly, transferred to the Ministry of Agriculture and, then, re-established as an independent agency. A law passed by the Russian Supreme Soviet on December 27, 1991, reaffirmed that 'natural resources within the territorial waters, exclusive economic zones, and continental shelf of the Russian Federation' remained the exclusive property of the Russian Federation government.[15] However, in 1990, many of Dal'ryba's management functions were decentralized to short-lived Basin Production Organizations. Beginning in mid-1991, as central authority collapsed, territorial governments took charge of quotas for harvesting marine resources, selling the rights to domestic and foreign harvesters. In 1992, the export of fish reached unprecedented levels, accounting for 50 per cent of the catch, leading to a drastic reduction in domestic supply.

In response, in 1992, a system of scientific-industrial councils was established to oversee management of the fishery resource and to make recommendations to the Federal Fisheries Committee. The Far East Scientific-Fishing Industry Council includes representatives of the Federal Fisheries Committee, Ministry of Environment and Natural Resources, scientific research organization, fish enforcement agencies (Glavryb), territorial councils, the fishing industry, and the territorial administrations. Within each territory, there is a territorial fishing industry council, appointed by the territorial government as a joint organization of the Federal Fisheries Committee and the regional government. This local organization is to 'develop recommendations to the territorial administration' on allocation of regional fishing quotas, fisheries regulations, territorial funding of fishing industry interests, licensing of fishing, etc.[16] (It, however, does not have authority to assign allocations.) The accompanying diagram (*Figure 6.1*) depicts the several administrative, scientific, and enforcement agencies involved in regulating the RFE fishery during the 90s. The outline is based on a diagram in Clarence Pautzke, *North Pacific Fishery Management Council Report to Congress*, September 30, 1997. The diagram shows that enforcement of fishing regulations was shifted from the fishing industry agency, Glavrybvod, to the Border Guard in 1998.

Far East fishing organizations were enormous in size. For example, BAMR, Marine Fisheries Base in Nakhodka controlled a huge fishing port, a ship repair yard, construction organizations, apartment buildings, and social overhead facilities. It employed more that 13,000 people. Despite (or, perhaps, because of)

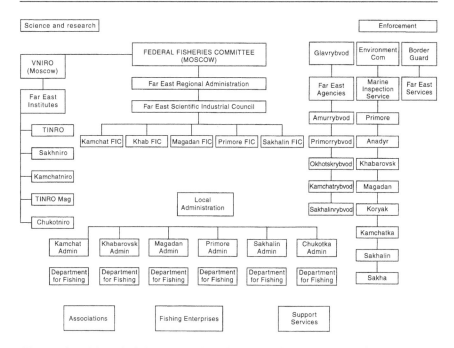

Figure 6.1 The administrative, scientific, and enforcement agencies involved in regulating the RFE fishery during the 1990s

their size, fishing associations were inefficient. Fleets faced bureaucratic regulations and excessive time in port. Fuel supply was uncertain. Fleets, ports, and repair yards had insufficient, aging technology.

As a result of privatization, the state organization, Dal'ryba and its sub-units became joint stock companies and most of the territorial production associations became independent commercial fishing enterprises. Some of these became joint stock companies and others remained state enterprises. The independent firms continued to participate as members of territorial associations in lobbying for access to quotas. Similarly, fishing cooperatives formed regional unions to represent their interests. The functions of Dal'ryba itself were redefined, allowing it to conclude contracts with producers, to oversee implementation of state orders and research, to set quotas, search out new stocks, and represent the interests of producers vis-à-vis the state (Minakir and Freeze 1996: 112–113).

After privatization, the new Dal'ryba included 54 organizations – some 40 state and private joint stock companies, four territorial unions of collectives, three limited liability partnerships, three joint ventures, and four state firms.[17] These organizations managed a large, but aging fleet of almost 1000 fishing ships, many of them big (3,500–6,000 ton) trawlers which engaged in open-sea expeditions using large fish-processing 'mother ships' supplied by a fleet of smaller seiners or trawlers. Most vessels in the Russian fleet had poor fuel efficiency, outmoded instrumentation, and were expensive to operate under market conditions.

Since privatization, access to fish in the Russian 200-mile zone has been based on contracts, or quotas. Access of Japanese and other foreign ships is negotiated annually in government-to-government agreements. Domestic allocations are determined in an administrative process. Rights are supposed to reflect the size of a firm or region's past catch, but lobbying and side-payments are reported to play a role as well. The Russian Federal Committee on Fisheries gives itself an allocation. Territorial governments receive separate quotas. Some, like Chukotka, have established commercial firms to exercise their quotas. Others re-sell their fishing rights to domestic or foreign bidders.

Today, joint ventures give Russian partners access to Western technology and capital markets, giving Western partners access to deep-sea processors and access to the Russian fishery resource. The earliest Soviet-US joint venture, Marine Resources, was incorporated in the US in 1978, after establishment of the 200-mile fishing zone. A partnership between Bellingham Cold Storage and Sovrybflot, the commercial arm of the Soviet Ministry of Fisheries, it fished in US waters, using leased Russian processors and American fishing boats and marketing the product internationally. After passage of the Soviet joint venture law in 1987, fishery joint ventures were established with partners in Japan, the US, South Korea, Hong Kong, Australia, and Vietnam.[18] At present, there are more than 100 Russian fishing joint ventures, including more than 30 with Japan.

In 1989, the Ministry of Fisheries, Minrybkhoz, set up a structure that would allow the Ministry to access foreign capital market for the construction of trawlers and transport vessels which would be leased back to Russian fishing organizations. The mechanism was a joint venture between the industry and an offshore firm, Bergen Industries and Fishing Co., owned by a sub-unit of the fishing Ministry.[19] With privatization, the industry reorganized into new commercial units. Russian firms with access to the Western capital market have been able to retrofit their ships with fuel efficient engines and state of the art technology. Firms acquired new supertrawlers, which can both catch and process fish, through leasing arrangements funded by Western banks.

However, in spite of the rising technical efficiency of the Russian fleet, reported catch has declined steadily from its reported peak in 1988, and the share of high-value products, such as salmon and crab, has fallen.

In part, the decline in production reflects overfishing – a consequence of high quotas and illegal fishing. In part, the decline in measured production reflects a growing volume of Russian catch, which is delivered offshore, going unrecorded by Russian customs authorities. (Japanese trade statistics report roughly 50 per cent higher landings than Russian data.) The movement offshore reflects the high costs of operating and selling in the Russian market where firms face high taxes, demands for informal payments, and customer arrears and non-payment.

Table 6.5 Russian Far East Production and Export of Seafood

	1985	1989	1990	1991	1992	1993	1994	1995	1996	1997
Total Seafood Production (Thousand Tons)	4193	4910	4628	4062	3176	2796	2299	2816	2964	2967
Sakha	9		10	7	6	6	4	3	2	2
Primorskii	1573	1946	1832	1586	1344	1171	1078	1322	1505	1470
Khabarovsk	317	395	370	301	243	226	171	223	214	240
Kamchatka	1242	1407	1348	1211	908	798	598	771	841	785
Magadan	93	122	140	97	97	102	67	83	43	30
Sakhalin	959	1032	925	857	576	486	378	414	357	442
Chukotka	4		5	4	2	2	4	1	1	1
Total Seafood Export ($ Mil)	179	282	361	413	629	688	649	1124	611	1080
Total Export to Japan ($ Mil)	99.76	238.651	310.721	375.466	582.225					
(Thous Tons)		36.729	56.376	109.201	174.661					

Sources: Promyshlennost, various years; Regiony Rossii, 1997, Nobuo Arai, 'Structural Crisis of the Marine Product Industry in the Russian Far East, 1993; Minakir and Mikheeva (1999), Dal'niy Vostok Rossii, Vladivostock: Dal'nauka.

An article by Viktor Tkachenko and Ernst Chernyi in *Sovetskii Sakhalin* in March, 1998, details the under-reporting of harvest and the opaque and allegedly corrupt allocation of quotas that had emerged.[20] They write that the Moscow office of the Fishing Committee received an allocation of 80,000 tons during 1994–97 (worth at least $1,000 a ton for fish or more than $10,000 a ton for crab.) This agency reported revenue of $15 million and received a government subsidy of 78.5 billion roubles to cover their costs. Scientific research quotas funded an extensive commercial harvest, while the staffs of the research institutes went unpaid. (In 1997, the Far East Fish Institute, TINRO-tsentr, received an allocation of 4,300 tons of crab, worth $43 million dollars.) In all, Tkachenko and Chernyi allege that the annual under-reporting of revenues in the fishing industry totaled more than $2.5 billion.

On January 1, 1998, the primary responsibility for monitoring and enforcement of fishing quotas was transferred from the Moscow fishing enforcement arm, Glavrybvod, to the Border Guard. Members of the industry questioned whether the Border Guard would, in fact, provide more effective enforcement. That organization, too, faced wage and payment arrears from the federal government. Sources in the fishing industry report incidents of theft of catch and other forms of 'hold-up' involving individuals in the Border Guard.[21]

In August, 1998, the Russian Fisheries Ministry announced that, in the future, 15–20 per cent of allowable catch of certain valuable species, such as salmon, sturgeon, and crab, would be offered to the highest bidder at regional auctions. They promised to consult the statistics of trading partners to monitor illegal export of fish. Industry observers countered that changes which gave allocators a better measure of the true value of access might increase, rather than reduce, corruption. Clearly, an annual auction would provide less incentive to undertake specialized investment than would a procedure involving the auction of a license or long-term right to access.

By 1999, many large fishing companies had disappeared, had become holding companies for smaller fishing units, or were drowning under huge debt loads and tax arrears. In 1997, fishery scientist Vlad M. Kasczynski reported that, out of 65 new and 19 reconditioned fishing vessels delivered to Russia under leasing arrangements with Western shipyards, 30 ships were in default on Western bank loans totaling $71.8 millions.[22] By 1999, many of these firms were bankrupt or in receivership.

One of the larger Russian companies, Vladivostok Base of Trawling and Refrigeration Fleet, ceased operation in January, 1998. This firm, which was owned, in part, by Dal'morproduct, the commercial arm of the Russian Fisheries Committee, had received Russian government guarantees for its bareboat of 12 Spanish-built trawlers. The trawlers were transferred to a new joint stock company, Super of Vladivostok, which received generous quotas for 1998.[23]

Super's subsidiary, Far East Maritime Services, operated 11 of these vessels for about a year, making leasing payments to the underlying owner, Bergen Industries and Fishing Corporation. (One vessel was destroyed in a fire.)

However, this turned out to be a troubled relationship as well. A total of $17.1 million of the lease payments Super paid to Bergen was intended for the federal government to pay off underlying loans. Another $19 million in insurance money for the twelfth trawler, was also never returned to the federal government. Super successfully sued Bergen in a London court, but on June 29, the Fishing Committee voided its contracts with Super and transferred the ships and their fishing quotas to Dal'moreprodukt. As Western creditors sued to recover their loans, the trawler captains were instructed not to put in at foreign ports where their vessels would be seized.

In sum, then, the interlinking state-commercial networks that provide access to the Russian pacific fishery contribute to a chaotic business environment. On the one hand, the emergence of offshore joint ventures allowed the industry to modernize its capital stock, something that did not happen in other industries. On the other hand, investors are withdrawing from the industry, alarmed by the declining resource, the uncertainty of Russia's economic environment, and the unpredictability of the administrative system for access to quotas and fishing rights.

There are a variety of ways in which a public decision-maker could try to manage the coastal fishery in order to limit overfishing, foster sustainable development, collect some share of the resource rents into the central or regional budget, and reduce the incentives for corruption or evasion. These mechanisms could include taxes on resources, taxes on fishing effort, imposition of quotas on aggregate catch, and individual quotas.

In the Soviet-era, the Ministry of Fisheries allocated regional and local access to resources politically. With domestic prices of fish products, ships and equipment, and fuel all very far from world prices, there was no way to determine efficient rates of harvest or underlying input efficiencies. There were considerable opportunities for corruption.

Today, the existing administrative framework suffers similar problems. quota allocation needs to be converted from an opaque lobbying process to transparent sale (and enforcement) of rights to fish. The experience of the US North Pacific Fisheries Management Council in creating a market for fishing licenses is far from ideal, but it is preferable to the pattern of corruption and criminalization which has emerged in the Russian Far East.

STATE MANAGEMENT OF RESOURCE STOCKS

At the beginning of the decade, in January 2000, the economic policies of a new president, Vladimir Putin, are still unclear. Until the presidential election on March 26, Putin's administration is likely to pursue policies with short-run political benefits. Members of the Union of Right Forces, like Yegor Gaidar, hope that the new government will quickly pass a Land Code providing a stronger framework for private property rights.[24] Other observers fear a nationalistic, anti-foreign bias in Putin's call for greater limits on access of foreign companies to Russian natural resources, telecommunications, and infrastructure companies.[25]

What most parties agree is that, to date, state management of natural resource stocks has led to decapitalization of assets and capital flight. Russia's government budgets, federal and territorial, and the communities in resource extracting regions receive scant benefits from the raw material wealth around them. Government administrative effort and private entrepreneurship are diverted from market liberalization to the battle for control of Russia's wealth.

Russia is stuck in a partial and incomplete reform in which the insider elites who were winners in the early privatization process seek to use government administrative controls to assure themselves continued control over Russia's resource wealth. Anders Aslund (1999) calls this system of interlocking political and commercial interests 'crony capitalism.' Aslund argues that it was not market liberalization per se which distorted Russian reform but capture of the reform process by self-serving elites. Aslund (199) argues that institutional capture of the government and the privatization process generated rent seeking, inequality, and management theft. For example, government control over access rights to export licenses, foreign exchange, quotas, and pipeline transport generated immense arbitrage profits and corruption.[26]

INSTITUTIONAL TRAPS

Is Russia locked in an institutional trap? It appears so. How does an economy develop institutions that yield a bad equilibrium? In December 1998 at the Annual Conference of the Eurasia Foundation's program of economic research, mathematical economist, Viktor Poltorovich, modeled the emergence of 'institutional traps' in the Russian economy. He defined institutional traps as stable institutional norms which impose high transactions costs on an economy but which may dominate other institutional arrangements because of the structure of costs or incentives.

Corruption is an example of an institutional trap when political institutions provide no other formal mechanisms for defining and enforcing property rights. Corruption serves to circumvent bureaucratic obstacles, allowing an administrator to 'sell' market access at a shadow price reflecting the market for bribes. If control over access to valuable assets becomes a significant source of political power or economic wealth in one market, then there will be significant incentives for regulators to extend regulatory control to other markets as well and to oppose legal changes that would reduce the value of their control (Schleifer and Vishny 1994).

Russia's crony capitalism appears to be just such an institutional trap. During privatization, political elites at the center and in the regions were able to turn their administrative control over resources into ownership. The first stage of voucher privatization was an attempt to co-opt economic interest groups by giving them partial ownership rights in their firms (Shleifer and Treisman 2000). However, a variety of non-transparent transfers – the closed privatization of oil and gas, the loans-for-share acquisition of the most valuable firms by insiders, and the opaque sale for rubles of the remaining shares of other large firms during the second stage of privatization – concentrated ownership in the hands of insider elites. Moreover, the inability to develop mechanisms to enforce corporate governance allowed insider managers to strip the profits and assets of their firms into their wholly-owned organizations.

Since Russia's legislative and executive branches had the responsibility for legislating and implementing privatization, it is not altogether surprising that political elites became the main beneficiaries of the process. Nor is it surprising that there is an extraordinary concentration of wealth in a few hands, given the extraordinary concentration of political power at the center in the former Soviet Union. Yegor Gaidar details the bad equilibrium that followed from government ownership of land and natural resources and government control of access to markets:[27]

> ... the main problem of present-day capitalism that has formed in Russia is as follows. It is the problem of the utmost intertwining of property and power. If we look at the operation of the Russian enterprises, the work of government agencies, in Moscow, in the regions, we will see constantly the closest intertwining of business and bureaucracy. In the majority of cases the success of an enterprise depends not on the ability of the director or the owner to organize normal production, but on his ability to correctly give bribes, on whether he has sufficiently high patrons, his ability in this connection to secure for himself a set of individual benefits and exceptions from the rule, his ability to get cheap money out of the budget, and so on.

Today, existing elites have an interest in preserving government administrative arrangements that provide access to underpriced resources and regulated markets and protect insiders from outside competition, domestic and foreign. Thus, it is the winners in the early reform process who have incentives to block further reforms which would introduce competition and reduce the value of their current rents.

How Do Institutions Change?

The potential for a bad equilibrium is obvious when the institutions that need to be restructured – the bureaucracy, security services, and parliament – are themselves the forces for implementing change. In a market system, the process of changing formal institutions is defined by the rule-making and rule-enforcing powers of executive, legislative, and judicial branches of government. The formal rules and their enforcement influence the costs of securing agreements between individuals and organizations. In particular, the definition and enforcement of clear property rights lowers transactions costs and makes assets more valuable. It provides incentives for investment and innovation, allows capital markets to move savings into productive use, and provides a framework within which individuals can get together to experiment with alternative form of governance for coordinating their activities.

Thus, the demand for institutional change comes from current or prospective owners who expect to receive the gains from moving resources to higher value uses. In addition, groups of individuals with differences in initial endowments and tastes for risk who hope to benefit from specialization and economies of scale will have incentives to try to improve structures of governance allowing them to partition property rights in a variety of different ways.

What are the incentives to escape from today's low-level equilibrium? The high level of capital flight in Russia reflects the uncertainty that those currently controlling assets feel about how long they expect to retain their control rights. So, although crony capitalism as a system seems to have considerable staying power, individuals in the system have a short-run time horizon.

The gain to Russia's citizens from developing a framework of rule of law should be immense. In 1999, the total value of the Russian stock market was less than 1 per cent of GNP and capital flight was estimated to exceed $20 billion annually. When we compare the low value of society's wealth under insecure property rights with the potential value of these assets in a secure economy with working markets, then there appears to be an enormous gain to be realized from further institutional reform.

THE RESOURCE CURSE

Why is it that many countries with large endowments of natural resources have poor economic performance? Sometimes, investment in a strong resource exporting sector raises exchange rates, making other sectors of the economy less competitive. More frequently, when the resources are state-owned, competition for access to natural resource wealth generates high levels of rent seeking. But rent seeking diverts the efforts of producers away from the production of new wealth and toward the capture and control of existing wealth. 'You wouldn't believe all the entrepreneurship that goes into gaining access to fishing rights,' the general director of one fishing company recounted in 1999.[28]

In Russia, with its large asset stocks and vast endowment of natural resources, the prospects of privatization diverted much of society's entrepreneurship to rent-seeking. Since the government, itself, was the legal owner of resources and determined the terms on which some would gain access to them, control of the government became the most valuable asset of all. Those who control the government can control the direction of institutional change.

CRONY CAPITALISM AND THE RELATIONSHIP SYSTEM

In the absence of market-supporting institutions, Russia's crony capitalism is based upon an intrusive regulatory bureaucracy which gives numerous governmental agencies the power to block economic activity and hold the producer hostage. Small entrepreneurs, like the wholesaler selling consumer goods to shops, are hostage to two groups – official regulators and tax agencies and informal

Table 6.6 Crony Capitalism

	Crony Capitalism	Competitive Capitalism
Goal	Rent-seeking, wealth-capture	Productivity, growth
Government Role	Control access to resources Subsidise, redistribute	Provide infrastructure Legal, financial, govt Provide social insurance Provide public goods
Foreign Trade	Protectionist, anti-foreign	Open
Foreign Investment	Passive foreign investment	Foreign direct investment Technology transfer
Domestic Investment	Closed capital market Capital flight	Open capital market Requires economic stability Requires secure property rights

protection rackets. 'I pay 25 per cent of my gross for protection,' one businessman in Vladivostok explained, 'but, at least, I get some services for my money. I pay 28 per cent of my gross to the government and get nothing at all.'[29]

In contrast, larger businesses reduce their uncertainty by relying on relationship systems, linking political and economic leaders in a single territory, and by constructing networks of vertical relations between local officials and producers and central authorities. Relationship systems, organized around the Communist party and the production ministries, played a vital coordinating role in the Soviet economy. In the Soviet regions, two plants subordinate to different ministries couldn't trade raw materials with each other. But if their directors were part of a local network, they could break bottlenecks, resolve disputes, and lobby the center. Between themselves, local officials and managers provided some of the local infrastructure that went unfunded from the center.

Similarly, today's relationship networks facilitate barter and extension of credits in a closed capital market. They can enforce agreements in the absence of legal mechanisms, but they can also allow insiders to block access to resources and markets. Since self-enforcing agreements work best when access to assets has a high franchise value, a relationship system will have incentives to restrict entry. Many of the peculiar institutions of Russia's virtual economy, such as reliance on barter and non-money means of credit, serve to enforce contracts within a relationship system and to evade taxes imposed by the center (Gaddy and Ickes 1998).

OWNERSHIP VERSUS ACCESS

Under Russia's regime for administering natural resources, a harvesting firm gains, not ownership, but access to resources. Therefore, its behavior is likely to differ from that of an owner.

How should a government owner of a resource stock maximize its rents? An owner of resource stocks would invest in resource development and exploration to the point where the efforts yield the rate of return on other investment. An owner would extract resources only if the marginal net return over variable cost of current extraction equals or exceeds the present value of expected future returns from not extracting. These future returns include the discounted net return from future use of existing stocks, the productivity of existing stocks in producing future yield, the effects of stock size on extraction costs, and the possible benefits derived from enjoying the stock in unharvested form. Current extraction may even compete in the manager's program with option demand – the desire to hold the stock until later in order to have the option of possible alternative uses.

When the state enforces its ownership rights as a principal and the harvesting firm is its agent, then the owner faces all the familiar agency problems that emerge when the agent has asymmetric information about local conditions and its own behavior. In the absence of effective enforcement, the agent will have incentives to provide biased information and to maximize its own wealth rather than the joint wealth of the principal and agent together.

In an uncertain world, the government, as principal, will choose to share some of the risk associated with extraction, if this reduction of risk leads the harvester to reduce the implicit risk premium that it requires from the project. A production-based tax or production-sharing arrangement would provide for sharing of risks.

One of the implications of efficient management is that the majority of resource rents should be captured at the point of production in a region. However, in Russia, one goal of the Federation government is to lower the price received by producers extracting resources in the regions. The federal government attempts to centralize the collection of rents, both to increase its share of the rent and to provide central control over information as to the size of the rent and the form of its capture. The Federal government also imposes in-kind taxes, forcing energy producers to supply fuel and energy at low prices to subsidized users. In-kind subsidies hide the size of implicit transfers and perpetuate inefficient resource use.

In consequence, resource use in Russia's partially-reformed system differs from market ownership in at least three ways. First, there are significant 'idiosyncratic' costs of maintaining control. Second, since central and regional authorities are competing for control of economic rents, the administrative arrangements will reflect this strategic interaction. Third, since tenure is insecure, a harvester will have a shorter time horizon and will attempt to move its portfolio into less risky assets, probably through capital flight. During a decade of economic reform, the partial and incomplete reform of rights to resources has impeded investment, fostered capital flight, and sown the seeds of conflict between the Federation government and Russia's regions.

IMPROVING RESOURCE MANAGEMENT

Achieving greater accountability and efficiency in the use and preservation of Russia's resource wealth will require further privatization, decentralization, and transparency in defining and enforcing a framework of laws and regulations.

In the case of agricultural land and forest land, a much larger sphere for private ownership is needed. Currently, the scale of farm management is divided between gigantic collective and state farms and minuscule private plots. Private farms owned by a single family or a small cooperative would improve food supply and productivity in agriculture and introduce flexibility into local labor markets. In the case of the timber industry, capital flight and tax evasion lead to overharvesting of high value, accessible stocks and diversion of cut timber to a large, informal market. Long term ownership rights would improve incentives to re-plant forests and to monitor theft of timber.

Decentralization of state ownership – increasing the rights of territorial governments to share in the management of publicly owned resources and to derive revenue from them – would improve the accuracy of information about resource use, reduce the incentives to tax evasion, and reduce the conflict of interest between the center and the regions over control of assets. Conflict over control of resource income and wealth was an important factor in the unraveling and collapse of the former Soviet Union.

There are both efficiency and fiscal reasons to increase decentralization of Russian resource management. As Russia has struggled to establish a tax-based government, the primary provision of social protection has fallen on territorial and local governments. For many categories of social protection, the roles of territorial and local (or municipal) governments is crucial. In 1996, regional and local governments provided 85 per cent of government educational funding, 90 per cent of funding for health, and 69 per cent of funding for social protection.[30] In 1998, about 3.6 per cent of GDP was spent on public health care, 93 per cent of the total by regional and local governments.[31]

Since formal tax shares fall short of budgeted expenditure at lower levels of government, each level of government is dependent on a higher level for transfers. Freinkman and Yossifov estimate that roughly 43 per cent of territorial expenditures were covered by federal transfers in 1996, while 35 per cent of local expenditures were transferred from the territory.[32] At all levels, lobbying and negotiation play an important role in determining the outcome.

In a more transparent system of resource management, there would be explicit charges for draw-down of valuable stocks which are presently unpriced, such as the offshore fishery. Royalties, stumpage charges, and production-sharing sharing taxation would replace current export taxes as the major form of government taxation of resource stocks. The regulatory procedures of government agencies would be brought into conformity with established law, and sanctions against corrupt practices would be strictly enforced.

CONCLUSIONS

The future of the RFE depends, in part, on whether the Russian government is able to develop resource management institutions which preserve stocks of reproducible resources, such as timber and fish and which provide sufficient security to generate investment in non-reproducible reserves, such as oil, gas, and minerals. Privatization of land and efficient reform of resource management are likely to emerge only when there is a renewed commitment to other elements of market reform – improved government administration, capital markets, rule of law, and market-supporting institutions.

There is a danger that a new nationalistic government under Vladimir Putin would not eliminate the intertwining of property and power that has caught Russia in an institutional trap. A stronger, more authoritarian government might well disenfranchise the current bevy of oligarchs only to transfer the rents in a more opaque form to other powerful political constituencies, such as government infrastructure monopolies, military and security forces, industrialists, or the immense government bureaucracy itself?

NOTES

1 Goskomstat rossiiskoi federatsii, *Khabarovskoe kraevoe upravlenie statistiki. Statisticheskii biulletenn' itogi raboty gorodov i raionov Khabarovskogo kraia za Ianvar'-dekabr' 1992 goda.* Khabarovsk, 1993, Goskomstat rossiiskoi federatsii, Khabarovskoe kraevoe komitet gosudarstvennoi statistiki. *Statisticheskii biulletenn' No 14. Chislennost' i zarabotnaia plata rabotaiushchikh ha krupnykh e srednykh predpriiatiiakh Khabarovskogo kraia za 1996 god.* Khabarovsk, 1997 and Prokapalo (1999: 30–31).
2 In addition, there are several taxes, discussed later.
3 An official who was responsible for privatization of municipal assets in Vladivostok argued that the most valuable city property was withdrawn from privatization when it emerged that the local committee could not be influenced. (Interview, October, 1995, Seattle.)
4 *Economic Life in the Russian Far East,* 'Privatization in Khabarovskiy Kray: Statistics for 1992–94 and plans for 1995,' 4 June 1995.
5 *Amurskaya Pravka,* 26 January, 1993.
6 *Vostochnyi Ekspress,* No 32, 1992, 8.
7 This process is described by Elisa Miller in Russian Far East Update, May, 1998, 6.
8 Goskomstat Rossii. *Khabarovskii kraevoi komitet Gosudarstvennoi statistiki. Sotsial'noekonomicheskoe polozhenie khabarovskogo kraia 1996,* p. 92.
9 *Osnovy lesnogo zakonodatel'stva Rossiiskoi Federatsii. Vedomosti c'ezda nar. deputatov RF i Verkhou Soveta RF.* 1993, 15, 851–881. Another provincial legal document, the Regulations for Timber Harvesting in Forests of the Far East (1993) was passed as well but was never fully enforced.
10 The following section relies on information in the Sheingauz et al (1996) and Wishnie (1997).
11 *Business Moskovskie Novosti,* 1995, No. 33, p. 10 (cited in Sheingauz et al 1996: 14.)
12 Visit to Dallesprom-Caterpillar Sales Center, Khabarovskiu krai, September, 1996.
13 In an authoritative discussion of changing foreign trade regimes, Pavel Minakir writes: 'With respect to the export contracts that replaced the former licenses, the Ministry of Foreign Economic Relations not only retained the main levels of control over the export of strategically important goods, but even reinforced its position.' Minakir and Freeze (1996: 106).

14 *Moscow Interfax Foreign Trade Report*, No. 1 (6 January 1998) and *Russian Far East Update*, March, 1998, p. 5.

15 Nobuo Arai, 'Fishery Development in the Russian Far East,' Conference paper, Monterey Institute of International Studies, October, 1993.

16 Clarence Pautzke, North Pacific Fishery Management Council Report to Congress, September 30, 1997, p. 7.

17 By comparison, the pre-reform industry included 60 associations and approximately 45 collectives, according to SOTOBO, *Chosa gepppo*, 4 (1990), 54–55.

18 Tsuneo Akaha, 'US-Russian Fishery Joint Ventures: A Curse in Disguise?' conference paper, Monterey Institute of International Studies, July, 1993.

19 Legal act (prikaz) of Minrybkhoz No. 499, 13 December 1989.

20 Viktor Tkachenko and Ernst Chernyi, 'Department of Abuse: Fisheries Department,' Sovetskii Sakhalin, No. 45 (11 March 1998), 2.

21 Interview in Seattle, Washington, September 2, 1998.

22 Vlad M. Kaczynski, 'Reconstruction of the Russian fishing fleet through leasing arrangements with Western shipyards,' Joint School of Marine Affairs-Fisheries Industry Seminar, February, 1997.

23 *Russian Far East Update*, Vol. VIII, No. 2, February, 1998, p. 3; *Interfax Business Report*, 21 Jan 1998 cited in *FBIS-SOV-98-022*, 22 Jan 1998.

24 Discussion with Yegor Gaidar, 18 January 2000, Seattle, Wa.

25 Andrew Jack, 'Russia turns back clock in plan for state controls,' *Financial Times*, 16 January 2000, 1.

26 Anders Aslund, 'Why Has Russia's Economic Transformation Been So Arduous?' World Bank Annual Conference on Development Economics (28–30 April 1999).

27 Press conference, Yegor Gaidar, Federal Information Systems Corporation, Official Kremlin International News Broadcast, October 12, 1995 (cited in James Leitzel, 'Rule Evasion in Transitional Russia,' Conference paper for the National Research Council workshop, Economic Transformation; The Reorganization of Production, Ownership, and Finance, Washington DC (November 2–3, 1995.)

28 Interview, Khabarovsk, October, 1999.

29 Interview Vladivostok, Russia August 1995.

30 Freinkman, Ibid., 14.

31 Russian European Center for Economic Policy, *Russian Economic Trends* (14 July 1999), 6.

32 Freinkman, op. cit. 25.

REFERENCES

Aslund, A. (1999) 'Russia's Collapse,' *Foreign Affairs*, 78 (5), 64–77.

Boycko, M. Shleifer, A. and Vishny, R. (1995) *Privatizing Russia*, Cambridge, Mass.: The MIT Press.

Gaddy, C. and Ickes, B. (1998) 'Russia's Virtual Economy,' *Foreign Affairs*, 77 (5), pp?

Gray, D. (1998) 'Evaluation of Taxes and Revenues from the Energy Sector in the Baltics, Russia, and Other Former Soviet Union Countries,' *IMF Working Paper WP/98/34*.

Minakir, P. and Freeze, G. (1996) *The Russian Far East: An Economic Survey.* Khabarovsk: 'RIOTIP'.

Prokapalo, O.M. (1999) *Sotsial'no-ekonomicheskiy potentsial sub'ektov federatsii rossiyskogo dal'nego vostoka*. Khabarovsk.

Sheingauz, A., Karakin, V. and Tyukalov, V. (1996) *The Forest Sector of the Russian Far East: A Status Report*. Khabarovsk-Vladivostok: Economic Research Institute RAN.

Shleifer, A. and Treisman, D. (2000) *Without a Map: Political Tactics and Economic Reform in Russia*, Cambridge, Mass.: MIT Press.

Shleifer, A. and Vishny, R. (1994) 'Corruption,' *Quarterly Journal of Economics* (November), 599–618.

Turner, W. (1994), 'Focus on the Russian Far East's Timber Industry,' *Russian Far East Update*, 4 (7), 7–10.

Wishnie, M. (1997) *The Centrally Planned Timber Sector in the Russian Market Economy: the Development of the Roskomlesprom Government Timber Monopoly* Seattle, Washington: Working paper, University of Washington.

Chapter 7

Demographic Change in the Russian Far East[1]

Timothy Heleniak[2]

INTRODUCTION

When the Russian State began to expand outward in the middle of the 16th century, its expansion across Siberia to the Pacific was accomplished with remarkable speed. However, throughout Russian and Soviet history, there have always been difficulties in fully incorporating the far eastern periphery region into economy because of the vast distances to central Russia. As the region and Russia enter the post-Soviet era, these difficulties are becoming apparent once again. The development practices towards the Far East employed in the centrally planned Soviet economy are no longer sustainable in the new Russian market or quasi-market economy. This fact is readily evident by the dramatic shift in migration patterns in the Far East between the 1980s and 1990s. The effects of the economic transition on the population of a periphery region such as the Far East is an overlooked feature in many recent books on the region in post-Soviet Russia (Akaha 1997; Minakir 1994; Stephan 1994; Valencia 1995). This chapter examines the effects of rapid economic shock and collapse of non-market development practices on the population and migration patterns in this peripheral region of Russia; it explains the causes of population decline in the region and examines the human and labour resource factors that might influence future economic development plans.

An important distinction for economic activity and post-Soviet migration patterns among the regions of the Far East is the classification of regions as being part of the Far North (*Kraynyy Sever*), regions equivalent to the North (*mestnosti priravnennyye k rayonam Kraynego Severa*), and other regions not in either of these two groups. The designation of these administrative regions was for the purpose of setting wage coefficients and others entitlements as part of a program to recruit workers for tours of duty and stimulate economic development of some of the least developed northern and periphery regions of the Soviet Union. Twenty-seven of the 89 Russian regions are classified as being either wholly or partially in the North. The classification of areas into these groups was based upon their northern latitude and remoteness, harsh climatic conditions, low population density and less developed industrial base, and greater expenditure of resources for the development of natural resources. Because much of the Far East was closed off from foreign trade ties with Pacific Rim neighbors and economic linkages were oriented towards western Russia, the attribute of remoteness was applicable to much of the region. Much of the Far East falls into either being in the Far North or regions equivalent to the Far North. All of the Sahka Republic, Magadan and Kamchatka oblasts, Chukotka and Koryak okrugs are entirely in the Far North. In this chapter, these five regions are referred to as the 'northern' portion of the Far East and the remainder as the southern. Magadan and Chukotka in the Far East have always had among the highest regional wage coefficients in the Soviet Union and Russia. The northern portion of the Sakhalin oblast is classified as being part in the Far North and the remainder being in 'regions equivalent to the Far North'. Portions of the Amur oblast and the Khabarovsk and Primorskii krais are included in the equivalent regions. None of the territory of the Jewish autonomous oblast is in either of these classifications.

HISTORICAL SETTLEMENT PATTERNS OF THE RUSSIAN FAR EAST

As the Far East enters a new phase in the post-Soviet era, it is useful to briefly review the past development and labour supply policies toward the region. As will be shown, many of the development dilemmas that confront the region today have been encountered before. Prior to the expansion of the Russian Empire into Siberia and the Far East, there were an estimated 230,000 natives living in the region engaged primarily in subsistence hunting and fishing (Mote 1998: 39). It was a desire for furs that prompted the early exploration and conquest of the region across the Urals. This expansion was extremely rapid; taking just 66 years from capture of Sibir in 1582 until the Pacific was reached in 1648 (Mote 1998: 41). By the late 1700s, while the population of Siberia was growing, partially through exile of prisoners, the population of the Far East was restricted from growing by the Treaty of Nerchinsk and was between 50,000 and 100,000 (Mote 1998: 45). The quest for North Pacific sea otters lead to the annexation of Alaska but difficulties provisioning the settlements there led to their sale to the United States in 1867 (Stephan 1994: 33). However, the Amur and Primorye regions were acquired in 1860 (Mote 1998: 45) and the present borders of the Far East were more or less established.

During the late 1800s, the population of the Far East began to grow rather rapidly, primarily through migration following the freeing of the serfs in 1861.

Between 1859 and 1917, a half million people moved to region, causing the indigenous population to fall to 45,000, or 5 per cent of the total (Stephan 1994: 62). When the Priamura governor-general was appointed in 1884, the Far East had a regional identity separate from that of Siberia for the first time (Stephan 1994: 55). The peasant migration to the region can be broken down into three phases. The first, lasting to 1882 was rather small-scale, was supported by exempting peasants from conscription, and most settlers were given small allotments of land. A second phase, lasting from 1882–1907 was marked by the increased use of sea transport and more state support of settlers. The third phase, lasting until 1917 was spurred by the Stolypin reforms and the state-sponsored resettlement consisted of primarily of poorer peasants. The flows were larger during this period, when 300,000 moved to the region, more than in the previous half century (Stephan 1994: 66). The expansion and completion of the Trans-Siberian railroad also contributed to increased flows.

The revolutions of 1917 had little impact on the day-to-day events in the Far East. Soviet rule came a bit later following abolishment of the Far East Republic, the buffer state that existed from 1917–1922. During the 1920s, the borders of the region were quite porous and people moved about freely. Because of the revolutions, civil war, and foreign intervention, the economy was in shambles and the population fell by 200,000 between 1913 and 1926. (Stephan 1994: 162–163). At the time of the first Soviet census in 1926, the population stood at 1,513,000 (*Figure 7.1*). Similar to the ideas that promoted this book, ideas were floated in the 1920s for developing the Far Eastern economy by developing links with neighboring Pacific countries (Stephan 1994: 164). For some time, such a situation existed but more because of the uncontrolled economy that existed in the 'Wild East' than explicit state policy (Mote 1998: 89). From 1926 to 1938, the Far East was a province known as *Dalnevostochny*

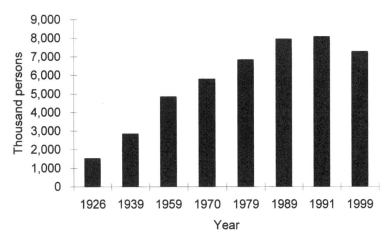

Figure 7.1 Population size of the Russian Far East, 1926–1999

krai or *Dalkrai*, and economic development plans were aimed at making the region self-sufficient. From 1931 to 1939, a million persons migrated to the Far East doubling the population size to 2.8 million. Between the censuses of 1926 and 1938, the population size of Vladivostok doubled to 206,432 and Khabarovsk quadrupled to 199,364 (Stephan 1994: 185). The effects of the immigration from elsewhere in the Soviet Union, along with migration from rural areas in Priamur and Primorye, gave the region the urban and industrial population that it has to this day.

Because of other priorities, distance, and a shortage of capital and labor, the Far East achieved none of its goals during the first five-year plan 1928–1932, (Stephan 1994: 189). In subsequent five-year plans the Far East received a much larger share of investment and as result industrial output doubled between 1937 and 1940 (Mote 1998: 92). This was partially the result of a perceived threat to the region because of the increased militarism of Japan. To solve a variety of 'Jewish problems' in the Soviet Union, the Jewish Autonomous District was created in the Far East in 1930. Few Jews were ever attracted to the region and their share of the population peaked at 23 per cent in 1936 (Stephan 1994: 193). A more important event was the first single-season navigation of North Sea Route from Archangelsk to Vladivostok in 1932. This lessened the Far East's isolation from European Russia. The 1930s were also the time when the industrialization drive picked up pace, regardless of the means. For the Far East, this was the beginning of the period of large scale forced labour. The Soviet government turned to forced labour when it encountered difficulty staffing new industrial projects in periphery regions such as the Far East (Nordlander 1998: 794–795). This was after another idea that is currently being circulated – importing Chinese labour – was rejected. Foreign exchange was needed to fund the industrialization drive and gold from the Kolyma region was a major source of this. The Far East Construction Trust, the notorious Dalstroy, was founded in 1931 with the responsibility for development of the Kolyma region and Okhotsk seaboard. The city of Magadan was founded in 1932 to serve as the base for mining operations in Kolyma and quickly grew to 15,000 by 1936. Between 2.5 and 4.0 million persons died either in or on route to the Kolyma mines.

Because of fears of a second front opening in the east, the region remained heavily militarized with one in seven persons being uniformed, a trend that would persist in the region throughout the Soviet era (Stephan 1994: 243). Over the period from 1939 to 1959, the population nearly doubled again from 2.8 to 4.8 million. Following the war, in 1948, much of the Soviet Union, to the east of the Urals, including all of the Far East was declared off-limits to foreigners (Stephan 1994: 250), another situation that would persist throughout the Soviet era. This policy, coupled with the direction of resource flows between the Far East and central Russia, served to almost completely isolate the region from Pacific neighbors, whom they were geographically closer to. Many parts of the region could only be entered with special permission, even by Soviet citizens. After the death of Stalin in 1953, forced labour ceased to be the primary means of staffing industrial enterprises in periphery regions such as the north and Far East. There was no longer an economic rationale for so many people in such distant regions and following the opening of the camps, there was a slight downturn in the population size, with Magadan loosing a quarter of its population size. Following the abolition of the *gulag* system, recruitment of a labor force to peripheral regions such as the Far East began to rely on wage incentives and other economic stimuli. These regional wage coefficients ranged from 1.2 to 2.0 times the base wage for the same occupation and length of service as in Central Russia (Sallnow 1989: 190). In the Far East, these coefficients ranged from 1.3 in the south to 2.0 in the north, the latter being the highest in the country. As a result, the population of the Far East continued to grow throughout the remainder of the Soviet era peaking in 1991 at 8,057,000.

The RFE is a classic example of a peripheral region, where inexpensive raw materials are extracted and sent to the core in exchange for expensive finished products. The local economy is based upon non-renewable resources such as gold, diamonds, and other minerals and renewable resources such as timber and fishing. The Far East produces over 60 per cent of Russia's gold, 90 per cent of diamonds, 65 per cent of fish products, 30 per cent of forest products, and small but increasing amount of the country's oil. In the centrally controlled Soviet economy, the region's extraction and distribution decisions were made by central ministries which distributed resources throughout the rest of the economy, and controlled profits. The investment policy was aimed at the extraction industries at the expense of more balanced development. Subsidy decisions were also made centrally. The region was forced to import a majority of its foodstuffs to support the large population and has traditionally been a major food-deficit region (Tikhomirov 1997: 179–180). With the withdrawal of transport and other subsidies, the food supply situation has deteriorated. The increased cost of shipping Far Eastern products to market has made many industries completely non-viable under market conditions. The development approach of the Gorbachev regime towards the Far East called for a greater return on investment. When Yeltsin liberalized prices, removed subsidies, and decentralized much fiscal responsibility, it proved catastrophic for the Far Eastern economy and its population. As a result, many have left and many of those who remain have seen their standard of living plummet even more so than the rest of the beleaguered Russian economy.

THE POPULATION OF THE FAR EAST AT THE END OF THE SOVIET PERIOD

A survey of the composition of the Far East reveals both past patterns of population change in the region, but also provides insights into the reasons for the current and possible future levels and direction of migration patterns. The 1989 population census (the most recent in Russia and the last conducted by the Soviet

Union) provides a useful benchmark for this as it was conducted just prior to the breakup of the Soviet Union and the onset of economic reforms in the country.

The spatial distribution of the population of the Far East is dictated by climatic and economic factors. As was mentioned above, a portion of the region lies above the Arctic Circle and much of the area consists of permafrost. As result, at the beginning of 1998, 68 per cent of the population of the Far East live in the three southern regions of Primorskii and Khabarovsk krais and the Amur oblast. The primary role of region's economy is resource extraction leading to a more urban population than Russia, 76 per cent versus 73 per cent in Russia. The two largest settlements are both located in the south, Vladivostok (population 675,000) and Khabarovsk (population 625,000). There are 8 other cities in the Far East with populations over 100,000. The typical settlement pattern within Far East regions is for there to be one large settlement in each oblast-level unit that serves as the administrative center, where a majority of economic activity takes place, and where a large portion of the population resides (between a quarter and half the population). This is true in all but the two smaller ethnic okrugs.

The ethnic composition of the Far East has some definite implications for migration patterns (*Table 7.1*). Four of the ten regions of the Far East are ethnic homelands – the Sakha Republic (homeland of the Yakuts), Chukotka (Chukchi), the Koryak okrug (Koryaks), and the Jewish okrug (Jews). The latter is an artificial homeland established in the 1930s that never had a Jewish share of the population of more than 23 per cent and by 1989 the Jewish share had dwindled to just four per cent. The Yakuts made up the largest titular share of any ethnic region, 33 per cent in 1989, and have been among the most vocal in advocating for increased local say in economic decision-making and in larger shares of the profits from economic activity remaining in the region. The Chukchi (7.3 per cent of Chukotka) and Koryaks (16.5 per cent of the Koryak okrug) are two of the 26 small Siberian and Northern ethnic groups that are classified as the 'Small-Numbered Peoples of the North (*malochislenny narod severa*). About half the 182,000 of these people live in the Far East. All the indigenous groups combined made up less than 6 per cent of Far East population in 1989. The shares for all three Siberian native groups are likely rising as it has been primarily the Russian and other non-native groups who are leaving the Far East.

The Russian share of the Far East population is similar to that of country. However, the Ukrainian share of the population is much higher, 8 per cent of the 1989 population in the Far East versus 3 per cent for the entire country. Ukrainians made up significant shares of every Far East region with the highest shares, about 17 per cent, in the northern regions of Magadan and Chukotka. When the Soviet Union broke up, many of these people returned to Ukraine because of fears of loss of citizenship or other privileges in newly independent Russia. There is difficult-to-substantiate anecdotal evidence of the return migration of some Ukrainians who encountered economic difficulties in Ukraine. *Table 7.1* also shows the minuscule Chinese population of only 784 in 1989 (more on this later).

Table 7. 1 The Ethnic Composition of the Russian Far East, 1989

Region	Nationality	Number	%
Russia	All nationalities	147,021,869	100.0
	Russian	119,865,946	81.5
	Ukrainian	4,362,872	3.0
	Belarussian	1,206,222	0.8
	Other FSU state titular nationalities	2,217,729	1.5
	Jews	536,848	0.4
	Yakuts	380,242	0.3
	Small-Numbered Peoples of the North	181,517	0.1
	Chukchi	15,107	0.0
	Koryaks	8,942	0.0
	Koreans	107,051	0.1
	Chinese	–	–
	Other nationalities	18,163,442	12.4
The Far East	All nationalities	7,950,005	100.0
	Russian	6,346,851	79.8
	Ukrainian	620,552	7.8
	Belarussian	99,438	1.3
	Other FSU state titular nationalities	24,271	0.3
	Jews	15,308	0.2
	Yakuts	365,236	4.6
	Small-Numbered Peoples of the North	87,912	1.1
	Chukchi	14,566	0.2
	Koryaks	8,203	0.1
	Koreans	53,898	0.7
	Chinese	784	0.0
	Other nationalities	335,755	4.2

Source: CIS Statistical Committee and East View Publications, 1989 USSR Population Census, CD-ROM.

Figure 7.2 shows a comparison of the age structure of the Far East versus that for Russia as a whole. The Far East has a much younger population than the Russian average, with an average age of 30 in 1989 versus 35 for all of Russia. At each age group from birth to age 50, the Far East has a relatively larger population. The difference is most pronounced in the prime working ages 25–44. This large working-age bulge is most pronounced in the northern regions of the Far East – Magadan, Kamchatka, Chukotka, and Yakutia. A young population with large shares in the young working ages is characteristic of a population with

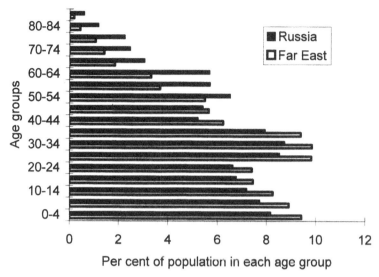

Figure 7.2 Age structure of the Far East and Russia, 1989

high levels of mobility. As will be discussed further below, the population of the Far East was formed largely through migration, which is the reason for the relatively younger population. This was also a contributing factor to the large exodus from the region when the economic reforms started. The Far East was viewed as region where people, induced by the high wage bonuses, would go to work for a period of time or an entire career, and then migrate back to European Russia. Because of this trend, the share of the population above the working ages in 1989 was much smaller in the Far East, 10.4 per cent, than it was for all of Russia, 18.5 per cent. Especially the northern regions were viewed as a place for working and many retired to Central Russia, where they came from.

Because of the age structure, industrial structure, and restrictions on migration to certain regions, the Far East had a much more educated population than the rest of Russia (*Table 7.2*). According to the 1989 census, there were 125 persons per thousand adults with higher education versus 113 per thousand adults in all of Russia and 225 persons per thousand with specialized secondary education in the Far East to 192 for the entire country. Again the northern regions of the Far East are more extreme in this area than other parts as Chukotka, Magadan, Kamchatka have much more highly educated populations. This is partially due to the fact that some of these regions were heavily militarized during the Soviet period and ordinary citizens were required to obtain permission to migrate to these regions. This gave hiring enterprises the ability to be selective and higher more educated and skilled workers. High education is another characteristic correlated with high mobility and it again affected the migration patterns during both the Soviet and post-Soviet periods.

Table 7.2 Level of Education of the Population of the Russian Far East, 1989 (Per 1,000 persons 15 and older, according to census data)

	Absolute totals		Per 1,000 persons 15 and older	
	Russia	Far East*	Russia	Far East
Number of persons 15 and older	113,037,728	5,834,189	1,000	1,000
Number of persons with a higher education:	12,739,509	726,569	113	125
Number of persons with an uncompleted higher education:	1,929,851	96,349	17	17
Number of persons with a secondary special education:	21,713,964	1,314,424	192	225
Number of persons with a secondary general education:	30,986,325	1,750,543	274	300
Number of persons with an incomplete secondary education:	23,744,434	1,225,039	210	210
Number of persons with a primary education:	14,574,309	509,224	129	87
Number of persons without a primary education or unknown:	7,349,336	212,041	65	36

Notes:
*In the 1989 census results, the figures for the Koryak autonomous okrug were included in those for the Kamchatka oblast, those for the Chukotka autonomous okrug were included with the Magadan oblast, and the figures for the Jewish autonomous oblast were included with the Amur oblast.
Source: CIS Statistical Committee and East View Publications, *1989 USSR Population Census*, CD-ROM.

Data from the 1989 census on the place of birth (*Table 7.3*) and length of residency (*Table 7.4*) further illustrate the transient nature of the Far East's population. The region had a much higher share of the population born outside of Russia, 14 per cent, than the country as a whole, 8 per cent, the majority of these born in Ukraine. Ukrainians, along with Russians, Belarussians, Jews, and a few other ethnic groups have long had high rates of mobility. Highly skilled Ukrainians have long left Ukraine to work in industrial enterprises in many of the newly industrializing periphery regions of the Soviet Union, including the Far East. Again, Magadan, Chukotka, and Kamchatka show up as outliers within the Far East with large shares of their populations born outside of Russia. Only 38 per cent of the population of the Far East were born in the region they currently reside versus nearly half, 48 per cent, for the country as a whole. None of the regions of the Far East had more than 40 per cent of their populations who had lived continuously in the region they were residing in at the time of the 1989 census. Only a quarter of the populations of Magadan and Chukotka had been born there. Of those not born in the region, 23 per cent had lived in their region

Table 7.3 Place of Birth of the Population of the Russian Far East, 1989 (According to Data from the Population Census)

Place of birth	Russia	Far East
Total population, 1989	147,021,869	7,950,005
Russia	135,549,786	6,819,998
Far East*	5,817,472	4,665,563
Region of current residence	–	4,104,872
Siberia**	21,668,646	730,274
Western Russia***	108,583,891	1,423,185
Outside Russia	11,472,083	1,130,007
Ukraine	4,595,811	626,438
Belarus	1,408,619	105,483
Other FSU states	4,473,565	326,165
Outside FSU or unknown	994,088	71,921
Total population, 1989 (per cent)	100.0	100.0
Russia	92.2	85.8
Far East*	4.0	58.7
Region of current residence	–	51.6
Siberia**	14.7	9.2
Western Russia***	73.9	17.9
Outside Russia	7.8	14.2
Ukraine	3.1	7.9
Belarus	1.0	1.3
Other FSU states	3.0	4.1
Outside FSU or unknown	0.7	0.9

Notes:
*In the 1989 census results, the figures for the Koryak autonomous okrug were included in those for the Kamchatka oblast, those for the Chukotka autonomous okrug were included with the Magadan oblast, and the figures for the Jewish autonomous oblast were included with the Amur oblast.
**Siberia refers to those born in the East and West Siberian economic regions.
***Western Russia refers to the rest of the country other than the Far East, East and West Siberian economic regions.
Source: CIS Statistical Committee and East View Publications, *1989 USSR Population Census*, CD-ROM.

of current residence for less than five years and forty per cent had lived in their region less than 10 years. The comparable figures for Russia are 14 and 27 per cent. Put differently, 80 per cent of the population of the Far East had either been born outside the region or had lived their less than 10 years, further reinforcing it as a place of newcomers with few ties to the region. If people have migrated once, they are more likely to use migration as a strategy of adaptation again. Thus, when economic conditions in the Far East began to deteriorate in the early

Table 7.4 Population of the Russian Far East by Length of Residency, 1989 (According to Data from the Population Census)

	Total		*Per cent*	
	Russia	*Far East**	*Russia*	*Far East**
Total population	147,021,869	7,950,005	100.0	100.0
Number who have lived in region since birth	71,768,212	3,038,399	48.8	38.2
Number who have not lived in region since birth	75,253,657	4,911,606	51.2	61.8
Of which:				
Less than one year	5,394,057	451,194	3.7	5.7
1 year	3,901,508	335,896	2.7	4.2
2 years	3,555,296	315,106	2.4	4.0
3 years	3,175,905	275,407	2.2	3.5
4 years	2,754,736	232,300	1.9	2.9
5 years	2,455,800	203,755	1.7	2.6
6–9 years	8,884,421	688,547	6.0	8.7
10–14 years	9,018,714	626,015	6.1	7.9
15–19 years	7,830,697	474,250	5.3	6.0
20 or more years	28,282,523	1,309,136	19.2	16.5

Notes:
*In the 1989 census results, the figures for the Koryak autonomous okrug were included in those for the Kamchatka oblast, those for the Chukotka autonomous okrug were included with the Magadan oblast, and the figures for the Jewish autonomous oblast were included with the Amur oblast.
Source: CIS Statistical Committee and East View Publications, *1989 USSR Population Census*, CD-ROM.

1990s, it should come as no surprise that many left. Since so many had either been born elsewhere or recently arrived, they still retained ties elsewhere in Russia or the non-Russian FSU states.

POST-SOVIET MIGRATION TRENDS IN THE RUSSIAN FAR EAST

The population of the Far East continued to grow during the 1980s, adding 1.2 million persons. Eighty per cent of this increase was due to natural increase and 20 per cent was attributable to net migration to the region (*Figure 7.3*). The rate of natural increase was about double the national level because of the young age structure of the population. There continued to be more persons migrating to each region in the Far East during the decade than leaving, with the exception of Sakhalin. While migration continued to be positive throughout the 1980s, it peaked in mid-decade and then began to decline. The *perestroika* and *glasnost* periods began when Gorbachev came to power in 1985. It was at this time that academics first began to openly question some of the economic development projects of the previous regime such as the Baikal-Amur Mainline, which was completed in 1984. Investment priorities began to be shifted away from such 'monuments of the period of stagnation' and the 10 industrial complexes planned along its path (Solovyova 1998, pp. 7–8). There was a growing realization of the lack of economic rational for the implicit subsidy given to periphery regions such as the Far East in the wage structure and that the wage bonuses did not match labor productivity. As a result, net migration into the Far East began to decline, becoming negative in 1989. It was also during this period that a limited amount of private business in the form of cooperatives began to develop. Peripheral regions such as the north, Siberia, and the Far East were no longer the only means that people had to be able to legitimately earn high wages, further stemming the tide.

The population of the Far East peaked in 1991, the last year of the Soviet Union's existence at 8,057,000. The population began to decline precipitously in 1992 following the liberalization of prices and the onset of market reforms. In

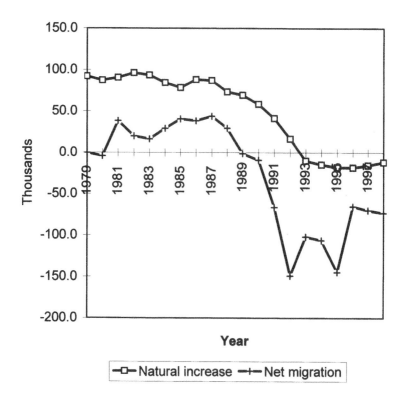

Figure 7.3 Population change in the Russian Far East, 1979–1999

that year, there was a net out-migration from the region of 148,800 and for the first time, there were more people leaving each of the ten Far East regions than arriving, a situation that has persisted to the present. In 1992, the natural increase of the population plummeted to just 16,800 more births than deaths from 41,200 in 1991 (through most of the 1980s, there were roughly 85,000 more births than deaths). In 1993, the natural increase of the population in the Far East became negative (more deaths than births) and has remained so. In the country as a whole, natural increase turned negative in 1992 and has contributed to the steep population decline. Positive but slowing migration into Russia from the near abroad has partially offset this.

Overall during the 1990s, the population of the Far East has declined by nearly 10 per cent, nearly all due to out-migration (*Table 7.5*). The exodus was heaviest during the first four years of independence when a half million more people left the region than arrived. The population has declined in every Far East region and there has been out-migration from each. In six of the ten regions, there was a population decline of more than 10 per cent between 1990 and 1999. The largest declines were in the northern regions of the Far East, entirely due to people leaving. In the furthest north are the extreme examples where there has been an out-migration of 43 per cent of the population of Magadan and over half of the population of Chukotka. The migration trends in these and other regions of the Far East are evidence of the dramatic reversal in migration direction within Russia between the 1980s and 1990s. During the 1980s, the general pattern was of continuing out-migration from central Russia to the peripheral regions, including at that time, the Baltic and other Slavic states. During the 1980s, the Far East had the third highest rate of in-migration of the eleven Russian economic regions. This situation has completely reversed itself with the breakup of the Soviet Union and onset of economic reforms so that the trend is one of net migration away from the periphery towards the core. This trend exists externally from the non-Russian FSU states back to Russia and internally from the north and Far East towards European Russia.

While the overall trend has been one of net out-migration from the Far East, there are still people coming to the region. From 1993 to 1998, there was migration of 718,000 persons to the Far East while 1,205,000 persons migrated away, resulting in the negative net migration of about a half million. For every 10 people coming to the Far East, 17 have been leaving. The peak year of both out-migration and in-migration to and from the Far East was 1994. This was the same in Russia as a whole in terms of both internal and externals migration. Since that year, overall migration turnover rates – the number of people moving – in the Far East as well as in the country have declined by nearly half. Over this period, about 70 per cent of migrants to the Far East have been from elsewhere in Russia and about 85 per cent of people who have migrated from the region have gone elsewhere in the country. Starting in 1994, the migration exchange with foreign, mostly other FSU states, has been positive. In 1993 (and probably 1992 as well if data were available), there was a net out-migration of 28,000 to

Table 7.5 Population Trends in the Russian Far East, 1979–1999)

Region	Total population			Per cent change, 1979–1989			Per cent change, 1990–1999		
	1979	1990	1999	Total	Natural increase	Migration	Total	Natural increase	Migration
Russian Federation	137,551	148,041	146,693	7.6	7.0	0.6	-0.9	-3.0	2.1
Far East	6,819	8,008	7,252	17.4	13.8	3.7	-9.4	0.3	-9.8
Sakha (Yakutia)	839	1,099	989	31.0	22.5	8.5	-10.0	6.3	-16.4
Jewish autonomous oblast*	190	218	203	14.9	–	–	-7.1	0.5	-7.6
Chukotka Autonomous okrug*	133	156	77	17.1	–	–	-50.7	3.2	-53.9
Primorskii krai	1,978	2,281	2,197	15.3	11.8	3.6	-3.7	-1.3	-2.4
Khabarovsk krai	1,566	1,840	1,737	17.5	13.5	3.9	-5.6	-0.9	-4.7
Amur oblast	937	1,066	1,015	13.8	14.2	-0.4	-4.8	0.3	-5.1
Kamchatka oblast	379	470	390	24.1	14.3	9.8	-16.9	0.8	-17.8
Koryak autonomous okrug*	34	40	30	16.2	–	–	-23.5	1.6	-25.2
Magadan oblast	466	539	317	15.8	12.0	3.8	-41.3	1.6	-42.9
Sakhalin oblast	655	713	608	8.9	10.3	-1.4	-14.8	-1.4	-13.4

Notes:

* The figures for the Kamchatka oblast include the Koryak okrug; the totals for the Khabarovsk krai include the Jewish autonomous oblast; and those for the Magadan oblast include the Chukotka autonomous okrug.

Sources:

1979 population totals: Goskomstat Rossii, (1997a) *Demograficheskiy yezhegodnik Rossii*, Moscow: Goskomstat. 24–26.

1980–1988 population totals: Goskomstat RSFSR, (1990a) *Chislennost', sostav i dvizheniye naseleniya v RSFSR 1990*, Moscow: Goskomstat. 9–11.

1989, 1993–1994 population totals: Goskomstat Rossii (1994) *Demograficheskiy yezhegodnik Rossiyskoy Federatsii*, Moscow: Goskomstat.

1990 population totals: Goskomstat SSSR, (1990) *Demograficheskiy yezhegodnik SSSR 1990*, Moscow: Finansy i statistika. Data for selected sub-units were subtracted from larger units to which they were subordinated to arrive at comparable level units according to Goskomstat RSFSR (1990b) *Chislennost' naseleniya RSFSR po gorodam, poselkam gorodskogo tipa i rayonam na 1 yanvarya 1990 g*, Moscow: Goskomstat.

1991–1992 population totals: Goskomstat Rossii (1995a) *Rossiyskiy statisticheskiy yezhegodnik*, Moscow: Goskomstat.

1995 population totals: Goskomstat Rossii (1995a) *Sotsial'no-ekonomicheskoye polozheniye Rossii 1993–1994 gg.*

1996 population totals: Goskomstat Rossii (1996) *Informatsiomyy statisticheskiy byulleten'* No. 6, June.

1997 population totals: Goskomstat Rossii (1997b), *Chislennost' naseleniya Rossiyskoy Federatsii po gorodam, poselkam gorodskogo tipa i rayonam na yanvarya 1997 g.*, Moscow: 10–12. Data are for the present (nalichnoye) population.

1998 population totals: *Goskomstat Rossii (1998a) Chislennost' i migratsii naseleniya Rossiyskoy Federatsii v 1997 godu: Statisticheskiy byulleten'*, Moscow: Goskomstat. 8–10.

1999 population totals: Goskomstat Rossii (1999a) *Chislennost' i migratsii naseleniya Rossiyskoy Federatsii v 1998 godu:* Statisticheskiy byulleten', Moscow: Goskomstat. 8–10.

1979–1988 births and deaths: Goskomstat RSFSR, (1990a) *Chislennost', sostav i dvizheniye naseleniya v RSFSR*, Moscow: Goskomstat. 92–93, 98–99. Absolute figures on births and deaths were based on CBRs and CDRs.

1989 births, deaths, natural increase: Goskomstat RSFSR (1991) *Chislennost', sostav i dvizheniye naseleniya v RSFSR, 1990*. Data for sub-units where totals are not available are estimated by taking same proportion of larger unit as in 1990. These estimates were then subtracted from the larger units.

1990–1993 births, deaths and natural increase: Goskomstat Rossii (1995a) *Demograficheskiy yezhegodnik Rossiyskoy Federatsii 1993*. Moscow: Goskomstat.

1994 births, deaths, natural increase: Goskomstat Rossii (1995a) *Sotsial'no-ekonomicheskoye polozheniye Rossii 1993–1994 gg.* Moscow: Goskomstat.

1996 births and deaths: Goskomstat Rossii (1997c) *Sotsial'no-ekonomicheskoye polozheniye Rossii 1996 g.* Moscow: Goskomstat.

1997 births and deaths: Goskomstat Rossii (1998b) *Sotsial'no-ekonomicheskoye polozheniye Rossii yanvar' 1998 goda*, Moscow: Goskomstat. 309–310.

1998 births and deaths: Goskomstat Rossii (1999b) *Sotsial'no-ekonomicheskoye polozheniye Rossii yanvar' 1999 goda*, Moscow: Goskomstat. 415–416.

1989–1998 net migration: Based on residual method.

outside Russia. The overall net migration with foreign countries during the period 1993 to 1998, has been a positive 16,000. There has been net out-migration to Ukraine, Belarus, Moldova, and to outside the FSU and net immigration from the other FSU states.

Not surprisingly, there is evidence of a north-south migration pattern within the Far East. *Figure 7.4* shows data on the destinations of migrants from the Far East for the period 1989–1996 illustrating the preference for a few select regions (the data include just those who have crossed an oblast-level boundary). Krasnodar and Rostov in the North Caucasus both received large numbers of migrants from the region. During the transition period, these two regions have become prime destinations of internal migrants from elsewhere in Russia, as well as external migrants from the other FSU states. Far East migrants are also settling in the southern regions of East and West Siberia. The three large southern regions of the Far East – the Amur oblast and Khabarovsk and Primorskii krais – have been magnets for people leaving the northern regions of the Far East.

Both the urban and rural areas of the Far East declined proportionally to their shares of the population over the 1990s. Half of the oblast centers had population declines with several of those in the north, Anadyr' (Chukotka), Petropavlovsk (Kamchatka), and Magadan city (Magadan) showing the largest per cent declines, by between 15 and 30 per cent (*Table 7.6*). In spite of the declines, the portion of the population residing in the oblast center in every region, except Petropavlovsk, has increased, in many cases rather dramatically. There is evidence in most cases of intra-regional migration away from rural areas towards the oblast centers and other large urban areas. This is not to indicate that these urban settlements are becoming growth poles. In most cases, they are better supplied with food and consumer goods and have slightly more stable economies than rural areas since the network of shipments of these goods to periphery regions has declined so precipitously during the reform period. A case in point is Magadan city, the oblast center of the Magadan oblast. In spite of the population declining by 21 per cent from 1989 to 1999, Magadan city's share of the oblast's population has increased from 28 to 40 per cent. The only other settlement with the status of urban in the oblast is Susuman, which is located in the western portion of the oblast in the Kolyma region with a population of 9,000. Many of the rural settlements based upon gold extraction have either become depleted or uneconomical during transition and have either died out or are in the process of being closed. While many leave the region, many choose to stay in Magadan city which was established as the base for the extraction of gold and other mineral products in the region.

At lower geographic levels, some of the northern rayons of Yakutia, Magadan, and Chukotka have had population declines of between 40 and 60 per cent between 1991 and 1998, as the economic base of these settlements have been proven completely non-viable in market conditions. There was discussion of the need for evacuation or emergency supplies following the financial crisis in August

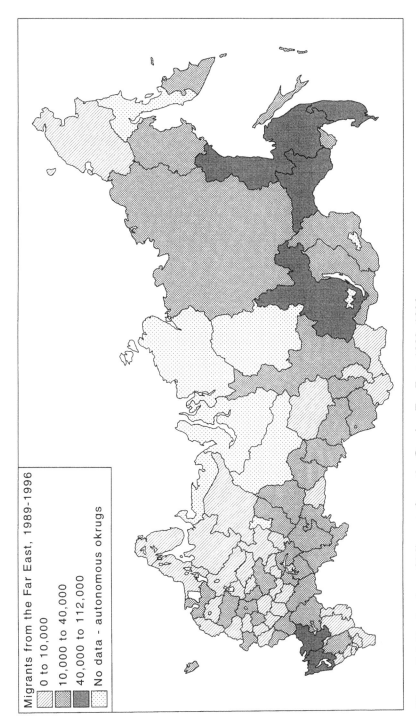

Figure 7.4 Destination of Migrants from the Russian Far East, 1989–1996

Migrants from the Far East, 1989-1996

0 to 10,000
10,000 to 40,000
40,000 to 112,000
No data - autonomous okrugs

Table 7.6 Population Change in the Urban Population and Regional Centers in the Russian Far East, 1989–1999 (beginning-of-year; in thousands)

Region (oblast center)	Per cent Urban		Per cent change, 1989–1999		Population in Oblast centre (ths.)		Oblast centre as Share of total Oblast population	
	1989	1999	Urban	Rural	1989	1999	1989	1999
Russian Federation	74	73	−1.1	0.3				
Far East	76	75	−8.5	−8.9				
Sakha (Yakutsk)	67	64	−10.6	−1.1	188	228	17.4	22.8
Jewish A. O. (Birobidzhan)	66	66	−5.3	−10.2	83	81	38.4	39.4
Chukotka A. O. (Anadyr')	73	72	−49.2	−41.4	18	13	11.5	16.1
Primorskii krai (Vladivostok)	77	77	−2.1	−5.6	631	640	27.9	28.9
Khabarovsk krai (Khabarovsk)	71	70	−4.3	−9.3	598	611	32.8	34.9
Amur oblast (Bladoveshchensk)	68	65	−7.8	1.6	204	223	19.3	21.8
Kamchatka oblast (Petropavlovsk)	81	81	−15.5	−12.6	273	210	58.6	53.0
Koryak A. O. (Palana)	38	25	−48.7	−3.7	4	4	11.1	13.2
Magadan oblast (Magadan)	60	68	−32.1	−58.7	152	131	28.0	40.0
Sakhalin oblast (Yuzhno-Sakhalinsk)	82	85	−10.2	−33.5	156	185	22.0	29.8

Notes: Population totals are for permanent population (postoyannoye naseleniye).
Sources:
1989: Unless otherwise noted, Goskomstat Rossii (1995b) *Goroda Rossiyskoy Federatsii*, Moscow: Goskomstat. 1995: 12–13.
1999: Goskomstat Rossii (1999c) *Chislennost' naseleniya Rossiyskoy Federatsii po gorodam, poselkam gorodskogo tipa i rayonam na 1 yanvarya 1999 g*, Moscow: Goskomstat.

1998 (Gordon 1999: A1, A4). Expenditures on the 'northern shipment' (*severny zavoz*) that supplied peripheral regions in the north and east with critical supplies of food, fuel, and consumer goods has gone from 1.58 per cent of GDP in 1992 to just 0.12 per cent in 1997. The Russian government, with lagging tax collection and other priorities, can no longer afford the massive supply effort to the periphery that the centrally-planned Soviet government could. A decision has been taken by *Goskomsever* (the Russian State Committee for Northern Development) to close approximately 16 per cent of these non-viable, hard to reach, settlements in the Far East. The largest shares of planned settlement closings are in Magadan, Chukotka, and on Sakhalin Island.

As has been shown above, while overall the population of the Far East has declined during the 1990s, it has not been uniform among geographic units. There has also been considerable variation in migration across age groups, educational levels, occupations and nationalities. The considerable variation in migration among these groups has implications for the populations that remain in the Far East, the local Far East governments and for the economic recovery of the region. In a normally functioning market economy, people respond to signals in local labor markets by migrating to where there is job growth, typically preceded by investment. This usually takes place at several different occupational levels simultaneously as there is differential demand for labor in different occupations. At the individual level, migration tends to follow a certain pattern along the life cycle, with people at certain ages being more mobile than others. Certain types of people also tend to be more mobile than others. For example, more educated persons tend to be more mobile and urban dwellers more so than rural residents. In a normally functioning economy, this redistribution of labor tends to take place over a protracted period of time. As a result, while there are labour shortages and labour surpluses in regions, these tend not to be that great and are alleviated by the sending of market signals and the ability of people to move freely. Because the process takes place over a long period of time, the age structure of sending and receiving areas tend not to become extremely warped with great 'excesses' or 'deficits' among any cohorts. In the case of the Far East during the transition period, the local labour market and standard-of-living variables changed rather rapidly resulting in the above mentioned mass exodus from the region. The population of the region had a rather unique age-sex and occupational structure to begin with. Below is a disaggregation of the migration streams by age and educational level to and from the Far East over this turbulent period followed by an analysis of the causes of this migration. Some of this is based upon migration data collected systematically by Goskomstat while others are based upon more anecdotal information.

There is considerable anecdotal evidence that it is the young and highly skilled who are abandoning the Far East in greatest numbers (Mote 1998: 192). Systematic migration statistics collected by Goskomstat partially substantiate this claim. While the *propiska* (resident permit) system was abolished in 1993, migrants in Russia are still required to register at place or origin and destination and provide information on their age, sex, and educational level. Data for 1994, in the midst of the mass exodus from the region, show that there was net out-migration at every age group except those 20 to 23. There is a large spike of net out-migration at age 17, when many students complete compulsory education. This net out-migration was largest between ages 30 and 45. The peak difference was at age 34, where there where more than 3 people of this age leaving the Far East for every one arriving. The net out-migration by age lessens up the age pyramid, until about age 55, when many retires leave the region. Over the period 1994 to 1996, there was a ratio of nearly two people leaving the Far East for every one arriving (1.90 to be exact). There were disproportionate numbers of people with specialized secondary and general secondary education leaving (the ratios of departures to arrivals was 1.97 and 2.12 respectively). Those with specialized secondary education are those who staff many of the industrial enterprises in the region.

A comparison of the age structure of the region both before (1989) the mass migration and recently (1997) show the effects of the age selectivity of migration to and from the Far East, leaving the region with a rather peculiar age structure (*Figure 7.5*). While the total population of the region declined by about 10 per cent over this period, those ages 25 to 40 declined by over 20 per cent. The

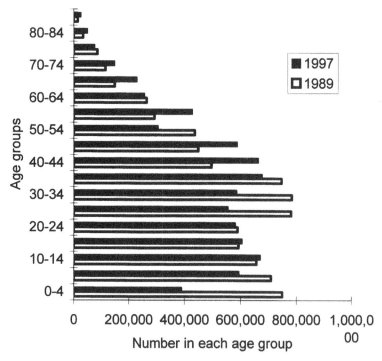

Figure 7.5 Age Structure of the Far East, 1999 versus 1997

number of children 10 years old and younger declined by over 30 per cent. This was partially due to the decline in the birthrate that affected all of Russia but the larger effect was the result of net out-migration from the region of their parents in the 25 to 40 age cohort. At the same time, the number of those above the working ages increased by nearly 25 per cent. Many of those in the older cohorts had savings they had accumulated from years of working in the Far East wiped out by the inflation of the reform period and were unable to leave. The government is no longer able to afford the system of state-sponsored migration assistance for those who had retired and wished to move to central Russia. The situation of people wanting to migrate but lacking the financial and other resources to be able to do so is most prevalent in the northern regions of the Far East.

To this point, this analysis of post-Soviet migration patterns in the Far East has described the levels and composition of the migration streams but has not discussed the causes of these patterns. The other chapters in this book, look more closely at economic change and prospects in the Far East during the transition period. This chapter looks at the impact of those economic reforms on the population of the region, specifically what about these economic shifts caused the region to so rapidly shift from being one of the largest in-migration regions in Russia to being by far the largest out-migration region.

As the region makes the transition from the Soviet Far East to the Russian Far East, a number of other processes are underway at the national level that have are having a severe impact on the region. The major one is the transition from a centrally planned economy to a market economy. In the planned economy of the Soviet Union, most economic decisions were made by the center but in a market economy, there is increased local decision making, which has had a deleterious effect on a peripheral region such as the Far East. During the Soviet period, much of the economic activity in the Far East was made possible by highly subsidised transport and energy costs. As these subsidies are withdrawn, much of the economic activity in the region has become unviable. During the Soviet period, the Far East was a closed economic space and the economic structure of the region was oriented towards resource extraction to be supplied to the rest of the country. The RFE is a much more open economy with increased integration with the Pacific Rim countries. But trading with these countries reveals the true costs resource extraction in high-latitude and distant regions. Food and other consumer goods were supplied to the region and other periphery regions with federal financing and subsidies. Local governments and enterprises are now responsible for food supply to region and the increased costs of shipping these products, often from abroad, are reflected in the highest consumer basket costs in the country.

When considering whether to migrate or not, individuals make a subconscious or conscious cost-benefit analysis of the standard of living and prospects in the region there are living and weigh this against other possible destinations. If the benefits other locations exceed the costs of making the move, the individual tends to migrate. Changes in the economy or standard of living in a region impact on individuals to alter the variables in their cost-benefit equation. If the variables change enough or enough to impact a large number of people, there will be large shifts in the number of people migrating into or out of a region. This is what has happened in the Far East during the transition period in Russia.

With the liberalization of prices and the reduction of transport and energy subsidies, the cost of living in the Far East has risen dramatically. The subsistence minimum in every Far East region is higher than the national levels. In 1994, in extreme northern regions of the Far East it was more than 3 times the national level. Even in the more accessible southern regions, it was more than 50 per cent the national level. The Soviet Union has long endeavored to make the Far East self-sustaining in food production. However, this would only be possible with continuous, uninterrupted and subsidised supply of the necessary inputs for agricultural production (Tikhomirov 1997: 157). This was only possible under the Soviet centrally planned economy and when that system collapsed, most agricultural production in the region became unprofitable and food imports to the region because very expensive. Even the region's legendary fish products became too expensive for local residents to consume. Between 1990 and 1996, per capita consumption of meat products fell by 30 per cent, milk products by 52 per cent, bread products by 15 per cent, and potato consumption increased by 27 per cent (Tikhomirov 1997: 184). Bread and potatoes became the main foodstuffs consumed, replacing more high quality items. Unlike other regions of Russia, turning to food produced on private plots has limited potential in much of the Far East because of climatic conditions.

The effects of price liberalization and the withdrawal of subsidies are not limited to food. Harsh climatic conditions made it necessary to provide heavily subsidised energy most of the year (Bradshaw and Kirkow 1998: 1043). The higher cost of food and other goods is not offset by higher wages, even though the Far East has among the highest nominal wages in Russia. The ratio of the average wage to subsistence minimum is lower in each Far East region than nationally. Poverty rates and per capita wage arrears are higher in every region as well. The share of unprofitable enterprises is much higher in the Far East than nationally as industrial production has proven unviable under market conditions. In sum, because the Far East was so heavily dependent on subsidised inputs and state support, and because production of many of the region's natural resources only made sense in the closed economic system of the Soviet Union, the economic collapse has been much greater in the Far East than in the rest of Russia. All of these factors contribute to greatly, and rather rapidly, change the variables in the migration equation of many Far East residents. Because many of them were young, educated, and from outside the region, all factors associated with a high propensity to migrate, it was not surprising that many quit the region during the 1990s. It is not surprising that these out-migration rates were higher from the northern regions of the Far East, which were relatively more subsidised and thus felt the effects of transition even more.

CONCLUSIONS: IMPLICATIONS OF MIGRATION PATTERNS AND FUTURE PROSPECTS

In the Far East, as in any region, the economy and the demographic size and structure of the population are inextricably linked. Among other factors, the size and growth prospects of a region dictate the size and composition of the population. As was pointed out above, given the gloomy prospects for the Far East, many are voting with their feet and placing their hopes elsewhere. In Soviet times, the Far East was a peripheral region highly dependent on the core. Though independence is probably not an option, there has been a distancing of the region from the rest of Russia. At the same time, the Far East needs a core of skilled workers in order to develop as a player in the 'Pacific Century' as it is supposed to do. Like any region in transition, there are labour market adjustments taking place at a number of levels simultaneously. There also seems to be a need for less-skilled workers, which is what lies behind much of the cross-border migration from China (more on this below).

The most recent set of population projections done by Goskomstat offer a clue as to the possible future population size of the Far East (*Table 7.7*). They project that population of the Far East will continue to decline so that by the end of the projection period in 2015, the population will be about the same level as in the late 1970s. After loosing 756,000 people between 1990 and 1998, the Far East is expected to loose another 670,000 people over the next 17 years, a 9.2 per cent decline. Slightly more than half of this decline is attributable to continued net migration from the region and a little less than half due to an excess of deaths over births. Every Far East region except Yakutia will have negative natural increase. If these projections hold true, this would be an 18 per cent decline from the peak population size in 1991. With the exception of Yakutia, all of the Far East regions will have lost more than 20 per cent of their populations. The population of Magadan will have declined nearly 60 per cent from its peak and that of Chukotka nearly two-thirds, to just 53,000. It is obvious that the Far East is in the midst of making a difficult transition from a population size and spatial distribution appropriate for a centrally planned economic system to one more appropriate for a market economy.

One of the major demographic issues in the RFE in the future will be the level of Chinese migration into the region. There has been migration of Koreans, Japanese and Vietnamese as well but, because of their sheer numbers, the issue of Chinese penetration is the most controversial. Described by some as 'Yellow Peril', there has been a great deal of hysteria, confusion and misinformation about the number of Chinese in the region, legally and illegally, and whether this should be viewed as threat or an inevitability that will serve as boon to the local economy. Most discussions of the issue start with the basic demographic fact that there are 7 million people in the Far East, 5 million in the southern regions bordering China, and 102 million in the three Chinese provinces bordering Russia (Zayonchkovskaya 1999: 137).

Table 7.7 The Projected Population of the Russian Far East, 1998–2015 (end-of-year; thousands)

Region	Total population		Population change, 1998–2015				Population change, 1990–2015	
	1998	2015	Total	Natural Increase	Migration	Per cent	Total	Per cent
Russian Federation	146,397	138,059	-8,338	-10,779	2,441	-5.7	-10,484	-7.1
Far East	7,282	6,612	-670	-301	-369	-9.2	-1,445	-17.9
Sakha (Yakutia)	1,011	1,018	7	66	-59	0.7	-91	-8.2
Jewish autonomous oblast	202	177	-25	-7	-18	-12.4	-43	-19.5
Chukotka autonomous okrug	88	53	-35	0	-35	-39.8	-101	-65.6
Primorskii krai	2,193	1,929	-264	-158	-106	-12.0	-370	-16.1
Khabarovsk krai	1,524	1,419	-105	-84	-21	-6.9	-432	-23.3
Amur oblast	1,003	848	-155	-48	-107	-15.5	-226	-21.0
Kamchatka oblast	401	376	-25	-16	-9	-6.2	-97	-20.5
Koryak Autonomous okrug *	31	31	0	-1	1	0.0	-9	-22.5
Magadan oblast	246	225	-21	-10	-11	-8.5	-309	-57.9
Sakhalin oblast	614	567	-47	-43	-4	-7.7	-150	-20.9

Notes:
* Data for the Koryak autonomous okrug are included with the Kamchatka oblast.
Sources: Data from Goskomstat Rossii (1998c) *Ob osnovnykh tendentsiyakh razvitiya demograficheskoy situatsii v Rossii do 2015 goda* (doklad), Moscow: Goskomstat.. Data are interpolated for years between 2000, 2005, 2010, and 2015.

Like many development and demographic issues confronting the Far East, the issue of foreign workers in the region is not new and has its origins in the past. There has long been an issue of Russian control over the region and during the Soviet period there were numerous borders skirmishes in the area. Even after the Amur and Primorye regions became a part of Russia in 1860, Chinese continued to enter the region across the rather porous borders (Stephan 1994: 71). In 1877, four out of five civilians in Vladivostok were Chinese or Korean. During the Soviet period, as border control became more rigid and much of the region was declared off-limits to foreigners, the number of Chinese dwindled. At the time of the 1989 census, there were just 784 Chinese enumerated in the Far East (*Table 7.1*).

Vladivostock officially reopened on January 1, 1992 and Chinese, Japanese, Koreans and Vietnamese flooded into Far East. Though there are certainly those who enter or over stay short-term travel permits, most Chinese and others working in the region seem to do so under rather carefully controlled conditions (Kim 1995: 79; Zayonchkovskaya 1999: 143). Claims on the part of border guards and other local officials who claim that there are up to 2 million Chinese living in the region, legally and illegally, are greatly exaggerated. Claims of this magnitude are based on fears that large numbers of Chinese will lead to a loss of control over the region and possibly loss of the territory. Though welcome by some because of the niche they fill in the local labour markets, this is not universally endorsed by all. Moscow's control over border crossings has largely been devolved to local Far East authorities. The best estimates are that there are between 30,000 and 70,000 Chinese in each of the Amur, Khabarovsk, and Primorskii regions (Zayonchkovskaya 1999: 143). Most Chinese tend to work in unskilled construction and agricultural jobs, and as petty traders in the large cities. Usually a labour contract is made between a local Russian enterprise and a Chinese team leader who keeps the workers under strict control and payment is made to the team leader, not directly to the workers. Many, like Zayonchkovskaya, believe that it is in Russia's and the Far East's best interest to take advantage of this demographic imbalance between the regions and allow more Chinese demographic expansion into the southern regions. She points out that this is inevitable and suits the mutual needs of both countries. However, given the low levels of migration now allowed by local officials, and the fears of more permanent Chinese expansion into the Far East at the national level, it is difficult to see how large scale Chinese migration much beyond the present levels would happen.

So what does the future hold for the Far East economy and thus the population of this region? Moltz lays out four different possible development scenarios: retention of peripheral status within Russian market economy; become a periphery resource supplier within Pacific Rim countries; greater regional autonomy and development of relations with both the rest of Russia and the Pacific Rim; and isolation from both Moscow and the Pacific Rim countries (Moltz 1996: 190–191). He says that the last is the worst, but most likely, scenario. If this proves to be the case, it will have extremely negative consequences on the region's population. The population will not see the results of the region's highly touted resource economy, incomes will remain stagnant, and poverty rates will increase. With little possibility for savings, those who would like to leave the region for better opportunities elsewhere in Russia will not be able to. The region's dim prospects will not attract the highly skilled workers it needs to realize its economic potential. In other words, the 'muddle along' scenario is the most likely for the people of the Far East, with too many people in the wrong places, too few skilled in the right places, increased poverty, and the region and its populace not realizing the potential that many saw for it in the coming Pacific Century.

NOTES

1 A preliminary version of this paper was presented at the 95th Annual Meeting of the Association of American Geographers, Honolulu, Hawaii, March 23–27, 1999.
2 The World Bank, 1818 H St., N.W., Washington, DC 20433. The views and opinions expressed herein are entirely those of the author and should not be attributed in any manner to the World Bank.

REFERENCES

Akaha, Tsuneo, ed. (1997) *Politics and Economics in the Russian Far East: Changing Ties with Asia-Pacific*, London: Routledge.

Bradshaw, Michael J. and Peter Kirkow, (1998) 'The Energy Crisis in the Russian Far East: Origins and Possible Solutions', *Europe-Asia Studies*, 50 (6), 1043–1063.

CIS Statistical Committee and East View Publications (1996) *1989 USSR Population Census*, *CD-ROM*, 1996.

Gordon, Michael R. (1999) 'Foresaken in Russia's Arctic: 9 Million Stranded Workers', *New York Times*, January 6.

Goskomstat Rossii (1999a) *Chislennost' i migratsii naseleniya Rossiyskoy Federatsii v 1998 godu: Statisticheskiy byulleten'*, Moscow: Goskomstat.

Goskomstat Rossii (1999b) *Sotsial'no-ekonomicheskoye polozheniye Rossii yanvar' 1999 goda*. Moscow: Goskomstat.

Goskomstat Rossii (1999c) *Chislennost' naseleniya Rossiyskoy Federatsii po gorodam, poselkam gorodskogo tipa i rayonam na 1 yanvarya 1999 g*, Moscow: Goskomstat.

Goskomstat Rossii (1998a) *Chislennost' i migratsii naseleniya Rossiyskoy Federatsii v 1997 godu: Statisticheskiy byulleten'*, Moscow: Goskomstat.

Goskomstat Rossii (1998b) *Sotsial'no-ekonomicheskoye polozheniye Rossii yanvar' 1998 goda*. Moscow: Goskomstat.

Goskomstat Rossii (1998c) *Ob osnovnykh tendentsiyakh razvitiya demograficheskoy situatsii v Rossii do 2015 goda (doklad)*, Moscow: Goskomstat.

Goskomstat Rossii (1997a) *Demograficheskiy yezhegodnik Rossii*, Moscow: Goskomstat.

Goskomstat Rossii (1997b) *Chislennost' naseleniya Rossiyskoy Federatsii po gorodam, poselkam gorodskogo tipa i rayonam na yanvarya 1997 g.*, Moscow: Goskomstat.

Goskomstat Rossii (1997c) *Sotsial'no-ekonomicheskoye polozheniye Rossii 1996 g.*, Moscow: Goskomstat.

Goskomstat Rossii (1995a) *Sotsial'no-ekonomicheskoye polozheniye Rossii 1993–1994 gg.*, Moscow: Goskomstat.

Goskomstat Rossii (1995b) *Goroda Rossiyskoy Federatsii*, Moscow: Goskomstat.

Goskomstat Rossii (1994) *Demograficheskiy yezhegodnik Rossiyskoy Federatsii 1993*, Moscow: Goskomstat.

Goskomstat RSFSR (1991) *Chislennost', sostav i dvizheniye naseleniya v RSFSR, 1990*. Moscow: Goskomstat.

Goskomstat RSFSR (1990a) *Chislennost', sostav i dvizheniye naseleniya v RSFSR 1990*. Moscow: Goskomstat.

Goskomstat RSFSR (1990b) *Chislennost' naseleniya RSFSR po gorodam, poselkam gorodskogo tipa i rayonam na 1 yanvarya 1990 g.*, Moscow: Goskomstat.

Goskomstat SSSR (1990) *Demograficheskiy yezhegodnik SSSR 1990*, Moscow: Finansy i statistika, Moscow: Goskomstat.

Kim, Won Bae, (1995) 'Migration', *The Russian Far East in Transition: Opportunities for Regional Economic Cooperation*, edited by Mark. J. Valencia, Boulder: Westview Press, pp. 65–86.

Minakir, Pavel A. and Freeze, Gregory, L. (eds.) (1994) *The Russian Far East: An Economic Handbook*, Armonk, New York: M.E. Sharpe.

Moltz, James Clay, (1996) 'Core and Periphery in the Evolving Russian Economy: Integration or Isolation of the Far East?', *Post-Soviet Geography and Economics*, 37 (3), pp. 175–194.

Mote, Victor L. (1998) *Siberia: Worlds Apart*, Boulder: Westview Press.

Nordlander, David J. (1998) 'Origins of a Gulag Capital: Magadan and Stalinist Control in the Early 1930s', *Slavic Review*, 57 (4), 791–812.

Sallnow, John, (1989) 'Siberia's Demand for Labour: Incentive Policies and Migration 1960–1985', *The Development of Siberia: People and Resources*, edited by Alan Wood and R.A. French, New York: St. Martin's Press, pp. 188–207.

Solovyova, Julia, (1998) 'From Nowhere, to Nowhere', *Moscow Times*, July 18.

Stephan, John J. (1994) *The Russian Far East: A History*, Stanford, California: Stanford University Press.

Tikhomirov, Vladimir (1997) 'The Food Balance in the Russian Far East', *Polar Geography*, 21 (3), 155–202.

Valencia, Mark J. ed. (1995) *The Russian Far East in Transition: Opportunities for Regional Economic Cooperation*, Boulder: Westview Press.

Zayonchkovskaya, Zhanna, (1999) 'Chinese Demographic Expansion into Russia: Myth or Inevitability?', *Population Under Duress: The Geodemography of Post-Soviet Russia*, edited by George J. Demko, Grigory Ioffe, and Zhanna Zayonchkovskaya, Boulder: Westview Press, pp. 137–148.

Chapter 8

Prospects for Multilateralism in Northeast Asia[1]

Vladimir I. Ivanov

INTRODUCTION

Northeast Asia (NEA) represents a subregion within the bigger Asia-Pacific region (APR). It is comprised of China, Japan, the Koreas, Mongolia, and Eastern Russia. The strong interests and presence of the United States also characterizes regional security, and political and economic relations. Despite a history of conflict and rivalry, as well as remaining problems, recent high-level dialogues have revealed issues and areas of mutual interest. Multilateral cooperation on these long-term issues, including new and improved transportation links, border-crossing facilitation, investment cooperation, environmental protection, and natural and energy resources development could reinforce stability and support economic development in NEA. Many opportunities are at hand, but the states that belong to NEA have yet to create the necessary bilateral mechanisms.

KEY QUESTIONS

There is already a growing community of advocates of a multilateral approach to some of the key economic problems that confront the region. Since the early 1990s, local, regional, and provincial governments have been trying hard to fill the gap that otherwise must be attended to by the central governments. Accumulated experiences, however, clearly demonstrates that most of these initiatives (a financial institution to promote viable investment projects of regional significance, for example) require the support of the central bureaucracies and the national political leadership. It is well known that some government officials in Tokyo, Beijing, and Moscow see these non-governmental initiatives as no more than a naïve 'countrified mentality.' Therefore, the bureaucrats from the central governments are likely to pose at least two questions: 'Why do we need multilateral cooperation in NEA?' and 'is it realistic to build the necessary framework for such cooperation?'

A conceivable answer to the first question could embrace a package of economic and other incentives that have normally accompanied cooperative multilateral relations in other areas and regions. Without exception, the countries, economies and territories in the 'integrated' Northeast Asian subregion would benefit from a better and more efficient allocation of available resources, more openness in trade and transportation links and multilateral development schemes. New prospects for trade and development will benefit the investment climate and more financial funds could flow in from various sources, including governmental, private, and the international lending agencies.

The second question is more complex. Could the political realities of NEA match the recently emerging opportunities for multilateral engagement? The primary task here is to envisage a comprehensive, politically realistic and economically feasible framework that will incorporate the wide-ranging interests of the states and constituent provinces in a unified action plan. Once assembled, such a framework could provide a road map for collaborative research efforts, business-oriented discussions and the exchange of far reaching ideas.

A NEW IMAGE FOR NORTHEAST ASIA

Meeting the interests of the national governments and appealing to the private sector is the only way to promote practical investment plans. Here is yet another problem – the image of NEA as an area of predominantly cool winds and cloudy skies. Although a number of summits in 1997–1998 between China and Russia, Japan and China, South Korea and Japan, Russia and Japan, and the United States and China provided evidence in favour of looking at the NEA more optimistically, skeptical views remained rather strong even when the political developments pointed to a different picture. The majority of international relations specialists still tend to emphasize security matters and historical legacies, and in so doing undermine new positive trends. Some people strongly believe that the existing conflicts and tensions complicate and even prevent normal region building in NEA. For many security experts the most significant issue is North Korea and from the standpoint of the majority of observers, the threat of proliferation and conflict it represents. Therefore, the cold-war perception of NEA ceaselessly affects practitioners and decision-makers in the capital cities. This negative vision influences political thinking and economic decisions and ultimately affects the investment climate.

This problem must also be taken into account in order to make future research and information dissemination efforts more efficient. Outside the limited circle of the general public and the experts involved in conferences on these matters, the understanding of the economic opportunities of the NEA subregion is still curbed. This is exactly why a greater effort is needed actively to contribute to creating and promoting a new positive image for NEA both within its borders and in particular internationally.

NORTHEAST ASIA AND THE ASIA-PACIFIC REGION

It is also desirable that any proposed scheme for multilateral cooperation in NEA is linked to broader Asia-Pacific realities. For decades, the name of Asia-Pacific served as a synonym for prosperity and economic dynamism. Northeast Asia is a specific subregion in Pacific Asia, but it is also a 'crossroad' between the major economic regions of the world, the APEC and the European economic zones – a linkage that could define and shape world economic trends the 21st Century. The European Union and the East Asian economies, for example, are uniquely linked through the Trans-Siberian Land Bridge. Imagine that Japan, South Korea, Russia, Poland, and Germany form an international body to operate this transcontinental transportation facility more efficiently and for the benefit of all users. This would be a major contribution to the future of the Japan Sea Rim economies, the Russian Pacific ports, the transportation infrastructure and economic activities in the subregion.

It also seems logical that the principles and techniques on which subregional economic processes could be based will be compatible with those of Asia-Pacific regional cooperation. For example, the academic network known as the Pacific Trade and Development Conference (PAFTAD) had its 25th meeting in Osaka in 1999.[2] This research-oriented and university-based community of individuals developed a conceptual base on which to track economic cooperation. The Pacific Economic Cooperation Conference (PECC) has been growing since 1980. The latter led to the creation of the Asia-Pacific Economic Cooperation forum in 1989. There are several subregional organizations represented at APEC, including the North America Free trade Association (NAFTA), the Association of Southeast Asian Nations (ASEAN), and the South Pacific Forum (SPF). After Russia became a member of APEC, the Northeast Asian subregion should have been seen also as an area for APEC's focus and programmes.

Moreover, some elements of technical and organizational expertise accumulated by existing regional bodies and frameworks could be tested in NEA to stimulate subregional dialogue. For example, the concept of 'action plans' aimed at trade and investment facilitation may be applicable to NEA. There is also an opportunity to coordinate Northeast Asian activities with those of APEC. The APEC members, for example, agreed to look at several wide-ranging issues as a part of their long-term agenda, including population, economic growth, food, energy, environment, technical cooperation in human resources development, infrastructure, and infrastructure projects financed by the private sector.

A MODULAR APPROACH TO MULTILATERALISM

At the same time as NEA is part of broader regional grouping, NEA is also a unique subregion – just borrowing knowledge from other regions cannot shape its future. Inventiveness must be encouraged and new approaches tested. Projects in NEA have traditionally explored prospects for cooperation based on a conventional approach – 'all the parties in all the areas.' Realistically, a viable multilateral process in this subregion should be issue-specific, accommodating miscellaneous demands and interests, and allowing various combinations of actors to participate, depending on the issue and their capacity.

However, a collective effort is needed to draw up a comprehensive list of issues critical to local and national economies. This list, for example, could include measures for developing subregional institutions for development financing. Both central and provincial governments must share the responsibility for supporting the private sector through national and subregional information networks, micro-level management dissemination techniques, market access information sharing, and small and medium enterprises promotion efforts. Special attention must be given to cooperative efforts in various issue-specific fields with the involvement of more than two countries using the concept of 'modular multilateralism.' One can assume that each 'module' means much more than a combination of bilateral economic issues and opportunities – rather each 'module' can encompass a number of collective or shared interests that cannot be effectively secured through unilateral or bilateral efforts. A regional process driven by such a concept can help to envision interdependent relations that are emerging in some sectors such as energy, transportation and the environment.

Positive developments in bilateral relationships make it possible to single out potential mutually beneficial country-linkages, for example the Japan-Russia-China 'triangle.' The focus on this 'module' is promising in exploring prospects for these three countries' long-term economic engagements as the core of a future framework of economic cooperation on a subregional level. If cooperation within this 'triangle' is successful, it will become a catalyst for the economic consolidation of the entire Northeast Asian subregion, incorporating other economies in various forms. Thus, the concept of 'modular multilateralism' can help to design an 'open' system of cooperative relationships among all economies of NEA, not only between Japan, Russia and China.

Bilateralism helps to identify 'modules'

Recently Russia, China and Japan have expanded their dialogues, moving away from solely security concerns with regard to NEA. For example, the Chinese and Russian central governments share ambitious plans for economic and technological engagements that will affect their border regions and NEA in general. On the part of China, there is a growing demand for transit transportation services – Russian Pacific ports will link Jilin and Heilongjiang with Japan and the United States. China's energy needs are expanding and Russia is ready to open its resources of natural gas and develop hydropower projects for China (more on this in Chapter 9).

During President Boris Yeltsin's visit to China in 1996 an agreement on cooperation in the field of energy was signed. In 1997, the Ministry of Fuels and Energy of the Russian Federation reached an agreement with the China Oil Corporation on the development of the Kovykta deposits and pipeline construction. The same year an inter-governmental agreement on cooperation in oil and gas resources development was concluded. It is expected that Russia will supply China with about 20 billion cubic meters of gas annually for 30 years.

As for Japan and Russia, progress in their bilateral dialogue also affects the nature of regional interaction. The Japanese government provided significant support (information, consultations and technical assistance) related to Russia's membership in the Asia-Pacific Economic Cooperation (APEC) forum and World Trade Organization (WTO). As a result of Prime Minister Keizo Obuchi's visit to Russia, the 'Hashimoto-Yeltsin Plan' was expanded to include the development of natural resources in Siberia (see Chapter 13). The role of the leading institution in shaping Russia-Japan bilateral dialogue on the energy sector development belongs to the Japan-Russia Inter-Governmental Commission. Under the auspices of this commission, a ministerial level dialogue on energy issues was launched.[3]

On 15–16 March 1999, the sessions of the Far Eastern Subcommittee of the Japan-Russia Intergovernmental Commission on Trade and Economic Cooperation and the private-level Japan-Far Eastern Russia Economic Conference took place in Tokyo. Six 'priority projects' were named for future joint efforts between Japan and the Far Eastern provinces, including five projects in the energy sector (gas pipelines construction and natural gas field development and hydropower station construction). A group of experts from the Japan Information Electric Power Center visited Russia in September–October 1998, followed by a research team dispatched in December of the same year to evaluate the conditions of the electric power sector in Eastern Russia and prospects and methods for privatization. Moreover, in the 1998 Moscow Declaration the sides confirmed their readiness to 'interact in fostering international cooperation in the field of power engineering in the Asia-Pacific region.' The understanding was that this would promote energy security, the resolution of the problem of global warming and the socio-economic development of the region.[4] In July 1998, 20 projects in Russia were named concerning possible joint actions to reduce 'green house gases' emissions.

For Japan, cooperation with Russia in the energy sector is a matter of prime and long-term interest. China's role in this relationship – in terms of the future demand-supply equation, environmental reasons and political considerations – is difficult to overestimate. Japan is keenly interested in joining the Russia-China gas pipeline projects.[5] There were also proposals originated in Tokyo for a concerted approach to the energy resources development and the environmental protection that envision Japan's close relations with both China and Russia.

Therefore, looking closely at Japan-Russia and China-Russia bilateral dialogues, we have a realistic opportunity to name the issue-specific 'building blocks' for the mid-term and long-term regional agendas. Firstly, it is desirable that they approach the problem of energy resources development and utilization in a joint, coordinated manner. This may require reviewing and modifying their energy policies. Secondly, a modern and expensive energy infrastructure must be planned and built for the transportation of natural gas, electricity, and possibly oil, with the massive participation of private investors and inter-governmental cooperation. Therefore, this cooperation must incorporate reliable and efficient mechanisms to encourage private participation in the projects. Thirdly, extensive multilateral cooperation will be needed in improving energy efficiency, including technological modernization of the existing facilities, efforts in energy conservation and environmental protection.

An immediate priority for multilateral actions

Ironically, the first formal multilateral organization to deal with the energy issues in NEA was born to prevent the threat of nuclear proliferation. In exchange for North Korea's freezing and ultimately dismantling its existing nuclear program the United States, Japan, and South Korea agreed to provide Pyongyang with fuel and two light water reactors under the 1994 Framework Agreement.

The Korean Peninsula Energy Development Organization (KEDO) was established by these countries with the purpose to assist the implementation of the Agreed Framework, manage all these transactions, including financing, fuel supplies, and the reactors construction. The mission of the KEDO was also to 'serve as an example of how a cooperative and targeted international diplomatic effort can lead to the resolution of regional security and political crises.'[6]

Officially, both the Framework Agreement and the KEDO are considered as successful policy measures in dealing with North Korea. Recently, however, some serious doubts surfaced with regard to the effectiveness of these agreements.[7] Moreover, the central element of this approach – 'financing and constructing in the DPRK two proliferation-resistant light water reactors' – was questioned as an expensive way to meet North Korea's energy needs, dubious from an economic perspective, and setting a high price for the DPRK's compliance with the non-proliferation regime.[8] In the joint paper published in May 1999 by the Atlantic Council of the United States and the Japanese Research Institute for Peace and Security, prominent experts pointed out that:

> the two light water reactors called for in the agreement may not be the most appropriate response to North Korea's long-term energy needs. They may be the wrong type of power plants in the wrong place and may be constructed too slowly to meet Pyongyang's pressing energy demand. Other forms of power generation facilities could be built more quickly and efficiently, at far less cost. The infrastructure is lacking and, even if

completed on time, North Korea lacks an effective electrical distribution system. Its energy needs could be better met by other means within the overall time and at less cost than the original deal – about $4 billion over more than 10 years.[9]

The joint paper also proposed that the United States, China, Russia and Japan should consider organizing a 'four plus two' (North and South Korea) effort at the United Nations that must not be perceived as a 'coalition' opposing North Korea, but as a forum and mechanism to ensure its vital interests as well as the interests and concerns of each of NEA's powers. A multilateral framework for cooperation in normalizing the energy supply situation in North Korea could provide support to the idea of subregional cooperation in NEA through the strategic partnerships of the great powers.

A long-term opportunity for all

Cooperation in the energy sector is likely to provide the most solid and long-lasting 'building block' for cooperation in NEA. Individual Northeast Asian countries dependent on external sources of energy supplies are looking for economically rational, diversified and reliable means to support their growing needs. In this context, the energy resources of Eastern Russia are attracting attention from both the governments and the end users in Northeast Asian countries. In Russia, also, the long-term 'look east' approach to energy resources development has gained momentum.[10]

At present, Russia and China have agreed to develop close links in the energy sector, focusing on the pipeline that will link the Kovykta resources with China. However, Japan is likely to play a role as a 'strategic investor.' Indeed, a shortage of investment funds will require the involvement of Japan and other third-party participants in this project. From December 1997, Japan, China, and Russia, as well as the Republic of Korea and Mongolia, has been participating in multilateral consultations on the prospects for the Kovykta natural gas development.[11] Energy resources exploration, development, and cross-border transportation are likely to continue to be on the agendas of the summits and high-level inter-governmental dialogues. These exchanges are taking place both on the intergovernmental level and through the multilateral expert-level conferences and other meetings. Non-governmental international organizations such as Pacific Economic Cooperation Council (PECC) and its Energy Forum and multilateral official bodies such as APEC have paid significant attention to the array of issues associated with the natural gas wider usage in the region, the international transmission systems, and trade and investment environment pertinent to the highly capital intensive natural gas projects, many of them are to be located in Eastern Russia.[12]

The NEA Natural Gas and Pipeline Forum (NAGPF) is less known compared with the PECC and APEC. This organization is rather young,[13] but it is tackling the issues of multilateral cooperation in the energy sector very actively, providing a stage for intensive professional dialogues for geologists, economists, engineers, business people, and the government representatives. The 5th International Conference on the Northeast Asian Natural Gas Pipelines held in Yakutsk from July 25–27, 1999 proved to be very important event not only for Yakutia, but in Russia as a whole. The conference has demonstrated the considerable interest that the economies of NEA share with regard to the huge deposits of natural gas in Eastern Russia, including Sakhalin, Sakha (Yakutia), Irkutsk oblast and Krasnoyarsk krai.

However, the most serious obstacle is the combination of the great distances between the resources and the markets, climate that complicates the construction projects and the astronomical financial resources that must be mobilized to initiate them. It seems that these differences in approaches, and the numerous technical and economic complications that surround the array of expensive gas pipeline projects cannot be effectively bridged without a core strategy based on the idea that brings all the interested parties and the involved actors together. Obviously, such a strategy should aim at ensuring adequate and equitable levels of domestic supplies. It should insure that adequate resources are left over for exports to NEA, providing a common ground for the potential importers and investors and stimulating their interest in delivery options through multilateral, joint efforts. In short, an infrastructure project should be envisioned that simultaneously serves domestic needs, stimulates large-scale exports to the Asia-Pacific markets, allows concentration of resources, and helps integrate multiple and competing strategies, options, and choices.[14] Hypothetically, a proposed super-pipeline could link Western Siberia with the Pacific coast.

A Trans-Siberian gas pipeline?

A super-pipeline could be faster to complete despite its gigantic length because the existing infrastructure of the Trans-Siberian railway would be fully utilized. The geological and permafrost conditions in the railway vicinity are also quite well known this would save time. The project would meet the domestic development needs to a maximum possible extent because economically and population wise Eastern Russia gravitates to the Trans-Siberian railway.

Such long-term plans could complement, integrate, and even facilitate the north-south gas pipeline projects currently under discussion. The gas fields in the northern areas of Krasnoyarsk krai, Irkutsk oblast, and Sakha (Yakutia) could step by step be linked to this transcontinental super-pipeline. A trans-continental gas pipeline system could then be connected with the north-south pipeline (Sakhalin-Komsomolsk-Khabarovsk-Vladivostok with likely extension to China), enhancing the foundations for a regional gas pipeline network that would include the Korean peninsula, northeastern and coastal areas of China, Mongolia, and Japan. It would, nevertheless, be a versatile system also supporting an LNG option aimed at potential users in Taiwan and other economies.

Among the important perceived advantages, that this long-term strategic design could offer is its capacity to mobilize financial resources from multiple sources. An 'west-east' super-pipeline system that could serve the domestic market in Eastern Russia, being quite neutral to potential suppliers and importers and open to potential users of LNG is likely to have more supporters and fewer opponents. Its strategic advantage woull be its super-large scale, with multiple deposits of natural gas at one end, and multiple users at the other end. Ideally, it should be an open-access transmission system, serving various users and customers without discrimination.[15] The proposed system could also ensure a choice (and economically and technologically optimal mix) for the final users of the natural gas for electricity generation, domestic use, electricity generation and transmission, generation and exports sales, etc.

The main point here is that an approach is needed that will allow for the fastest possible introduction of Russian natural gas in the Asia-Pacific markets. It will also ensure a strategic export potential to attract major potential customers and stimulate the devclopment of gas resources in Eastern Siberia and Yakutia. It will allow supply of gas to domestic users, and, at the same time, provide natural gas in strategic quantities and on a long-term basis to the cities in northeastern and coastal China, the Koreas, and Japan. Such a system, aimed at both increased scale and profitability, and can only be designed and implemented in cooperation with neighboring countries and international lending agencies.

CONCLUSIONS

Various factors, including environmental and economic merits, regional and global challenges, national and local needs, favour a much wider use of natural gas in NEA, including Eastern Russia. These same factors demand the utmost attention on the part of the Russian federal and regional authorities, and non-governmental organizations to the problems that must be resolved in order to integrate Eastern Russia's energy potential with neighboring markets. There are several issues that deserve priority attention:

First, the incorporation of the natural gas resources of the northeastern regions of Western Siberia in any export-oriented gas pipeline plans for Eastern Russia will greatly reduce the time taken for feasibility studies and facilitate funding and implementation.

Second, a long-term strategy for a 'west-east' delivery system must be considered to combine the development needs of the southern regions and industrial areas in Eastern Russia with potential multiple export opportunities (through the supplementary 'north-south' pipelines) to users in Mongolia, Northeastern China, the Koreas, and Japan. Alternatively, the new sources of natural gas in the northern regions could be connected to this system facilitating new gas projects in Eastern Russia.

Third, if this approach is adopted, the best possible 'corridor' for a trans-continental gas pipeline will be the Trans-Siberian railway and the adjacent development areas along this mainline. As a result, a 'multiple sources-multiple users' system for natural gas production and 'domestic-export' transmission could be created with a 'strategic' export capacity to ensure long-term and large export quantities of supplies, including both LNG and electricity-for-export generation options.

Fourth, there is an opportunity to combine domestic gas pipeline projects – already approved by the Russian government and supported by Japan – with the private sector's interest in supplying Sakhalin gas to northeastern China. Making this project regional will facilitate its funding and reduce implementation time, assisting the economic recovery if the main production areas in the Far East and generating export earnings.

Finally, this approach could solidly support Russia's new position as the fully-fledged member of APEC, responding to its recent initiatives and contributing to both economic and environmental cooperation in NEA. In this context, the opportunities for Japan-Russia-China economic interaction need priority attention. Healthy bilateral ties within this 'triangle' focused on energy resources development, environment, and trans-border links could be a major catalyst for a New NEA.

Long-term prospects for energy demand and supply in NEA and prospects for the export-oriented energy projects in Eastern Russia are likely to play a pivotal role in forming mutually beneficial linkages in NEA. There are, however, critical issues to consider. The scale of these projects is being measured in tens of billions of dollars and their implementation could be estimated at a minimum of five-ten years. Nonetheless, the expectations are high and enthusiasm is building up despite some serious technical constraints, economic impediments, and even political uncertainties at the national level and those of foreign origin.

NOTES

1 Earlier versions of this chapter appeared in two parts in the *ERINA Report*, vol. 28, June 1999 and vol. 30, October 1999.

2 See: *APEC: The Challenge and Tasks for the Twenty First Century, Summary and Recommendations of the 25th Pacific Trade and Development Conference*, Kansai Economic Research Center, July 1999.

3 In September 1997, a delegation from the Japan Forum of the Nuclear Power Industry visited Russia and a protocol on cooperation was signed encompassing various bilateral programs such as fast-breeder reactors, spent fuel reprocessing, and Japan's involvement in the BN-800 nuclear reactor project designed in Russia. Several high-level Russian delegations representing the energy sector visited Tokyo in 1997–1998, including a visit by the former minister of the Energy and Fuel Industry of the Russian Federation, Sergei Kiryenko, in March 1998.

4 'On Establishing Constructive Partnership Between the Russian Federation and Japan,' Moscow, November 13, 1998, *Rossiyskaya Gazeta*, November 22, 1998.

5 See Katsuhiko Suetsugu and Tatsu Kambara (1998) 'Geopolitics and Energy Development in Northeast Asia,' *Cambridge Review of International Affairs*, XII (1): 115 and 121.

6 *The Korean Peninsula Energy Development Organization.* Annual Report, 1996/1997, p. 1.

7 See Richard L. Armitage (1999) 'A Comprehensive Approach to North Korea,' *Strategic Forum* Washington, D.C.: Institute for National Strategic Studies, no. 159.

8 Peter Hayes, (1997) 'Supply of Light-Water Reactors to the DPRK,' in Young Whan Kihl and Peter Hayes, eds. *Peace and Security in Northeast Asia: The Nuclear Issue and the Korean Peninsula*, Armonk, N.Y.: M.E. Sharp, p. 45.

9 *Building an Asia-Pacific Security Community: The Role of Nuclear Weapons* (1999) Washington, D.C.: The Atlantic Council of the United States, Policy Paper, May, p. 7.

10 By 2010 a shortfall between the demand and supply of liquefied natural gas (LNG) in Japan, the Republic of Korea, and Taiwan is estimated at 44 million tons or about 60 Bcm and could reach 100 Bcm by 2020 because of the declining popular support for the nuclear power generation. For China the demand in natural gas uncovered by the domestic production is estimated at 60 Bcm by 2010 and is expected to rapidly reach a 160 Bcm mark by 2020. Depending on various factors, particularly China's energy policy and the scale of efforts to move away from coal towards cleaner sources of energy the demand for natural gas could be even higher – only the three northeastern provinces of China are projected to consume between 20 Bcm and 40 Bcm of natural gas by 2020. These estimates and projections allow foresee a regional demand for imported natural gas to be about 260–300 Bcm. Even if half of this demand will be met through the LNG supplies, the remaining part is unlikely to be covered by the natural gas from the gas fields of Eastern Siberia, Yakutia, and Sakhalin even if all natural gas produced there is exported.

11 In November 1997, an international symposium on regional cooperation in the energy sector was held in Tokyo with the participation of Russia, China, South Korea, Mongolia, and the International Energy Agency. The meeting was organized by the Asian Energy Community Support Committee, and sponsored by, among other influential bodies, the Ministry of Foreign Affairs, MITI, Japan National Oil Corporation, and JEXIM. In December 1997, ministerial-level representatives in charge of energy policies from China, Japan, South Korea, and Mongolia met in Moscow at the Russian Ministry of Fuels and Energy to discuss prospects for cooperation.

12 In The APEC, October 1988, Energy Ministers' initiative on investment in natural gas supplies, infrastructure and trading networks called for removal of unnecessary barriers to natural gas utilization, taking into account the environmental benefits of natural gas compared with other fossil fuels. This document also called for a predictable legal, regulatory and trade frameworks governing the natural gas sector, as well as fiscal regimes that recognize risks involved to natural gas projects. Private (domestic and foreign) ownership of natural gas facilities were proposed to be permitted, and the property rights of private (domestic and foreign) investors/operators in natural gas facilities clearly defined and protected. It also called for policies that facilitate development of domestic and cross-border trading networks and proposed the establishment for formal consultations between APEC economies involved in cross-border projects to ensure an equitable treatment for domestic and imported sources of natural gas. The document has also indicated the need of competition between all sources of energy.

13 The Northeast Asian Gas and Pipeline Forum has organized its regular annual meetings since 1997. The organization took its roots from a conference on the Trans-Asian gas pipeline network held in Tokyo in 1995 with only Japan, China, Russia (Yakutia), and the ROK involved. The second conference on prospects for the Northeast Asian natural gas pipelines took place in Beijing in 1996. Representatives from Australia, Canada, the United States, the United Kingdom and other countries also joined this meeting. The National Pipeline Research Society of Japan, serving as a coordinator for these two conferences, proposed to establish a Northeast Asian Gas and Pipeline Forum to promote regional cooperation in expanding natural gas utilization in the region. The third conference held in Seoul in 1997 adopted the statute of the proposed forum as a non-profit organization for international cooperation. The government of Mongolia hosted the fourth conference in 1998 that attracted 110 participants from 11 countries, including representatives of the DPRK and Chinese Taipei. The decision to begin joint research activities and the

presentation made by a representative of Gazprom on the feasibility of natural gas supplies to China were the highlights of the meeting. See *NAGPF Newsletter*, Northeast Asian Gas & Pipeline Forum, Tokyo, March 1999, vol. 1/no. 2.

14 Yakutia's President Mikhail E. Nikolaev noted in his address at the conference that 'when alternative gas pipeline projects are considered, it is obviously desirable to proceed with joint development of the deposits available in Sakha Republic, Irkutskaya Oblast, and Krasnoyarskiy Kray as a useful starting point. See Mikhail E. Nikolaev, (1999) 'Russia and Asia-Pacific Region: Energy Integration as a Foundation of an Economic Breakthrough,' Speech at the 5th International Conference on Northeast Asian Natural Gas Pipeline, Yakutsk, July 25–27, p. 8.

15 It has been argued that an 'open-access' transportation system could solve at least one problem 'the great lobbying dance over which company shall win the right to build a pipeline to serve a new market' that could be easily resulted that no infrastructure gets built. It is common that each and every candidate, many of which are gas producers, fear being severely disadvantaged (if not shut out of the gas game entirely) by failing to win the right to build the delivery infrastructure. See Robin Baldwin, Geoffrey Roberts, and Terrence H. Thorn (1998) 'If You Build It, They Will Come: Strategies for Implementing APEC's Natural Gas Initiative,' in Dona K. Lehr, ed., *Natural Gas in Asia: Facts and Fiction*, Singapore: PECC Energy Forum, pp. 70–73.

Chapter 9

Energy Developments in Northeast Asia: a role for Russia?

Keun-Wook Paik

INTRODUCTION

The end of Cold War opened the door for Russia's active participation in the Northeast Asian (NEA) region, but despite its relatively large geographical presence, Russia is still an alienated player in the region. In November 1998 the summit of the Asia Pacific Economic Co-operation (APEC) forum officially accepted Russia as a full member of APEC, and, as the pervious chapter argued, the early development of energy resources in Russian Asia (RA) comprised of East Siberia (ES) and Russian Far East (RFE) could help Russia's early integration into the Northeast Asian economy.

The price of delay in developing RA's abundant oil and gas development has been an energy crisis in RA. The dire energy situation is expected to continue for the time being even though early oil production from Sakhalin offshore started in July 1999. It will take time to develop the related infrastructure needed for RA's oil and gas trade with the neighbouring countries in NEA. Meanwhile, the priority of the neighbouring countries in NEA is to stabilise energy supply, to diversify supply sources, and to further sustainable economic development. In fact, Japan, Korea and China are set to increase their heavy dependence on Middle East oil and gas in the coming decades, and oil and gas from RA could contribute to balancing this high dependence on the Middle East.

This chapter focuses on the problems and implications of RA's oil and gas development. First, it examines oil and gas supply sources in RA and discusses the problems of energy shortage in RA. It then explains where the main market of RA's oil and gas exports lie. Finally, it briefly touches on the possibility of the appearance of circular natural gas pipeline connecting RA with neighbouring countries in the coming decades.

RUSSIA'S OIL AND GAS SUPPLY FOR NORTHEAST ASIA

The summary of a study for a comprehensive energy plan in East Siberia and Far East of the Russian Federation, jointly undertaken by the Energy Research Institute (now Energy Systems Institute, Irkutsk) from Russia and the Institute of Energy Economics, Japan during 1992 and 1995 confirmed the following points:

- ES and RFE have confirmed reserves of 640 million tonnes (mt) of oil and 2.5 trillion cubic metres (tcm) of gas.
- Some 38 billion tonnes (bt) of confirmed bituminous coal reserves and some 8.8 bt of confirmed brown coal reserves have been found in the region.
- The total amount of hydroelectric power available and for which it would be economically feasible to construct hydroelectric power generation facilities comes to as much as 534 billion kilowatts hour per year.

According to the study, plans were laid for the implementation of a total of 16 projects to be completed by 2010, and these projects include 4 oil resource development projects and 2 gas resource development projects to be implemented in the region extending from the northern shores of Lake Baikal to the Republic of Sakha (Yakutia), a total of 6 coal resource development projects to be implemented in the area along the BAM Railroad, and a total of 3 hydroelectric and 1 thermal power development projects. The estimated cost for these developments, totalled $14 billion during 1995–2000 and $90 billion during 1995–2010.[1]

These findings confirm the abundance of energy sources in ES and RFE. Strictly speaking, there are two major oil supply sources and three major gas supply sources for the NEA region. Their combined proven reserves are sufficient to meet the regional energy demand in Russian Asia, Northern China, North and South Korea and Japan.

SAKHALIN OIL AND GAS[2]

Sakhalin offshore development was first discussed in the 1960s, but until the early 1990s no real development was undertaken, partly because of uneasy relations between the former Soviet Union and Japan and partly because of poor development economics. As shown in *Table 9.1*, the combined of oil and gas reserves in Sakhalin I (Exxon 30 per cent Sodeco 30 per cent, Rosneft 17 per cent and Sakhalinmorneftegas 23 per cent), and Sakhalin II (Marathon 37.5 per cent, Shell 25 per cent, Mitsui 25 per cent, and Mitsubishi 12.5 per cent) are 463 mt and 833 bcm. Besides this, the estimated oil, gas and condensate reserves of the Kirinskii block in Sakhalin III are 1.8 billion tonnes, 873 bcm, and 62 million tonnes respectively. If the estimated 800 bcm of gas reserves of Sakhalin IV are added, the total of gas reserves are big enough to promote both LNG and pipeline gas development options.

Table 9.1 The Sakhalin Offshore projects

No.	Fields/Blocks	Consortium name	Partners	RR*	Development Costs (exploration)	PSA	Production schedule
I	Odoptu & Chaivo & Arkutun-Dagi	Sakhalin I Consortium	Exxon 30%, Sodeco 30%, SMNG 23%, Rosneft 17%	O/C: 323 mt Gas: 425 bcm	$15.2 bn	Implemented in 1996	2005: 7.7 mt, 2010: 20.9 mt, Peak: 26.5 mt & 21 bcm
II	Piltun-Astokskoye & Lunskoye	Sakhalin Energy Investment Corp.	Marathon 37.5%, Mitsui 25%, Shell 25%, Mitsubishi 12.5%	Oil: 140 mt Gas: 408 bcm	$10 bn	Implemented in 1996	July 1999 start: 045 mt & 2000 0.74 mt, 2005: 9.05 mt & 15.5 bcm, 2010: 6 mt & 15.5 bcm
III**	Kirinskii	Exxon-Mobil (formerly Pegastar-Neftegaz)	Exxon-Mobil 33.3%, Texaco 33.3%, SMNG & Rosneft 33.3%	Oil: 450 mt Gas: 720–970 bcm	$6.4 bn ($151 mn)	Awaiting	
III	East-Odoptinsky & Ayashsky	Exxon-Mobil	Exxon-Mobil 66.7%, SMNG & Rosneft 33.3%		($202 mn)	Negotiation	
IV*	Astrakhanovsky & Shmidtovsky		Arco 49%, Rosneft 25.5%, SMNG 25.5%	Gas: 800 bcm	($300 mn)	Negotiation	
V	East-Shmidtovsky		BP-Amoco 49%, Rosneft 25.5%, SMNG 25.5%				
VI	Pogranichny			Oil: 80–90 mt, Conden: 17 mt, Gas: 220 bcm			

Notes:

*RR means recoverable reserves. DC means development cost and DC (figure) means projected exploration cost.

**The Sakhalin regional administration is reported to have acquired a 10% stake in the Sakhalin III project.

**In the spring of 2000 ARCO announced that it was withdrawing from Sakhalin IV for the time being. It may return to the project one Bp-Amoco's takeover of ARCO has been completed.

Source: Keun-Wook Paik, 'Sakhalin-Hokkaido Gas Pipeline Introduction and its Implications towards Circular Pipeline Development in Northeast Asia', presented at an International Conference on Advancing the Japan Pipeline Project for introducing Sakhalin Natural Gas, held in Sapporo, 2 April 1999.

Regardless of the oil and gas potential in exploration blocks offshore Sakhalin, the already proven reserves in Sakhalin I and II are big enough to make Sakhalin Island a major energy supply source for NEA. Sakhalin II's oil production was expected to reach 90,000 b/d in 1999, and combined Sakhalin I & II oil and gas production in 2005 is projected at 17 mt and 15.5 bcm respectively. The figure for 2010 is projected at 27 mt and 36 bcm. Quite a significant volume of this oil production could be easily exported to the neighbouring countries in the region. Japan alone could provide a sufficient market.

Although Sakhalin II is currently targeting the LNG market in Japan (and South Korea and China), the Sakhalin I project is looking at both Japanese and Chinese pipeline gas markets. As for the Japan option, Japan's Ministry of International Trade and Industry (MITI) minister, Shinji Sato, announced at the International Energy Agency ministerial meeting held in May 1997 in Paris that Japan is considering the construction of Sakhalin offshore gas import pipeline.

This was the first official remark by a Japanese minister on the international development of a pipeline between Russia and Japan.[3] The state-owned, Japenese National Oil Company (JNOC), Japex, the steel companies and major trading companies have been investigating the possibility of constructing a 2,225 km pipeline connecting Sakhalin Island and mainland Japan. The pipeline is composed of three sections: the first section with 625 km from Katangli to Prigorodnoye, the second section with, 1300 km from Prigorodnye to Niigata and the last section of 300 km from Niigata to Tokyo.

In early December 1998 it was announced that a company was set up by Japex (50 per cent), Marubeni (25 per cent) and Itochu (25 per cent) to conduct a feasibility study on this Sakhalin gas pipeline via Hokkaido to Northern Japan, 30 per cent of the study cost will be covered by Exxon.[4] Despite these efforts, within Japan the forces supporting this pipeline option are still facing strong resistance from the conservative, powerful electricity companies, and LNG industry sectors.

As for the China option, in 1997 Exxon has undertaken a feasibility study on the delivery of Sakhalin offshore gas to Northeast provinces in China. In terms of location, the northeastern provinces of China are well positioned to be the beneficiaries of Sakhalin offshore gas development. It is worth noting that CNPC aimed at using part of the imported gas from Irkutsk for injection into the Daqing oil field to enhance its production. Recently it was reported that the Khabarovsk Administration officials are supporting a proposal to pipe natural gas from offshore Sakhalin Island to China via Khabarovsk krai. Northeast China is one of a number of potential markets for natural gas exports now under study by Exxon Neftegas.[5]

If the reserves in Sakhalin III and IV are proved as projected, there is the possibility of constructing a gas pipeline connecting northern Sakhalin with Kyushu, southern Japan via Khabarovsk krai and Primorskii krai and North and South Korea. This Korean option could lay the ground for a circular pipeline that will eventually combine the areas surrounding the Sea of Japan (see *Figure 9.1*).

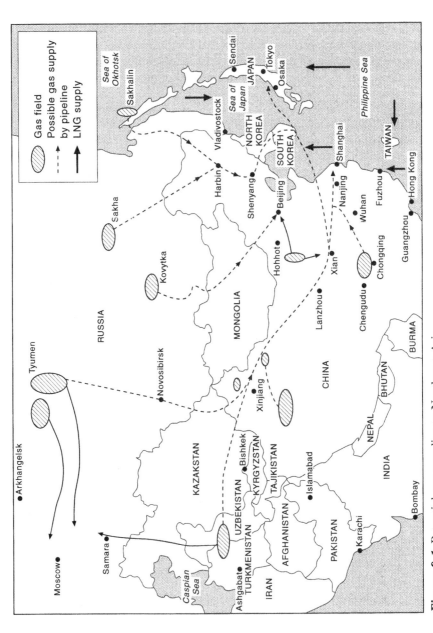

Figure 9.1 Potential gas supplies to Northeast Asia

SAKHA GAS AND OIL[6]

It is not an exaggeration to say that the initiative on East Siberian gas export to Northeast Asian market was first taken by the Sakha Republic (Yakutia). It was as early as the 1960s that the possibility of Yakutian gas export to Japan was explored and promoted. It was suspended in the wake of the Soviet Union's invasion of Afghanistan in late 1979. In the late 1980s Korea's Hyundai group revived the forgotten project. In 1995, a preliminary feasibility study was commissioned for Sakha gas development, at a cost of $10 million, funded by Russia and South Korea. Unfortunately, the outcome was not very encouraging, and no further steps have been taken. The conclusion was that Sakha gas export to Korea would not be acceptable for the time being due to remote location, harsh environment and consequently poor development economics. However, the Sakha Republic does have substantial proven gas reserves (over 1.5 tcm). According to Vasiliy Moiseyevich Efimov, president of Sakhaneftegas, the currently registered C1 category reserves in Vilyuisk region (10 fields: 437.8 bcm) and Botuobinsk region (21 fields: 586.3 bcm) are 1 tcm. Besides this, the reserves of Chayandinskoye field in Botuobinsk region are estimated at 755 bcm (previously 208 bcm), of which 535 bcm is exploitable. Already 64 wells have been drilled in the field, and the figure could reach 1 tcm with further exploration. If the proven reserves of the Kovyktinskoye gas project fail to reach 850 bcm, after comprehensive exploration, the Sakha Republic is well positioned to add enough proven reserves to justify long-distance and transnational pipeline development.

In an interesting development, Sakhaneftegas has proposed an East-Siberian consortium based on Irkutsk oblast, Sakha Republic and the Evenki autonomous orkug of Krasnoyarsk krai. This proposal is being supported by Rosneft, the Chita oblast Administration, JSC Unified Electrical System of Russia, the Administration of Evenki Autonomous okrug and Rusia Petroleum (the company that holds the rights to the Kovytka project). Sakhaneftegas has signed an agreement with Rusia Petroleum for the joint development of Kovyktinskoye and Chayandinskoye fields. If this approach is realised, at least 40–50 bcm of gas will be exportable to the NEA market. The significance of this proposal lies in a fact that the combined development of Kovyktinksoye and Chayandinskoye fields will guarantee enough gas reserves to justify a 4000-km long pipeline development.

Sakhaneftgas has another export option. As shown in the *Figure 9.1*,[7] there could be a direct gas pipeline from Sakha Republic to Heilongjiang province in northern China. This route is a hybrid of the Vostok route of the 1970s. The advantages of Sakha gas to China as opposed to Irkutsk (Kovyktinskoye) gas, lies in the following points: firstly, the majority of Sakha gas is exportable while the considerable portion of Irkutsk gas can be absorbed by the local market; secondly, the pipeline route connecting Butuobinsk region and Harbin can bypass Mongolia and consequently does not need to take care of the transit tariff issue; and thirdly, a Sakha gas pipeline to China could provide enough gas to revitalise China's three northern provinces (see Chapter 11).

The weak points of this route are as follows: firstly, the distance is longer than the Irkutsk line; secondly, the pipeline section that would pass through the permafrost region is quite lengthy and thus the pipeline development cost is very high.

Reportedly, Sakhaneftegas and CNPC have agreed to form an alliance to undertake a preliminary feasibility study of the Chayandinskoye gas deposit. The agreement, signed on March 17th 1998, names the study as the Sakha-China project and states that, if the results of the study are positive, a joint venture named Chayanda-Gas will be formed between the two companies and 10 per cent of the JV will be owned by CNPC to compensate for performing the study.[8] In January 1999, the Sino-Russian energy sub-commission meeting confirmed the 1998 agreement and the one-year preliminary feasibility study was started. It remains to be seen whether the result of the study will open the door for the direct export of Sakha gas to China.

Unlike this gas pipeline option, Sakha's biggest Talakanskoye oil field looks very likely to be combined with Verknechonskoye oil field as the Talakanskoye oil reserves, but they are not big enough to promote the parallel gas and oil pipeline from Sakha to Heilongjiang province.

IRKUTSK GAS AND OIL[9]

The centre of the East Siberian gas development is the Kovyktinskoye gas and condensate field, discovered by parametric well 281 drilled in 1986 by Vostsibneftegasgeologiya, a subdivision of former Ministry of Geology of Russian Federation. The field is located in the Zhigalovsky region, 350 km to the north-northeast of Irkutsk. As of July 1 1995, the Kovyktinskoye field's gas and condensate reserves were recorded in the state balance at 870 bcm and 0.4 billion barrels. After the drilling of 28 exploratory wells and geological modelling, the Siberian Far East Petroleum Company Ltd. (Sidanco) has estimated the field's reserves at more than 1.2 tcm and 0.6 billion barrels respectively.

In 1991, the Baikalekogaz consortium and BP/Statoil alliance conducted a study on the oil and gas resources in East Siberia. At that time BP/Statoil concluded that the study identified no incentive for taking further steps due to the lack of an immediate market for East Siberian oil and gas export. In 1992, the Baikalekogaz consortium was converted into Rusia Petroleum. The same year Canada's SNC and Lavalin, under the sponsorship of the Canadian Bitech Corp., carried out a pilot feasibility study on the Irkutsk region's gas supply project based on Kovyktinskoye.

In September 1993, CNPC began to negotiate with the Russia for the exploration of Markovskoye and Yaraktinskoye oil and gas fields in Irkutsk region. (These two fields are located between Kovyktinskoye and Verkhnechonskoye fields.) CNPC's Russian counterpart was a group consisting of Irkutsk's Petroleum and Gas Geological Company and Geophysical Research Institute, together with 14 other local companies and organisations. Two exploratory wells were drilled in the two virgin fields.

The same year, Russia was also promoting plans to develop Irkutsk oblast's gas fields and the export of electricity to China. Vladimir Yakovenko, then the First Deputy Head of the Administration of Irkutsk oblast, has pointed out that the regions's oil and gas development has two main strengths:

- It can replace fuel oil and local brown coal with gas from Kovyktinskoye in the region's power stations, reducing emission of pollutants by 0.4 mt/y and freeing 16 mt/y of coal for delivery to the RFE, and;
- Electricity from the 4,500 megawatt Bratsk and 3,840 megawatt Ust Ilinsk hydro-stations and 1,050 megawatt Irkutsk CHPP No. 10 thermal power station, plus a large number of smaller coal-fired stations could be exported to China.[10]

In early November 1994, a milestone in the development of East Siberian gas was laid when CNPC and MINTOPENERGA signed a memorandum of understanding for the construction of a long distance pipeline to promote East Siberian oil and gas resources. The 1994 agreement was the first official expression of their determination to develop the pipeline option. In late June 1997, when a Russian delegation led by Premier Viktor Chernormyrdin visited Beijing, a governmental framework agreement was signed between Russia and China to export natural gas and electricity from East Siberia to China. Under the natural gas deal, Russia would export 25 bcm/y of gas from the Irkutsk region over 30 years. The $1.5 electricity deal over 25 years envisages a supply of 20 billion KW/h of electricity from Irkutsk to either Shenyang, Liaoning province or to Beijing.[11]

During 10–11 November 1997, a Memorandum of Understanding was signed between the government of the Russian Federation and the government of the People's Republic of China on the main principles of the preparation of the feasibility study on the construction of a gas pipeline to deliver gas from the East Siberian region of the Russian Federation to China as well as to potential consumers in third countries and the development of Kovyktinskoye gas and condensate field in Russia.

The Kovyktinskoye Development Plan and the BP-Amoco Factor

The starting point for the East Siberian transnational pipeline is the Kovyktinskoye gas field. The blue print was revealed by Anatoli Sivak, then president of Sidanco in February 1997 (see *Table 9.2*).[12] According to Sivak, the development of the Kovyktinskoye gas field is part of federal programme named 'Fuel and Energy' and is within the framework of sub-programme titled 'Oil Production and Oil and Gas Construction Complex Stabilisation'. The Kovyktinskoye development plan comprises both local (within the Russian Federation) and federal (international export pipeline) programmes.

Until late 1997, due to lack of finance, no major step had been taken to realise the regional development programme covering the 1994–2001 period. However,

Table 9.2 The Kovyktinskoye Field Development Plan

	Period	Required Investment	Planned Work
Regional Programme	1994–2001	$725 million, of which	
• 1st Stage	1994–98	$357 million	– 1.56 bcm gas production – 720 mm diameter gas pipeline to Angarsk Petrochemical Complex – condensate pipeline to Magistralnaya railway station – provide condensate refining facilities
• 2nd Stage	1998–99	$220 million	– 5.5 bcm gas production – construct gas-fired power generation
• 3rd Stage	2000–01	$148 million	– gas supply to industrial enterprises, residential areas, and agricultural consumers
Federal Programme	?	$7.64 billion	– Develop 3,364 km (of which 1,027 km in Russia, 1,017 km in Mongolia, and 1,320 km in China) gas pipeline, with 1420 mm diameter & 15 compressor plants. – The delivery capacity is 32 bcm/y.

Source: Keun-Wook Paik and Jae-Yong Choi, 'Pipeline Gas in Northeast Asia: Recent Developments and Regional Perspective', RIIA Energy and Environmental Programme *Briefing Paper, no. 39,* January 1998, p. 2.

partial financing for the regional programme was enabled after the East Asia Gas Co. (EAGC), a subsidiary of the South Korean Hanbo Group (which subsequently went bankrupt in January 1997) paid $44 million in July 1996 for 27.5 per cent of the equity shares of Rusia Petroleum.

As shown in *Table 9.2*, the total investment required for the regional programme is projected at $725 million. According to EAGC calculation, the regional programme requires a 430 km (with a 28 inch diameter and 1 compressor station), pipeline development would cost $721 million, of which $294 million is for wellhead development and $324 million for pipeline development. Surprisingly, projections put the IRR (internal return rate) at over 30 per cent with a payback period of 8 years.[13]

In November 1997, BP Exploration's decision to form a strategic partnership with Sidanco by taking a 10 per cent equity stake through a $571 million investment, and to acquire 45 per cent of Sidanco's interest in Rusia Petroleum by meeting the $172 million cost of appraising the Kovyktinskoye field, heralded a major breakthrough in terms of financing the programme.[14] As shown in *Table 9.3*, BP-Amoco is the only player that can handle the field's development plan. Despite Sidanco's bankruptcy problems, BP-Amoco has invested an

Table 9.3 Russia Petroleum's equity share composition, as of late May 1999

Shareholders	(%)
Burovik East Siberia Holdings Ltd (BP–Amoco)	22.32
Sidanco	6.62
Parthenon (Sidanco)	15.31
KM Technologies (Sidanco)	6.45
Irkutsk Administration	16.04
Irkutskenergo	12.79
Angarsk Petrochemical Plant	9.97
East Asia Gas Co	8.37
Others	2.13

Source: Dr. Paik's interview.

estimated $50–60 million to confirm the gas reserves of Kovyktinskoye field. So far three wells have been completed and the technical evaluation on the field's reserves is expected to be completed by 2001.

As far as the international pipeline project is concerned, no progress has been made. At the end of December 1997, a multilateral memorandum among five countries, Russia, China, Mongolia, Korea and Japan, was signed at a Moscow meeting. The memorandum calls for a co-ordinated approach to improving reserves estimates, further developing the field, defining the market for the gas and carrying out a feasibility study of the transnational pipeline project.[15] However, this multilateral approach was suspended after one-year of negotiations, and both Russia and China have decided to start the work on a bilateral basis. In late February 1999, when the Chinese premier Zhu Rongji visited Moscow, an agreement was reached on a feasibility study for the development of the Kovyktinskoye field and the construction of a gas pipeline to China.[16]

The two-year study will be completed in 2001 and the final decision on the international pipeline project is expected before the end of 2001. The study will review the three routes studied by RNGS International, a Rosneftegaztroy subsidiary (See *Table 9.4*).

ENERGY SHORTAGE IN THE RFE

Despite the great potential for oil and gas supply to NEA, the current level of oil and gas production from Sakhalin and Sakha at present is relatively small. Even thought the RFE's two major refineries have a 10 mt refining capacity, the majority of the refineries' feedstock needs had to be covered by crude oil from West Siberia as the indigenous oil production in the RFE is inadequate (See, *Tables 9.5, 9.6* and *9.7*)

Table 9.4 RGNS Study on Russian gas export routes to China

Option 1	**Kovyktinskoye field – Irkutsk Ulan Bator – Beijing: 2645 km** – of which Russia section 985 km, Mogolia section 990 km, and China section 670 km – total cost: $8–8.4 billion – compressor stations: 22 – pipeline diametre: 1220–1420 mm
Option 2	**Kovyktinskoye field – Irkutsk Ulan Ude – Chita – Harbin – Beijing: 4485 km** – of which Russia section 2170 km (Irkutsk oblast 575 km, Buryat Republic 750 km, and Chita oblast 845 km) and China section 2315 km. – total cost: $10.2–10.6 billion – compressor stations: ? – pipeline diametre: 1220–1420 mm
Option 3	**Yamburg field – Surgut Krasnoyarsk – Irkutsk – Ulan Bator – Beijing: 5665 km** – of which Russia section 4005 km, Mongolia section 990 km, and China section – total cost: $12 billion, of which $7.5 billion for pipeline, $2.5 billion for compressor stations, and $2 billion for infrastructure. – compressor stations: 47, of which 34 in Russia, 8 in Mongolia, 5 in China.

Source: The Petroleum Economist, Sep 1997, supplement section.
It is worth noting that a Sino-Russian joint technical and economic study confirmed that a 3400 km transnational pipeline connecting Irkutsk and Rizhao, a port city in Shandong province is feasible. The pipeline with 1420 mm diameter and 7.5 Mpa operation pressure could transport 32 bcm of gas, of which 10.5 bcm/y for Irkutsk oblast and Mongolia, 10 bcm for China, and 10 bcm for the third country. The pipeline also requires steel in garde X-65 and 15.7–23.7 mm wall thickness. The total cost of this pipeline development with 14 compressor stations is estimated at $10 billion. Only when a comprehensive exploration on Kovyktinskoye field is completed, however, can the true scale for transnational pipeline development be measured.

Table 9.5 Oil Refining by the RFE Refineries

	Khabarovsk	*Komsomolsk-on Amur*	*Total (mt)*
1990	4.20	5.60	9.80
1991	4.50	5.60	10.10
1992	4.10	5.00	9.10
1993	3.30	4.50	7.80
1994	1.90	3.10	5.00
1995	1.70	1.70	3.40
1996	1.70	1.69	3.39
1997*	1.79	2.28	4.07

Note: An alternative total figure for 1997 is 3.24 mt. (Oil & Gas Journal, 19 July 1999, p. 43)
Source: Energy Systems Institute (Irkutsk).

Table 9.6 Oil and Gas production in Sakhalin oblast

	Oil (mt)	Gas (bcm)
1990	1.93	1.83
1991	1.86	1.89
1992	1.68	1.73
1993	1.56	1.62
1994	1.49	1.48
1995	1.49	1.63
1996	1.43	1.78
1997	1.44	1.84

Note: Gas production by Yakutgazprom in Sakha Republic during 1993–1998 was 1.52–1.63 bcm/year.
Source: Energy Systems Institute (Irkutsk).

Table 9.7 Oil Import to the RFE

	Volume (mt)
1990	8.87
1991	8.24
1992	7.42
1993	6.24
1994	3.51
1995	1.91
1996	1.96
1997	2.63

Source: Energy Systems Institute (Irkutsk)

Interestingly, the RFE's level of oil products self-sufficiency actually increased during the 1990s when the RFE recorded a dramatic decline in its energy consumption. In 1992, the RFE's consumption of motor gasoline, furnace fuel oil, and diesel fuel were recorded at 2.3 mt, 6.6 mt and over 9.1 mt respectively, but in 1997 those figures dropped to 1.2 mt, 2.4 mt and 1.9 mt respectively. Despite the dramatic fall in indigenous refinery output, the lower oil demand has resulted in a generally higher level of self-sufficient in meeting liquid fuel needs. Consequently, the RFE's self sufficiency in furnace fuel oil, diesel fuel, refinery feedstock (crude oil and condensate) was recorded at 61 per cent, 57 per cent and 45 per cent in 1997, far higher those of 51 per cent, 32 per cent and 18 per cent in 1992.[17] This increase in self-sufficiency in the midst of weakened oil demand indirectly reflects the impact of transitional recession on the region's economy.

There are only 606 filling stations in RFE, as of October 1996, to service a population of about 8.0 million, as a consequence the retail price for oil products in the region was nearly twice the national average,[18] RFE is paying a very high price for delays in oil and gas development.

The energy shortage situation in ES is not so different from that of RFE. For example, the Angarsk refinery, whose design capacity is 65,000 tonnes/day (23.3 mt/y), received only 17,000 tonnes/day (6.1 mt/y) during November and December 1998. Due to this reduction in crude oil supply, the Angarsk petrochemical plant had to reduce the supply volume of refined products to Primorskii krai (from 2 mt/y to 0.6 mt/y), Amur oblast, Khabarovsk krai and Sakhalin (from 5.1 mt/y to 1.3 mt/y), and Irkutsk, Chitinakaya oblast, and Buryat Republic (from 4.3 mt/y to 3.0 mt/y).[19]

Strictly speaking, the physical shortage of oil and gas is not the main source of the energy crisis in RFE as coal is the primary fuel in the energy complex.[20] The RFE's energy shortage crisis could be summarised as being the result of the persistent failure of both the federal and local authorities to reconcile expensive energy supplies with insolvent energy requirements. Early, and comprehensive development, of RA's oil and gas resources and its export to the neighbouring states can only help ease regional energy supply shortages and strengthen RA's position as a reliable oil and gas supplier to Northeast Asian countries, like China, Korea and Japan. The soonest that RFE consumers will begin to get the benefit of RFE oil and gas development will be the second half of the this decade.

THE MARKET FOR RUSSIAN ASIA GAS AND OIL

Until the early 1990s, Japan was always regarded as the only market for oil and gas from the RFE. China was never seriously considered as a major market. The situation has changed considerably during the last few years. Not only the RFE, but also East Siberia and West Siberia are aiming at China's oil and gas market.

China became an oil importer in 1993 and is set to import quite a large volume of oil and gas in the coming decades. The US Department of Energy has projected that China's oil demand in 2010 and 2020 would be 6.4 mb/d and 8.8. mb/d respectively, while the figure of oil production would be 3.5 mb/d and 3.6 mb/d respectively (based on the reference case)[21] Chinese specialists from the Ministry of Geology and Mineral Resources, and CNPC have projected that its oil production will peak at 4 mb/d in 2010. As for gas, the Energy Research Institute under the State Development and Planning Commission (SDPC) has projected that natural gas production in 2010 and 2020 would be 60–74 bcm and 100–120 bcm, while demand would be 98–125 bcm and 231–309 bcm respectively.[22]

These projections strongly indicate that Russia is very well positioned to export a relatively large amount of oil and gas to China in the coming decades. At present, six pipeline gas supply sources are targeting China's gas market. The combined volume of exportable gas from these six sources could reach

100–160 bcm: 10 bcm from Sakhalin offshore, 20–40 bcm from Sakha Republic, 20–30 bcm from Irkutsk oblast, 20–30 bcm from West Siberia, 20 bcm from Kazakhstan and 20–30 bcm from Turkmenistan. In other words, there will be fierce competition among these potential supply sources.

The final decision on this transnational pipeline gas option will be made after the feasibility study that will be finished in 2001. It is too early to predict how the import of LNG and pipeline gas will be balanced and whether the pipeline route passing through the northern provinces will be chosen, but it looks quite certain that the scale of pipeline gas import will be much bigger than that of LNG.

The keys to this transnational pipeline development are market availability and financing. Despite the huge potential of the gas market in China, it is very desirable to connect both Chinese and Korean gas markets to promote the early realisation of transnational gas pipeline development. Japan seems very unlikely to provide a market for transnational pipeline gas in the early stage. Assuming that Japan will implement the pipeline from Sakhalin to Japan, the transnational pipeline grid links among China, Korea and Japan will open the door for the establishment a Circular Pipeline Network in NEA. This circular pipeline network connecting Sakhalin, Heilongjiang and Liaoning provinces, the Beijing area and Hebei province, Shandong province, Jiangsu province and the Shangahi area, South Korea and Japan could deliver 100–120 bcm of gas annually.[23]

To minimise the supply security burden, this network could develop two inner circular pipelines:

- Sakhalin Island – Japan –Korean Peninsula – Primorskii and Khabarovsk Krais
- Liaoning province – Korean Peninsula – Shanghai area – Shandong province and Beijing area

China is very well positioned to be the driving force behind the development of the circular pipeline network in NEA, but the roles of Korea and Japan are equally important. The priority sections of this circular pipeline are the section between East Siberia and northern China, together with the section between Sakhalin and the West Coast of Japan. Based on a nation-wide pipeline network, South Korea could play an important role in linking the network. The most important factor in this circular pipeline will be a confidence and consensus building among the related parties (see discussion in the pervious chapter).

CONCLUSIONS

The year 1999 witnessed early oil production from offshore of Sakhalin and it is the first signal that Russia is set be a crude oil supplier to NEA in the coming decade. As Japan, Korea, Taiwan and China are all major oil importers and anxious to diversify their crude oil supply sources, there is a considerable market for crude oil exports from the RA region.

When it comes to natural gas trade, the story is somewhat different. It is not the supplier, but the consumers that will deliver the final say on Russian gas exports to NEA. Due to the Japanese utility companies' reluctance to open the gas market to Russian pipeline gas, China is in the driving seat at this stage. It remains to be seen what sort of decision China will make later this decade with regard to pipeline gas imports. It is worth noting that a number of Russian companies are also exploring the possibility of exporting its surplus electricity from RA region to China and Japan, and this electricity export option could affect the natural gas export option to some extent.

In short, RA has abundant oil and gas supply sources in its frontier areas, but is lacking of the capital and the market to justify the massive oil and gas related infrastructure development. During the 1990s, Russia missed an excellent opportunity to attract western investors due to its rigid investment environment and its failure to understand the principles of a market system. The abundance of energy resources in RA is a great asset, but it will have no value if it remains untapped. In consideration of the fierce global competition to attract foreign investment for frontier oil and gas development, and the diversified supply options available to NE, Russia is still one of the countries with huge untapped energy resources. The decision-makers in Russia's central and local authorities need to pay a special attention to early and comprehensive oil and gas development in RA region. No party benefits from further delays in development, and the benefits are too big to miss.

NOTES

1 Executive Summary of a study on Comprehensive Energy Plan in East Siberia and Far East of the Russian Federation prepared by Energy Research Institute, Russia and Institute of Energy Economics, Japan, September 1995.
2 Keun-Wook Paik (1995) *Gas and Oil in Northeast Asia: Policies, projects and prospects*, London: Royal Institute of International Affairs; Pacific Russia Oil & Gas Report, 2, (1), *The Oil and Gas Industry of Sakhalin Island Annual Review,* Spring 1999.
3 *Mainichi Shimbun*, 22 May 1997.
4 *Nihon Keizai Shimbun*, 1 December 1998.
5 *Pacific Russia Oil and Gas Report*, 1 (4), Winter 1999, p. 11.
6 Proceedings of the 5th International Conference on Northeast Asian Natural Gas Pipeline, held in Yakutsk (Sakha Republic) during 25–27 July 1999.
7 The map came from Miao Chengwu and Liu Hequn, 'Northeast Asia Gas Demand and Transportation in the 21st Century', paper presented at the 15th World Petroleum Congress, Beijing, October 1997.
8 *Russian Far East Update*, September 1998, p. 11.
9 Quan and Keun-Wook Paik (1998) *China Natural Gas Report*, Xinhua News Agency and Royal Institute of International Affairs, London pp. 103–122.
10 Keun-Wook Paik, 'Energy cooperation in Sino-Russian relations: the importance of oil and gas', *The Pacific Review,* 9 (1): 83.
11 *Reuters News Service*, 27 June 1997.
12 Siberian Far East Petroleum Company Ltd. (Sidanco) was established by ordinance 452 of the Russian Federation in May 1994 and has incorporated the following companies based

on the ordinance: Varyeganneftegaz, Kondpetroleum, Chernogorneft, Udmurtneft, the Angarsky Petrochemical Company, the Saratovsky Refinery, and Sakhalinnefte-produkt.

13 Author's interview with EAGC senior officer.

14 *The Times*, 18 Nov 1997.

15 *Interfax Petroleum Report*, 6 (9)15 Jan 1998, p. 10.

16 *Interfax Petroleum Report*, 8 (9) 5–11 March 1999, pp. 4–6; *China OGP*, 7 (6) 15 March 1999, pp. 1–3.

17 Eugene M. Khartukov, 'Energy Security in Northeast Asia: A Russian Perspective', presented at the 5th International Conference on Northeast Asian Natural Gas Pipeline, held in Yakutsk (Sakha Republic) during 25–27 July 1999.

18 David C. Wilson, (1999) 'Russian Far East holds huge Resource Potential', *Oil & Gas Journal*, 19 July, p. 43.

19 R. N. Diyashev, E. S. Ziganshin, and V. N. Ryabchenko, (1999) 'Verkhnechonsky field shows Eastern Russia's Potential', *Oil & Gas Journal*, 19 July, p. 58.

20 Michael J. Bradshaw and Peter Kirkow (1998) 'The Energy Crisis in the Russian Far East: Origins and Possible Solutions', *Europe-Asia Studies*, 50 (6): 1043–63.

21 Energy Information Administration, US Department of Energy, International Energy Outlook 1999, with projections to 2020, DOE/EIA-0484(99), March 1999, pp. 145 & 201.

22 Keun-Wook Paik, (1999) 'Trans-National Pipeline Gas Introduction and its Implications towards China's Gas Expansion', presented at IEA-China Conference on Natural Gas Industry: Market Development, Regulatory Framework and Financing Needs, Beijing, 9–10 Beijing November.

23 Keun-Wook Paik, (1999) 'Sakhalin-Hokkaido Gas Pipeline Introduction and its Implications towards Circular Pipeline Development in Northeast Asia', presented at an International Conference on Advancing the Japan Pipeline Project for introducing Sakhalin Natural Gas, held in Sapporo, 2 April.

Chapter 10

Chinese Relations with the Russian Far East

David Kerr

INTRODUCTION

It is impossible to separate China's relations with the Russian Far East (RFE) from its relations with Russia as a whole. There will be distinctive contacts between Russian and Chinese regions in the future as development and mutual opening progresses, but this will take place within the matrix of the overall Sino-Russian relationship, as well as the wider context of regional relations in Northeast Asia. Given that relations between Russia and China have only recently embarked upon a new era following a long period of political, military and ideological confrontation, it is even more important to begin by outlining the factors that are shaping the broader relationship before focusing on China's relations with the RFE. This will be done in four stages – geopolitics, the strategic partnership, national economic relations, and finally the regional dimension.

THE POLITICS AND ECONOMICS OF SPATIAL CHANGE

The heightened concern with geopolitics in the early years of the foreign policy debate in Russia was a natural reaction to the dissolution of the historic boundaries of the Imperial Russian and Soviet states.[1] The debate was intense because the forces that propelled the Soviet Union to disintegration – ethnonationalism, economic regionalism, and ideological polarisation – did not halt at the boundaries of the Russian Federation so that perceptions of internal instability and external vulnerability persisted after 1991 generating concern with geopolitical change and weakness. A further factor was the need to fill the values vacuum left by the implosion of Soviet ideological structures.

Clearly the dominant group in the political elite at that time believed that unconditional adoption of the political and economic values of the Atlantic powers would expedite Russia's integration into the principal international institutions, as well as strengthening their domestic power. There was a contradiction, however, between this attempt at strategic convergence with the West and the widespread feeling that the country was further from the West geopolitically, and in terms of power and influence, than at any time in the modern era. This was to be compounded by the trajectory of reform in Russia that raised doubts as to how far it could adopt the values and institutions of the advanced capitalist democracies.

Russian foreign policy since 1994 has been driven by the need to adjust to the new geopolitical realities. The year after the crushing of the parliamentary revolt was arguably the watershed because internally it marked the determination of the centre to end doubts about spatial instability within Russia, evident in the promulgation of the new Federal Constitution and the first Chechen war. Externally it marked the beginning of the absorption of the Central European states into the European economic and Atlantic security systems. Russia was offered mechanisms through which it could comment on these processes but there was never the illusion that it could prevent them (Pierre and Trenin 1997). At least part of the function of the interlocutory mechanisms developed by the West was to channel Russian grievances into control systems rather than have them expressed through traditional power politics. Since 1994, however, Russia has accepted the challenge of developing new relationships with which it can counterbalance and influence developments in the West, at the same time as giving expression to its enhanced geopolitical identity as a Eurasian power (Voskresenskii 1996; Abazov 1997).

Much of this effort has gone into developing the relationship with China with which Russia announced a strategic partnership in April 1996.[2] China's importance to Russia is manifold but its rising geopolitical significance can be noted here. The perception of Russia's geopolitical shift being primarily to the East is correct from a European perspective; but Russia has also shifted northwards. Most of the countries of the CIS are on Russia's southern periphery and Russia is now more than ever wedged between this unstable southern belt and the Arctic north. This process has been reinforced by change to internal settlement and economic activity during the transitional crisis, which has seen the severest retrenchment in the north and east. The region which represents the largest proportion of the krainii sever – the Far East – has been the worst effected. China's importance in this dimension is not only that it dominates eastern Eurasia, but it is the single most important factor influencing access to the south – to the economies of the Asian rim from the Yellow Sea to the Bay of Bengal – for most of Asiatic Russia. The geopolitical balance between Russia and China is not exclusively west-east, therefore, but also crucially north-south.

These changes to Russia's geopolitical and geoeconomic perspectives would of themselves have encouraged concentration on China but they are complemented by equivalent processes within China itself. It has been argued that Chinese history has been dominated by the dual impulses of northern defence and southern expansion (Fitzgerald 1972: 1), but the latter in particular has been modified in the modern era. As well as international factors, changes to China's social order have meant that internal expansion – that is demographic growth and economic development – has taken the place of expansion overseas. The coastal development strategy pursued since 1978, the latest chapter in this process, is commonly viewed as reinforcing spatial disparities between coast and interior,[3] but it is also re-establishing the developmental differences between North and South China, which the planned economy had gone some way to eroding. North and Northeast China, the site of some of the country's most important extractive and heavy industries, were beneficiaries of the developmental strategy pursued up to the reform era, and have necessarily lost ground since. A number of northern coastal provinces are prospering under the new strategy, notably those of the Bohai rim, but they are loosely integrated and internally competitive in comparison with the other key growth zones centred on the Chang (Yangtze) and Zhu (Pearl) River deltas.[4] The new relationship with Russia supposes that the requirement of northern defence, operative until very recently, can be replaced by a strategy of mutual opening and development that will allow China's border areas to become the functional equivalents of the coastal provinces and cities, and thus one factor offsetting imbalances between North and South (Ma and Zou 1991).

As in Russia, China's concerns with spatial development are tied to geopolitical perspectives. China understands the implications of Russian Eurasianism and accepts the resumption of Russia's role in Asia provided this is now founded on a recognition of the equality of sovereign states. Equally important, China is aware that the Eurasianist trend is part of a broader conception that expresses Russia's desire for a foreign policy which can be formulated and implemented independent of the West (Li 1997: 25–26). This lessens the likelihood that China will be faced with a strategic alliance between the Atlantic powers and the former Soviet Union, necessitating the resumption of the northern defence imperative. Eurasia in this view is heading towards tripolarity between the EU, the CIS and the Asian states, in which China will have a pivotal role, and the US by implication will be less able to exert unilateral influence.

As far as the spatial dimension of the Sino-Russian relationship is concerned there are two predominant problems. Firstly, the fact that Northeast Asia was until recently a region of closed borders means that Russia and China adjoin in regions that have at best uneven experience in economic opening. The problems of re-orientating to meet demand from international markets instead of the central plan are multiplied when two transitional economies are attempting this. Secondly, because of the role of the plan and the concentration of heavy industry in Northern China, these regions are not only comparable in terms of economic model, but in economic structure also. As regards these two factors, however, China stands on the brink of radical change following the decision of the 15th

CCP Congress in September 1997 to finally embark on structural reform of the state sector.[5] This increases dramatically the need to find external markets for the products of the state-owned enterprises (SOEs), both those large and medium ones that have been restructured, and the many smaller ones that have been turned over to collective management.

In summary, therefore, the Russian and Chinese experience can be seen as distinctive variants on wider processes of regional and global change, in which they have certain common characteristics arising from transition from the planned economy in regionally diverse continental states. The major difference in spatial terms between them is that the centrifugal forces released by the combination of domestic transition and external opening have in China's case been confined within existing boundaries and institutions while in Russia they have recast both. It is against this process of comparative geopolitical and geoeconomic change that the strategic relationship should be viewed.

THE STRATEGIC PARTNERSHIP

The fact that improvement in bilateral relations, which began in the early 80's and reached its Soviet-era high point with normalisation in 1989, has continued in the wake of Soviet dissolution points to two inter-related factors – the relative balance of power between the two states and changed elite perspectives. In terms of perspectives both countries have seen a decisive shift away from ideologically – driven internationalism and towards a concentration on national interests. This is prompted not by isolationism, though this remains an undercurrent, but increasing external awareness and interaction, including in relation to the costs and benefits of integration into the world economy. This latter concern has two dimensions: the model of economic interaction and the place the countries will occupy in the structure of the world market economy. In both instances the experience of the Asian economies has been a powerful influence, although necessarily more so for China than for Russia. This said, Russia's social and economic model is still being contested, and there are distinctively Asian characteristics evident, notably the weakness of institutions in the face of informal group and personal allegiance. These came to the fore in the political and economic crisis of 1998 when comparisons between Russia's oligopolistic capitalism and the Asian NIEs crony capitalism were made. However, the Asian model had at least demonstrated its ability to generate sustained growth, a relatively decriminalised economy, and distribution of wealth outside elite circles, none of which can as yet be claimed for Russia. In the regional crisis, China's managed exchange rate and capital controls initially provided notable protection but there was evidence by 1999 that export growth and direct investment were under pressure, which, when combined with the fall-out from SOE reform, suggested that China might again resort to devaluation.

As both states move towards political and economic nationalism as an interpretative and legitimating doctrine (essentially what western international relations theory would identify as a realist-mercantilist approach) there is the danger of friction, hence both countries concern at the possibility of extreme nationalism in the other.[6] However, a common approach based on national interest has at least the virtue of applying a standard of predictability which was absent in the recent past. It also means that a great deal depends on the relative balance of power between the two powers.

In military terms Russia retains dominant nuclear capability at the same time as its conventional forces, including those in Siberia and the Far East, and the MIC that supported them, undergo marked deterioration (Arbatov 1998; Clarke 1995). Russia is unlikely to forfeit military advantage before 2010, although relative capability must move in China's favour.[7] One of the more controversial aspects of the bilateral relationship has been whether Russia should actually be abetting this change by military transfers to China, which have included submarines, aircraft and surface vessels. Such transfers may account for about a third of China's imports from Russia (Tian 1999: 86), and include exports of the Far East MIC, such as SU-27 parts from Komsomolsk. Two points should be made about this trade: it may be unsustainable as present weapons systems are the product of Soviet-era research and development which has since degraded due to declining investment. In this perspective, military exports, including to developing countries where Russia has half the market share of the US (Bickers 1997), far from diluting relative capabilities may be a vital source of finance for sustaining them.

The second factor is relative economic capability. *Table 10.1* indicates that China's GDP reached $811 bn in 1996 when converted at the average exchange rate, some 80 per cent greater than Russia's although only a fifth in per capita terms. However, the limitations of using the exchange rate for international comparisons of transitional economies is evident in the fact that this method implies that China's economy shrank relative to the Russian between 1992 and 1996, when the opposite must be true. Valid comparisons can only be made using purchasing power parities. Goskomstat has begun to issue PPP estimates of GDP which indicate that the ratio of exchange rate GDP to PPP GDP declined from 8.5 to 1.4 between 1992–96 as Russia has its prices. On this basis PPP GDP had fallen to $625bn by 1996, with per capita GDP down to $4235. In the most comprehensive study to date of China's GDP in comparative perspective Ren has provided a benchmark PPP GDP for China in 1986 and a weight against other transitional economies (Ren 1997). This has been adapted to provide a time series using official growth figures, although these undoubtedly suffer from insufficient deflation. On this basis China's PPP GDP reached $3332bn in 1996, five times greater than Russia, although per capita GDP at $2723 remained around two-thirds.[8] Equally notable is the relative change since 1992: GDP and per capita ratios had increased from 2.9 and 0.36 in only four years. Two factors argue against this divergence being maintained: the return of growth in the Russian economy and, in per capita terms, relative population growth.

Table 10.1 Russia and China, comparative GDP and projection to 2010

	GDP (R/Yn bn)	DP/XR ($ bn)	Pop (m)	DPpc/XR ($)	PPP/ XR	R/Yn PPP$	GDP/PPP ($ bn)	GDPpc/ PPP ($)
1992								
Russia	19006	86.4	148.3	582.5	8.55	25.7	738.6	4980.4
China	2663	483.0	1183.6	408.0	4.45	1.2	2149.0	1815.6
Ratio		5.59	7.98	0.70			2.91	0.36
1996								
Russia	2256120	440.6	147.7	2982.8	1.42	3606.3	625.6	4235.6
China	6779	811.8	1232.1	658.8	4.10	2.0	3332.1	2704.4
Ratio		1.84	8.34	0.22			5.33	0.64

	Growth (p.a.)	Pop (m)				Growth (p.a.)	GDP/PPP ($ bn)	GDPpc/ PPP ($)
2010								
Russia	−0.5%	137.7				4.0%	1083.3	7867.1
China	1.0%	1416.3				7.0%	8592.0	6066.5
Ratio		10.29					7.93	0.77

Sources: Goskomstat Rossii (1997) *Sotsialnoe-Ekonomicheskoe Polozheniye Rossii, 1996 g.* Moscow: Goskomstat.
Ren Ruoe (1997) *China's Economic Performance in Comparative Perspective*, Paris: OECD.
IMF (various issues) *International Financial Statistics.* Washington D.C.: IMF.

Growth in the Chinese economy to 2010 was being predicted at a lower rate of 7 per cent p.a. before the Asian financial crisis, but there is as yet no firm basis on which to lower this further. Growth in the Russian economy remains the great unknown. Estimates varied between 3 per cent and 6 per cent p.a. before the financial collapse of 1998. The estimate chosen here is an optimistic 4 per cent over the review period. On this basis China's GDP will be some eight times greater than Russia's by 2010, but with differing population growth rates per capita ratios will only have increased to three-quarters. The data in this estimate and projection are evidently somewhat soft, but the divergence is wide enough to support clear policy implications. Russia may be in what is a unique situation in that it adjoins a country whose economy is several times bigger than its own but whose population is relatively less well off. On the regional level, if contribution to national industrial output can be accepted as a proxy for GDP, we can estimate that the economy of Northeast China (the provinces of Liaoning, Jilin, and Heilongjiang) was some eleven times larger than that of the RFE in 1996 (9.6 per cent and 4.6 per cent of industrial output respectively). It cannot be assumed the regional ratio will follow national projections to 2010, however, since changes to regional output under growth in China have exceeded those under recession in Russia: the Northeast's share of industrial production fell 2.7 per cent from 12.3 per cent in 1991, compared to 0.4 per cent from 5 per cent for the RFE. The divergence in regional economic performance will be less marked than that at national level, therefore, and the economy of Northeast China will exceed that of the RFE somewhere between the parameters of the present regional and implied national ratios (11:16). Two provisos can be added to the above. Russia will continue to enjoy a technological advantage, certainly in terms of the applied technology in society and economy, and advantages in educational levels and skills base. Secondly, China's rising real incomes must be seen as a stabilising factor internally and an opportunity for China's economic partners. Most economies are aware of the dual consequences of China's economic revolution – the threat to industrial competitiveness but also the potential of the market. In Russia's conditions of economic vulnerability, the latter has not received due attention.

It remains to consider the relative weight that Russia and China enjoy in international politics. This is the core of the strategic partnership. The policy statements emanating from the regular bilateral summits do not point only to a leveling of status between the two powers, but a convergence of strategic perspectives. Most notable has been the declaration on a multipolar world signed in April 1997 which announced agreement on the 'necessity of mutual respect, equality, and mutual benefit and not hegemonism and power politics' as the basis of international relations (Diplomaticheskii Vestnik, 1997a: 19–21). In the case of Russia and China multipolarity means placing limits on US unilateralism by adjusting relations between themselves, and between themselves and Japan and Europe. The war over Kosovo was opposed by Russia and China as just such an example of US unilateralism made all the more unacceptable to two continental, multi-ethnic states because the principle of territorial sovereignty was set aside by NATO in favour of minority rights to self-government. The result of the strategic convergence is that the foreseeable factors which might destabilise the partnership are predominately regional, or what might be termed peripheral – the points at which the interests of the two states overlap in Eurasia, particularly with regard to Korea, South Asia, Central Asia, Taiwan and their own border area in Northeast Asia. In the case of the division of Korea and between Pakistan and India these hardly qualify as foreseeable factors since their danger in part arises from their very unpredictability. Suffice to say that Russia and China have nothing to gain from an escalation of these conflicts, although there may be a contradiction between Russia's attempt to form strategic partnerships with both India and China unless the latter is prepared to downgrade its sponsorship of Pakistan in favour of the benefits of better relations with both Moscow and Delhi. Central Asia has the potential to cause friction between the two powers as they compete for influence and economic advantage, but China has intrinsic interests in regional stability within and between the Central Asian states, arising from the geopolitical and ethnic sensitivity of its western provinces especially the Xinjiang-Uighur AR, including through limiting the influence of extra-regional powers.

These interests are entirely compatible with that of Russia and are likely to outweigh the competitive dimensions in the triangular relationship. The status of Taiwan remains the *cassus belli* of China's relations with other powers, but, to date, Moscow has been scrupulous in its adherence to a One-China formula. This does not inhibit Russia's development of economic relation with Taiwan provided there is no linkage between trade and investment and political recognition.[9]

It has been claimed that contemporary China's policy towards its periphery is imperial both in origin and in its 'fundamental impulses towards exercising control over neighbouring peoples consonant with available Chinese power' (Hunt 1976: 19). Since the Russian Far East not only neighbours China, but some fifth of its territory, constituting over half the crucial southern zone which contained 64 per cent of FE population and produced 52 per cent of economic output in 1996, was at one time part of the Chinese imperial system this should imply extreme geopolitical vulnerability. However, neither the historical record nor contemporary policy appears to support this conclusion. Relations between Russia and China were marked by pragmatism and mutual benefit until 1858 when the Tsarist regime abandoned the principle of equality between sovereign states in pursuit of its territorial ambitions. The Soviet Union openly admitted that the 19th century treaties were unequal and in 1924 committed itself to redemarcate the boundary on the basis of 'equality, reciprocity, and justice',[10] although no serious attempt was made at this until 40 years later. The Chinese position in 1964 and thereafter was not that the Soviet Union should return the territory it had gained under the treaties but that the line of control gave it possession of territory not defined by those treaties, principally the islands of the Amur and Ussuri rivers, and that therefore it should be redemarcated on the basis of equality and consent (Tsui 1983; Ginsbergs 1993). It is this which has finally been achieved in the demarcation process between May 1991 and November 1997 which has established the eastern frontier under the thalweg principle, save three islands which will be open to joint development. Along with the multilateral agreements signed between China and the other states of the CIS (the Shanghai five) leading to the progressive demilitarisation of the border zones, this can be taken as evidence of a return to the pragmatism that previously characterised Sino-Russian relations.

It is difficult at this stage to asses how the balance between Russia's military and technological advantage and China's economic power will be played out. What is clear is that the agenda between the two states now operates on a series of complex interlocking levels, in which relations between Northern China and the Russian Far East are by no means the primary determinant. This is in effect a continuation of the previous model of regional relations, where these were largely a barometer of the overall relationship. Thus, the Sino-Russian territorial dispute never determined the bilateral relationship in the way the Kuriles/Northern Territories dispute has with Japan. That the model of regional relations has not changed significantly as yet is primarily due to the role of economics. Political and military change is always easier to achieve than economic change even without the barriers and distortions presently operating between Russia and China. These include: the long period of isolation between the two economies; the differing pace and direction of reform; the effects of transition at the regional level; and the absence of precedents from the past for regional relations – neither the Russia Imperial penetration into Manchuria nor the years of proletarian alliance offering much that is useful to the international political economy of Northeast Asia (Kerr 1996). The two countries are faced with the need to construct a new model of relations so that economics can take its place alongside the military and political understanding in the strategic partnership. Regional level relations can take an increasingly important role in this, although they must be set within the context of the overall complementarity between the two economies.

ECONOMIC RELATIONS

Assessing future economic complementarity between Russia and China is complex not only because of the nature of absolute change in both countries but also its interregional and intraregional variations. Disparities in regional growth, investment and restructuring will continue to shape external orientation. There will also be distinctive intra-regional biases within areas such as Northeast China (Dongbei) and the RFE which are too often regarded as homogeneous. The highly volatile trade relationship between the two countries since opening in 1992 reflects these factors, as well as change in the mechanism and structure of trade.[11]

Table 10.2 indicates the degree to which Russia's current trade profile with China runs against the trends of the open economy. The bulk of Russia's trade is conducted with border provinces whose openness (measured as exports + imports/ as share of nominal GDP) is less than half the national average. Only 18.5 per cent of China's exports to Russia originate in the open coastal regions although an increasingly higher share of imports are directed there. Clearly these figures disguise much province-level diversity. *Figure 1A* shows that six provinces

Table 10.2 Economic Characteristics of Russian trade partners, 1996

	GDP	National Exports	Russia Exports	National Imports	Russia Imports	FDI Exports	Opening Nat = 17.5%
Coastal	57.9%	86.6%	18.5%	88.5%	42.6%	96.9%	23.3%
Central	31.6%	9.9%	18.6%	6.0%	5.9%	2.1%	4.1%
Border	10.5%	3.5%	69.6%	5.4%	54.1%	1.1%	6.3%

Sources: Almanac of China's Foreign Economic Relations and Trade, 1997–98; Statistical Yearbook of China, 1997.

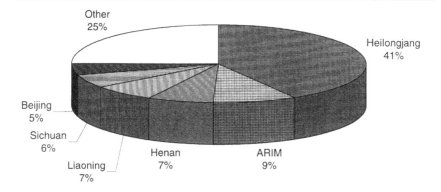

Figure 10.1a China's exports to Russia

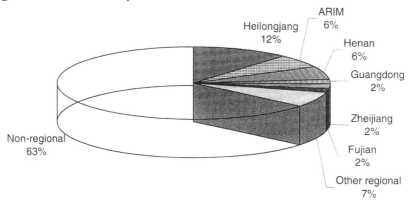

Figure 10.1b China's imports from Russia

accounted for over 75 per cent of China's exports in 1996: three northern provinces, two central agricultural provinces and Beijing. The corresponding import figure is notable in two regards: four out of the top six regional partners are now coastal provinces, a change from the early years of opening when the north dominated imports as well as exports. Secondly, these six provinces account for only a third of national imports with 64 per cent of Russian goods not being registered against any province of final use. There is undoubtedly under-reporting of regional imports in these figures; nevertheless, it can be concluded that a majority of Russian imports are still taken by state-level corporations, including those of the defence sector, as in the Soviet era.

Figure 10.2 indicates the role of the key border regions of Heilongjiang and the RFE in bilateral trade between 1992 and 1996. Chinese exports have been constrained by a succession of factors. Within Russia by the transitional crisis; the saturation of Russian markets, including the RFE, with Chinese goods and the collapse of re-export trade; and the diversification of Russian and FE imports,

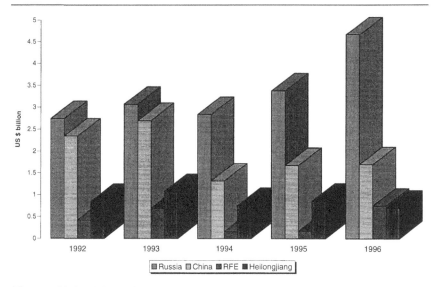

Figure 10.2a Bilateral Exports

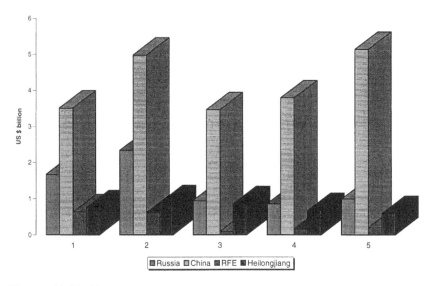

Figure 10.2b Bilateral Imports

including from elsewhere in Asia. On the domestic side by problems with the quality of goods and the end of the twin-track foreign exchange system in January 1994 which had encouraged the barter boom of 1992–93. It should be noted that the data provided does not contain estimates of China's informal exports to Russia which may amount to $2bn p.a. Heilongjiang's exports have not been as adversely effected as national exports and as a result its share of exports has risen. Conversely, its share of imports has declined as other provinces and trade corporations have developed direct ties with Russia. The RFE's share of Russia's exports was never that high even in the years of the barter boom (22.5 per cent in 1993) and has since declined dramatically, only rising in 1996 due to the inclusion of regional arms exports for the first time. As a result of these changes 25.7 per cent of RFE exports went to China in 1996 (6.9 per cent in 1995 with civil commodities only) and 11.6 per cent of imports originated there. 32.8 per cent of Heilongjiang's exports were sent to Russia in the same year and 34.7 per cent of its imports originated there. This data points to the changing regional bases of trade with distinctively different patterns in the two economies. In China, whilst stagnating exports are concentrating in the North, imports from Russia are expanding and diversifying, most importantly towards the newly industrialising provinces. In Russia, the RFE appears to have a paucity of goods which it can export to China, although it continues to take a limited number of imports. On this basis the RFE could not expect to have an advanced trade relationship with China, with the bulk of Russian exports originating elsewhere and a limited interest in Chinese imports dependent on improving quality. The scenario for Heilongjiang is also rather negative; its own exports are constrained whilst its re-exporting role is undermined. Clearly, therefore, the regional bases of Sino-Russian trade have already changed with the concentration on border regions in the early years of opening arising primarily from the barter mechanism giving way to a more diversified direction of trade. Given the continued stabilisation of the new mechanism of hard currency settlements the primary factor influencing the development of the regional bases of trade must be the commodity structure.

The commodity structures of national and regional trade for 1995 are set out in *Table 10.3*. Manufactures now constitute 85 per cent of Chinese exports and 81 per cent of imports, but these figures disguise the fact that China remains most competitive in labour and resource intensive goods and least competitive in technology intensive or high technology manufactured goods; hence the continuing deficit in machinery. Moreover, the share of primary products is set to rise as China encounters resource constraints, with iron ore, fuels, grain and cotton all likely to be imported in increasing proportions (Wang 1996). The two most important categories of primary imports in 1996 were foodstuffs (4.5 per cent) and minerals/fuels (4.9 per cent). China's energy intensity has declined remarkably in the reform era, but primary energy production increases have still failed to keep pace with soaring consumption. Production increased by close to 53 per cent over the ten years to 1997 but consumption increased even faster at 60 per cent. The imbalance has been particularly noticeable since 1991 with production growth at 4.0 per cent p.a., only marginally up from 3.9 per cent p.a. in the previous period, whilst consumption increased at 5.0 per cent p.a., up from 3.7 per cent. As a result China recorded its first deficit in primary energy in 1997, albeit a minor one equivalent to 0.7 per cent of consumption. Given that China's

Table 10.3: Commodity structure of foreign trade, 1995 (billion $)

	China and Heilongjiang			*Russia and RFE*		
National Exports	Textiles	35.9	24.1%	Energy	30.9	39.9%
	Machinery	27.6	18.6%	Metals	13.7	17.9%
	Metals	12.1	8.1%	Machinery	4.6	6.0%
Share		75.6	50.8%		49.2	63.8%
National Imports	Machinery	47.0	35.6%	Machinery	15.5	33.4%
	Metals	12.2	9.2%	Foodstuffs	5.5	11.5%
	Chemicals	10.4	7.9%	Beverages	2.0	4.5%
Share		69.6	52.7%		23.0	49.4%
Bilateral Exports	Foodstuffs	0.626	37.4%	Metals	1.337	35.2%
	Textiles	0.434	25.9%	Fertilizers	0.950	25.0%
	Shoes	0.037	2.2%	Machinery	0.410	10.8%
Share		1.096	65.5%		2.697	71.0%
Regional Exports	Textiles	n/a		Fish	0.649	40.3%
	Electrical	n/a		Timber	0.309	19.2%
	Soybean	n/a		Fuels	0.248	15.4%
Share		0.516	24.6%		1.206	74.9%

Note: *RFE figures are for 1994.*
Sources: *Almanac of China's Foreign Economic Relations and Trade, 1996–97; Statistical Yearbook of China, 1996; Russian Economic Trends,* various issues; Institut Dal'nego Vostoka (1997) *'Ekonomika KNR v preddverii XXI veka',* Moscow; P.A. Minakir (1996) *The Russian Far East: an economic survey',* Khabarovsk: Institute of Economics RAS.

per capita energy consumption is only 43 per cent of world average and its fuel structure is dominated by coal, and the remainder by oil (75.4 per cent and 20.5 per cent in 1997), there is considerable potential both for growth and diversification of sources of supply (Kerr 1999). Russia's new energy companies are anxious to expand in to Asian Pacific markets, although projections suggest that this will be based predominantly on Russia's unique endowment in gas, not oil. Although China does import some fuels from Russia at present, energy is principally imported in embodied form. Much effort currently is being directed towards agreement on the first fixed supply, most likely gas from Irkutsk oblast (Diplomaticheskii Vestnik 1997b: 11–12). The energy dimension aside both countries will be most concerned with advancing industrial competitiveness through trade in machinery and technology.

The perspective for regional trade in this outlook is mixed. Heilongjiang has a much more diversified trade structure than the FE and its exports can expect to find a market in Russia provided they are quality competitive. The major problem the Dongbei faces is that of industrial reform. The number of SOEs in total industrial enterprises is not significantly greater than the national average; it is share of output and size of enterprises that is disproportionate. The national share of SOEs in GVIO had shrunk to 44 per cent by 1996; but it was 64 per cent in the Dongbei and 70 per cent in Heilongjiang. Large-scale enterprises contributed 38.2 per cent of GVIO nationally but 57 per cent in the Dongbei (SSB 1997). These structural problems emphasise the shared inheritance of the planned economy in the Dongbei and the FE and the distance that must be travelled before either region develops the non-state SMEs that are crucial to growth in China's coastal south. The RFE's trade limitations are evident in the high share of a limited number of predominately primary commodities, some of which its shares with the Dongbei. The latter produced 30 per cent of China's timber in 1996 and in fuels – 12 per cent of coal, 22 per cent of gas and 48 per cent of oil (for Heilongjiang the figures are 19 per cent of timber and in fuels: 5.8 per cent, 11.6 per cent and 35.6 per cent respectively). The fact that commodity structure is similar should not inhibit trade given the general trend to overseas resourcing: there are physical and environmental limits to timber production in China for example (Waggener and Backman 1997). On the key question of energy, however, it is evident that the regional position is in effect the reverse of the national: Russia may be resource rich and China facing energy constraints but at the regional level Heilongjiang has been the most important source of China's energy exports for the last generation whilst the RFE is notoriously energy deficient. Developments on Sakhalin, and at some point of the future in Sakha, may yet produce an energy relationship between the RFE and China but at present, as noted in previous chapters, discussions are concentrating on East Siberia. On this basis expanding trade relations between the RFE and China is dependent on increasing the diversification of the export structure and the sources of investment to sustain this. These factors are evident to most commentators in the FE. Where they diverge is on the regional strategy that is most likely to achieve this and how far open or closed regionalism, perhaps particularly with regard to China, meets FE interests.

In summary, the present economic relationship between Russia and China is still being shaped by internal dynamics. The high profile accorded to regional level economic relations after 1992 was principally a consequence of the way opening was conducted and the different trajectory of reform in the two economies. The role of border areas is arguably declining in importance as relations between the respective core regions and sectors are widened and systematised. Therefore, what appeared to some in the RFE as a problem of excessive interdependence in the first years of opening may be becoming the opposite – border regions may be in danger of becoming little more than trade conduits with limited prospects for using bilateral relations to influence restructuring and development. In essence, the transitional model of regional relations may be passing but a new model is not yet in place. The last section will examine the options for such a model.

REGIONAL RELATIONS

The first point that must be made about any future regional relationship between China and the RFE is that competition is unavoidable. This is natural given that internally Russian and Chinese provinces already have highly competitive relationships.[12] In China this competition has two dimensions: as important as the benefits and costs arising from participation in the open economy are those which exist within the centre-region relationship. As the government's use of fiscal transfers and supplementary grants to equalise growth between provinces has declined in effectiveness it has employed two further methods: low-cost loans through the banking system and variable de-centralisation of policy-making (World Bank 1995). To the extent that interior regions are the recipients of these measures they can be used to advance regional opening and development. RFE regions will recognise in these measures some of their own demands against the centre in Moscow, but they must also realise that they represent one set of factors which now make regionalism in China a multilayered phenomenon, involving provinces, recognised development regions, and central actors. This regionalism will shape relations with the Chinese provinces, for example in the committee of Siberian, Far Eastern and northern Chinese provinces promoted at the time of Yeltsin's November 1997 visit, if it is successfully established.

The central question here is what constitutes the natural economic territories of the regions surrounding the Yellow Sea and the Sea of Japan? At present the Chinese Northeast is divided, in terms of development regions and economic activity, into two distinct zones: the Bohai rim and the northern interior. Cumulative FDI in the Dongbei 1983–96 was $11.042bn, 6.4 per cent of national total, but two-thirds of this was in Liaoning; Heilongjiang's share was 1.1 per cent and Jilin's 0.9 per cent. Exports of enterprises with foreign investment in the Dongbei in 1996 were $3.682bn, 6.0 per cent of national total, but these were even more concentrated in Liaoning at $3.179bn; Jilin's total was $260m and Heilongjiang's $242m (*ACFERT,* various years). Thus, Northeast China remains a product of the era of closed boundaries. Interior opening would not erode the natural and economic advantages of regional growth poles such as the Liaodong peninsula and the greater Vladivostok region but it would allow more rapid and balanced economic development than is possible within exclusive spheres, which means that the protectionist inclinations of the past must be left behind (Lu 1993). There are two dimensions of regionalism to be considered – the factor dimension related to the economic features that regional economies bringing to the relationship; the spatial dimension relates to defining geographic areas for opening, and in particular whether these should be bilateral or multilateral (*Problemy Dal'nego Vostoka* 1995: 16–35).

As argued the natural resource bases of the Dongbei and the RFE are rather similar indicating potential cooperation over the extraction and processing of common resources.[13] The principal area of competition will be over the attraction of investment. but there is an assumption behind the concept of open regionalism that this investment may be easier to find for collaborative projects. This may be as true for bilateral investment as external sources. China is not yet thought of as a major overseas investor. MOFTEC's figures for China's approved foreign investments to 1996, excluding Hong Kong, was $2.118bn. Investment stock in Russia was put at $95.965m (which constituted 49 per cent of JV capital) in 228 enterprises. This represented 4.5 per cent and 11.8 per cent of respective totals indicating that the average investment in Russia at $0.42m was only 40 per cent of the national average (*ACFERT*, 1997–98). Some Russian estimates for investment in the FE suggest that much of this activity was taking place there (Kostyunina 1997). Russian investment stock in China, 1992–96, was of a similar order – $134m. This data indicates an emerging investment relationship and in China's case, when taken with the resource constraints identified above, indicates the means as well as the motives towards external resourcing. China's other primary interests in regional opening will be labour supply and transport.

China has the largest labour force of any country in the world at 688m, 56.3 per cent of the population, in 1996. The Dongbei's labour force was 48.6m but the share of the labour force in the population was lower at 46.5 per cent (and for Heilongjiang only 42.1 per cent) indicating problems of unemployment and under-employment exceeding the national average (SSB 1997). China has always seen labour contracts as one of the major advantages of opening with Russia, and in particular with Siberia and the RFE. In the first years of opening, however, this issue became embroiled with that of cross-border migration. In excess of a million people a year were moving between the two countries, with Russian sources claiming that an unknown number of Chinese were not returning. Even after the sharp reduction in crossings in 1994 due to the collapse in barter trade and the introduction of a new visa regime the issue persisted, being reported in the Russian media in terms of the 'silent colonisation' of the FE. This was unsupported by the numbers of the illegals seized, however, and attitudes to the Chinese varied depending on provincial perspectives. Thus, V. D'yachenko of Amur oblast' administration, the centre of much of the re-export trade, told *Izvestiya* in 1995 that 'the priming of anti-Chinese hysteria looks very much like planned activity' (Skosirev 1995). The motivation behind this activity was largely to defend the interests of sections of the regional elite from Chinese business operations. The RFE was not being singled out for unusual practices. The Chinese were conducting business as they do throughout East Asia, although as is well known this can cause problems with indigenous populations. Even so, there was no hard evidence of anti-Chinese feeling among general population in the RFE: data gathered in 1994–95 indicated that fewer than a quarter of Far Easterners were hostile to Chinese, although two-thirds considered there to be a threat of Chinese expansion (Larin 1997; Lukin 1998). The issue of migration should be receding, however: Head of the Border Guard Service, A. Nikolyaev, was reported by Xinhua in mid-1997 as saying that illegal crossings had been reduced by five-sixths in two years (*BBC-SWB-FE/2962, G/1,*

4 July 1997). This issue can now, perhaps, be disentangled from that of labour cooperation. China had around 10,000 personnel in the RFE in 1997 working mainly in construction and agriculture but there is an expectation that this figure can be substantially increased in the future.

The last area of cooperation is likely to be transport. The interior of the Dongbei is constrained by its lack of access to the Sea of Japan. This infrastructural problem has of course been influenced by the border issue. With this settled the possibility of creating an open transit region arises, west to east – Chita-Harbin-Vladivostok – and north to south – Zabaikal'ya and RFE to Liaodong (Li 1994). This question is clearly linked to the other, spatial dimension of regionalism – creating open areas where goods are not only exchanged but processed.

The most ambitious plan for open regionalism is of course the Tumen River Delta Project. A great deal has been written about this because it seems to answer the combined questions of investment location, resource processing and access to the Sea of Japan. However, the barriers to its realisation, both political and economic, remain formidable. Politically balancing the interests of China, Russia, and North Korea is highly complex, particularly when the centre-region dimension in each country is taken into account.[14] In the case of China it should be recognised that the project lacks the support of powerful regional forces on which so much of China's development strategy depends, although this is self-fulfilling – the provinces of the interior are less powerful precisely because they lack external access. Economically, it can be questioned whether Tumen is a natural economic territory; the boundary between the three states is a rather arbitrary political one, lacking in geographic or infrastructural features, though Jilin is doing much to overcome the latter. Certainly, Liaodong does not view Tumen as its future competitor in the north; this position is held by Vladivostok. The TRDP may yet be realised but in the present circumstances it is not surprising that most attention is being paid to bilateral opening, although even here progress is limited.

The combined border exports of Heilongjiang, Jilin and Inner Mongolia were $997m in 1995, equivalent to 24.5 per cent of total exports, and $1011m imports, or 30 per cent of total imports. The share of the four main open areas in border exports and imports was 16.2 per cent and 28.3 per cent respectively. The main export area was Heihe with Amur oblast' (7.8 per cent of border exports) and the major import areas were Suifenhe with Primorskii krai and Manzhouli with Chita oblast' (10.3 per cent and 13.6 per cent of border imports respectively) (*ACFERT* 1996–97). As this suggests border trade played an important part in local economies, and for Heilongjiang at provincial level, but there was no evidence as yet of open areas having a decisive impact. This is supported by data on investment with contracted FDI in the open areas at $60m for 1995, compared with close to $2bn for the three provinces as a whole. Thus the open areas should presently be characterised as entrepots rather than export-processing zones equivalent to those of the coast. Liaoning's four development zones in contrast contracted $1.35bn in FDI and contributed $1.14bn in exports in 1995.

On this basis the regional dimension of China's relationship with the RFE appears at a very early stage of development but the impetus towards increasing engagement on the Chinese side is very strong. It is driven at the central level by the need to expand and diversify resource access and, in time, to maximise investment potential. At the regional level it is driven by pressures to maintain pace with national development and meet the challenges of economic reform through increased external orientation. What is not clear is how the development of regional level relations will fit into the overall economic relationship between the two countries. Regional relations have the potential to become a genuine vehicle for deepening that relationship but a succession of problems must be overcome, only some of which are exclusively economic. Many exist in the interface between centre and regional government, particularly on the Russian side. The major obstacle may be the divergence of interests, and consequently the strategy of engagement, in developing relations with China. Above all the fear at the regional level that the Far East will be Sinified, economically and demographically, must be overcome. The answer to this lies in stable development of mutual advantage. It should also be made clear that the alternative, continuing protectionism, is not really viable in the context of the future East Asian economy – none of China's neighbours are going to be immune the consequences of living next to one of the world's pivotal economies. Rather constructive engagement may be both inevitable and ultimately beneficial. These arguments are put so concisely by V.G. Gel'bras (1995: 43) that they merit citation at length:

> Fear paralyses the will and in no way enables sober judgement and considered action. It is impossible to found positive strategies of development on defensive concepts. Only offense and not defence can be the key to success. That truth is obvious and has long been known. The 'offensive' for contemporary and future Russia may, and should, mean one thing – the consistent management of Siberia and the Far East.
>
> China is our neighbour and Russia must not be shut off from it, bristling with bayonets and missiles, but promoting the resolution of the complex problems of that country, mindful of its own interests. Russia is vitally interested in a flourishing China. The primary path to the realisation of the strategic interests of Russia lies above all in the creation of complex of export-oriented production on the basis of in-depth processing of domestic resources, along with the information, consultation and specialisation of foreign trade organisations, operating in close interaction with the equivalent structures of the PRC.

CONCLUSIONS

As in the past, China's relations with the Russian Far East will both reflect the wider Sino-Russian relationship and influence it. The challenge for regional relations in the future is to establish a more stable and beneficial influence on the overall relationship than has been possible previously. This above all means economic interaction. There is no question that this will present real challenges to Russian policy-makers and enterprises. These will include: competition over foreign investment; high demand for primary resources and intermediate goods produced with these resources, especially energy; problems of adaptation on both sides given what Tian (1999, p. 88) identifies as the 'clash of cultures' (*wenming de chongzhuang*); and, an important area which it has not been possible to develop, the environmental consequences of China's industrialisation. However, given that the principal obstacles to development of the RFE in the past have been investment sources, labour supply and market access, China should be seen as presenting at least as many solutions as it does problems.

At present, too much emphasis is being placed on the differences in scale between the future Chinese economy and Russia and its regions. This has been discussed here but the essential factor to keep in view is the developmental gap between macroeconomic change in China and the economic reality as it exists in the villages, townships, cities and provinces, of which Northeast China is a compelling example. The problems presented by the need to close this gap will absorb China's efforts well into the next century and, since the open door is now irreversible, present unequalled opportunities for neighbouring economies to participate. An effective and stable model for the participation of the RFE awaits development, but the potential for cooperation must eventually outweigh the problems of interdependence.

NOTES

1 A discussion of early debates in Kerr (1995). A later assessment in International Affairs (1998).
2 For evidence that the partnership was orginally proposed by Russia see, Kuang Chiao Ching (1994). On China's attitude to change in European security structures see, Bogoliubov (1998).
3 Spatial inequality in China is much debated. Ash concludes that the 'proposition that growth polarisation has been an outcome of mainland China's open-door strategy can be accepted, but with qualification.' Ash (1995) p. 14.
4 Johnston (1999) argues for the superiority of a manufacturing zones framework, as opposed to the conventional regional analysis framework (MZF/RAF), for interpreting spatial change in China. This approach highlights more the north-south, as opposed to coast-interior, division.
5 On the relationship between regional and industrial reform see,China's Foreign Trade (1998).
6 On China's concern's for political and ethnic stability in Russia see, Hsin Pao (1996).
7 The data from Arbatov (1999) and Wang (1999) indicate that Chinese military expenditure as a share of GDP is still less than Russian (1.9 per cent and 2.97 per cent in 1998), though

the gap is closing markedly (1.9 per cent and 5.6 per cent in 1994). The 1998 figures imply approximate equality in nominal terms; in purchasing power parity terms the gap widens considerably. See discussion below.

8 Official growth figures have been used to allow comparison for individual years. If World Bank estimates with revised deflation for China's average growth between 1986–96 are used the differences are, for our purposes, minimal: GDP would have reached $3152.9bn by 1996 and per capita GDP $2556, giving ratios of 5.04 and 0.60 respectively (as opposed to 5.33 and 0.64).

9 On China's acceptance of non-state relations between Russia and Taiwan see Foreign Minster Qian Qichen's press conference in Moscow in April 1997, in *BBC-SWB-FE/2904*, *G/1*, 28 April 1997.

10 Cited in Tsui (1983), p. 30.

11 On the bilateral economic relationship see, Kerr (1998). A Russian assesment in Kulik (1997). Chinese assessments in Shi (1996) and Tian (1999).

12 On 'the local competition state' in China, and the role of FDI see, Breslin (1996).

13 Assessment of comparative resources in Sheingauz and Ono (1995).

14 Zabrovskaya (1995) can be contrasted with Xia (1994).

REFERENCES

Abazov, R. (1997) 'Politika Rossii v ATR: smena paradigm', *MEiMO*, Moscow. 2, 23–34.

Almanac of China's Foreign Economic Relations and Trade (ACFERT) (1997–98) Beijing.

Arbatov, A. (1998) 'Military reform in Russia', *International Security*, 22 (4) 83–134.

Arbatov, A. (1999) 'Russia: Military Reform', *SIPRI Yearbook 1999*, pp. 195–212.

Ash, R. (1995) 'Mainland China's emerging role in the world economy', *Issues and Studies* (Taipei), 1, 1–26.

Bickers, C. (1997) 'Bear market', *Far Eastern Economic Review*, 4 September, pp. 25–26.

Breslin, S. (1996) 'China in East Asia: the process and implications of regionalisation', *The Pacific Review*, 9 (4), 463–487.

Bogoliubov, G (1998) 'NATO's Eastward drive: How it affects Russian-Chinese relations', *Far Eastern Affairs*, 1, 38–52.

British Broadcasting Corporation, *Summary of World Broadcasts – Far East*, (BBC-SWB-FE).

Clarke, D.L. (1995) 'A hollow Russian military force in Asia?' *Transition*, 22 September, pp. 24–27.

China's Foreign Trade (1998) 'China's Regional and Industrial Development', Beijing, April, pp. 4–8.

Dibb, P. (1995) *Towards a New Balance of Power in Asia*, London: IISS, Adelphi Paper 295.

Diplomaticheskii Vestnik (1997a) 'Rossisko-Kitaiskaya Sovmestnaya Deklaratsiya o mnogo-polyarnom mire i formirovanii novogo mezhdunarodnogo poryadka', 5, pp. 19–21.

Diplomaticheskii Vestnik (1997b) 'Memorandum', 12, pp. 11–12.

Fitzgerald, C.P. (1972) *The Southern Expansion of the Chinese People*, London.

Foreign Broadcast Information Service-China (FBIS-CHI).

Gel'bras, V.G. (1995) *Aziatsko-Tikhookeanskii Region – Problemy Ekonomicheckoi* Moscow: Bezopasnosti Rossii.

Ginsbergs, G. (1993) 'The end of the Sino-Russian territorial disputes?', *The Journal of Northeast Asian Studies*, 2 (1), 261–320.

Hsin Pao, (1996) 'Sino-Russian relations as viewed from internal report', in *FBIS-CHI 96-129*, 3 July, pp. 9–11.

Hunt, M.H. (1976) 'Chinese Foreign Relations in Historical Perspective', in H. Harding (ed) *China's Foreign Relations in the 80's*, Yale: Yale University Press.

International Affairs (1998) 'Is the World Becoming Multipolar? A Roundtable Discussion', 1, 1–20.

Johnston, M.F, (1999) 'Beyond Regional Analysis: Manufacturing Zones, Urban Employment and Spatial Inequality in China', *China Quarterly*, March, pp. 1–21.

Joint Publication Research Service – China Area Report (JPRS-CAR). Washington DC: Government Printing Office.

Kerr, D. (1995) 'The New Eurasianism: The Rise of Geopolitics in Russian Foreign Policy', *Europe-Asia Studies*, 47 (6), 977–988.

Kerr, D. (1996) 'Opening and Closing the Sino-Russian border: trade, regional development, and political interests in Northeast Asia', *Europe-Asia Studies*, 48 (6), 931–957.

Kerr, D. (1998) 'Problems in Sino-Russian Economic Relations', *Europe-Asia Studies*, 50 (7), 1133–56.

Kerr, D. (1999) 'The Chinese and Russian Energy Sectors: Comparative Change and Potential Interaction', *Post-Communist Economies*, 11 (3), 337–372.

Kostyunina, G. (1997) 'Rossiya i integratsionnye protsessy v aziatsko-tikhookeanskom regione: problemy i vozhmozhnosti uchastiya', *Dal'nii Vostok Rossii*, 1, 10–15.

Kuang Chiao Ching (1994) 'Inside story on Yeltsin's letter to Jiang Zemin, Russian leader's recent visit to Beijing', in *FBIS-CHI-94-130*, 7 July, pp. 9–11.

Kulik, A. (1997) 'The economic carriages have fallen behind the political engine', *Business in Russia*, December, pp. 46–47.

Larin, V. (1997) 'Russia and China on the Threshold of the Third Millennium', *Far Eastern Affairs*, 1, 17–32.

Li Jingjie, (1997) 'Razvitie kitaisko-rossiskykh otnoshenii: ot druzhby k strategicheskomu partnerstvu', *Problemy Dal'nego Vostoka*, 3, 20–33.

Li Xiangping, (1994) 'Liaoning and Economic cooperation in Northeast Asia: opportunities and policy recommendations', *Bohai Shangbao, Shenyang* in *JPRS-CAR-94-37*, 17 June. pp. 18–20.

Lukin, A. (1998) 'The Image of China in Russian Border Regions', *Asian Survey*, 38 (9), 821–835.

Lu Zhongwei (1993) 'Northeast Asia's Economic Cooperation and its Prospects', *Xiandai Guoji Guangxi*, in *JPRS-CAR-93-002*, 14 January 1–4.

Ma Jun, Zou Gang, (1991) 'On opening up China's inland border provinces and autonomous regions to the outside world', *Jingji Yanjiu*, in *JPRS-CAR-91-043*, 19 July, 45–53.

Pierre, A.J., Tremin. D, (1997) 'Developing Russia-NATO relations', *Survival*, 39, (1), 5–18.

Problemy Dal'nego Vostoka (1995) 'Interesy Rossii v Severo-Vostochnoi Azii i perspektivy ispol'zovaniya mnogostoronnego sotrudnichestva so stranami regiona dlya razvitiya rossiiskogo Dal'nego Vostoka', 2, 4–37.

Ren Ruoen, (1997) *China's Economic Performance in International Perspective*, Paris: OECD.

Sheingauz, A., Ono, H., (eds) (1995) *Natural Resources and Environment in Northeast Asia: Status and Challenges*, Tokyo: Sasakawa Peace Foundation.

Shi Ze (1996) 'On Sino-Russian relations in a new era', *Guoji Wenti Yanjiu*, in *FBIS-CHI-96-148*, 31 July, pp. 7–10.

Skosirev, V (1995) 'Grozit li nashemu Dal'nemu Vostoku kitaiskaya kolonizatsiya?', *Izvestiya*, 16 March, p. 3.

State Statistical Bureau of PRC (SSB, 1997) *Statistical Yearbook of China 1997*.

Tian Chunsheng (1999) 'Zhong-E jingji guanxi de zou shi ji qi yinsu fenxi' (The Changing Situation in Sino-Russian economic relations and its causes analysed) *Taiping Yang Xuebao*, 1, 85–89.

Tsui Tsien-hua (1983) *The Sino-Soviet Border Dispute in the 1970's*, Canada: Mosaic Press.

Voskresenskii, A (1996) 'Veter s zapada ili s vostoka?', *Svobodnaya Mysl'*, 9, 89–100.

Waggener. T.R., Backman C.A., (1997) 'Russian Trade with links with China: Research Report on Forest Products', *Post-Soviet Geography and Economics*, 38 (1), 47–58.

Wang Shaoguang (1999) 'The Military Expenditure of China, 1989–98', *SIPRI Yearbook 1999*, 334–349.

Wang Yueping, (1996) 'Conflicts and Options facing China's Overgrown Foreign Trade', *Guoji Maoyi Wenti*, in *FBIS-CHI-96-057*, 22 March, 33–39.

World Bank (1995) *China: Macroeconomic Stability in a Decentralised Economy*, Washington: The World Bank.

Xia Youfu (1994) 'Comparing Development Models for Tumen Jiang', *Shije Jingji*, in *JPRS-CAR-94-026*, 27 April, 16–21.

Zabrovskaya, L. (1995)'The Tumangang Project: A View from the Primorie', *Far Eastern Affairs*, 1, 34–51.

Chapter 11

South Korean Relations with the Russian Far East

Chung-Bae Lee

INTRODUCTION

During the Cold War, economic and political interaction between South Korea and the former Soviet Union was severely limited. Gorbachev's policy of Perestroyka had a considerable impact on the former Soviet Union's relations with Northeast Asian countries, including South Korea. As a part of Gorbachev's Asian initiatives, the Soviet Union sought to establish economic relations with South Korea. In line with the Soviet Union's economic interest in South Korea, Seoul saw political benefit in establishing ties with Moscow. The perceived mutual benefits for both countries led to the establishment of diplomatic relations in September 1990, after which bilateral economic and political relations rapidly improved. During the early 1990s, a boom in economic relations between South Korea and the former Soviet Union resulted from their political interaction with each other. South Korean businesses rushed to visit Moscow and other cities in the Soviet Union in order to seize business opportunities. In particular, the Soviet (Russian) Far East attracted South Korea's business community because, not only is it very close to the Korean peninsula, it also had a vast resource base. South Korea, with few raw materials of its own, hoped to obtain raw materials from the Russian Far East (hereafter RFE).

However, little time was taken by the South Korean business community to understand the realities of the RFE. They lacked knowledge and experience regarding the region. They also lacked the technology to overcome the harsh realities of doing business in the RFE. The high expectations of South Korea towards Russia, including the RFE, declined as rapidly as the boom had arrived. Some companies abandoned their opportunities without hesitation while others became more cautious in carrying out their potential projects in Russia. For those

204

that remained, the Asian financial crisis and then the Russian financial crisis brought the end to their investment interests in Russia.

SOUTH KOREA-SOVIET RELATIONS DURING THE SOVIET PERIOD

Official diplomatic relations between Korea and Russia (Imperial Russia) date back to 1884 when the two countries concluded a Mutual Commercial Protection Agreement. However, relations were halted in 1910 after Japan's victories in the Sino-Japanese War (1894–1895) and Russo-Japanese War (1904–1905), because Japan annexed Korea by force. After the end of the Second World War, Japanese forces were expelled from Korea and the peninsula divided into North and South Korea by the Soviet Union and the United States respectively. With the onset of the cold war, South Korea became associated with the West, being led by the United States, while North Korea was under the Soviet Union's influence. South Korea was devastated by the North Korean invasion of 1950; which has the support of the Soviet leader. Consequently, the Soviet Union resisted any contact with South Korea.

The short-lived period of East-West détente during the early 1970s provided Soviet leaders with an opportunity to deal with Seoul more flexibly and, in tandem with changes in Soviet foreign policy, the South Korean government responded positively. With Japan's participation in resource development in Siberia and the Soviet Far East, motivated by the oil crisis at that time, South Korea also hoped to establish economic relations with the Soviet Union. However, this did not happen because the Cold War revisited the international political arena due to Soviet Union's military intervention of Afghanistan in 1979. Furthermore, the shooting down in 1983 of a Korean 747 Airline, with 269 passengers aboard, by Soviet jets led Seoul to shift to a firm anti-Communist position.

Gorbachev's perestroyka paved the way to reconcile the antagonism between Seoul and Moscow. Gorbachev attempted to improve relations with East Asian countries, including South Korea, during late 1980s because he thought it would help his reform policy by activating economic relations between the two countries. His speeches in the RFE aimed to display warm gestures towards neighboring countries to the east that responded positively to them. In particular, the South Korean government, which was pursuing a policy *nordpolitik* at that time, responded positively through frequent visits by business people, scholars and government officials to Moscow.[1] Although the two countries had different expectations regarding the interaction between them, they were ready to compromise with each other. A compromise in which Seoul expected to gain political support from Moscow and the Soviet Union hoped to gain economic benefits from South Korea. This led to the establishment of diplomatic relations in September 1990.

SOUTH KOREAN TRADE AND INVESTMENT WITH RUSSIA

Boom in Economic Relations (1988–1991)

Improved political climate in Soviet-South Korean relations was followed by development of economic relations during the early perestroyka period. In the initial stages of their relations the South Korean business community expected that access to Soviet Union's market would provide great business opportunities, because of its big market, high technologies and a vast resource base. Therefore, prior to and after the opening of diplomatic relations, a number of South Korean businesses, especially South Korea's *Chaebol*, rushed into the Soviet Union proposing numerous megaprojects. The major projects outlined in the media between 1988 and 1991 were valued at nearly $5.6 billion; amounting to 48 projects and averaging $118.6 million per project (Lee C 1995:. 185–188). Many planned investment projects focused on Siberia and the Soviet Far East, in manufacturing (45.7 per cent in terms of case number), construction (16.1 per cent), resource development (18.5 per cent), construction (15.1 per cent) and fishery and food (4.9 per cent) and the business sector.

South Korea, deficient in energy resources, also hoped to develop fuel and power projects in the Soviet Union. The large-scale development projects proposed by the South Korean government and industrial conglomerates included the Yakut Natural Gas Project in Sakha and offshore oil, liquefied natural petroleum development offshore of Sakhalin and coal project in Elginskoe. Among the South Korean *Chaebol*, Hyundai, led by Chung Ju-yong, the honorary chairman of the Hyundai Business Group, was the most impressive in terms of the scale of planned projects. He frequently visited the Soviet Union to announce mammoth investment projects including an aluminum refinery in East Siberia and a petrochemical complex at Tobol'sk, both worth nearly $1 billion (see also Randolph 1990: 1171–72). However, doubts were already emerging concerning the realization of some projects, particularly the large-scale projects, because they were poorly prepared without due consideration of their economic feasibility (Chon 1989: 1183–85). The reasons for the poor performance of South Korea's investment strategy in the Soviet Union are as follows. Firstly, South Korean firms had little knowledge regarding the Soviet economic system, commercial practices, investment environment and infrastructure conditions. Secondly, the gloomy outlook for the Soviet economic and political situation. Thirdly, due to the Soviet Union's chronic shortage of hard currency, South Korea was required to self-finance any projects they initiated in the Soviet Union. Considering that South Korean companies were in a weak financial position, they could not proceed without the government's full financial support. Finally, the unsatisfactory performance of most Japanese projects in Siberia and the Soviet Far East during the 1970s had a negative influence in South Korea's investment decisions (Lee C 1995, p. 189).[2] This became more evident when examining the projects actually invested in. Total investment up to

1991 was $17.5 million in six projects. Investments such as Hyundai's Svetlaya project had symbolic meaning politically, rather than being feasible in money terms (see *Table 11.1*).

In comparison, with the insignificant amount or actual investment, growth in bilateral trade was real. Although trade between the two countries began in 1979, it was very limited until the late 1980s, due to political factors and systemic discrepancy. Since that time it has increased sharply. In 1979, the volume of trade accounted for a mere $11.6 million, but from 1979 to 1986 trade increased steadily, exceeding $100 million in 1985. During the same period the average annual growth was 39.2 percent and the volume increased ten-fold. Warm gestures towards the East Asian countries by the Soviet Union, such as Gorbachev's speech in Vladivostok, provided confidence to those in the South Korean business community involved in trade with the Soviet Union. Consequently, the volume of trade increased considerably reaching $200.3 million in 1987, 70.2 per cent up from the previous year and $289.9 million in 1988, up 44.7 percent. The reasons for the expansion was the improved political climate, which contributed to reducing risk in trade and the establishment of institutional and technical frameworks for trade. A bilateral trade agreement was signed in December 1990. In the late 1980s, trade and consular offices were established in Seoul and Moscow and maritime transport routes were established between Pusan and Vladivostok to facilitate bilateral trade. Following the opening of Hyundai's office in Moscow in 1990, other large South Korean companies rented office space in the Soviet Union, so that by the end of 1991 six companies had established their branches in Moscow and other Soviet cities.[3]

Trade relations between the two countries reached a turning point in 1988 when Gorbachev announced the possibility of economic relations with South

Table 11.1 Trends of South Korean Investment in Russia (1990–97)

Year	Number of Projects			Amount of Investment (thousand dollars)		
	Planned	Actual	Cumulative Actual	Planned	Actual	Cumulative Actual
~1990	5	2	2	9,261	480	480
1991	3	4	6	9,210	16,989	17,469
1992	12	7	13	7,386	3,247	20,716
1993	24	13	26	5,199	3,296	24,012
1994	26	20	46	29,645	11,922	35,934
1995	14	23	69	48,273	30,502	66,436
1996	20	12	81	61,901	41,336	107,772
1997	12	3	84	19,209	7,901	115,673

Source: The Korea Federation of Bank (1998) *Overseas Direct Investment Statistics Yearbook*, Seoul, p. 22.

Korea in his Krasnoyarsk speech. Between 1988–1991 the average annual growth rate of trade was 68.1 percent, rising from $151 million in 1987 to $599 million in 1991.[4] South Korea diversified its import and export items, although a few of them still dominated the total trade, especially in the case of imports. Marine products, including fish (23.2 per cent), mineral resources (8.1 per cent) and steel products (19.0 per cent) were the dominant imports of South Korea while manufacturing products such as electronic and electronics (32.4 per cent), daily necessities (17.1 per cent) were the main exports to the Soviet Union.

From 1979 to 1983, South Korea enjoyed a trade surplus with the Soviet Union. However, during the period 1983 to 1990 South Korea had a negative trade balance. In 1989 alone a deficit of $184 million was recorded, accounting for 30.7 percent of the two-way trade between the two countries. Such a deficit was caused by an increase in raw material imports from the Soviet Union. In 1990 the trade balance changed again this time, reaching $149.5 million in favour of South Korea. In the following year the balance narrowed to $47.8 million partly due to increased imports of consumer products from the Soviet Union. It was clear that the Soviet Union had the potential to play a major role as the source of raw materials for South Korea, rather than as an export market for South Korea's manufactured goods (see *Figure 11.1*).

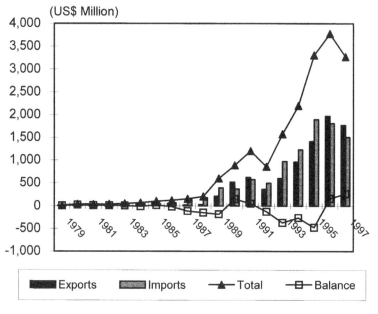

Figure 11.1 South Korea's Trade with the former Soviet Union (Russia) (1979–1997)

South Korea hoped to diversify the source of its resource imports when it had begun to trade with the Soviet Union. In 1988, South Korea imported 1.4 million tons coal from Russia worth $62 million. Although imports of coal were stable for the next 2 years but fell reduced sharply to 0.5 million tons worth 25 million in 1991 and then stopped. In 1991, South Korea also imported small amount of oil, worth $5.4 million, but this also stopped because it is not economical. When South Korea discovered that there were severe limitations to importing raw materials from Russia, it attempted to become directly involved in resource development in Russia, particularly in the RFE.

The Geopolitics of South Korean-Russian Relations

The development of economic relations between South Korea and the Soviet Union had a favorable impact on their political relations. After the two countries established diplomatic relations, political relations developed significantly, isolating North Korea diplomatically. As requested by the South Korean government, the Soviet Union encouraged Pyongyang to develop contacts with Seoul.

The South Korean President Roh, encouraged by the establishment of diplomatic relations with the Soviet Union, paid a hasty visit to Moscow in November 1990 in order to strengthen ties. At the meeting with Gorbachev, Roh asked Moscow to play a more active role in promoting inter-Korean relations, promising South Korea's economic support for the Soviet Union's economic reform. Roh promised to encourage the South Korean business community to establish business links, focusing on Siberian development projects. In January 1991, Seoul announced a $3 billion loan package to support Soviet economic reform. This included $1 billion in cash loans, $1.5 billion in tied loans for the purchase of South Korean consumer goods, and $500 million for deferred payment for the procurement of industrial plant and equipment.[5]

The development of Soviet-South Korean relations produced tangible achievements in inter-Korean relations. Firstly, North Korea, fearing isolation from other socialist countries, accepted talks with Seoul. As a result the premiers of both Koreas have met five times in Seoul and Pyongyang respectively to discuss inter-Korean affairs. Although the talks failed to produce an expected summit meeting, they produced two accords, 'The Agreement on Reconciliation, Non-aggression, and Exchanges and Cooperation,' and 'The Joint Declaration of the Denuclearization of the Korean peninsula' at the end of 1991. Secondly, both Koreas, neither of whom had had a seat in the United Nations (UN), mainly due to the veto of two members of Security Council, the Soviet Union and the United States, became members of the United Nations in September 1991. The simultaneous entry of the two Koreas into the UN had been rejected by North Korea. Therefore, the decision by the UN can be regarded as the victory of South Korean diplomacy over North Korea. With improved relations between North and South, many South Korean businesses paid visits to North Korea to express their intention to do business with the North. However, those warm inter-Korean relations ended with the nuclear issue initiated by Pyongyang in 1992.

The Honeymoon is Over?

Gorbachev's reform policies did not always progress smoothly. The domestic economic reform program, not clearly defined, crippled the later period of Gorbachev's leadership. Economic hardship and demands of independence from several Republics made hard-liners attempt to reverse the reforms. The August Coup of 1991, led by several hard-liners, ended in failure but speeded up the collapse of the Soviet Union, which broke into fifteen republics at the end of 1992. As a result Yeltsin, the President of the Russian Federation succeeded Gorbachev. The collapse of the Soviet Union further aggravated the internal and external economic conditions in the former Soviet republics. The foreign trade system of the Soviet Union, already damaged by the collapse of the CMEA system, was paralyzed by the collapse of inter-Republican trade (Smith, pp. 172–175).

Gorbachev's pro-Seoul foreign policy had been criticized by some politicians in the Soviet Union. They argued a one-sided pro-Seoul policy would weaken the Soviet Union's influence on the Korean peninsula as a whole. They urged the government to maintain an equi-distance stance, improving relations with Pyongyang and China (*Far Eastern Economic Review*, Nov. 30 1995, pp. 28–29). Similarly, South Korea was not always satisfied with its relations with the Soviet Union, expressing dissatisfaction with Moscow's influence over North Korea. In fact, since perestroyka, North Korea had attempted to strengthen links with China in both political and economic spheres, in turn Moscow's leverage over Pyongyang has declined. The extension of the loan to the Soviet Union was already being criticized by many scholars and politicians in Seoul. Although few expressed these views, the relations between the two countries obviously declined, compared to the boom period prior up to 1991. The uncertainty caused by the August 1991 coup, the disintegration of the Soviet Union, and subsequent creation of fifteen newly independent states further diminished prospects for bilateral trade and economic relations.

South Korea's loan ($1.53 billion) to the Soviet Union, suspended by the Coup, was canceled due to the default of interest payments and the South Korean government's doubts on repayment of the loan's principal.[6] Consequently, the volume of trade dropped because South Korea's trade was highly dependent on the loans guaranteed by the government. They needed to seek new partners to continue their businesses with the former Soviet Union. Furthermore, the South Korean business community was confused by events in the former Soviet Union. For example, the representatives of the Republics and local governments emerged as new business partners, replacing the Soviet government. South Korean business had to become accustomed to doing business in new business environments that had new institutions, regulations and laws.

In 1992 South Korean trade with the former Soviet Union decreased by 28 per cent compared to the previous year. Total trade amounted to $859.1 million, a reduction of 40 per cent compared to the previous year. The decline of exports (71.4 per cent) was worse than that of imports (18.9 per cent) mainly because of a shortage of hard currency in all the republics of the former Soviet Union. This reduced the Russian importers' ability to pay for goods and was compounded by the South Korean government's suspension of credit for exports (see *Figure 11.1*). Although South Korea's trade statistics were divided by the republics of the former Soviet Union in 1992, they were incomplete. Complete data were published in 1993, when trade between the former Soviet Union and South Korea recovered, up to 117.5 per cent of the previous year, valued at $1.8 billion. Russia's was the dominant trade partner, occupying about 83 per cent of the former Soviet trade with South Korea. However Russia's proportion declined gradually and occupied 70 per cent in 1996 (see *Table 11.2*).

A small amount of South Korean capital was invested in Russia between 1992–93. Although the number of projects increased compared with the previous years, the total amount of investment decreased during this period. This meant that the size of the projects declined. The volume of actual investment stood at $5.4 million in 8 projects, averaging $0.68 million in 1992, but this fell to $2.27 million, 16 cases, and $0.14 million per project in 1993 (see *Table 11.1*).

Table 11.2 Korea's Exports and Imports to the CIS (1996) ($ Million, %)

Country	Exports	Imports	Total	Percent of Total
Russia	1,967.5	1,810.3	3,777.8	70.6
Uzbekistan	493.8	196.1	689.9	17.7
Ukraine	104.4	109.7	214.1	3.7
Kazakhstan	105.4	124.7	230.0	3.8
Byelorussia	18.0	6.0	24.0	0.6
Moldova	1.1	0.1	1.3	0.0
Tadjikistan	4.4	6.1	10.6	0.2
Turkmenistan	1.6	1.1	2.6	0.1
Azerbaijan	8.7	2.8	11.5	0.3
Georgia	10.5	1.9	12.4	0.4
Kirghiz Rep	3.5	2.5	6.1	0.1
Armenia	1.1	0.4	1.5	0.0
Estonia	8.3	2.6	10.9	0.3
Lithuania	51.2	27.5	78.7	1.8
Latvia	6.6	8.8	15.5	0.2
Total	2,786.3	2,300.5	5,086.9	100.0

Source: Korea Foreign Trade Association (1997).

It was increasingly clear that South Korean interest in Russian business opportunities had declined. During this period, few South Korean businesses had optimistic views on the Russian economic climate. In addition, the importance of political factors, which had encouraged the South Korean firms to take risk under the government's financial guarantee, had declined. This was not only because the South Korean government had already achieved its main goal, the establishment of diplomatic relations with the Soviet Union but because the influence of Russian-South Korean relations on inter-Korean relations was also declining.

New Geoeconomic and political relations with Russia

With the collapse of the Soviet Union, South Korea sought close relations with Russia and at the same time Moscow still needed financial aid from Seoul. Yeltsin visited Seoul in November 1992, to restore the faith of South Korean investors presenting 23 potential projects in the RFE with the opportunity for cooperation.[7] Yeltsin stressed Russia's Asiatic roots and its desire to participate in Asian affairs, expressing a desire to join the Asia-Pacific Economic Cooperation (APEC). He declared Russia's military aid to North Korea would halt, and gave his support for the non-proliferation of nuclear weapons on the Korean peninsula.

Despite these gestures of support from Yeltsin for South Korea on the nuclear issue with North Korea, Russia's evident intention was to exercise its influence over both Koreas. Pointing to the fact that Russia has assisted North Korean nuclear technology, Russia proposed an eight party conference between the US, Russia, China, Japan and North and South Korea to solve the nuclear issue on the Korean peninsula (*Far Eastern Economic Review,* Dec. 29 1994: 14–15; *Korea Time* 17 Apr. 1996).

After Yeltsin's visit to attract South Korea's investment, South Korea's investment activity increased steadily. Between 1993 and 1997 total investment by South Korea in Russia amounted to $91.6 million, averaging $18.3 million per year (see *Table 11.1*). However, it is worth noting that the amount fell sharply to $7.9 million in 1997, just 20 per cent of the previous year due to the financial crisis in South Korea. Up to 1997, cumulative investment was $115.7 million in 84 projects. Despite the increase in South Korea's investment in Russia, this amount is very modest, constituting 0.7 per cent of South Korea's total investment around world in 1997. Furthermore, Russia's share, although similar to Kazakhstan, fell behind that of Uzbekistan within the CIS.[8]

In terms of the number of projects, the sector of greatest interest to the South Korean businesses was manufacturing (31.3 per cent), followed by trade (30.1 per cent), fishery (7.2 per cent). In term of amount of investment, the focus was also on manufacturing (41.1 per cent), followed by mining (21.7 per cent) and the trade sector (5.3 per cent) (see *Table 11.3*).

Hyundai's Svetlaya project (timber processing in the Far East region) was the largest of the South Korean investments in Russia, and was started in 1990.

Table 11.3 South Korean Investment in Russia by Sector (As of 1997)

Sector	Number of Projects			Amount of Investment (thousand dollars)		
	Planned	*Actual*	*Percent(Act.)*	*Planned*	*Actual*	*Percent(Act.)*
Mining	2	1	1.2	25,140	25,121	21.7
Forestry	2	2	2.4	1,500	493	0.4
Fishery	7	6	7.2	5,568	2,481	2.1
Manufacturing	41	26	31.3	64,999	47,549	41.1
Trade	33	25	30.1	13,294	6,148	5.3
Others	27	23	27.7	78,159	33,807	29.2
Total	112	83	100.0	188,660	115,599	100.0

Source: The Korea Federation of Banks (1998) *Overseas Direct Investment Statistics Yearbook*, p. 41.

South Korea's investment projects were dominant by the *Chaebol*, Hyundai, Samsung, LG (previously named 'Lucky-Goldstar') and Daewoo. As illustrated in *Table 11.4*, the total value of the top ten projects was $51.9 million, which accounted for 78.7 per cent of the total capital investment in Russia.

In contrast to investment, increases in trade were apparent in South Korean-Russian economic relations. Between 1994–97, the volume of trade increased by 50 per cent reaching $3.27 billion in 1997 (exports: $1.77 billion, imports: $1.50 billion). However, it is worth noting that between 1996–97 the volume of

Table 11.4 Major Investment Projects of South Korea in Russia (As of 1995) ($1,000)

Investor	Location	Permitted Date	Sector	Share (%)	Capital invested
Hyundai	Vladivostok	10/90	Timber	50	16,000
LG	USSR	1/92	Telecommunication	50	1,500
KAIST	Petersburg	6/92	Technology devel.	42	1,500
Hyundai	Vladivostok	2/94	Hotel	70	13,470
Young Distribution	Moscow	8/94	Manufacturing	70	4,865
Dacom	Russia	2/95	Telecommunication	50	1,937
Samsung Electronics	Moscow	2/95	Telecommunication	49	2,118
Jinro International	Moscow	5/95	Food	70	3,587
Korea Steel	Russia	7/95	Base Metal	38	5,000
Samsung Electronics	Russia	10/95	Telecommunication	71	1,900

Source: Bank of Korea.

bilateral trade dropped by 13.4 per cent for the first time and the balance of trade turned positive in South Korea's favour in 1996. The commodity structure of Russia-South Korea trade has been relatively stable. Electronics and electrical products still dominate South Korea's exports to Russia, accounting for 52 per cent, followed by machinery & movement vehicles (14.8 per cent) and primary products (13.3 per cent). Major South Korean imports from Russia consist of steel and metal products (45.7 per cent), followed by agro-fishery products (21.9 per cent) and chemicals (19.5 per cent) (see *Table 11.5*). This trade pattern is akin to that between a developed and less developed country.

The RFE soon emerged as the focus for South Korean investment in Russia. As shown in *Figure 11.2*, most of South Korean investment projects were located in the RFE (58.2 per cent), followed by the central region, including Moscow, (30.9 per cent), and East Siberia, both in terms of total value as well as number of projects. Russia also encouraged South Korea to set up closer economic relations with the RFE as demonstrated in the proposed projects.

South Korean President, Kim Young-Sam, who succeeded Roh, visited the RFE on route back to Seoul after he met Boris Yeltsin in Moscow in June 1994. During ameeting with Yevgenny Nazdratenko, Governor of the Primorskii Krai, President Kim emphasized the importance of economic cooperation between the two regions. He pointed out the potential investment areas as follows, the fishing industry, utilization of natural gas resources in the Sakha Republic and the development of an industrial estate exclusively for South Korean business in the port of Nakhodka. It is, therefore, not surprising that the South Korean business community concentrated on the RFE, rather than other regions in Russia.

Table 11.5 Structure of South Korean-Russian Trade (1996)

Exports	%	Imports	%
Primary products	13.31	Agro-fishery products	21.90
Chemical goods	1.15	Mining products	4.43
Plastics, rubber and leather products	1.67	Chemical products	19.49
Non-metal mineral products	3.26	Steel, metal products	45.70
Clothes & textile	9.10	Machinery & vehicles	5.19
Necessities	2.81	Electronics & electrical goods	0.31
Steel, metal products	1.74	Clothes & textiles	2.71
Electronics & electrical products	51.81	Others	0.26
Machinery & movement vehicles	14.78		
Miscellaneous products	0.38		
Total	100.00		100.00

Source: Korea International Trade Association (1997).

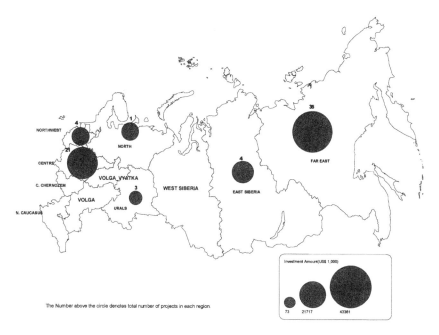

The Number above the circle denotes total number of projects in each region.

Figure 11.2 Geographical Distribution of Actual Investment Projects of
South Korea in Russia (As of 1995)

INVESTMENT ATTITUDE OF SOUTH KOREAN BUSINESSES TOWARDS THE RFE

South Korea's Economic Interaction with the RFE

The possibilities of economic benefits being shared between the RFE and
Northeast Asian countries had already been proposed as early as the late 1960s
(See Khun 1996 and Li 1997).[9] As early as the first half of the 1970s, Japan
displayed considerable interest in developing Siberian and Soviet Far Eastern
resources. But before perestroyka, the political environment presented many
obstacles to the development of economic relations with Northeast Asia. The
subsequent change in the political climate ushered in new opportunities for
economic cooperation between Russia and its neighbours (Segal 1993, p. 69).
The share of total Russian trade with the Asia-Pacific region increased from less
than 10 percent in 1991 to 16.5 percent in 1993. However, the trend reversed
between 1993–1995 because of a sharp decline in Russian imports, principally
from China. This was despite the fact that Russia's declining trade with its
former CMEA partners in Central Europe tended to enhance the relative
importance of the Asia-Pacific Region.

According to Russian trade statistics (*Goskomstat Rossii*, each years), the share of Northeast Asian in Russian foreign trade turnover increased from 4.8 percent in 1986 to 7.25 per cent in 1990 and again expanded to 8.64 per cent in 1995. Furthermore, those four countries made up 80.4 per cent of the RFE trade turnover in 1992, accounting for $2.74 billion. Although there were some fluctuations in trade between the two regions, the predominant position of the Northeast Asian countries in trade with the RFE was still maintained, accounting for 73.7 per cent in 1994. As a Northeast Asian country, South Korea was active in increasing economic cooperation with the RFE. Of total South Korean trade with Russia, 23.9 per cent and 24.5 percent flowed from the RFE in 1992 and 1996 respectively (Minakir 1992; *Russian Far East Update*, October 1997: 15).

According to the ROTOBO statistics, by mid-1993 the number of registered investment projects in the RFE was 915, although only 485 projects were actually in operation. More than half of these investment projects were from three countries in Northeast Asia, China, Japan and South Korea. Therefore, there is clear evidence of increased integration between the RFE and the Northeast Asian economy.[10] As shown in *Figure 11.2*, it accounted for the bulk of South Korean investments in terms of cases as well as value, followed by the Central region, which included Moscow (with 30 percent), and East Siberia.

One of the factors cited as grounds for closer economic relations between South Korea and the RFE was the assumed natural fit in their economic structures. Increased opportunities for interaction can also be traced to geographic proximity (the distance from Seoul to Vladivostok is 750 km, as opposed to 10,000 km from Seoul to Mosocw), as well as the fact that nearly 60,000 ethnic Koreans live in RFE. As for the RFE, it has a strong desire to develop its economic relations with Northeast Asian countries to revitalize what is a relatively backward region within Russia. In 1991, as a part of Russian efforts to boost the RFE's economy, the Russian government proclaimed Nakhodka and Sakhalin as Free Economic Zones (FEZ). Yeltsin also signed a decree in April granting the RFE preferential treatment and greater autonomy in foreign economic activities (*Interfax*, 28 May 1992). Furthermore, Yeltsin Russia proposed a number of potential projects focused on the RFE during his visit to Seoul in 1992, as mentioned earlier.

Accordingly, many observers appeared to believe that South Korea and the RFE could benefit from an economic complementarity in which South Korea supplies consumer goods, while the RFE exports raw materials to South Korea's industries (Lho 1989: 1163; Andrianov 1991: 248–251; Drysdale 1991: 3). South Korea, furthermore, hoped to develop natural resource base for its own needs, while the RFE needed foreign capital for its regional development as well as exploitation of its resource base.

In June 1997, the first meeting of the Korean-Russian Joint Committee on Economic, Scientific, and Technological Cooperation was held in Seoul. The construction of the industrial complex in the Nakhodka Free Economic Zone was identified as an important project to serve as the centerpiece for Russian-Korean investment in the Far East. Within the RFE, Primorskii krai dominates South Korean foreign investment, as shown in *Figure 11.3*. According to the Bank of Korea, Primorskii krai received over $33 million from South Korean investors through the mid-1990s, more than 10 times the amount invested in Sakhalin. Given Korea's interest in the Nakhodka Free Economic Zone (e.g., see Kirkow 1997: 310–311), Primorskii krai is likely to remain the key location, especially since Korean companies, thus far, have failed to gain a share of Sakhalin's oil and gas. Even after the financial crises in Asia and Russia, South Korea remains committed to the idea of an industrial park in Nakhodkha (more on this below). However, the project is still far from reality, few foreign companies, let alone South Korean companies, are looking to locate in Primorskii krai at present.

Major Projects of South Korea in the RFE

In the early 1990s, with the improved political climate between South Korea and the former Soviet Union, many companies advanced into Russia to take advantage of the opportunities available there. Due to the relatively favourable economic climate of the RFE, several of the mega-projects under consideration by South

Figure 11.3 South Korean investment in the Russian Far East at the end of 1995

Korean conglomerates were located in the RFE. They included development of resources such as timber, coal, iron ore, aluminum, tin etc. Fishery processing was also attractive to South Korean companies. However, almost of all the projects pronounced at that time were later canceled without any explanation. The projects that have survived are the projects planned at the government level or at least under the South Korea government's support which includes the gas project in Sakha and Irkutsk and the industrial park in Nakhodka. Hyundai, as a private company, is the only Korea *Chaebol* that is involved actively in investment in the RFE. However, Hyundai's investments in the region never proceeded smoothly. From the onset, it faced both local and international environmental opposition to its Svetlaya forestry project (see Lee, C 1995: 323–24, for more details). Eventually, Hyundai pulled out of Svetlaya, a harsh reminder to other South Korean companies of the problems of doing business in Russia.

South Korea also attempted to develop a Yakutia gas field which had been studied by Japan as well as the United States during 1970s (see Egyed 1983; Sagers 1995: 279). Yeltsin's visit to Seoul sought cooperation with South Korea rather than Japan due to political constraints between Japan and Russia (Murakami 1997: 116). In order to realize the project, South Korea conducted a preliminary feasibility study of the Yakutia gas field with Russia and South Korea investing $10 million respectively in 1995. Although its economic viability was not confirmed, South Korea has not abandoned the desire to decvelop these energy resources. The Kovyktinskoye gas condensate deposit in Irkutsk Oblast was found to be more viable in terms of economic potential. In August 1996, the South Korean Company Hanbo Steel joined the Kovytka project by investing $25 million to acquire a 27.5 per cent share of Rusia Petroleum. However, the subsequent bankruptcy of Hanbo forced it to sell off a large part of its equity share to the Siberian Petroleum Company (Sidanko), which then sold it to British Petroleum as part of the deal between BP, Sidanko and Oneximbank. Consequently, South Korean interests now have a very small share (7.5 per cent) of a potential mega-project to deliver natural gas from Siberia to China (Lee and Bradshaw 1997: 475 and Chapter 9). Now, because of the scale of the problems in their domestic economy, South Korean companies are unable to take the kind of risks expected of major players in Russia's resource economy.

As noted above, South Korea agreed to establish an industrial park in the Nakhodka free economic zone with Russia to encourage investments from South Korean companies during Yeltsin's visit to Seoul in November 1992.[11] President Yeltsin approved a plan for Russia and South Korea to set up a joint industrial area, in the RFE in March 1996(*Korea Time*, 12 Mar. 1996). However, many difficulties have arisen between the two sides. Although Russia has promised tax breaks for the project, they were considered as not being satisfactory to South Korea.[12]

Hyundai opened a 13-story Business Center in Vladivostok in cooperation with Vladivostok City municipality in August 1997.[13] Hyundai expected this center to serve as a foothold for the company's ventures in Russia. Although it is too early to assess performance of the project, it was known that Hyundai was suffering from heavy taxation by federal government (Interview, Aug. 1998). Given that Hyundai's Svetlaya timber project is under liquidation; they have little to show for their investments in the RFE. The company plans are now focused on the trade of second-hand cars, construction materials and clothes. No large-scale projects are under consideration due to the recent financial problems in South Korea and Russia.

In sum, there are no examples of South Korean projects that have been successful. Therefore, South Korea's economic interest in the RFE has declined. This was made quite clear while interviewing South Korean companies in August 1998. They were quite pessimistic about the prospects of South Korean companies' investment in the RFE. Although they agreed that there were some profitable projects in the RFE, such as in timber processing and fishing, they still felt it too risky and costly under the current investment climate.[14] They suggested that the best option to take would be trading, rather than direct investments in the RFE. The South Korean financial has also made South Korean companies more reluctant to invest in the RFE. It is also worth mentioning that South Korean companies have many other options for investment, if they have enough, capital to invest in the future. They argued that Southeast Asia and China have better conditions for their investment. Furthermore, with improved relations with North Korea, South Korean companies are more likely to make investments there rather than in the RFE. Considering these factors, without significant improvements of investment climate in the RFE, it is very unlikely that South Korean companies will become major investors in the RFE.

CONCLUSIONS: PROSPECTS FOR
SOUTH KOREAN-RFE ECONOMIC RELATIONS

Since the advent of perestroyka in the 1980s, South Korea and Russia (and the former Soviet Union before) have developed closer economic and political relations. During the initial period of their relations, both countries recognized the potential benefits of closer ties, with South Korea expecting political benefits from Moscow, and Moscow expecting to receive economic assistance. However, South Korean hopes to develop closer economic ties with the Soviet Union proved unrealistic, likely because they were motivated by political considerations at the expense of sound economic planning. Accordingly, only a few investment projects planned by the South Korea during that early period managed to survive. Although the total volume of bilateral economic activity was increasing before the financial crisis befell several Asian countries (and particularly South Korea) in the fall of 1997, the increase seems to have been due to South Korea's desire to gain market access, notwithstanding the deteriorating investment climate in Russia.

Some large-scale projects focusing on natural resource development in Siberia and the RFE were still under consideration in 1997, but they are now likely to take a long time, if ever, to materialize (see also Paik 1995: 236–237). The pessimism surrounding prospects for direct investment is not as evident in bilateral trade, at least prior to the Russian financial crisis. The volume of trade with the RFE, however, may be limited in the near future because the region's market is relatively small compared to South Korea's export potential. However, South Korean businesses did have an interest in the RFE prior to the crisis. That interest, prompted by the need for raw materials, also reflected the comparative price advantage of South Korean consumer goods vis-à-vis Japanese exports to Russia.

Interviews in Seoul in mid-July 1998 revealed a very pessimistic assessment of commercial opportunities in the RFE (and that was before ruble devaluation). The realization of South Korean projects in the RFE is unlikely without government financial support (much of it borrowed in the first place). One notable exception is Hyundai, which recently opened a $100 million business center in Vladivostok. However, the other flagship project, the Korean Business Park in Nakhodka, has yet to break ground and the Korean Land Corporation is struggling to find potential tenants. Now due to the financial crisis in South Korea, the corporation has stopped the project, although there is possibility to continue if the situation improves in the future. When one adds the increasing realism of the South Korean business community regarding the problems of doing business in the RFE to the financial problems at home, it is difficult to sustain much optimism about the prospects for Korean investment in the region. As recent events have shown, economic relations between Russia and South Korea are increasingly based on economic rather than political considerations. In such an environment, the prospective absence of politically motivated government support for trade with Russia will likely prompt the South Korean business community to become even more cautious. Under the new Korean government created in 1998, which is pursuing a policy of reducing direct government intervention into business affairs, South Korea's investment in the RFE could be even more limited in the future. This is because the new government is unlikely to underwrite business with Russia. Furthermore, Russian-South Korean diplomatic tensions caused by the expulsion of a South Korean diplomat from Moscow on spy charges, have also had negative impacts on South Korea's economic relations with Russia (*Korea Time*, 10 Jul. 1998).

In sum, one natural conclusion is that South Korea's investment in Russia and the RFE in particular has waned not only because its interests in the RFE has declined but also because South Korea's ability to secure capital for investment has been reduced. Furthermore, due to financial and political crises in Russia, existing South Korean projects in the RFE have been shelved. At present, the South Korean business community would prefer to trade with the RFE rather than investment there.

NOTES

1 'Nordpolitik' denotes Seoul's foreign policy towards the socialist countries linking between economics and politics and is analogous to the 'Ostpolitik' articulated by Willy Brandt of West Germany in 1970s (see Sanford 1990; Joo 1993).

2 It is also worth noting that most of the projects announced were very similar to projects in which Japan expressed interests during 1970s (see Mathieson 1979).

3 The number increased significantly totaling 125 offices at the end of 1995.

4 According to Russian trade statistics, during the same period Russia's total trade decreased by 16.3 percent.

5 In return for the loan Moscow reportedly offered the following three commitments: firstly, a written commitment on support for South Korea's membership of the UN; secondly, assurances that offensive weapons would no longer be supplied to North Korea; and thirdly, withdrawal of the Soviet assistance in the building of nuclear power facilities north of the demilitarised zone (*FEER*, 7 Feb 1991: 44).

6 The proponents for continuing loans to Russia, mainly officials in diplomatic and political affairs within the government contended that it could continue to help Russia's economic difficulties and would also contribute to the development of relations in the long run. Those against further loans, mainly government officials in economic and financial affairs, argued that the loan should be stopped since Russia could not even afford to pay the interest aside from the debt principal considering the economic situation and foreign debt in Russia.

7 Twenty three investment projects were proposed in November 1992 when Yeltsin visited Seoul included mining (6 projects), timber processing (5), construction (2), fishery processing (2), light industry, ship repairing, tourism etc. in the Russian Far East (*Chosun Ilbo*, 21 Nov. 1992).

8 In 1997, total investment of South Korea is $184 million in Uzbekistan and $110 million in Kazakhstan.

9 For example, Mieczkowski(1968, p. 78) suggested that the economic development of the Soviet Far East could be linked to export of natural resources to the Asian Pacific neighbouring countries rather than the European Soviet region.

10 According to the statistics, in terms of number of companies in operation, Japan accounted for 22.5 per cent, followed by China (15.5 per cent) and South Korea (2.27).

11 According to the initial plan, South Korea was to develop an industrial park renting 330 hectares for 50 years from Russia while Russia was supposed to provide infrastructure such as electricity and water. The total construction cost of the industrial park was estimated at $150 million.

12 The measures provided a 5-year tax holiday for all local taxes after the first return has been reported, and 50 per cent tax reduction for 5 years afterwards.

13 Hyundai's equity share of the project is $8.8 million.

14 The major obstacles to investment in the RFE mentioned in the interviews included incomplete and unpredictable institutional system such as regulations and tax system, distribution system, conflicts between Moscow and local governments, hyperinflation, financial system, unreliable partner, organized crimes and a massive foreign debt.

REFERENCES

Ahn, Byung-joon (1980) 'South Korea and the Communist Countries,' *Asian Survey*, 20 (11), 1098–1107.

Akaha, Tsuneo (1997), *Politics and Economics in the Russian Far East. Changing Ties with Asia-Pacific*, London: Routledge.

Andrianov, V.D. (1991) 'Soviet-South Korean Trade and Economic Cooperation: Possible Avenues and Prospects,' *Sino-Soviet Affairs* (Hanyang University, Seoul), 50 (1), 241–51.

Bae, Young-shik, (1992) 'Soviet-South Korean Economic Cooperation Following Rapprochement,' *Journal of Northeast Asian Studies*, 11 (1), 19–34.

Bradshaw, M.J. (1990) 'Soviet Far Eastern Trade,' in A. Rodgers, ed., *The Soviet Far East. Geographical Perspectives on Development*, London: Routledge, pp. 239–268.

Bradshaw, M.J. (1991) 'Foreign Trade and Soviet Regional Development,' in M.J. Bradshaw, ed., *The Soviet Union. A New Regional Development*, London: Belhaven Press, pp. 165–86.

Bradshaw, M.J. (1993) 'Economic Relations of the Russian Far East with the Asian-Pacific States,' *Post-Soviet Geography*, 35 (4), 234–46.

Chon, Soohyun, (1989) 'South Korea-Soviet Trade Relations: Involvement in Siberian Development,' *Asian Survey*, 29 (12), 1177–87.

Dorian, J.P. (ed) (1993) *CIS Energy and Minerals Development. Prospects, Problems and Opportunities for International Cooperation*, Dordrecht (Netherlands): Kluwer Academic Publishers, pp. 293–313.

Drysdale, P. (1991) 'Soviet Prospects and the Pacific Economy,' in P. Drysdale, ed., *The Soviets and the Pacific Challenge*, Canberra: M.E. Sharpe, pp. 1–15.

Egyed, P. (1983) *Western Participation n the Development of Siberian Energy Resources: Case Studies*, Ottawa Carleton University: Research Report.

Hauner, Milan (1990) What *is Asia to Us? Russia's Asian Heartland Yesterday and Today*, Boston: Unwin Hyman.

Ivanov, Vladimir I. (1991) 'The Soviet Far East Development Prospects: Illusions, Contradictions, Solutions', *A Paper for International Conference of KIEP*, Seoul: KIEP, pp. 58–77.

Khun, K.S. (1996) 'Sostoyaniye I prioritetnyye napravleniya vneshneekonomicheskogo sotrudnichestya mezhdu Rossiye I Respublikoye Koreya ', *Problemy Dal'nego Vostoka*, 3, 86–96.

Kim, Euikon, (1991) 'The Significance of the Opening of Seoul-Moscow Diplomatic Relations and Its Effects on Korean Unification,' *East Asian Review*, 3 (1), 22–36.

Kirkow, P. and Hanson, P. (1994) 'The Potential for Autonomous Regional Development in Russia: The Case of Primorskiy Kray', *Post-Soviet Geography*, 35 (2), 63–88.

Klyuchnikov, Y. (1988) 'The Soviet Far East in the "Pacific Century". Towards Elaboration of a New Concept of the Region's Development', *Far Eastern Affairs*, 4, 3–14.

Kovrigin, E.B. and Smoliak, V.G. (1991) 'Economic Development of the Russian Far East and Korean Participation: Present Situation and Future Prospects', *Sino-Soviet Studies*, 17, 57–83.

Kovrigin, E.B. (1992) 'The Problems of Economic Rapprochement of the Russian Far East with Japan and Other Asia-Pacific Countries', Hokkaido University: *Acta Slavica Iaponica*, pp. 143–66.

Kovrigin, E.B. (1991) 'Economic Development of the Russian Far East and Korean Participation: Present Situation and Future Prospects', *Sino-Soviet Affairs*, 50(12), 57–83.

Lee, Chang-Jae (1992) 'Current Status and Prospects for Korean Investment in Russia,' in Jehoon Park, ed., *Russia's Reform and Economic Cooperation between Korea and Russia*, Seoul: Korean Institute for International Economic Policy (KIEP), pp. 85–96.

Lee, Choongbae and Bradshaw, M.J. (1997) 'South Korean Economic Relations with Russia', *Post-Soviet Geography and Economics*, 38(8), 461–77.

Lee, Choongbae (1995) *The Geopolitics of South Korean Trade with the Former Soviet Union, 1988–1993*, School of Geography, University of Birmingham, England: Unpublished Ph.D thesis.

Leitzel, J. (1995) *Russian Economic Reform*, London: Routledge.

Manezhev, Sergei A. (1993) *The Russian Far East*, London: Royal Institute of International Affairs.

Mieczkowski, Z. (1968) 'The Soviet Far East: Problem Region of the USSR', *Pacific Affairs*, XLI (2), 214–29.

Mikheeva. N.N. (1998) 'Development of The Russian Far East and Korean-Russian Cooperation', in Sejong Research Institute (ed), *Dongbook-a Kyeongjekwon Kusangkwa Hankookeoi*, Seoul: Sejong Research Institute, pp. 119–135.

Minakir, P.A. (1995) 'Economic Reform in Russia', in Valencia, M.J. (ed), *The Russian Far East in Transition*, Boulder: Westview Press, pp. 49–64.

Minakir, P.A. and Freeze, G.L. (eds) (1994), *The Russian Far East. An Economic Handbook*, Armonk, New York: M.E. Sharpe.

Murakami, T. (1997) 'The Present Situation and Future Problems of Energy Production in the Russian Far East', in Akaha, T. (ed), *Politics and Economics in the Russian Far East*, London: Routledge, pp. 110–119.

North, R.N. (1978) 'The Soviet Far East: New Centre of Attention in the U.S.S.R.', *Pacific Affairs*, 51 (2), pp. 152–215.

Oh, Kook Hwan (1996) 'Nakhodka Free Economic Zone and Korea-Russia Industrial Park', in *Russian Economic Prospects and Effective Strategy for the Investment*, Seoul: Korea-Russia Far East Siberian Association, March 26, pp. 111–20.

Paik, Keun-Wook (1995) *Gas and Oil in Northeast Asia. Policies, Projects and Prospects*, London: The Royal Institute of International Affairs.

Rehbein, Robert E. (1989) 'The Japan-Soviet Far East Trade Relationship: A Case of the Cautious Buyer and the Overconfident Seller', *Journal of Northeast Asian Studies*, 8 (2), 38–64.

Russian Far East Update, (1996) *The Russian Far East: A Business Reference Guide 1996*, Seattle: Russian Far East Update.

Saeki, K. (1992) 'Towards Japanese Cooperation in Siberian Development', *Problems of Communism*, 21 (3), 1–12.

Sagers, M.J. (1995) 'Prospects for Oil and Gas Development in Russia's Sakhalin Oblast', *Post-Soviet Geography*, 36 (5), 274–90.

Sanford, D.C. (1990) *South Korea and the Socialist Countries. The Politics of Trade*, Basingstoke: MacMillan Press, Ltd.

Segal, G. (199??) 'Russia as an Asian-Pacific Power', in Thakur, R. and Thayer, C.A. (eds), *Reshaping Regional Relations. Asia-Pacific and the Former Soviet Union*, Boulder: Westview Press, pp. 65–84.

Simonia, N.A. (1992) 'Socio-Economic Changes in the Soviet System and Possibilities of Russian-Korean Relation,' in Ericson, R.E. and Lee In-Sung (eds.) *Economic Reform and Political Change in Russia*, Seoul: Hanguel Publishing Company, pp. 76–98.

Skorokhodov, Yu (1988) 'The Soviet Far East: Problems and Prospects. Gorbachev's Interview with Liaowang', *Far Eastern Affairs*, 3, 1–17

Smith, A. (1993) *Russia and the World Economy: Problems of Integration*, Routledge, London.

Stolyarov, Yu.S. (1991) 'The Soviet Far East: The Economy and Foreign Economic Relations', *Journal of East and West Studies*, 20 (1), 1–15.

Swearingen, Rodger (ed) (1989) *Siberia and the Soviet Far East. Strategic Dimensions in Multinational Perspective*, Stanford: Hoover Institution Press.

Tsuneo Akaha (ed), (1997) *Politics and Economics in the Russian Far East, Changing ties with Asia-Pacific*, Routledge: London.

Chapter 12

Japanese Relations with the Russian Far East

Kazuo Ogawa

INTRODUCTION

It is commonly said that Japan's economic and trade relations with the Former Soviet Union and Russia are determined by the nature of political relations between these two countries. Does this statement reflect reality? Among the various relations between Japan and the Soviet Union and Russia that developed after the Second World, the most important one, which promotes mutual benefit and interest most, is that of the economy and trade. After the Second World War Japan adopted a new Constitution prohibiting it from having any military power. Instead, Japan chose the economy as the basic national strategy for future development. By pursuing this strategy, Japan has become one of the richest countries of the world. Japan has pursued multi-directional peaceful relations with the rest of the world, making the most of its economic power as an instrument for attaining diplomatic ends in negotiating with its partners. The Soviet Union, having built up its military power to match that of the United States during the Cold War, was mainly interested in Japan's industrial, technical and financial resources. The Soviet Union, and more recently Russia, have sought to integrate Japan's capital and technology to promote its own economic and industrial development. In the light of this, it is a quite natural that a mutually beneficial and stable economic relationship has been maintained between Japan and Russia in the post-war years. From the Japanese viewpoint, the Russian Far East (hereafter RFE) is the nearest region of Russia's vast territory, and the region with which Japan has had historical relations and the most frequent human exchanges. Notwithstanding the dispute over the 'Northern Territories', the Japanese people are very interested in the RFE and business relations with the RFE dominate Japanese trade with Russia.

In 1970, Japan was the largest trade partner of the Soviet Union amongst the Western countries and all through 1970s it held the position of the second largest trade partner, after the Federal Republic of Germany. However, in the 1980s Japan lost this position and lingered in fifth or sixth place, in the 1990s its position declined even further. At the same time East-West confrontation disappeared and the globalization of the world economy gathered pace. Today in Northeast Asia, once the front line in the Cold War between the East and the West, tensions have eased and multilateral economic cooperation projects in the Japan Sea Rim Economic Zone are now discussed seriously. The Sea of Japan has been transformed into a sea of peace and cooperation. All economic relations around the Japan Sea used to be built on a bilateral basis, that is the Japan-Soviet (Russia), the Japan-China, the Japan-South Korea, the Japan-North Korea relations, etc. Now multilateral economic relations have started to develop and some of the multilateral cooperation projects are being to materialize.

The first phase of Japanese diplomacy toward Russia after the war was marked by the principle of 'economy and policy linkage'. This then shifted into 'balanced expansion' and now, since 1996, Japan has been pursuing a 'multi-layered approach' to Russia. Favourable political relations have been formed between Japan and Russia, as a result of the direct talks between the leaders of both countries, which took place in Krasnoyarsk, Russia (November 1997) and in Kawana, Japan (April 1998). The basic policy line of Japan with Russia has continued despite the change of the Japanese Prime Minister from Mr. Ryutaro Hashimoto to Mr. Keizo Obuchi. However, it remains to be seen if President Putin will follow the steps of President Yeltsin. This rapid improvement in political relations has created a favourable environment for the further development of business relations between Japan and Russia. But, in reality, Japanese trade with Russia has remained stagnant, especially Japanese exports to Russia which linger at the level of $1.1–1.3 billion a year, in sharp downward contrast to the early 1980s when exports amounted to more than $3 billion a year.

Although the improvement of the political relations has not been reflected in the development of economic relations so far, the trade and economic relations between Japan and Russia will be activated, with the future recovery of the Russian domestic economy. The sites of many promising large scale cooperation projects between Japan and Russia, such as the oil and gas projects on the shelf of Sakhalin Island for example, are located mainly in the RFE.

JAPAN-RUSSIA RELATIONS IN THE 1990S: FROM COLD WAR TO WARM RELATIONS

The year 1996 marked the 40th anniversary of the normalization of official relations between Japan and the Soviet Union (Russia) after the Second World War. Both countries commemorated the date with various ceremonies and activities and the past forty year history of Japanese-Russian and Russian-Japanese relations was reviewed. At the same time, the prospects, and concrete measures, for the future development were discussed. Ten years is sufficient time for people to look back and perceive the passage of a generation or era. However, in 1996 people reacted positively to the occasion of the fortieth year. It was quite visible then that political and the business circles, along with the mass media, in Japan looked forward toward the improvement of Japan's relations with Russia. There were evident reasons for the good mood at the time. A new age was about to emerge in the world history. The end of the Cold War between the East and the West followed by the strong tide of globalization all over the world. These factors facilitated a new track in Japanese-Russian relations. With only a few years left before the start of the 21st century both Japan and Russia were making quiet, but substantial, efforts to construct real friendly relations.

All through the post-war period to the end of 1980s, there was almost no time when the political relationship between Japan and the Soviet Union was good. After the war severe confrontation continued over the issue of the Northern Territories. In contemporary world diplomacy the resolution of a serious problem between nations is normally sought through face-to-face talks between the leaders of the nations concerned, but in case of Japanese-Russian relations mutual visits of the leaders of both countries very rarely took place. Just after the beginning of Perestroyka, President Gorbachev (then) made an official visit to Japan (April 1991). That was the first visit of a Russian head of the state to Japan in the long history of the Japan's relations with Russia and the Soviet Union, which had started in the middle of 19th century. This single fact is enough to prove of how bad political relations between Japan and Russia were.

Japan was concerned about the huge Soviet military presence deployed in the RFE and considered it a threat to Japanese national security. This concern about the 'Soviet threat' culminated in early 1980s when the Soviet Union invaded Afghanistan (December 1979) and even now many people remember that in the big book stores of Tokyo, Osaka and Sapporo special areas were dedicated to books on the Soviet threat. In September1983, the shooting down of the Korean Airline's passenger plane by a Soviet fighter plane over the Sea of Okhotsk further increased Japanese anxiety.

In the autumn of 1996, the 40th jubilee year, the situation was completely different and much improved. The Cold War between the East and the West was over. In Russia, transition of the political and economic system was underway. The fact that both the presidential election in June1996 and the final election in July had gone smoothly proved the establishment and the development of democracy in Russia. The national economy of Russia still suffers from the painful transition process; however, a return to the centrally controlled planned economy is now impossible. The diplomatic policy of the Japanese government has also shifted from 'the linkage of diplomatic and economic policies', followed by 'the balanced expansion of relations', to today's 'multi-layered approaches.' A package of Japanese governmental support programs worth $4.3 billion is now being carried out with Russia in the form of the Japanese governmental trade insurance and the export credit from the Japanese Ex-Im Bank and other measures. Almost all of the factors impeding the development of normal relations between Japan and Russia have disappeared, except for the unsolved 'Northern Territories' dispute. No time has ever existed in the Japanese-Russian history when the number of factors causing hostile confrontation between Japan and Russia has been reduced to minimum as today. Both Japan and Russia should be sensitive enough to perceive the emergence of a new era.

Japanese Prime Minister Mr. Hashimoto's talk with President Yeltsin, on the occasion of Mr. Hashimoto's participation in the Moscow Summit on Nuclear Energy in April 1996, was a good example of the long term change in global international relations. The result of the talks vividly showed that the international multilateral framework was more directly influential than the bilateral one in relations between Japan and Russia. Obviously, the mutual personal understanding that developed between the leaders of Japan and Russia resulted in further successful meetings in Krasnoyarsk, Russia and Kawana, Japan. Also in May 1996, the then Japanese Defence Minister Mr. Shirai made the first visit of Japan's Defence Minister to Moscow in the history of Japanese-Russian relations. This opened a channel for direct mutual dialogue on military matters, which had never existed before between Japan and Russia (the USSR). In return, the Russian Defence Minister made the first visit to Japan in March 1997.

DEVELOPING JAPANESE TIES WITH THE RUSSIAN FAR EAST

During the Cold War, the Sea of Japan was the front line between East and West. It was a sea of confrontation and tension. As the East-West confrontation disappeared, the obstacles impeding the natural development of normal relations between Japan and the RFE have greatly decreased and exchanges in a variety of fields have been activated.

Both the Japanese and Russian sides are taking active measures, including grass roots private exchanges which were impossible in the Cold War era. The Japanese Government opened the Japan Centre on Sakhalin in September 1996, following the opening of Centers in Vladivostok in April 1996 and in Khabarovsk in 1995. These centers aim to enforce Japanese assistance to the regional governments of the RFE by promoting administrative reform, developing local industry and privatization as part of an overall Japanese assistance scheme for introducing a market system to Russia. These inconspicuous quiet efforts of the Japanese Government do not seem to be given due evaluation. It is also a good example of the implementation of the new policy, which was impossible even to think of in the 1980s. At that time, the strict linkage of policy and economy was the basic line of Japanese diplomacy towards Russia. The main target of the then Japanese policy was above all to demand the return of the Northern Territories.

It should also be noted that direct regional communication and exchanges have been developing quickly in many fields between the prefectures of Japan and the regions of the RFE on the Japan Sea coast. The Prefecture of Hokkaido of Japan has opened its own independent representative office in Yuzhno Sakhalinsk, the capital of Sakhalin. At the same time, the Republic of Sakha (Yakutia) has established a representative office in Tokyo. Regular mutual visits of the governors of the local governments of both countries and other types of human exchange and the organization of various international conferences are very frequent these days.

In July 1996 ships of the Japanese Self-Defence Navy were invited to Vladivostok to take part in the ocean parade to commemorate the tri-centennial jubilee of the Russian Navy and were welcomed very warmly. This was the first port call of a Japanese vessel to Russia since the end of the Second World War, something that was also completely unthinkable during the Cold War. In September 1997 a Russian cruiser returned the call to the Port of Tokyo and won the popularity of the people in Tokyo as well. Many Japanese people saw a Russian military ship for the first time with their own eyes.

Everyday Russian fishing boats fully loaded with their catch, mainly crabs, from Sakhalin, Magadan and Kamchatka and other fishing ports of the RFE come to the fishing ports on Hokkaido, such as Wakkanai, Abashiri and Nemuro. They dump their load directly at the piers of the fish markets of these Japanese ports. The local Japanese importers instantly make up the import invoices on the spot and pay the Russian fishermen in Yen. The Russians then buy Japanese cars, refrigerators, washing machines and other daily household commodities at the local secondhand markets, or even fresh vegetables and fruits and so on. Many Japanese shops designed for Russian customers have opened in these Japanese port cities and are doing good business.

The number of the Russian tourists visiting the island of Hokkaido for sightseeing and shopping is rapidly increasing. According to the official annual figures issued by the Otaru branch of the Bank of Japan, some thirty two thousand Russians visited Otaru city in 1997 and the amount of money exchanged into Japanese Yen reached to 1,838.81 million yen, which was as 6.2 times that in 1993, when the branch started to issue such statistics. This amount of 1.8 billion Yen is a considerable sum and can bring sizable economic benefit to a small city like Otaru. The *Druzhba*, a free shopping information journal in Russian is published in Otaru for Russian tourists.

It is now very clear times have been changed and we can expect new good neighbor relations to be formed in the future. If we are able to form new positive relations, then old doubts about the Soviet military threat to Japan created by the deployment of the carriers Novorossiisk, Minsk, and other vessels of the Far Eastern Fleet, will disappear. In 1989, during my first visit to Vladivostok, the author had the chance to see the huge body of the Minsk close-up, moored at the buoy in the Bay of Amur. Several years later both the Minsk and Novorosiisk were retired and sold to a Korean company as scrap. Russia is still a big country, but is not a super-power as the Soviet Union used to be. The country does not need strong military power, more than that; it does not have enough money to sustain its military forces. For Russia today it is far more important and effective to build favorable international relations, rather than to enforce military confrontation. It goes without saying that such a choice for Russian diplomatic policy is also favourable for Japan.

JAPAN-USSR RELATIONS IN THE LATE SOVIET PERIOD: FROM COOPERATION TO LEVERAGE

In 1970 Japan was the largest Western trade partner of the USSR and kept second place, after West Germany, all through 1970s. The stagnation of Japanese-Russian (Soviet) trade only began in the 1990s (see *Table 12.1* and *Figure 12.1*).

The government and industrial circles in Japan cooperated in promoting economic relations with the USSR and several large-scale resource development projects were realized by providing big Japanese bank loans. This positive attitude was in marked contrast to the passive nature of policy in the mid-1980s and early 1990s. Two large economic cooperation projects between Japan and the USSR were stimulated by the visit of then Prime Minister Mr. Tanaka to the USSR in 1973 and signed in 1974. These gave impetus to the further expansion

Table 12.1 Japan–Russia trade, 1984–1999[a] ($m; % of previous year or same period)

	Export		Import		Total		Trade Balance
1984	2,518.3	(89.3)	1,394.0	(95.7)	3,912.3	(91.5)	1,124.3
1985	2,750.6	(109.2)	1,429.3	(102.5)	4,179.8	(106.8)	1,321.3
1986	3,149.5	(114.5)	1,972.0	(138.0)	5,121.6	(122.5)	1,177.5
1987	2,563.3	(81.4)	2,351.9	(119.3)	4,915.1	(96.0)	211.4
1988	3,129.9	(122.1)	2,765.8	(117.6)	5,895.7	(119.9)	364.1
1989	3,081.7	(98.5)	3,004.5	(108.6)	6,086.2	(103.2)	77.2
1990	2,562.8	(83.2)	3,351.0	(111.5)	5,913.8	(97.2)	−788.2
1991	2,113.7	(82.5)	3,316.8	(99.0)	5,430.5	(91.8)	−1,203.1
1992	1,076.7	(50.9)	2,403.0	(72.4)	3,479.7	(64.1)	−1,326.3
1993	1,500.8	(139.4)	2,769.2	(115.2)	4,270.0	(122.7)	−1,268.4
1994	1,167.2	(77.8)	3,490.4	(126.0)	4,657.5	(109.1)	−2,323.2
1995	1,170.1	(100.3)	4,763.3	(136.5)	5,933.5	(127.4)	−3,593.2
1996	1,024.7	(87.6)	3,948.8	(82.9)	4,973.4	(83.8)	−2,924.1
1997	1,014.9	(99.0)	4,018.4	(101.7)	5,033.3	(191.2)	−3,003.5
1998	969.3	(95.5)	2,892.1	(72.0)	3,861.4	(76.7)	−1,922.8
1999	478.4	(49.4)	3,747.0	(129.6)	4,225.4	(109.4)	−3,268.6

[a]1984–1991: Former Soviet Union.
Sources: customs statistics, the Ministry of Finance.

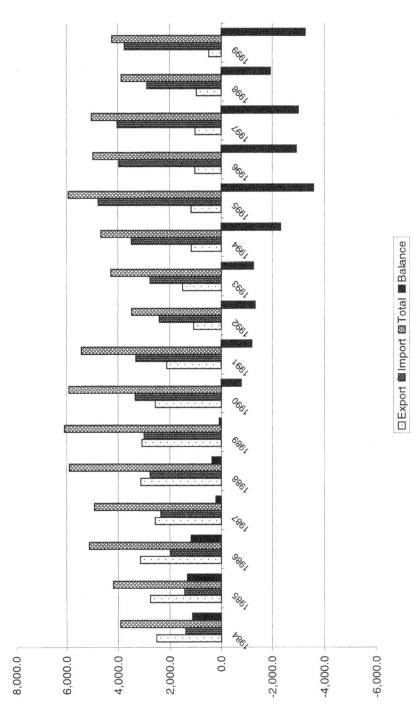

Figure 12.1 Japan–Russia Foreign trade

of the Japanese-USSR trade. They were the South Yakutia coal resource development project and the Second Far East forest-resource development project, to which the Ex-Im Bank of Japan granted loans totaling $1.05 billion. Following these projects, bank loans were provided to enable large diameter steel pipe export and the export of large petrochemical plants. The total amount of Japanese bank loans given to the USSR during 1974–1977 reached $3.2 billion US dollars (more than $10 billion in current prices).

At that time, when Japan was still a comparatively small national economic power, an active trade policy with the USSR had the merits of developing a new export market for Japanese industrial goods and also securing stable sources of the energy imports from resource-rich Siberia. Therefore, at that time economic-relations between Japan and the USSR were driven strongly forward by purely economic and commercial factors. At that time, the principle of Japanese diplomatic policy toward the USSR was the 'non-linkage' or 'separation' of political and economic relations. Because of the problem of 'the Northern Territories' and in the context of the East-West confrontation, the only way for Japan to implement a positive trade policy towards the USSR was to separate economic policy from diplomacy. Only later in 1970s, with the growth of its national power and accompanying upgraded international position, did Japan start to insist on the 'linkage' or 'non-separable' policy. In the 1980s, Japan enforced the principle of 'linkage' when Japan joined with the industrial countries of the West and imposed economic sanctions on the USSR, under the initiative of the United States, to protest Soviet military intervention in Afghanistan. Japan's resolve hardened with regard to the territorial dispute. Japan required the immediate collective return of the four Northern Islands, which were Japanese territory and which were illegally occupied by the Soviet Union. This was the number one question unresolved in Japan's relations with the USSR. Until the territorial question was resolved in favour of Japan, it would not take any active measure for the development of economic relations with the Soviet Union. Naturally, the Soviet Union saw this as a fundamental shift in Japanese diplomatic policy toward the USSR. At that time, economic cooperation between Japan and the USSR stagnated. After the $1 billion contract for the Third Far East Forest Resource Development Cooperation Project was signed in 1981, no further economic cooperation projects materialized between Japan and the USSR until the end of 1980s.

During the 1980s Japanese-Soviet trade was under the strong influence of the political situation between two countries. Even after the arrival of the Gorbachev era, when relations between East and the West improved, the deadlock in economic relations between Japan and the USSR remained. Furthermore, the confusion in the Soviet foreign trade system caused by hasty liberalization brought about the failure of payment for Japanese exports and Japanese companies suffered financial damage. Because of the collapse of the Soviet economy and, later, the problems associated with economic transition in Russia, both domestic production and imports from abroad fell sharply in Russia and

Japanese industrial circles quickly lost interest in Russia. Japanese business transactions in the Russian market diminished.

Through 'balanced expansion' to a 'multi-layered approach'

Various ways of getting out of the deadlocked situation were discussed and sought, but no significant solutions were found. However, in accordance with the resolution at the Munich G7 Summit in 1992 which proposed economic assistance measures to Russia, the Japanese government revealed a package of supports for Russia worth $4.32 billion, third in its size only after Germany and the United States. This action was the result of a major shift in diplomatic policy toward Russia from that of 'linkage' to that of 'balanced expansion'.

By 'balanced expansion' was meant the expansion of economic relations with Russia in return for progress on the political problem of the Northern Territories. Thus, a lack of political relations no longer inhibited economic cooperation. Still the situation was confined within the limits of the 'linkage' principle, because without improved political relations economic relations could not be expanded. It was obvious that this 'linkage' principle did not match the global consensus, as the G7 countries offered total support for Russia to convert its economic system after the collapse of the USSR. The Japanese government, namely the Japanese Ministry of Foreign Affairs, was therefore forced to find a good excuse in order to change the basic principle of the Japanese diplomacy toward Russia.

The 'multi-layered approach' gradually began to gain currency in the summer of 1996 and in early 1997 the *Yomiuri*, the largest newspaper in circulation in Japan, used this term in the front page headline as the keyword in regard to the new diplomatic policy toward Russia. Though the recovery of the Northern Territories still remains the question of first priority, other areas of relations between Russia Japan are now seen as being no less important. Today such a multi-layered approach toward Russia forms the basis for dialogue between the two countries leaders on political, as well as security matters, cooperation in the introduction of the market economy in Russia, the promotion of economic exchange with the RFE, cooperation in environmental protection and so on. The governmental support program for Russia is closely linked with the implementation of large scale private export contracts and may well result in success, if the Russian economy recovers.

RUSSIA-JAPAN SUMMITS AND THE HASHIMOTO-YELTSIN PLAN

As Japan's approach toward Russia shifted, in July 1997, the then Japanese Prime Minister, Mr. Hashimoto revealed new guidelines for diplomacy with Russia based upon the three principles of 'reliance', 'mutual benefit' and a 'long range view'. His statement was accepted by the Russian side and the Hashimoto-Yeltsin summit took place in Krasnoyarsk in November 1997, where both sides agreed to make efforts towards the targeted conclusion of a peace treaty between Japan and Russia in 2000 (a target date that has not been met). In February 1998 the Japanese Foreign Minister Mr. Obuchi visited Moscow, in April President Yeltsin came to Japan and summit was held in Kawana. The meeting in Kawana resulted in the considerable enlargement of the 'Hashimoto-Yeltsin Plan', the main body of the Japan's economic support package program for Russia. Japan and Russia agreed upon the promotion of Japanese direct investment to Russia; Japanese support for the Russian official participation in APEC and WTO; a grant of a untied loan by the Japanese Ex-Im Bank to the amount of $1.5 billion; support for the development of small- and medium-sized enterprises in Russia; the invitation of Russian trainees to Japan; the introduction of ministerial dialogue in the energy field; and, the promotion of peaceful utilization of nuclear energy.

The greatest achievement of the Kawana summit was that it laid out the basis upon which to establish a regular channel for dialogue between the leaders of Japan and Russia by exchanging mutual visits. Mr. Hashimoto resigned from the premier's post and Mr. Obuchi took over, but this line of mutual dialogue is firmly maintained.

In July 1998 the new Russian Premier Mr. Kiryenko made his first visit to Japan. In the long history of the Japanese-Russian relations, this was the first visit by a Russian Premier to Japan. Mr. Kiryenko also supported the 'Hashimoto-Yeltsin Plan' and made it clear that he would continue the dialogue in future. On this occasion both sides agreed upon the conclusion of an investment protection agreement between Japan and Russia and the establishment of a Japanese-Russian investment company. However, further progress was blighted by the Russian Financial Crisis and then President Yeltsin's ill health and it remains to be seen if President Putin will maintain the dialogue.

TRENDS IN JAPAN'S TRADE WITH RUSSIA

Japan's trade with Russia constitutes only a very small portion of its total trade volume (see *Table 12.2*). In 1997, exports to Russia were only 0.24 per cent of total exports and import only 1.18 per cent. However, the FSU used to be a major market for Japanese exports of industrial plants and steel pipes. Russia is still a relatively important supplier of non-ferrous metals and lumber to Japan. From the Russian point of view Japan is a major trading partner among the Western countries along with Germany, Finland and Italy. When examining trade relations between Japan and Russia, it is necessary to understand correctly these ambiguities. That is to say, from the Japanese view Russia's share in the total trade is very small and from the Russian side, Japan is an important Western trade partner. In addition, we must note that for certain commodities both countries play a very important role for each other.

In recent years, Japanese exports to Russia have stagnated; the official trade statistics shows that in 1994–1997 they were at the low level of $1–1.2 billion dollars annually (see *Table 12.1*). This means that the Japanese exports to Russia

Table 12.2 The share of Japan–Russia Trade in foreign trade of Japan[a] ($m)

		Total	USA	Great Britain	Indonesia	China	Russia	Weight of Russia (%)
Export	1987	229,221	83,580	8,400	2,990	8,250	2,563	1.12
	1988	264,917	89,634	10,652	3,054	9,476	3,130	1.18
	1989	275,175	93,188	10,741	3,301	8,516	3,082	1.12
	1990	286,948	90,322	10,786	5,040	6,130	2,563	0.89
	1991	314,525	91,538	11,040	5,612	8,593	2,114	0.67
	1992	339,650	95,793	12,287	5,576	11,949	1,077	0.32
	1993	360,911	105,405	12,047	6,022	17,273	1,501	0.42
	1994	395,599	117,560	12,734	7,672	18,681	1,167	0.29
	1995	442,937	120,859	14,141	9,971	21,931	1,170	0.26
	1996	477,313	121,771	13,580	9,860	23,824	1,027	0.22
	1997	423,003	117,663	13,775	10,216	21,846	1,019	0.24
	1998	385,632	117,795	14,504	4,645	19,957	969	0.25
Import	1987	149,515	31,490	3,057	8,427	7,401	2,352	1.57
	1988	187,354	42,037	4,193	9,497	9,859	2,766	1.48
	1989	210,847	48,246	4,465	11,021	11,146	3,005	1.43
	1990	234,799	52,369	5,238	12,721	12,054	3,351	1.43
	1991	236,737	53,317	5,017	12,770	14,216	3,317	1.40
	1992	233,021	52,230	4,890	12,244	16,953	2,403	1.03
	1993	240,670	55,236	4,951	12,478	20,565	2,769	1.15
	1994	274,741	62,659	5,914	12,917	27,566	3,490	1.27
	1995	336,094	75,408	7,151	14,214	35,922	4,763	1.42
	1996	379,934	86,310	7,799	16,532	43,997	3,954	1.04
	1997	340,196	75,997	7,221	14,697	42,044	4,013	1.18
	1998	279,011	66,820	5,819	10,781	36,894	2,892	1.04

[a]1984–1991: Former Soviet Union.
Sources: customs statistics, the Ministry of Finance.

fell by one third compared with the 1980s when they recorded about $3 billion annually. Furthermore, Japan is not a major investor in Russia. It is not counted among the top-ten investing countries in Russia, despite being one of the world's largest sources of foreign investment. Nonetheless, Japanese imports from Russia have been doing rather better. In 1995, Japan imports from Russia amounted to $4.7 billion dollars the highest recorded level of Japanese-Russian trade since the Second World War. Major import items include fish and marine products, aluminum, nickel, platinum, paradigm, lumber and coal (see *Table 12.3* and *Table 12.4* for the commodity structure of Japan-Russia trade).

Table 12.3 The commodity structure of Japanese exports to Russia
($m; % of total)

	1992	1993	1994	1995	1996	1997	*(% of 1997)*
Total	1,076.7	1,500.8	1,167.2	1,170.1	1,026.8	1,018.6	99.2
	(100)	(100)	(100)	(100)	(100)	(100)	
Light Industry	95.1	98.0	77.7	91.2	110.6	122.2	110.4
	(8.8)	(6.5)	(6.7)	(7.8)	(10.8)	(12.0)	
of which; Textile	19.0	15.8	6.5	9.1	10.5	11.2	106.7
	(1.8)	(1.1)	(0.6)	(0.8)	(1.0)	(1.1)	
Chemical Industrial Product	890.7	1,332.3	1,019.8	1,025.3	857.5	843.8	98.4
	(82.7)	(88.8)	(87.4)	(87.6)	(83.5)	(82.3)	
of which; Chemicals	78.4	109.2	35.6	29.1	27.9	24.5	87.8
	(7.3)	(7.3)	(3.1)	(2.5)	(2.7)	(2.4)	
Metals	108.8	375.8	243.0	98.2	63.8	43.6	68.3
	(10.1)	(25.0)	(20.8)	(8.4)	(6.2)	(4.3)	
Machinery & Equipment	703.5	847.3	741.2	898.1	765.8	775.7	101.3
	(65.3)	(56.5)	(63.5)	(76.8)	(74.6)	(76.1)	

Sources: customs statistics, the Japanese Ministry of Finance.

Japanese exports and investment are hampered by the depressed state of the Russian economy as well as the unstable Russian foreign trade system. In addition, the unclear arbitrary taxation system discourages Japanese investment. Non-payments for previous Japanese exports are also unresolved, which also discourages Japanese trading firms from developing new business with Russia. However, if we look at the present poor situation from a different angle, we may say that we can expect big business opportunities with Russia in future. When the Russian economy recovers, demand for the import of industrial machinery and equipment will increase. If a reliable Russian foreign trade system is formulated the commercial contracts already signed between the Japanese and the Russian companies, but not implemented due to the lack of the finance from the Japanese Ex-Im Bank, will be realized. For example, two major contracts were signed in the autumn of 1995, one for the modernization of an oil refinery plant in Yaroslavl ($200 million dollars) and the other for the supply of equipment for the new diesel motor plant for the Kama Truck Factory ($150 million dollars), but they are yet to be implemented.

Things will eventually improve and we have to start to prepare measures now. Japanese business tends to be overly cautious in dealing with Russia. Such caution stems from Japan's relatively long and rich experiences of trade with the Soviet Union since the Second World War and, therefore, Japan is lagging behind relative newcomers like the United States and South Korea. In the Cold

Table 12.4 The commodity structure of Japanese imports from Russia
($m; % of total)

	1992	1993	1994	1995	1996	1997	*(% of 1996)*
Total	2,403.0	2,769.2	3,490.4	4,763.3	3,953.5	4,013.0	101.5
Fish & shells	582.2	710.0	1,024.8	1,320.5	1,246.5	1,055.1	84.6
	(24.2)	(26.3)	(29.4)	(27.7)	(31.5)	(26.3)	
Cotton	6.4	11.2	0.6	2.6	1.1	0.3	27.3
	(0.3)	(0.4)	(0.0)	(0.1)	(0.0)	(0.0)	
Iron & steel scrap	2.6	1.9	4.1	4.3	7.3	8.6	117.8
	(0.1)	(0.1)	(0.1)	(0.1)	(0.2)	(0.2)	
Timber	465.6	616.6	618.6	769.0	689.5	785.5	113.9
	(19.4)	(22.3)	(17.7)	(16.1)	(17.4)	(19.6)	
Coal	237.5	202.1	211.9	260.7	266.5	237.4	89.1
	(9.9)	(7.3)	(6.1)	(5.5)	(6.7)	(5.9)	
Machinery & Equipment	5.1	6.8	6.1	5.1	9.2	10.6	115.2
	(0.2)	(0.2)	(0.2)	(0.1)	(0.2)	(0.3)	
Platinum	223.4	179.2	302.2	402.2	318.8	121.0	38.0
	(9.3)	(6.5)	(8.7)	(8.4)	(8.1)	(3.0)	
Nickel	25.1	26.8	58.3	193.9	77.4	95.5	123.4
	(1.0)	(1.0)	(1.7)	(4.1)	(2.0)	(2.4)	
Aluminium & aluminium alloy	149.9	335.5	484.9	807.5	690.9	931.5	134.8
	(6.2)	(12.1)	(13.9)	(17.0)	(17.5)	(23.2)	
Gold	63.9	71.7	58.0	150.7	–	12.5	–
	(2.7)	(2.6)	(1.7)	(3.2)	(–)	(0.3)	

Sources: customs statistics, the Ministry of Finance.

War era trade between South Korea and the Soviet Union was almost nil due to the lack of official diplomatic relations (see Chapter 12). Thanks to active business promotion, trade between South Korea and Russia reached almost $3 billion dollars in 1996. However, recent experience might suggest that South Korea could have learnt lessons from Japan's cautious approach to Russia.

DEVELOPING NEW BUSINESS CHANNELS

The future prospects for trade between Japan and Russia is considered limited. However, all is not lost and in certain sectors further growth can even be expected. First, new business channels are being developed between Japan and Russia and consequently new relationships and business expertise are being formulated. Large amounts of Japanese electric and electronic home appliances (colour TVs, VTRs, air conditioners) and office equipment are now supplied to

Russia through the third countries like Finland, Dubai, Singapore and others. The previous structure of Japanese exports to the Soviet Union, which mainly consisted of machinery and equipment for industrial plants, large diameter steel pipes and drilling pipes for resource development projects, has been completely changed.

Today consumer appliances are one of the most important export items to Russia. During the period of 1994–96, Japanese electronic manufacturers exported 2 million colour televisions a year. The annual export value was estimated at more than $20 billion. In 1997 this trade increased further to 4 million sets. Television sets made in Japan conquered the Russian market. They were sold in the department stores and shops of cities in the Far East and the North, not to mention Moscow and St. Petersburg. Russians are brand conscious and choose high quality colour TVs manufactured on the Japanese mainland. The newly emergent middle class in Russia was the chief generator of the boom. If we take into consideration these exports through third countries, Japanese exports to Russia prosper despite the depressed impression. National Panasonic, Sony, Sharp, Sanyo, Funai–all of these Japanese manufacturers have already studied the Russian market and built up their own business channels and know-how and are making big profits. The Japanese company NEC is one of the most successful foreign investors in the Russian telecommunications market. NEC steadily contributes to the modernization of the communications system in Russia through large-scale projects. This surge of demand for Japanese electronic goods was caused by the yearn for Japanese products at lower prices and of higher quality; but the imperfect Russian taxation system helped amplify the tendency as well. Normally these consumer products were taxed 25 per cent of their value on import into Russia. However, some charitable organizations were granted special duty free import rights. Under cover of this special agreement, skillful brokers brought Japanese goods into Russia without paying import duties. Of course this illegal business was known to the Russian government and the special duty free import right was abolished. In the summer of 1997 it was announced that these privileges would be stopped in 1998, as a result Japanese consumer electric products began to sell very fast and sales reached twice the volume of the pervious year. Since May 1998 the Russian government has placed controls on the import of colour TVs in the hope that it might foster domestic production to substitute for imports. A goal that was further aided by the devaluation of the ruble in the summer of 1998. Of course, Russia can produce colour TVs. The Japanese electronic manufacturers are ready to switch to direct investment in Russia, as soon as the Russian government shifts its policy to foster the domestic industry. However, the result of research conducted in Russia by the Japanese electronic manufacturers in 1996–1997 concluded that time was not right for direct investment. Electric consumer goods are not the only Japanese products manufactured in third countries. Many Japanese cars made in third countries are also sold in Russia. The question here is whether these trade transactions via third countries should be included in Japanese exports to Russia or not? In an age of industrial globalization it is difficult to evaluate trade relations between two countries only relying upon the official customs statistics which simply show the figures derived from the countries of origin. To capture the whole picture it is necessary to include not only trade via third countries, but also the amount of foreign investment and other factors.

THE PLACE OF THE RUSSIAN FAR EAST IN CONTEMPORARY JAPANESE-RUSSIAN ECONOMIC RELATIONS

The RFE is of greatest significance in Japan's economic relations with Russia. Products from the RFE account for a large share of Japanese imports from Russia. Most of the Japanese resource development cooperation projects within Russia are located in the RFE. In 1995, Japanese imports from Russia recorded a post-war peak with the total value of $4.7 billion. The major import items from Russia were fish and marine products (crabs and cod roe) $1.3 billion dollars (28 per cent), lumber $770 million (16 per cent), aluminum $800 million dollars (17 per cent), platinum 400 million dollars (8 per cent), palladium $320 million dollars (6.7 per cent), and coal $260 million dollars (5.5 per cent). Most of the above mentioned Russian products are from the RFE and much of the remainder from East Siberia (alumnium and platinum-group metals). The crabs and cod roe from the RFE enrich the dinner tables of Japanese families, traditional Japanese wooden houses are built by the lumber from the RFE and the key components of the most advanced Japanese electronic technology are sustained by the rare metals from the RFE and Siberia.

If we look at this from the Russian side, about half of the exports of the RFE are directed to Japan. Trade between the RFE and China and the United States is growing fast and the South Korea is energetically expanding its business. In contrast, the trade with Japan seems to be declining in significance in the RFE, nevertheless, Japan will likely remain the largest trade partner for the RFE in the near future. If any of the proposed large scale economic cooperation projects between Japan and Russia in oil, gas, coal or lumber resource exploration are realized, then exports from the RFE to Japan will soar; as will the purchase from Japan of the materials and machinery for resource development. Consequently, the role of the RFE in the overall economic relations between Japan and Russia will become more important.

Russian statistical data concerning the foreign trade of the RFE are now much improved. Unfortunately, Japanese Customs do not issue detailed separate data on Japanese trade with the RFE. It is impossible to obtain figures for trade with the RFE, even from the offices of the Japanese prefectures. Though it may seem to be an easy problem to solve, in fact it is really a difficult question. In 1996 the total foreign trade turnover of the RFE was $5.37 billion (exports –$3.34 billion, import $2.03 billion dollars), which exceeded the amount of 1995 in both export and import. Foreign trade appears to be the most lively sector in the depressed economy of the RFE (an observation confirmed by the analysis in Chapter 2).

Three regions, namely, Primorskii ($1.89 billion), Khabarovsk ($1.21 billion) and Sakhalin ($840 million) accounted for almost 70 per cent of the total foreign trade turnover of the RFE in 1996. Here Japan is the largest trade partner and the largest purchaser of the products of the RFE. The largest single export commodity from the RFE is fish and marine products, which account almost 45 per cent of total exports. In second place comes lumber, which accounts for 16–20 per cent. More than half of the exports to Japan from the RFE is fish and marine products. In return, the RFE imported from Japan the modest amount of 190 million dollars of goods in 1996.

The real extent of business relations between the RFE with Japan are more extensive than those captured by the official statistical and these ties are being strengthened. It is widely known that every day the Russian fishing boats fully loaded with marine products from Sakhalin, Magadan, Kamchatka and other regions call at the ports of Hokkaido and unload the cargo directly to the local fish markets. We can witness here borderless economic relations in action in a simple primitive form. It also clearly demonstrates the increasing dependency of the local economy of the RFE on Japan. Japan imported fish and marine products from Russia worth $1.3 billion dollars in 1995 (see *Table 12.5*) and $1.2 billion dollars in 1996, and a large portion of this business was carried out in the above mentioned form.

The number of registered enterprises with foreign capital (joint and total foreign investment) in the RFE increased by 460 from 2208 at the end of 1994 to 2661 at the end of 1995. Only 30 percent of them are said to be really working. The number of established companies in 1995 by country was 236 for China, 72 for the United States, 30 for Japan and 16 for South Korea. The boom in the establishment of joint ventures took place in 1992–1993. In 1993 alone, 789 joint ventures were registered. Since then the pace has slowed, especially in 1996 when there almost no newly established companies and the number of already registered companies shrank mainly because of harsh taxation enforcement by the Russian Tax Office. Interest was further dampened by Russian economic crisis in August 1998, which reduced the purchasing power of Russian consumers.

The number of Chinese joint ventures exceeds others, but most of them are small and medium-sized enterprises and therefore they do not contribute so much to the economy of the RFE. The number of joint ventures with Japan reached more than 300 at the end of 1995. The amount of hard currency earned by the exports of these joint ventures reached $150 million dollars in 1995, the largest amount of foreign currency earned by foreign participants.

Joint ventures with Japanese companies are mostly in the service sector, commerce, processing and sale of marine products and lumber. At present, the Japanese presence in the RFE remains modest, as Japanese companies are simply unwilling to invest. Both the Japanese and Russian governments began to cooperate in taking realistic active measures for the expansion of the Japanese investment in Russia. Both agreed to conclude an investment protection agreement and to establish a Japanese-Russian investment company. Never-

Table 12.5 Foreign Trade of the Russian Far East by country, 1992–1997

	Year	Export		Import	
		mil. USD	*%*	*mil. USD*	*%*
Japan	1992	730.0	47.4	230.6	19.4
	1993	892.1	48.2	208.1	17.5
	1994	995.0	62.0	110.0	16.9
	1995	1,173.3	48.3	188.0	10.7
	1996	1,036.7	36.6	160.1	9.2
	1997	1,071.2	32.8	534.8	24.1
China	1992	419.5	27.3	564.6	47.5
	1993	511.5	33.0	576.8	48.4
	1994	156.0	9.7	94.6	14.6
	1995	172.4	7.1	155.6	8.9
	1996	707.4	25.0	218.8	12.5
	1997	399.9	12.3	262.7	11.8
Korea,	1992	108.2	7.0	139.4	11.7
Republic of	1993	117.3	6.3	71.2	6.0
	1994	163.3	10.2	98.6	15.2
	1995	253.5	10.5	212.2	12.1
	1996	328.7	11.6	307.0	17.7
	1997	423.1	13.0	461.8	20.8
USA	1992	59.2	3.8	47.3	3.9
	1993	28.0	1.5	76.1	6.4
	1994	63.6	4.0	112.4	17.3
	1995	220.9	9.1	376.3	21.5
	1996	128.2	4.5	413.3	23.8
	1997	395.4	12.1	481.5	21.7
Germany	1992	2.3	0.1	12.0	1.0
	1993	5.5	0.3	41.9	3.5
	1994	19.3	1.2	17.4	2.7
	1995	50.4	2.1	198.5	11.3
	1996	21.4	0.8	57.8	3.3
	1997	132.1	4.1	52.7	2.4
Korea,	1992	2.1	0.1	1.1	0.1
Democratic	1993	9.8	0.5	1.5	0.1
People's	1994	1.9	0.1	3.6	0.6
Republic	1995	9.7	0.4	1.4	0.0
	1996	–	–	–	–
	1997	44.3	1.4	56.1	2.5
United	1992	0.2	0.0	1.3	0.1
Kingdom	1993	1.6	0.1	6.6	0.6
	1994	2.3	0.1	6.9	1.1
	1995	20.6	0.8	17.4	1.0
	1996	–	–	–	–
	1997	37.9	1.2	46.8	2.1
Switzerland	1992	–	–	1.8	0.2
	1993	5.1	0.3	6.4	0.5
	1994	15.5	1.0	19.7	3.0
	1995	39.8	1.6	8.6	0.5
	1996	–	–	–	–
	1997	28.7	0.9	93.4	4.2

Sources: compiled from various data issued by the Administrations of RFE

theless, Japanese business circles are still maintaining a cautious posture towards Russia. Without quickly eliminating existing problems and drastically improving the investment climate, no further development can be expected.

Problems of investing in Russia

- Unstable political and social systems
- Lack of macro economic control
- Very poor infrastructure
- Discrimination against foreign capital
- Too frequently changing laws and orders
- Excessive legislation and taxation to foreign capital

THE POTENTIAL FOR JAPANESE ECONOMIC IN THE RUSSIAN FAR EAST

The RFE is a vast uncultivated field for new promising economic cooperation projects on both a bilateral and multilateral basis. The projects with the greatest potential are listed below.

Major fields of economic cooperation in the Russian Far East:

- Development and exploitation of energy resources–natural gas, oil, coal, hydroelectric, power and pipeline construction
- Development and exploitation of other resources–gold, diamonds and copper
- Development and processing of marine resources
- Development and processing of forest resources
- Development of tourism (including the construction of hotels)
- Development of agriculture
- Construction and expansion of infrastructure–urban infrastructure, seaports, airports, railways and roads
- Free economic zones

Large scale international projects feasible for realization in future:

- The Yakut natural gas development project
- The Sakhalin shelf oil and gas development project
- The East Siberian Kovytka natural gas development project
- The RFE port facility improvement project
- The Amur river railroad bridge reconstruction project
- The greater Vladivostok economic zone project
- The Tumen river development project and its Russian portion (Port Zarubino, railroad)
- The Blagoveshcensk-Heihe automobile bridge construction project

In the immediate future, the development of the rich resource base of the RFE should be the focus of cooperation between Russia and Japan. This will be an essential factor both for the development of the local economy of the RFE and for the expansion of the Japanese trade relations with the RFE. This scenario of the development of Japanese economic cooperation with the RFE is favourable not only for neighboring Japan and Russia but also for the development of economy of the countries and the regions in the Japan Sea Economic Zone, that is to say for the development of the whole Northeast Asia. The economic development of Northeast Asia will respond to and stimulate strongly the local economy of the RFE in return. In the light of this interrelationship, economic cooperation between Japan and Russia will stimulate large-scale cooperation projects of international nature. The countries, the regions, the people of the North-Eastern Asia should be well aware of the significance of these international projects and understand the meaning of economic cooperation of Japan with Russia correctly. They should also support and strive for the realization of these projects. For the smooth development of the local economy and the natural resources of the RFE it is necessary to build and expand such basic infrastructures as railroads, roads, ports, airports, urban facilities and so on. This is another promising area for future Japanese economic cooperation with Russia.

Some of the more feasible projects of cooperation between Japan and Russia have been already started or are under practical negotiation. They include the Sakhalin shelf oil and gas development projects, the Yakut (Sakha) natural gas development project, the East Siberian Kovykta natural gas development project, port improvement and expansion projects in the RFE and coal development projects in Sakhalin and the coastal regions. The fourth RFE forest resource development project, which had been negotiated for many years, became impossible in the autumn of 1997 because of conflicting interests on both the Japanese and the Russian sides. Below we examine two projects in detail. One is the Sakhalin shelf oil and gas development project which is the largest economic cooperation project between Japan and Russia, the other is the East Siberian Kovykta natural gas field development project which has recently attracted attention.

The Sakhalin shelf oil and gas development projects

Both Sakhalin I and Sakhalin II were officially started in 1996. The fact that these projects have been realized at last implies something more than the start of ordinary business transactions. As noted by the then Russian Minister of Fuel and Energy Mr. Shafranik, they are the largest foreign investment projects ever developed in Russia with a total possible investment of $25 billion dollars for two projects. The scale of these huge projects far exceeds the limit of bilateral cooperation and they have now become large-scale international cooperation. In Sakhalin I take part three countries, namely Japan (Sodeco), Russia (Rosneft and SMNG), and the USA (Exxon). Sakhalin II also involves four countries, namely Japan (Mitsui and Mitsubishi), the USA (Marathon) and the UK and the Netherlands (Shell) (see Chapter 9 for more details). The basic contracts of these two projects were signed in Washington, DC in the presence of Mr. Chernomyrdin, then the Russian Premier and Mr. Gore, the American vice-president. Both projects plan that the oil and gas produced in the waters of the northern land shelf of Sakhalin Island will be supplied not only to Russia but also to other countries. Sakhalin II has pursued a strategy of early oil production and the first offshore production started in the summer of 1999. Commercial natural gas production and supply to Japan should be beginning by 2010 at the latest. Since both projects started, labour, capital and goods have started to flow into Sakhalin. Uncertainty in the future of the Japanese-Russian trade is now removed. In Russia, in April, 1996 President Yeltsin signed 'The long term program for the development of the economy and society of the RFE' which indicated the guidelines for a concrete regional development programme until 2005. It was approved by the Russian government as an official plan of the government. According to this long-term plan, these two projects are expected to play an important major role in the economic development of the whole the RFE. Out of the total cost of $25 billion, $17 billion dollars are allocated for the purchase of machinery and equipment necessary to exploit the resource. The Production-Sharing Agreement (PSA) for Sakhalin II contracts requires that 70 per cent of this amount should be spent on Russian products. Sakhalin I is also committed, but not bound, to a 70 per cent local content. Many factories in the RFE are scarcely alive and desperately struggling for survival. Many failed to adapt themselves to the new market economy and went bankrupt, victims of the extraordinary strict monetary policy of the Russian government enforced by the IMF. Potentially, orders from these two projects offer a lifeline to the industrial base of the RFE.

These are national projects in the scale and nature, but the site of the projects is limited to a local area. It is expected that these projects will create a new form of mutually beneficial cooperation that will not be confined within the rigid framework of traditional concepts inter-state relations. Instead, the regions and the central government of the state will receive fair portions of the benefits. The recent rise of localism in both Russia and Japan may help formulate a new form of cooperation, if the regions of both countries skillfully cooperate with each other.

The East Siberia Kovytka gas field development project

The large scale Russian-Chinese joint project for the development of the Kovykta gas field in Irkutsk oblast has captured considerable attention. The gas will be supplied to China by pipelines through Mongolia. Japanese business circles show an interest in it because the Russian side seeks sizable Japanese participation in the project. The total construction cost is estimated at $7–8 billion dollars which is impossible for Russia and China to finance by themselves. Therefore, Japanese financial and technical cooperation is sought. It is planned that Russia will supply China 20–25 billion cubic meters of natural gas every year through a 3,400-kilometer pipeline system from Russia to the Chinese port of Liushan in Shangdong Province via Beijin and Tenjin. It is also proposed that gas will be provided to South Korea and Japan. Russia has requested Japanese cooperation in this project at every possible occasion. The then Russian Minister of Fuel and Energy Mr. Kiryenko openly expressed his desire for Japanese participation in the project when he visited to Japan in March 1998.

In Japan the then Prime Minister Mr. Hashimoto referred to the possibility of rendering Japanese assistance to the 'Irkutsk gas development plan' in the summer of 1997 when he revealed his new diplomatic policy toward Russia. His statement attracted the attention of the various Japanese interests linked with the project. There is support in Japan for the advancement of this project. This support is based on the possibility of a future energy crisis in North Eastern Asia due to the rapid growth of China's energy consumption. There is also the possibility of the direct supply of the gas to Japan itself. Nevertheless, we should also take into consideration the following factors. First, we have to keep in mind the fact that Japan is not and will not be the leading partner in the project and it is difficult to think that the gas will be supplied to Japan. Above all this is a deal between Russia and China and Japan is the third party in it. Since 1995 this project has been one of the main subjects of negotiations between China and Russia. At the time of President Yeltsin's visit to Beijing in November 1997, the project was mentioned extensively in the joint statement signed by President Yeltsin and Chairman Zhao. As for Japan, the matter has been discussed only with Russia. Japan must consult with China on this subject as well. The length of 3,400 kilometers of the pipelines is not a problem at all. Many of the main pipelines in Russia are of the same length. But to transport 25–30 billion cubic meters of gas annually, steel pipes of the maximum diameter in production in the world (1,420 millimeters) are required. This also means that if China receives 20–25 billion cubic meters and Mongolia demands its own share for transit, small amount will remain for South Korea and will leave no room for Japan at all. In order to secure the supply for Japan it will be needed to double the pipelines and recalculate from the beginning the basic parameters of the project such as the construction costs and the estimated reserve of the Kovytka gas field itself. It should also be noted that manufacturers in only three countries in the world (Russia, Japan and Germany) are capable of producing steel pipes of the required diameter. The decision on Japanese participation in the project should be discussed with due consideration of the above mentioned factors.

CONCLUSIONS

Until it was opened in 1992, Vladivostok had been a closed city for a long time. Now the city is open to the world and is connected with Niigata, Toyama, Seoul, Pusan, Harbin, Anchorage and Seattle by regular flights. Times have certainly changed. Today it is possible to build new ways of direct communication and ties with counterparts across the Japan Sea at the level of cities and prefectures. Thus, in the future the scale and scope of economic cooperation in Northeast Asia may be determined by regional, as much as national, governments.

Chapter 13

America's Pacific Northwest and the Russian Far East in the 1990s: A tumultuous decade, a tumultuous relationship

Elisa Miller

EDITOR'S INTRODUCTION

This chapter is somewhat different from the other country case studies presented in this section. The author, Dr Elisa Miller is the former founder and publisher of the monthly business newsletter *Russian Far East Update* (1991–1999) and, quarterly *Pacific Oil and Gas Report*, (as well as the annual publication *The Russian Far East: A Business Reference Guide*).

During the 1990s, Dr Miller and her team monitored developments in the Russian Far East (hereafter RFE) from their offices in Seattle, Washington State. She traveled throughout the region, often as a consultant assisting American companies interested in potential investment projects. Eventually, even Elisa Miller's optimism was crushed by the problems of doing business in the Russian Far East. In 1998 Dr Miller accepted an offer from London-based Business Monitor International to acquire the Update which is now incorporated in their *Russia and FSU Monitor*. The *Pacific Oil and Gas Report* is now published by the Sakhalin-Alaska Consulting Group.

What follows in this chapter are Elisa Miller's reflections after several decades of close involvement in US-RFE relations. While the chapter lacks the supporting statistics and graphs of the other case studies, it does explore the sense of disappointment now felt by US business, government agencies and non-governmental organization who rushed to the region in the early 1990s. It also identifies the underlying psychological barriers that have hindered the integration of the Russian Far East into the Asia-Pacific region.

THE PAST AS PRELUDE TO THE PRESENT: THE STATE'S VIEW OF THE RUSSIAN FAR EAST: GARRISON AND GULAG

It has always been (in Tsarist times and in Soviet times) that the people of Russia, as subjects of the State, were obligated to serve the state; but the state was not obligated to serve the people. It has also always been that the regions of Russia, as subjects of the State, were obligated to serve the State; but the State was not obligated to serve the regions. An exception has been the Russian Far East, where the State chose to take on an obligation to the region in the form of subsidies to it, because, in the State's view, the region had specific military and defense significance important to its interests. The commitment of the State to provide specific subsidies to the region was, foremost, a commitment to maintain a defendable border and frontier.

In addition to its obligations to the region for military and defense purposes, the State (in Tsarist and in Soviet times), saw the region as a territory which could also provide valuable mineral wealth to the State, if such wealth could be extracted. The harsh conditions in which was located that mineral wealth, however, meant that labor to extract it would either have to be induced, or forced.

Early in the 18th century, the idea surfaced that the remoteness and harsh environmental conditions of the trans-Baikal and Russian Far Eastern regions would make a most convenient destination for the exile and banishment of political or criminal deviants. It followed that these people (sent into the region as punishment) could comprise a labor force to extract the mineral wealth of the region. The idea, which surfaced early in Tsarist times, was implemented in the late 19th century with the settling of Sakhalin Island as Russia's farthermost penal colony and later in the 20th century with the establishment of the gulag system under Stalin.

In sum, the Russian Far East, from the point of the State, is both garrison and gulag. It is our intent to show how this point of view imbues federal policy (yesterday's, today's, and tomorrow's) with a negativism toward regional autonomy, and a cynicism or, at best, an indifference, toward regional economic development.

As long as the State sees the region as garrison, regional autonomy can not be a priority for Moscow. Regional autonomy would conflict with the aim the State has fixed for the region: one of defending and protecting the State's borders. A move toward regional autonomy could imperil, threaten or even subvert the state's purposes for the region. An independent, autonomous region would mean a lack of predictability, the possibility of open borders, an invitation to foreign influences – all of which, from the State's centrist point of view run counter to a strong, defendable border which must project strength, stability, predictability.

Neither can the State be much interested in regional economic development, as we know and define it in the West. A program whose goal is economic development for the Russian Far East region would require massive federal subsidies. Given scarce investment resources, and the priorities for military and defense, funds for these subsidies do not exist. Although the state has proclaimed many development programs over the decades past, the state's actual disbursements of financial resources for investment have been only a small fraction of what it has promised. What support the State has provided in the past under the guise of economic development can better be understood as providing infrastructure and that industrial capacity needed to continue to support a military and defense position.

In addition, the State's view of the region as gulag, and the historical experience of the region as gulag, can not help but color any programmatic thinking about economic possibilities and development. To wit, pessimism, not optimism, about the local environment and its possibilities creates the view that the labor needed for large-scale infrastructure projects and natural resource extraction – if it can not be forced – must be induced with promises of higher wages and other benefits.

THE CRISIS OF THE 1990S: THE STATE DEFAULTS ON ITS OBLIGATIONS TO THE RUSSIAN FAR EAST AND OTHER CONCEPTS RESURFACE: REGIONAL ECONOMIC DEVELOPMENT AND INTEGRATION WITHIN ASIA

These attitudes of the State – that the region is Garrison and Gulag – imbue the policies of local officials. Local leaders in the region have always known that because the Russian Far East is garrison, the State will not abandon it, yet abandonment is almost exactly what happened in the 1990s. Despite the commitment of the State to provide the region with needed military and defense infrastructure, the State failed to meet its obligations in the 1990s. Subsidies were in name only, transfer payments (those that occurred) were always late, and almost always involved complicated and clumsy barter arrangements. Direct investment in infrastructure was cut back to almost nil. *The region in fact was left to fend for itself. The State in the last decade of the 20th century could barely support Garrison and had no interest in Gulag.*

The Russian federal budget crisis of the 1990s allowed other concepts regarding the region to resurface. Despite the traditional purposes the State had set for the region, the reality of a much weakened and financially bankrupt central government meant otherwise. Local governors and the local population – left on their own as the Soviet state capsized – simply had to 'cope' as best as they could. Coping meant survival behavior: grabbing, and then squirreling away, whatever resources were loosened during the chaotic destruction of the Soviet state.

The primary occupation, then, of local political leaders and the Russian Far East populace in the first half of the 1990s was to deal with the realities of acquiring sufficient food, shelter, and clothing when all the usual support systems of the Soviet State had collapsed. Beyond that, focus and concentration went to satisfy a long pent-up demand for quality consumer goods and, where possible, travel.

At the same time, the incoherence and instability of the newly created Russian State and the collapse of powerful hierarchies created an extreme political cautiousness on the part of local leaders and populations: no one wanted to be caught on the losing side of any Russian squabble or power struggle. To many, the collapse of the Soviet hierarchies was puzzling for some hierarchies collapsed in name only (but not in reality). And it was difficult to judge between those Soviet hierarchies that, in appearance only, were powerless and those that had become, in fact, powerless. Most politicians along with the local populations opted for a kind of political paralysis to avoid being on any 'losing side;' a paralysis especially as regards real movement toward regional or market reform.

It was at this time, early in the 1990s, that two concepts resurfaced to gain popular currency: the concept of regional economic development and the concept of integration into Asia. There was little reality behind the rhetoric as we shall see below, but for both the foreigners looking in and the local leaders looking out, the rhetoric fit the situation at the time. For the foreigners, these concepts (Regional Economic Development and Asian Integration) were the slogans with which they could, in good conscience, come 'marching in.' Americans living on the U.S. West Coast believed that an economic relationship with the Russian Far East was a 'natural.' Their enthusiasm was based on the belief that the resources within the Russian Far East, coupled with the markets in Asia could jumpstart the Russian Far East economy. Entrepreneurial help in the USA was but a short distance away; a shorter distance and more reliable, in this opinion, than help from Moscow.

For local Russian leaders too, these two concepts were also useful: a new set of masks, behind which their reality could be hidden: the reality that the region was in a desperate situation and the reality that in fact Moscow would not, and probably could not, offer any help at all. For local governments, the maintain transportation, communications and other infrastructure, without help from Moscow was not possible. The situation was deteriorating and these leaders were without any realistic strategy. A regional partnership between the Russian Far East and the U.S. West Coast might help, and thus the equation was created: from the Americans living in the U.S. Pacific Northwest would come enthusiasts and entrepreneurs (supported by the American government); from the Russian Far East would come a stated willingness to accept foreign help (technology, capital), to learn market methods, and to contribute land and resources for the development of joint projects. Given the enthusiasm of the Americans, local leaders had little reason not to act compliantly. Perhaps Asian Integration and Regional Economic Development could provide the goods and investment strength the region needed?

THE U.S. WEST COAST / RUSSIAN FAR EAST PARTNERSHIP IS CREATED: FALSE ASSUMPTIONS AND FALSE PROMOTIONS

Americans came to the region, wrote and signed agreements, brought their new Russian partners and friends to America for visits. Handshakes became the basis of new visions, new projects. The American optimism was based on a set of assumptions about the Russian Far East, its leaders and its peoples.

These assumptions were:

- Regional decision makers, without undue influence from Moscow, would make 'rational' (market-rational), and even 'autonomous' favourable decisions;
- Moscow's policies would coincide with and enable progress toward establishing a rule of law, creating a friendly foreign investment climate and toward building a firm resolve to fight corruption;
- American offers of finance and investment capital would be based on sound business plans and sound profit projections and these offers would be accepted, and projects would be realized;
- A commonality of experience in frontier, arctic-type development challenges would aid cooperative efforts, and that the Russian partners would come to see the American way and come to accept it as better.

By the end of the decade, the Americans entrepreneurs came to understand that their optimism had been misplaced and their assumptions had been false and illusory.

What the Americans came to understand was:

- Local administrations are not easy to deal with; *that regional decision makers do not make 'rational' (market-rational) favourable decisions.* An attitude prevailed that a host region has a right to part of the take, and takes what it can without regard for mutual economic benefit;
- Moscow's policies did not enable 'progress' toward establishing a rule of law, creating a friendly attitude toward foreign investment, and fighting corruption;
- Corruption was rampant and endemic, and there was little or no progress toward a rule of law and toward changing a corrupt court system;
- American offers of finance and investment capital, while accepted, were not based on sound business plans and sound profit projections. Projects failed to become profitable. Expectations of profit were unfulfilled because of cost overruns resulting from lack of infrastructure, pressure from the Russian partner to spend for extraneous purposes, lack of support from Moscow for infrastructure or environmental essentials, and a lack of an economic development policy which favored commerce – as defined in the West.
- *And, finally, despite a commonality of experience in frontier, arctic-type development challenges that could aid camaraderie and cooperative efforts, the Russians did not come to accept the American way as better.* And, in fact, Russian views rejected the

American concept of progress, in favour of passive stoicism to accept a situation as is, because 'we [Russians remember that] we have suffered much worse.' (. . . 'And it is an insult to us that you Americans act as you know better than we do.')

So what happened? How do we explain the difference between the optimism early in the decade and a change in mood at the end of the decade. Our explanation returns to the twin concepts of Garrison and Gulag. What the American entrepreneurs failed to see as they came marching into the region at the beginning of the 1990s was the region's primary and immutable relationship to the State. A relationship – garrison and gulag – that created constraints as regards the region's future, especially the ability of the region to absorb direct foreign investment.

A COLLISION OF CONCEPTS. BUSINESS IN THE 1990S. THE PAST HAUNTS THE PRESENT AND PREVENTS THE FUTURE

We have already seen that the concept of the region as garrison begets a set of priorities that overwhelm and even preclude all other goals. Scant resources (whatever that amount) must go to defense and the military, leaving very little for anything else. Asian Integration, Regional Economic Development, are slogans used to encourage foreign investors, but the overarching fact is that lack of financing for the massive requirements of these programs (particularly, infrastructure) both inhibit and constrain even the best possibilities.

Besides garrison, the concept of the region as gulag also infects and limits the ability of the region to absorb direct foreign investment. The legacy from the region's past acts on the present in the sense that the regional economy is even today riddled with projects begun with forced labour. Labour for project development in the Russian Far East (in Tsarist times, in Soviet times) has always been drawn from four pools of people: penal labour, escaped convicts, military conscripts, and finally, free men induced to move to the Russian Far East by the promise of high wages, land, other benefits. With a few exceptions (brief interludes where concessions were given to private entrepreneurs including foreigners), the State has always been the owner and manager involved in extraction of the region's mineral wealth and other natural resources. (An exception is the artel, which are long-standing independent miner-prospector cooperatives.) Therefore, the origin and planning of State projects was based on the premise that the State would also arrange for the labour. Labour would not be a problem: it would be available, one way or another. Investigations into early mining and logging projects, early road and railroad construction in the 18th and 19th centuries indicate that the labour force that the State provided was weighted heavily toward forced labour.

Today, one can see the legacy of this past: a local economy riddled with projects started with forced labour (not only in Stalinist times, but projects that go back to Tsarist times when penal labour was also prevalent). It so happens that many of these are the very projects that local leaders now want to resurrect or save.

When a foreign investor comes forth with a new proposal, local leaders usually counter that proposal with one of their own, hoping the foreigner might be persuaded to release some resources for projects that the local officials happen to favour. The foreigner's vision (or version) of development projects is often shunned or even rejected in the hopes that the foreigner might be convinced to look at some of the projects that local leaders are backing. (There are times when a foreign company, in order to get the foot in the door, will try to accede to local requests with regard to projects of local interest. This strategy usually fails.)

It is most noticeable that the list of projects favoured by local officials are usually those that were started in the past and have since been abandoned. These are usually in localities in which there is no present employer, leaving populations desperate. It is these kinds of projects that local governors wish to save. In the tug-of-war that ensues (between local officials and foreign investor), this aspect of the region's past creates an architypical discordance between the partners, limiting the possibilities of success.

(An exception is those instances when a project proposed by a foreign investor may in fact be accepted by local officials, especially if it can be justified in terms of a defense benefit. Coastal projects, for instance, benefit both the foreign investor (interested in commercial benefit) and local and federal authorities interested in the defense or military benefit that might result from such a project. Coastal infrastructure can serve military and defense interests thus serve a dual purpose, if the situation warrants.)

From the point of view of local Russian leaders, it is difficult to start something new when there is so much already started now languishing. Gold mining at Mnogovershinnoye, a small town just North of Nikolaevsk-na-Amure, is an example. The area is known for gold and was mined in the Stalinist era with penal labor. (It was also mined in the late 19th century, and indications show mined with penal labor.) At Mnogovershinnoye about 1,000 workers have been without wages as the operator of the mines has been unable to come up with their wages. Hunger strikes there create a political problem for the Governor of Khabarovsk krai and the krai Administration put forth extra effort to find a new partner for the mine, with some results: a show of interest from a French/Canadian consortium.

Another way to look at how the concepts of gulag and garrison limit the ability to absorb direct foreign investment and otherwise interfere with business success is to analyze the way these concepts grip present thinking, preventing rationality both about the present and about the future. In order to explain, I must digress.

I live in a neighborhood where, one block from my house, lived a family that in 1985 became victims of a heinous crime committed by an insane man believing that he was carrying out his mission to eliminate 'enemies of the people.' The day of that crime is seared in my memory. And to this day, I can not walk by this house without remembering. I am unable to set that moment aside when I walk past; I am unable to think in any other way about that house. Nor can I freely talk about it with my children if we are walking together. I say nothing. And I feign that nothing is the matter. I evade; I hide the truth. I am a prisoner of this past event and yet I can not reveal it. Nor can I, as I walk by, concentrate in the present moment, I only think about what happened in that house, to that family decades ago.

The above is true, I employ it here as a parable. So many projects in the Russian Far East were started with forced labour, labour that was expelled from Russia's western regions without judicial process and sent to work under the harshest of conditions. This is a past that also creates an involuntary shudder. It is a past that is almost never spoken about, yet affects almost everyone. It is a past with an overwhelming hold on the present. It forces a silence, an evasion, and as any great obsession, greatly interferes with the ability to concentrate on the present.

POSTSCRIPT
BUSINESS IN THE 1990S: A CONUNDRUM AND A PERSONAL STORY ABOUT THE AUTHOR AND HER GUIDE, LUBA

Luba (the name has been changed) was assigned to help me on many of my visits to the Russian Far East during the 1980s and early 1990s, when I was an official guest of the Soviet Academy of Sciences and later when I was a guest of the Russian Academy of Sciences. Luba's job was to be sure my travel arrangements went smoothly and that I encountered no particular problems. Luba always did her job well. Over time I became comfortable and respected her requests of me as part of the job she was assigned to do. Otherwise, I knew little about her, certainly less than she knew about me.

Luba recently revealed her story to me. In 1933 her grandmother, grandfather and mother were resettled (by Stalin's order) from their home in Latvia to a gulag camp near Mnogovershinnoye (about 70 km north of Nikolaevsk-Na-Amure). Luba's grandfather, ill on arrival, was sent to Blagoveschensk and never heard from again. Luba's grandmother was assigned to a group of people who served the gulag camp. 'Hearty and spirited,' says Luba, her grandmother lived to raise Luba's mother and then Luba herself. Neither Luba's mother nor her grandmother has ever spoken to Luba about their camp life. Only from her father did Luba learn about her family's past, and this just before his death.

In the mid-1990s, I very briefly advised the French/Canadian company who, for a short time, held an equity involvement in Mnogovershinnoye gold fields. At the time of my conversations with the company, I did not know that Mnogovershinnoye and the adjacent Lake Chyla area were, in the first decades of 20th century, proffered as concessions for foreign involvement, just as they were being proffered again to the Canadians. Nor did I know that in past times these gold mines were worked with forced labour. I also did not know that Luba's family had been interned near Mnogovershinnoye.

At the time of my consultancy to the Canadian company, what if Luba had been at my side? What would she have done had we visited the very area of her family's past history? I am certain that Luba would have not told me anything at all. But, I ask, if she had remained silent about this, what other silences had there been between us? And if she could not at times tell me the truth, what was the nature of what she did tell me? Lies? And what about everyone else tied to an unspeakable past one way or another?

Chapter 14

Pacific Russia and Australian Business

David Lockwood and Vladimir Tikhomirov

INTRODUCTION

It is fairly clear that Pacific Russia will not be a 'resource supplier' for Australia, since many of the potential resources of the area are replicated within the Australian economy. In fact, the attention of Australian Governments was first drawn to the RFE (hereafter RFE) (now Pacific Russia in official parlance) because of the potential competitiveness of this resource rich and relatively under-populated area. However, in the more immediate term, if Bradshaw and Lynn are correct in contending that resource-based industrialisation ('the further processing of natural resources, such as minerals and metals') may be one of the few options for the development of Pacific Russia, then access to capital and technologically advanced equipment (for the extraction and processing of natural resources) from outside the area will be necessary.[1]

This accounts for the second aspect of Government interest in the area: the encouragement of Australian companies to invest in and sell advanced technology. It is argued that Australian industry cannot 'impede' the development of the area, and since someone is likely to develop the resources, it would be in the interests of the Australian economy that Australian companies are involved in the process. The experience gained by Australian enterprises that are used to working with low population densities over large areas is said to give them a competitive edge over the Japanese, Korean and even American firms working in the area.

A third reason for Government interest is the continuing need for Pacific Russia (and the Russian Federation in general) to import food. Russia is by far the largest importer of grain and dairy produce, and the Russian market is of vital importance to Australian rural industry (which has exercised considerable

254

influence over Australian governments, past and present). As a result of Russia's current trials, the question of food is likely to assume an even greater importance. As short falls in the supply of food for the Russian population increase, the Russian government will almost certainly be forced to enlarge the role of the state in ensuring that food stocks are somewhere near adequate. We can expect an increase in state purchases of food from outside Russia. This will be of considerable interest to Australian exporters, since the stocks for such exports to Russia are readily available.[2]

During the last days of the Soviet Union, Australian government circles were aware of the potential for a changing trade relationship were the Union to break up. The Senate Standing Committee on Foreign Affairs, Defence and Trade submitted a report in December 1990 entitled *Perestroika – Implications for Australia-USSR Relations*. The Committee reported that 'Australia has made some efforts to respond to Soviet interest in getting Pacific countries to invest in the Far East.' In 1987 there had been an Australian trade mission to the Soviet Far East, which was the first to the area for well over a decade. This was followed by a further mission in 1989 and a trade fair in Vladivostok in July 1990.[3] However, the Department of Foreign Affairs and trade pointed out to the Committee:

> Expansion of trade between the Soviet Far East and regional countries has been hampered by lack of local authority over economic decision-making and hard currency, and poorly developed infrastructure.

Possibly with an eye to the future, the Senate Committee concluded that the decentralisation of Soviet trade was 'a key part of opening up the Soviet Far East and Siberia to foreign investment'.[4] Nevertheless, although it recommended 'a more vigorous trading relationship' with the USSR, it was not optimistic about Australian prospects in the Soviet Far East:

> The Far East and Siberian region offers fewer prospects for Australian exports in general than the rest of the USSR. The size of the market alone is a disadvantage.[5]

Overall, the Committee identified the USSR as a potential competitor in agricultural produce (especially 'to the extent that Australia succeeds in its efforts to export food handling and processing technology to the USSR'), and in the longer term in the export of minerals extraction and processing technology.[6]

The collapse of the Soviet Union, followed by the collapse of the Russian economy, wrought great changes in the trade relationship between Australia and Russia. The broad trade figures for the period are shown in *Table 14.1*. Eventually the argument that Russia or the RFE would be a competitor with Australian exports would be rejected, and there would be a revival of interest in a special economic relationship between Australia and the region. In the period immediately following the collapse however, there seemed to be at most a 'wait and see' attitude on the part of the Government and its advisors. Paradoxically enough, this attitude continued throughout the initial period of the Keating

Table 14.1 Dynamics of Australia–Russia Trade, 1986–1994 (Million Australian dollars)

	Exports	*Imports*
1986–7	688	15
1987–8	630	22
1988–9	1010	54
1992	43	15
1993	192	21
1994	275	21

Source: Department of Foreign Affairs and Trade, Canberra.

government's much-expressed enthusiasm for greater ties with North East Asia and the Pacific region.

The 1992 Raby Report included Pacific Russia in the North East Asian region,[7] but did not discuss it at any length. In the chapter on Australia's economic relations with North East Asia, Pacific Russia was only mentioned in the context of possible Australian collaboration with Korean mineral exploration and development in the area.[8] Raby noted the events in Eastern Europe and the former Soviet Union but argued that in the next five years those countries' 'demands on world capital markets and the consequent impact for Australia will be relatively minor.' He did, however, concede that 'if the transition can be managed, Pacific Russia should begin to play a larger role economic role in the region'.[9]

One of the reasons for the apparent indifference of the Keating government to Pacific Russia was revealed only recently in a speech by Mr Keating on the subject of Indonesia in which he argued against Pacific Russia's inclusion in the region. He said:

> But more basically, APEC has been hobbled by the agreement to add Russia to its membership ... Under no conceivable stretch of the imagination is Russia currently part of the Asia Pacific economy.[10]

Perhaps the reawakening of Government interest in Pacific Russia was occasioned by the independent activities of Australian business itself; six out of the ten companies surveyed for this paper reported having commenced their activities in the region in the early 1990s. What ever the reason, the geographical area of the East Asian Analytical Unit (EAAU) of the Department of Foreign Affairs was expanded to include Pacific Russia at this time, and the Minister for Trade and Overseas Development paid a visit to the area at the end of 1992.

In 1996 the EAAU published a major report, *Pacific Russia: Risks and Rewards.* Characterising Pacific Russia as 'a slow moving blip on East Asia's economic radar screen',[11] the promise of which had yet to materialise, the report nevertheless pointed to certain limited opportunities in the area for Australian companies (many of which were already being taken advantage of). The report rejected the notion of Pacific Russia as a competitor with Australian exports:

> Russia's current difficulties mean that Pacific Russia is unlikely to be able to develop rapidly enough to threaten Australia's exports in the short to medium term.

And in the longer term, such a possibility was balanced by the expected rise in demand as North East Asian economies expanded. Indeed, if Pacific Russia was integrated into the region, this would in itself have a dynamic impact on regional growth, and would increase demand for Australian exports. In the short term the EAAU believed that Australian opportunities lay in niche markets, particularly food and beverages. In the longer term they argued that the mining sector would be Pacific Russia's main area of comparative advantage and therefore a promising avenue for Australian investment. This, however, depended on Moscow and on a more stable policy environment.[12]

THE POLICY OUTLOOK

There was no dramatic change of attitude towards economic relationships with the RFE with the election of a Liberal/National Party government in 1996. In an interview in that year, the new foreign minister, Alexander Downer, was clearly more enthused about prospects in central and eastern Europe, than any developments in Russia. Nevertheless, he supported Russian integration into the Asia Pacific region, and repeated the EAAU's optimistic prognosis on the effect of Pacific Russian development on the region. He also gave support to Russia's efforts to join the ASEAN regional forum and APEC. This was not, however, purely economic encouragement. Government sources suggested that, if Russia (as a predominantly European country) was included in these bodies, it would lessen Australia's vulnerability to 'Asians only' arguments put forward by, among others, Malaysia.[13] A trade delegation led by David Brownhill (Assistant Minister for Trade and Minister for Primary Industries and Energy) visited central/ eastern Europe and Russia in September 1996. Once again, while optimistic about the former areas, Senator Brownhill was wary about the latter. He declared that the return of Russia as a major component in Australia's trade scheme was some years off.[14] In the Government's major White Paper on foreign policy, released in 1997, Russia as a Pacific power was ignored. Only the US, Japan, China and Indonesia were listed as being of interest to Australia in the Asia Pacific region.[15]

From the business point of view, however, Australian investors were becoming tentatively more optimistic and more conscious of the advantages of geographic proximity to the RFE. John Evans, president of the Australia-Russia and Newly Independent States Business Council (ARNISBC), described Pacific Russia as 'the easiest area [in Russia] for most of our members to concentrate on . . . The Europeans can get into Moscow and St Petersburg a lot easier than we can, because of the distance.'[16] On the food import side, ARNISBC reported that Russian trade officials believed that foodstuffs would retain their high Russian market share through 1998 – because the Russian food and food processing industries were still not capable of a substantial increase in output.[17] For minerals, it was not so easy. Evans reported: 'At the moment foreign companies are expected to go in and explore, and if they find anything then the discovery is put out to open tender.'[18]

That was not the only inhibiting factor on the Russian side. Budget constraints made it less likely that the Russian authorities would seek out increased trade relationships with middle-level powers like Australia. In August 1996, the Russian government announced that it was closing the offices of Russian trade representatives in thirty five countries, Australia among them.[19]

At the same time, protectionist measures were increased by the Russian government, including measures against imported food and beverages, despite the need for imports to satisfy consumer demand. John Helmer of the *Business Review Weekly* suggested a number of reasons for this. Firstly, the new measures were designed to force Russian consumers to buy local products – but not the same ones. Thus, Alexandr Zaveryukha (deputy premier with responsibility for agriculture and food production), said that if a tariff was placed on imported bananas, Russian would be forced to eat . . . local apples. A 20 per cent import duty exists on fine-micron Australian wool, which has no comparable Russian competitor. Secondly, the new protectionism can be seen as a pay-off of political debts to local authorities that encouraged their regions to vote for Yeltsin rather than Zyuganov (of the KPRF) in the last presidential elections (see Chapter 4). Thirdly, it results from pressure by local 'nomeklatura directors' to protect their inefficient industries. And finally, it results from the communist/nationalist majority in the Duma.[20] Measures to protect the Russian sugar beet industry against Australian imports for example were introduced by the former premier Kirienko as part of the price for his approval by the Duma.[21]

Dynamics of Bilateral Foreign Trade

According to the official Soviet statistical series, Australia's share in overall USSR exports and imports in the late 1980s was rather low (*Table 14.2*). Soviet exports to Australia constituted only 0.03 per cent of the total volume of Soviet exports in 1989 and by 1991 this share dropped even further to just 0.02 per cent. Australia's share in overall Soviet imports was slightly higher: in 1989 it was 0.8 per cent and in 1991 it increased to 0.9 per cent. The bulk of Soviet exports to Australia was machinery (around 80 per cent of the total volume), which included vehicles, metal-cutting equipment, photo cameras, etc. The major items that the USSR imported from Australia were wool (50–70 per cent of all imports) and food products (wheat, meat, diary). Bauxites were another

Table 14.2 USSR–Australia Foreign Trade, 1989–91 (Million current roubles)

	1989	1990	1991
Exports to Australia	17.7	17.6	15.3
Machinery	15.0	16.0	12.0
Imports from Australia	587.4	225.9	691.2
Wool	429.4	97.0	346.5
Bauxite	66.7	54.2	56.2
Wheat	27.0	0.0	134.3
Total Soviet exports	68741.6	60756.8	81418.9
Total Soviet imports	72137.0	70727.6	79230.1
Russia's share in exports, %	58.2	68.5	78.9
Russia's share in imports, %	58.2	67.6	56.4

Sources: Vneshnie ekonomicheskie svyazi SSSR v 1990 g. (1991) Moscow: Goskomstat, p. 8, 274; *Vneshnie ekonomicheskie svyazi SSSR i Sodruzhestva Nezavisimykh Gosudarstv v 1991 g.* (1992), Moscow: EVIK.

important item of Australian exports to the USSR with a share of 11.4 per cent in gross exports in 1989 and 8.1 per cent in 1991.

The major part of Australian non-food exports to the Soviet Union was consumed in Russia. In the late 1980s the Russian share in the gross Soviet imports was varying between 56 per cent and 58 per cent, while its share in exports was significantly higher (up to 80 per cent). Australian food exports to the USSR were distributed between Russia and other Soviet republics, while the major part of Australian meat exports (mutton) was consumed primarily by the population of the Soviet Central Asia.

The collapse of the Soviet Union and the start of market reforms in Russia resulted in dramatic changes in the dynamics of Australian trade with the former Soviet Union. First, the disintegration of the USSR meant that Australia had to diversify significantly its trade operations between 15 ex-Soviet republics. Second, decentralisation and privatisation of foreign trade in the majority of former Soviet republics led to a rapid decline of importance of the former state-controlled trade organisations. Australian exporters had to find new trading partners which in many cases turned out to be a difficult and, given the instability of the post-Soviet markets a risky business. Third, reforms in the former Soviet Union had led to a rapid fall in the living standards of the population, which forced many local importers to search for cheaper and lower quality products. In this situation planning of trade operations and long-term strategies became more complicated and at times impossible. Fourth, the removal of state subsidies from local industries and transportation companies in the former Soviet Union had resulted in growing incapability of ex-Soviet industrialists to pay for much needed imported components, like unprocessed meat, wool or bauxites. At the same time, delivery of imported goods from Australia became much more expensive than in the Soviet period. This made many Australian products significantly less attractive for internal consumers, particularly when they could buy cheaper low-quality goods from Asia or quality goods from much closer European countries. A flow of imports from Western Europe and the USA, many of which were subsidised through various export enhancement or aid programs, also had a negative effect on the dynamics of Australian exports to the post-Soviet markets.

The result was an immediate and large fall in the volumes of Australian trade with the former Soviet Union. While Russia remained the largest trade partner of Australia among all ex-Soviet republics, its exports to Australia in 1992 were significantly lower than Soviet exports in 1991. If we recalculate the Soviet trade data from roubles into US dollars using the official exchange rate, than the gross volume of Soviet exports to Australia in 1991 was about US$24 million. In 1992 Russian exports to Australia amounted to only about US$8 million, or 3 times less than the Soviet exports a year earlier. The share of machinery in Russian exports had fallen from 80 per cent in the Soviet period to about 47 per cent in 1992 and 36 per cent in 1993 (*Table 14.3*).

However, the decline in imports was even more astounding: while in 1991 the Soviet Union imported about US$1,000 million of Australian goods, in the next year Russian imports from Australia amounted to just US$52 million. Such a fall was a manifestation of the total collapse of the earlier trade relations. All major

Table 14.3 Russia–Australia Foreign Trade, 1992–96, Goskomstat Series (Million US dollars)

	1992	*1993*	*1994*	*1995*	*1996*
Exports to Australia	7.9	10.0	37.6	29.5	8.3
Machinery	3.7	3.6	–	–	–
Imports from Australia	52.4	80.9	191.0	135.0	102.0
Wool	4.0	4.9	–	–	–
Bauxite	10.1	11.5	40.2	62.4	–
Wheat	0.0	6.7	67.4	–	–
Total Russian exports	42376.0	44297.0	53001.0	65607.0	71874.0
Total Russian imports	36984.0	26807.0	28344.0	33117.0	31798.0

Sources: *Rossiiskii statisticheskii ezhegodnik, 1996* (1996) Moscow: Goskomstat, 1996, p. 343; *Rossiiskii statisticheskii ezhegodni, 1997* (1997) Moscow: Goskomstat, p. 578; *Vneshneekonomicheskaya deyatel'nost' gosudarstv Sodruzhestva v 1995 godu.* (1996) Moscow: Statkom SNG, p. 147; *Vneshneekonomicheskaya deyatel'nost' gosudarstv Sodruzhestva v 1994 godu* (1995) Moscow: Statkom SNG, pp. 275, 286, 288, 292; *Vneshneekonomicheskaya deyatel'nost' gosudarstv Sodruzhestva v 1993 godu* (1994) Moscow: Statkom SNG, pp. 224, 231; *Vneshnie ekonomicheskie svyazi Rossiiskoi Federatsii v 1992 g. Moscow* (1993) Goskomstat, pp. 243–244; *Vneshneekonomicheskie svyazi Rossiiskoi Federatsii v 1993 godu* (1994) Moscow: Goskomstat, pp. 145–46.

items of Australian exports to Russia/USSR had recorded sharp falls, with the most dramatic decline registered in the wool trade (down 135 times). It is important to note that these falls in trade came not only as a result of the changes in the organisation of the Russian foreign trade, but were also a consequence of the inability of the post-Soviet Russian government to honour financial commitments in accordance with trade contracts signed by the Soviet government.

The changes that occurred in 1992 have led to the de facto disappearance of large-volume and organised trade between Russia and Australia. In the post-Soviet period small export-import operators came in as the major driving force of the bilateral trade. Volumes of their trade operations were often in the range of a few million dollars and sometimes equalled just one or two cargo containers a year. The composition of trade became greatly diversified and included various pre-packed and processed foodstuffs, like canned food, wine and other alcoholic beverages, small quantities of meat and meat products, dairy products and butter, etc. Some non-food consumer goods like textiles, clothing and shoes, were also exported to Russia, although in very small quantities. Among industrial goods bauxites were the largest item; their share in Australian exports to Russia during 1992–96 varied between 20 per cent and 50 per cent.

These negative trends affected the shares of Australia in the total volume of Russian foreign trade operations. Australia's share in Russian exports in 1992 was less than 0.02 per cent and by 1996 it fell to just 0.01 per cent. The share in imports was only slightly higher: in 1992 Australia's imports constituted 0.1 per cent of the total Russian imports and in 1996 the percentage was 0.3 per cent. According to Australian trade statistics, similar trends were recorded on the Australian side as well. The difference in trade figures derived from Russian and Australian sources can be explained by the fact that Australian data series do not list some confidential items, which include aluminium ore (bauxites). Data from the Australian Bureau of Statistics (ABS) demonstrates that in the 1990s importance of Russia as Australia's trade partner was also extremely low. In 1992 Russian share in the gross volume of Australian exports was just 0.07 per cent; by 1997 it increased to 0.18 per cent (*Table 14.4*). During the same period the share of Russia in the gross volume of Australian imports of goods has fallen from 0.03 per cent to just 0.02 per cent.

The composition of Australia-Russia trade could be drawn from trade statistics that are gathered in the *TradeData* database at the Victoria University of Technology. This database is based on information provided by the Australian customs; however, it also does not include some classified items. As *Table 14.4* demonstrates, if we take out Australian exports of bauxites from the total volumes of exports to Russia, the largest single group of items in the remaining part of exports are foodstuffs: in 1993–94 they constituted between 62 per cent and 74 per cent of non-classified Australian exports to Russia. Australian statistics also show a significantly lower share of machinery in the gross amount of imports from Russia than the Russian sources (see *Table 14.5*). This, however, could be explained by differences in trade classifications that were used in the two countries.

Table 14.4 Australia–Russia Foreign Trade, 1992–97, ABS Series (Million Australian dollars)

	1992	1993	1994	1995	1996	1997
Exports to Russia	43	192	275	146	74	158
Imports from Russia	15	21	21	36	19	20
Total Australian exports	58265	62772	64776	71664	77229	87362
Total Australian imports	55874	62402	68099	77469	78429	85081

Source: Australian International Merchandise Trade, Canberra: ABS. Quarterly.

Table 14.5 Australia–Russia Foreign Trade, 1992–94, TradeData Series (Million US dollars)

	1992	1993	1994
*Exports to Russia**	15.1	88.7	94.6
Wool	–	–	–
Bauxite	n/a	n/a	n/a
Foodstuffs	2.7	55.0	69.8
Imports from Russia	12.6	19.2	18.2
Machinery	1.9	8.6	3.9

*Totals do not include classified items.
Source: TradeData, Centre for Strategic Economic Studies, Victoria University of Technology, Melbourne, Australia.

The data series presented above demonstrate that from both the Australian and the Russian perspective bilateral trade relations were never a high priority particularly in the post-Soviet era. Internal Russian developments and the restructuring of Russia's trade relations were the main factors in blocking the development of this trade. A second factor was the changes in Australian economic orientation, particularly in the first half of the 1990s, when many Australian exporters became actively involved in East Asian markets. And the third factor were general economic structures of the two countries that forced them often to compete, but not to co-operate, on the world market.

ECONOMIC RELATIONS BETWEEN AUSTRALIA AND PACIFIC RUSSIA

Given the small scale of Australia-Russia trade, it would be correct to assume that volumes of Australia's trade operations with any particular region of Russia will have to be even smaller. However, because of its importance as one of the major trade gateways in the USSR/Russia, the RFE has always had a special status. Significant volumes of Soviet foreign trade went through Far Eastern port destinations, like Nakhodka, Vladivostok and Vostochnyy. In many cases foreign trade partners of the Soviet Union had no other route information about their exports except the first Soviet destination, and many Australian exporters thought that a significant part of their exports was actually destined for consumption in Pacific Russia. That, of course, was often not the case. Much of the goods that were imported through Far Eastern ports, were later shipped via rail to other internal Soviet destinations, like the European parts of Russia or Central Asia.

The rise in transportation costs that occurred simultaneously with price liberalisation in 1992 led to a rapid decline of the attractiveness of the Far Eastern destinations for Russian traders. The volumes of Russian imports via pacific ports started to sharply fall since 1992. On the other hand, the Pacific part of Russia with a population of about 7.5 million people had a very limited potential for any increase in trade operations. Economic depression that hit the Far Eastern economy in the post-Soviet period also had a negative impact on the expansion of local foreign trade.

Data collected from a variety of local Far Eastern statistical publications show that Pacific Russia had a rather modest shares in the gross volume of Russia's foreign trade operations (*Table 14.6*). The share of the region in Russia's exports in 1992 was just 3.3 per cent; it remained virtually unchanged in 1995. During the same period the share of the region in Russia's gross imports had increased from 2.1 per cent to 5.1 per cent.

The bulk of Pacific Russia's exports come from five territories: Primorskii and Khabarovsk krais, Sakhalin, Kamchatka and the Republic of Sakha (Yakutia). These exports predominantly consist of metals, coal, timber and fish products. The major destinations of these exports are neighbouring countries of Pacific Asia (Japan, China, South Korea) and North America (the US and Canada).[22] The latest available combined data for the whole region is for 1995. It shows that in that year 24.8 per cent of Pacific Russia's exports came from Khabarovsk krai, 21.8 per cent from Sakhalin, 21.5 per cent from Primorskii krai, 17.3 per cent from Kamchatka and 11 per cent from Sakha (*Table 14.6*).

The same five territories are the major importers in Pacific Russia; however, the share of Primorskii krai in the gross volume of imports into the region is significantly higher which reflects the importance of port infrastructure of Primorskii krai. In 1995 this area had a share of 32.2 per cent in the total imports of Pacific Russia. Other significant importers included Sakhalin (17.2 per cent), Khabarovsk krai (17 per cent) and Sakha (13 per cent). Food products had the largest share in Pacific Russia's imports: in 1993 it was 40.4 per cent. In Primorskii krai food amounted to over 70 per cent of all imports, while in Magadan and Sakha it was only 10–15 per cent.[23] The major imported item in the two latter areas was equipment for the local mining industry.

The fact that both Australia and Pacific Russia have similar export structures with minerals, timber and fish products making the bulk of their exports,

Table 14.6 Foreign Trade of Pacific Russia in 1991–96 (Million US dollars)

	1991	*1992*	*1993*	*1994*	*1995*	*1996*
All exports including:	*(443.9)*	*1411.5*	*1837.3*	*1615.2*	*2186.7*	*(1153.0)*
Primorskii krai	126.8	230.8	442.3	441.7	469.4	600.8
Khabarovsk krai	–	371.1	515.9	385.6	543.3	–
Sakhalin	306.6	206.8	284.0	251.3	475.9	552.2
Amur	–	231.2	233.2	69.1	48.5	–
Kamchatka	–	137.2	185.1	288.0	378.0	–
Magadan	10.5	81.1	18.4	13.9	30.2	–
Sakha	–	153.3	158.4	165.6	241.4	–
All imports including:	*1154.0*	*784.4*	*1146.7*	*1275.2*	*1704.6*	*(913.6)*
Primorskii krai	183.8	181.0	237.0	581.2	549.0	629.7
Khabarovsk krai	414.0	125.7	357.3	118.6	289.0	–
Sakhalin	204.3	102.9	124.9	262.1	292.6	283.9
Amur	60.0	185.3	174.4	36.6	76.0	–
Kamchatka	133.0	69.8	75.0	85.0	147.0	–
Magadan	5.9	60.4	49.2	59.7	130.0	–
Sakha	153.0	59.3	128.9	132.0	221.0	–

Sources: *Primorskii krai v 1996 godu* (1997) Vladivostok: Goskomstat, p. 105; *Primorskii krai v 1995 godu* (1996) Vladivostok: Goskomstat, pp. 196–197; *Primorskii krai v 1994 godu* (1995) Vladivostok: Goskomstat, pp. 197–198; *50 let Sakhalinskoi oblasti* (1996) Yuzhno-Sakhlinsk: Goskomstat, p. 192; *Sakhlinskaya oblast', '96* (1997) Yuzhno-Sakhlinsk: Goskomstat, p. 33; *Statisticheskii sbornik vneshneekonomicheskoi deyatelnosti predpriyatii i organizatsii Sakhalinskoi oblasti za 1993 god. Chast' 1,* (1994) Yuzhno-Sakhlinsk: Goskomstat, p. 11; *Sakhalinskaya oblast' v tsifrakh (1970, 1985–1992 gg.)* (1993) Yuzhno-Sakhlinsk: Goskomstat, p. 22; *Vneshneekonomicheskaya deyatelnost' Amurskoi oblasti* (1995) Blagoveshensk: Goskomstat, p. 5; *O razvitii ekonomicheskikh reform v Amurskoi oblasti, yanvar-dekabr 1995 g.* (1996) Blagoveshensk: Goskomstat, p. 46–47; Pavel Minakir, Gregory Freeze (eds.), (1996) *The Russian Far East: An Economic Survey (2nd E,.),* Khabarovsk: RIOTIP, p. 455–68.

precluded low levels of their mutual trade. The other important items that Australia could supply to the RFE were food products, but availability of supply of these products from countries next to the borders of the Far East has greatly limited export opportunities for Australian traders. As *Tables 14.7* and *14.8* demonstrate, the levels of Australia-Pacific Russia direct trade in the post-Soviet period were rather low. Pacific Russia's exports to Australia topped just US$3 million in 1995, or only 10.3 per cent of the gross Russian exports to Australia that year. A major part of Pacific Russia's exports to Australia came from Primorskii krai; these were mainly metals and fish products.

In the post-1991 period Australia's exports to Pacific Russia were always significantly higher than its imports from the region. By the mid-1990s the share of Pacific Russia in the total volume of Russian imports from Australia increased to 20–25 per cent. This was a reflection of the growing dependency of the Far

Table 14.7 Dynamics of Trade between the Russian Far East and Australia (Million US dollars)

	1991	1992	1993	1994	1995	1996
Exports to Australia including:	*(0.83)*	*0.60*	*1.84*	*0.66*	*3.05*	*(0.30)*
Primorskii krai	0.83	0.60	1.80	0.60	3.00	0.30
Khabarovsk krai	–	0.00	0.00	0.00	0.00	–
Sakhalin	–	0.00	0.04	0.06	0.05	0.00
Amur	–	0.00	0.00	0.00	0.00	–
Kamchatka	–	0.00	0.00	0.00	0.00	–
Magadan	0.00	0.00	0.00	0.00	0.00	–
Sakha	–	0.00	0.00	0.00	0.00	–
Imports from Australia including:	*(3.34)*	*0.06*	*3.57*	*37.60*	*33.07*	*(19.90)*
Primorskii krai	–	0.00	3.00	37.60	32.80	19.90
Khabarovsk krai	–	0.00	0.00	0.00	0.00	–
Sakhalin	3.34	0.06	0.39	0.00	0.27	0.00
Amur	–	0.00	0.00	0.00	0.00	–
Kamchatka	–	0.00	0.19	0.00	0.00	–
Magadan	0.00	0.00	0.00	0.00	0.00	–
Sakha	–	0.00	0.00	0.00	0.00	–

Sources: See Table 14.6 above.

Table 14.8 Australian Trade with Pacific Russia in 1992–94, TradeData Series (Million US dollars)

	1992	1993	1994
Exports to the RFE*	0.4	46.2	38.0
Wool	–	–	–
Bauxite	n/a	n/a	n/a
Foodstuffs	0.4	36.7	33.3
Imports from the RFE	0.8	1.4	4.1
Machinery	0.0	1.1	0.2

*Totals do not include classified items.
Source: *TradeData*, Centre for Strategic Economic Studies, Victoria University of Technology, Melbourne, Australia.

East on foreign suppliers that were replacing traditional suppliers from European parts of Russia and the former Soviet Union. The highest volume of imports from Australia was recorded in Pacific Russia in 1994 (US\$37.6 million). According to the *TradeData* database, food products made the bulk of Australia's non-classified exports into the region: in 1993 their share in overall exports was 79 per cent and in 1994 it has grown to 87 per cent (*Table 14.8*). Almost all of these exports entered the region through ports located in Primorskii krai.

Despite the fact that there was a certain increase in foreign trade dynamics between Australia and Pacific Russia in the mid-1990s, their bilateral trade operations continued to remain on very low, almost non-existent levels. For instance, the peak of Pacific Russia's exports to Australia in 1995 was equal to only 0.005 per cent of the gross Russian exports that year. And the largest volume of Pacific Russian imports from Australia, recorded in 1994, amounted to just 0.13 per cent of the gross Russian imports. The importance of Pacific Russia in Australia's foreign trade operations was at the same low level. Imports from Pacific Russia in 1995 constituted just 0.006 per cent of all Australian imports, while exports to this region a year earlier had a share of 0.08 per cent in the gross volume of Australian exports to all destinations.

The difficult financial situation of Russia, the continuing decline of its national economy and the gross underdevelopment of its market institutions have created major difficulties for the operations of Australian traders. Dramatic rise in costs of transportation of goods from Pacific to European parts of Russia had effectively cut off Australian exporters from the most populated areas of Russia. In addition, high levels of competition on the Russian market from low-quality and/or subsidised exports from other foreign destinations also put major obstacles to Australian trade businesses in Russia. Apart from trade, in most other areas Russian and Australian exporters often found themselves as competitors in the same markets, be that in Asia or in Europe. All that led to a situation when many large Australian companies became less and less interested in the Russian market. The trade dynamics as presented above clearly reflected that process.

THE EXPERIENCE OF AUSTRALIAN INVESTMENT IN THE RUSSIAN FAR EAST

In the decade up to 1989, Australian trade with the Soviet Union was dominated by the export of wool and wheat. Trade in manufactured goods was negligible, although Australia did import limited numbers of tractors and passenger cars (over $6 million worth of each from 1988–1989). The 'Perestroyka' report was of the opinion that this pattern of trade was unlikely to change in the short term.[24]

Change it did, however – but not for the better. After the Soviet collapse, the Russian Federation was unable to service its debts. Australia closed off trade credits with the result that Australian exports to Russia fell by over 90 per cent between 1991 and 1992. Wool (for which the Soviet Union had been Australia's second largest export destination) was hit hardest. By 1994 Russian wool mills could only afford to operate at 20 per cent of their former capacity. With demand from the military sector dropping and imported woollen goods from Asia increasing, this situation continued into 1995.[25]

Food: In food exports, things appeared a little brighter. One of the effects of the Soviet decline was the need to import unprocessed and processed food. Russian imports of wheat continued and increased. In 1996, Viktor Khlystun, the Minister of Agriculture, announced that Russia would buy another three to four million tonnes of wheat on international markets and an additional 500,000 tonnes of food wheat for Primorskii *Krai*. He pointed out that it was cheaper to buy abroad to supply the needs of the *RFE* than to import from southern Russia by rail. A significant amount of the imported wheat would come from Australia.[26] A month later first deputy minister of Agriculture Vladimir Shcherbak said that the Russian Federation would import 4.5 million tonnes of maize and soybeans from Australia, Canada and the United States.[27]

But processed food was the big winner in exports to post-Soviet Russia – especially to the RFE. By 1996, processed food had become Australia's major export to the area, along with sugar and aluminium. As living standards and the quality of life declined in Russia, Australian processed foods had established a reputation for high quality and clean produce. It competed successfully with imports from South Korea and China, probably because the tastes of Russian consumers were closer to those in Australia than in Asia.[28]

Australian meat trade with Russia has followed the pattern of other food exports. Its gross volume in the post-Soviet period had decreased significantly, mainly due to the inability of Russian importers to pay for quality meat supplies from Australia, but also due to the fact that a significant proportion (mainly mutton) of the meat previously supplied to the USSR was consumed not in Russia but in Soviet Central Asia. In the 1990s Australian meat exports to Pacific Russia were limited to small quantities of assorted pre-packed and fancy meats, which were targeted for consumption in restaurants or small delicatessen style shops. In 1994–1996, the Australian Meat Research Corporation funded a research project on the potential meat market in the RFE. The report found that the immediate prospects for increased volumes of meat trade with Pacific Russia were low.[29] Notwithstanding this, James Hardie Industries has constructed two cold stores on Sakhalin and the Kuriles.[30] Before the August 1998 rouble devaluation, meat exports were rising, reaching five times their 1996/7 level by the end of the 1997/8 financial year ($A100 million). The immediate impact of the crisis was a cancellation of some orders and payment difficulties with others. *Austrade*, however, was confident that the trade would continue since Russia's ability to produce meat was limited. By September 1998, with the crisis easing somewhat, the Russian government was considering cuts in import duties on Australian meat in order to speed up supplies for Russian citizens.[31]

Meanwhile, as a class of nouveaux riches developed in Russia, sales of Australian bottled wine have increased.[32]

The success of Australian food exports is well illustrated in the case of butter. The Soviet Union was the world's largest producer and consumer of butter, with each of its citizens consuming an average 7.5 kilo a year (4.4 for Western

Europeans). Little wonder then that Australia had been selling small amounts of butter to the RFE for several years before 1991. After that, the Russian government was under domestic pressure to maintain supplies; imports of Australian butter increased. The situation was exacerbated as Russian herd size began to decline (at a rate of about 12 per cent per year) and the dairy industry moved to cut butter production more sharply than milk or cheese.[33]

The International Food Processing Group (IFP) had been the largest Australian exporter of butter to the Soviet Union for a number of years. When markets increased, IFP opened a butter recombining plant in Komsomolsk-na-Amure in 1993, using Australian butter making equipment to manufacture product from Australian butter fat imports. Taking advantage of Australia's 'clean' image, IFP also entered the marketing arena. In 1994 it reached an agreement with GUM to operate its outlet in Vladivostok as a western-style supermarket, exclusively stocked with Australian goods. The following year, a second supermarket along these lines was opened in Nakhodka. In 1996, production of butter was doubled with the opening of a second plant in Khabarovsk. Each factory employed around 26 people.[34] IFP seemed well aware of the advantages for Australian companies in Pacific Russia. According to the managing director, Mike Murray:

> The long term future for Australian companies in Russia is on the Pacific side. In Western Russia we can't compete with Western Europe from a freight point of view.[35]

Minerals: Mineral exploration and exploitation presents an altogether gloomier prospect from the Australian point of view. Risks and Rewards *predicted:*

> Over the medium to long term, exports related to investment in the resources sector (such as technology and equipment) are also likely to be a growing focus for Australian trade.[36]

Both BHP and CRA were considering joint venture activity in the mining sector in the RFE. BHP, together with Amoco and Hyundai, put in a bid for the Sakhalin-2 oil and gas project. But differences between Moscow and the local authorities ensured that the project went to another company. BHP subsequently transferred its interests to other parts of Russia.[37] The company has, however, increased its presence in Magadan in recent years and has obtained a license to explore for minerals there.[38] CRA had a technology agreement with the Siberian Geological Survey for the exchange of information on petroleum exploration techniques, and an understanding with the Far Eastern Research Institute of Raw Materials for discussions on mineral resources in the region.[39] The company did carry out some exploration in Siberia, but ran into problems with property rights and what it described as: 'an extremely difficult operating environment'. Following the merger of CRA with its major shareholder, the UK based RTZ, it ceased exploration activities in Russia altogether.[40]

Steel: The Amurstal plant, situated in Komsomolsk-na-Amure (Khabarovsk oblast), was the only steelworks in the RFE. By 1993, it was heavily in debt, owing US$31.9 million to the Nizhne Amursky Commercial Bank alone. The bank insisted on opening up the plant to foreign investors, and the Australian companies Asia-Pacific and Parmelia Resources stood ready to lease capacity.[41] It was then revealed that Amurstal in fact owed US$56 million to the banks, suppliers and to their own workers. By this stage, the potential Australian investors had been joined by Hankook Steel of South Korea. It was proposed to split Amurstal in two, with one joint venture (with the Australian companies) taking over the newer divisions, while the other (with the South Koreans) would lease the older section.[42] Negotiations broke down in 1995 over the amount of money the foreign companies were prepared to put up.[43] The Australians withdrew from the joint venture, but acquired 10 per cent of Amurstal itself. However, in May 1996, Amurstal was placed in receivership. Nizhne Amursky Bank wanted it sold to foreign companies to pay off its debts (not least to them), but the Russian courts decided otherwise.[44] The Australians packed up and left.

Gold: According to Glenn Whiddon of Pinnacle Associates (an Australian merchant bank, based in Moscow and advising two Australian gold mining companies in Siberia):

> We believe gold is waiting for a huge jump start. Everything is now set for a major push in the Russian gold industry ... The first wave of Australian interest here peaked some time ago. Now there is another wave.[45]

Part of that 'first wave' was the Australian company, Star Mining. Whether its experience constituted a 'peak', however, is open to question.

The Sukhoi Log deposit of gold (and possibly platinum) is located in the Bodaibo district of the Irkutsk region. Discovered in 1961, its potential was proved in 1980, earning a Lenin prize for the six geologists who proved it. The Soviet state company Lenzoloto began preparation work to exploit the site in the 1980s. It was estimated that the production cost per ounce would be below that in similar Russian deposits (for example, RTZ/CRA's potential site at Svetlinskoye), and that Sukhoi Log would yield 40–60 tons of gold annually until the middle of the next century.[46] After the Soviet collapse and the end of state financing, Lenzoloto and the Irkutsk regional authorities sought outside help – and found Star Mining. The company, with its team of Australian and South African geologists, metallurgists and engineers, had to obtain the co-operation of no less than eleven Russian engineering, mining and metallurgical organisations in order simply to prepare a feasibility study. Eventually this was achieved, and agreement was reached with Lenzoloto in 1992 to form a joint stock company to exploit Sukhoi Log.

By 1994, however, the Irkutsk regional authorities had decided that the Star/ Lenzoloto agreement had not taken enough account of the region's right to a share in the profits. They declared that the agreement breached Russian privatisation legislation – and they gained support for this view from within the Presidential Administration, the Ministry of Justice and the Procurator's office. They managed to block further work on the site. The Russian government set up a special commission to sort out the conflict.[47] In May 1995, the Federation Committee for the Management of State Properties finally granted a licence to Star and Lenzoloto under which Star would hold 34.9 per cent of the shares, the Russian government, 38 per cent, the employees, 17 per cent (and presumably the region the other 10 per cent – DL). Star would invest US$250 million by mid 1996. It was proposed that by late 1996, the open pit at Sukhoi Log would start operation.[48] In its first quarter report for 1996, Star reported substantial progress in the verification of the ore body and plans for computer-based analysis of resources. US$250 million had by this stage been committed.[49]

But opposition lingered on. In May 1995, the newspaper *Rossiiskiye Vesti* had questioned the reputation of the Australian company and speculated as to why there had been no international or domestic tendering process for the exploitation of Sukhoi Log. The article hinted at some kind of underhand deal between Star and Lenzoloto.[50] Worse was to come. Petr Mostovoi was the Russian government representative at Lenzoloto before becoming first deputy chairman of the State Property Committee. At a meeting at the Procurator General's office in July 1996, he was accused of helping Star acquire their interest in Sukhoi Log at a substantial discount. His accuser, Yuri Chaika (first deputy Procurator General) went on to say that the State Property Committee was one of the main centres of government corruption, and to allege that Mostovoi had cost the state a huge sum of money by allowing Star to buy its shares at an artificially low price.[51] Mostovoi was arrested and prosecuted over the privatisation of Lenzoloto and another company, Rybinskie Motory.

The corruption allegations did not affect Star's investment directly, but they did revive Moscow's interest in the project. By this stage, the chairman of Lenzoloto's Board of Directors was Boris Yetskevich – who was also first deputy Minister of Natural Resources. He announced in early 1997 that Lenzoloto would in fact form a subsidiary company (Sukhoi Log Mining Company) to mine Sukhoi Log. Star meanwhile would withdraw its interest in Lenzoloto, but would have a 'pre-emptive right' (first option) to buy 49 per cent of the subsidiary. For this privilege, Star would have to pay US$50 million to settle some of Lenzoloto's debts, make a commitment to invest another US$200 million and provide banking guarantees for a further US$500 million.[52] All of which Star did.

This further re-organisation and demonstration of good (investment) faith did not extract Star from the complicated embrace of Russian politics and competing interest groups. In March 1997, the Higher Arbitration Court granted the protest lodged by the Procurator general against the irregularities in the privatisation of Lenzoloto. The Court concluded that the government officials concerned had not observed the correct legal procedures for denationalisation, and had therefore deprived the workers of their rights to concessions and involvement in management.[53] Nevertheless, Premier Chernomyrdin signed a government order in June which, according to Yatskevich, 'essentially legalises the company and had initiated the reversal of the situation' [i.e. the Higher Arbitration Court ruling]. He said that the premier's decision confirmed that 'the joint stock company exists and has not been liquidated'.[54] Lenzoloto had survived – but what of the Sukhoi Log Mining Company and its operations? Under the same government order, developments on this score depended on negotiations between the shareholders and the Irkutsk authorities. Star warned that additional funds would not be released until the shareholders had made up their minds. The majority of the shareholders started negotiations with the Irkutsk administration on the possible surrender of their licence to mine Sukhoi Log, subject to compensation.[55] The Irkutsk administration finally decided to re-tender for the development of gold deposits in Sukhoi Log on the basis of conditions that they promised to announce early in 1998. They had failed to provide them by March and said that they would not be ready for a further six months.[56]

A number of other companies had now discovered that the Sukhoi Log project was an attractive investment proposition. Foreign competitors included De Beers, Barrick Gold (Canada) and a large US company represented by the law firm of Baker and McKenzie.[57] But there were also a number of Russian companies showing interest: Menatep, Rossiiskii Kredit, Uneximbank, Eurozloto and Almazy Rossii Sakha. *Kommersant-Daily* pointed out that Uneximbank already controlled the obast's Kovyktinsk gas deposit, and were it to gain control of Sukhoi Log it would have considerable power over the oblast administration (3 April 1998).

The Irkutsk administration had, in fact, been overly pessimistic in their time frame for the new tender conditions. They managed to send a list to the Ministry of national Resources in April 1988. It demanded US$50,000 for the preliminary geological data, US$50 million to be paid to Lenzoloto for work 'it has already done', and 5 per cent of the mine to be owned by the oblast. These conditions were considered harsh, given that it was now known that the gold content of the ore was relatively low, that platinum deposits were unconfirmed, and that the world market price of gold was also relatively low.[58] In the survey conducted for this paper in March 1998, Star Mining confirmed that it was likely to withdraw from the project – and from the RFE.

However, the 1998 financial crisis opened the prospect of asset selling by the Russian government and the reduction of costs for prospective miners. There was, therefore, a renewed interest in Russia's gold deposits. A number of Canadian corporate geologists turned up at Sukhoi Log, replete with payments for any local officials willing to back their bid in the new tendering process. Rio Tinto was also expected to make a return to the area as a bidder for Sukhoi Log. Star's strategy meanwhile had switched to a consideration of legal challenges to the various decisions of regional and federal authorities, and to the possibility of taking action against the successful bidder.[59]

Services: Australian companies have provided services in aviation (Australian Jet Charter to the Sakhalin-2 project) and software (currency exchange in Vladivostok).[60] Australian Telstra (Telecom's semi-privatised successor) has, since 1992, contracted with Rostelecom to provide investment capital and build the necessary infrastructure to modernise international telecom services in the RFE. In 1993 this involved building a satellite earth station on Sakhalin to route international calls through Sydney. In 1996 Telstra commenced construction of an enhanced system to provide reliable communications for companies going into Sakhalin for investment and exploitation purposes.[61]

Upgrading port facilities has also constituted an important aspect of Australian service exports to the RFE. P&O Australia took up a 25 per cent share in a joint venture company (along with Sea-Land Services (US) and the Port Authority) to take over and upgrade the Vostochny international container terminus. Vostochny is the major eastern rail terminus of the Trans Siberian Railway.[62]

Further involvement in port upgrading has resulted from Australia's exports of bauxites to Russia. In 1994 these were worth between $70 and 90 million (the precise figures were confidential). Bauxites are transported to Vostochny and Vanino ports, and then to smelters in Siberia (including the Bratsk smelter, which is the largest in Russia). In 1995, Comalco and Alcoa agreed with the Far Eastern authorities to upgrade the bauxite handling facilities at the two ports in order to increase the amount of bauxites handled and to speed its delivery to the smelters. The export and processing of bauxite combines Australia's advantages as a raw material supplier with the energy price advantages of the Siberian producers.[63]

Australian Business Attitudes towards Pacific Russia

In general terms, the structure of foreign trade and their traditional export orientation make Australia and Russia competitors in raw materials markets and natural trade partners in agricultural commodities' markets. However, because of the underdevelopment and technological backwardness of many Russian mining enterprises, there are also good prospects for Australian investments in the area of primary industries.

These factors have led to the concentration of Australian business interest towards Pacific Russia in two major areas: trade and mining investment. In the early 1990s, immediately after the disintegration of the Soviet Union and the start of market reforms in Russia, there was a significant increase in Australian business interest towards Russia. Business trips to Pacific Russia became frequent and discussions on a number of possible investment projects were started.

However, very soon the initial euphoria had started to give way to growing pessimism. Australian trade with this region of Russia was seriously undermined by the increasing decline in population's living standards, when the majority of Russians could not afford to purchase imported foodstuffs and consumer goods, not at least on a daily basis. At the same time, many mining investment projects never materialised because of continuing political, economic and legal instability in Russia, which made any investment there a highly risky business.

In the post-Soviet period trade and financial flows between Australia and Russia were extremely unbalanced due to the fact that only few of commodities that were produced in Russia could find a market in Australia. At the same time, an acute crisis in the Russian agriculture had stimulated growth of food imports and ensured a stable, albeit small, volumes of Australian food exports to Russia. In general, Australian exports to Russia, and to Pacific Russia in particular, were significantly higher than its imports from the area (see tables above). It was hoped that general economic relations between the two countries would become more balanced with the growth of Australian investment in Russia, but this did not happen.

Consequently, the number of Australian companies active or interested in developing their business in Pacific Russia was constantly falling during the last few years. Since 1995–96 the majority of business operations between Australia and Russia were carried out by just a handful of companies. At the same time the general business interest in the region became extremely low.

In the framework of the current research project, we have carried out a survey of Australian companies, which have been or continue to be active in Pacific Russia. The results of this survey are presented in *Table 14.9* below. The total number of companies that were surveyed was ten, which amounted to between a third to a half of all Australian companies involved in business operations in Pacific Russia. Eight of these companies had an independent status, while two were subsidiaries of larger companies. Six companies were based in Victoria and three in New South Wales. Four of the surveyed companies were large (with a total turnover of more than US$1 bn in 1995/96), three – medium (turnover between US$100 mln and US$1 bn) and the remaining three – small (turnover of less than US$100 mln). These latter figures corresponded to employment levels: four companies employed a total of over 1,000 people, three – between 100 and 1,000 and three – less than 100 people.

The nature of business of surveyed companies reflected the general pattern of Australian business interest towards Pacific Russia. Six companies were exporters, two were involved in mining business, and one each listed as main business profile transportation and manufacturing.

In general, four companies assessed their business in Pacific Russia as profitable and prospects as good, while two companies said that they suffered losses there and three stated that prospects for their business in the region were very poor (*Table 14.9*). At the same time, only two companies stated that they had an intention to expand their business operation, while three said that they intended to terminate their business in Pacific Russia in the near future. All of the surveyed companies have listed legal and economic problems as the main disincentives for business in Pacific Russia. Political and financial considerations came second, while logistic problems were stated as the least important for business.

Table 14.9 Australian Business Attitudes towards Pacific Russia: A Survey (March–May 1998)

Total surveyed	10
Assessment of business prospects in Pacific Russia	
Good	4
Very poor	3
No answer	3
Main discentives for business in Pacific Russia (priority number)	
Legal	1–2
Economic	1–2
Political	3–5
Financial	3–5
Logistic	4–5
Profitability of investment in Pacific Russia	
Yes	4
No	2
No answer	4
Overall success rate of business operation(s) in Pacific Russia	
Very good	2
Good	2
Fair	2
Total failure	2
No answer	2
Future plans in Pacific Russia	
Expand	2
Maintain	2
Terminate	3
No answer	3

The results of this survey have confirmed other findings of this research. Internal developments have become a major stumbling block for a normal operation, let alone expansion, of any business in Russia. Legal chaos, economic decline and the consequent falls in living standards of the population have distracted many foreign businessmen, including Australians, from investing or trading with Russia. Until Russia sorts out its internal problems chances for the growth of Australian business interest in Pacific Russia will continue to remain slim.

CONCLUSIONS

From the above it would seem clear that Australian trade and investment with the RFE remains patchy and hesitant in most areas outside those of wheat and processed food. Given the well-documented disasters of Amurstal and Sukhoi Log, it is little wonder that Australian investors are wary of any long-tern involvement in the region. In 1997, Robert Purves, of the Hong Kong-connected White Tiger Investment Company attempted to raise capital for investment in Russia. 'For an investor,' he enthused, '[Russia] is a fabulous story. Russia has an educated population, with literacy above 90 per cent and huge natural resources.' But the attempt failed. Purves concluded: 'The Australian market has not caught up with changes in Russia in the past two years'.[64]

Possibly the reason for the success of processed food is that its export is a simpler kind of operation than exploration for, and exploitation of mineral wealth (much the same could be said of services). Food exports have not encountered the problems of property rights, the size of the shares of conflicting interest groups, and jealous eyes being cast at the resource once the initial work has been done – all of which have plagued the minerals area. Nevertheless, dangers lurk for Australian food exporters. One of them is Russian protectionism. In 1994, Russian dairy farmers demanded and received a 15 per cent tariff on butter imports.[65] 'Disguised' protectionism (dubious 'quarantine' on vessels and the like) has also been noted.[66] Furthermore, even for food exporters, there is the constant threat of default on the Russian side.[67]

Perhaps the only safe way in the volatile markets of the RFE is to specialise in nothing at all – except trade itself. This has certainly been the experience of the Rangedale company based in Victoria. Rangedale started in the Far East before the Soviet collapse counter-trading Soviet steel for foodstuffs and medical equipment, providing the steel to Japanese, Taiwanese and Chinese companies which wanted Rangedale to take the market risk on their behalf. This lasted until 1994 when the amount of Russian steel available for export declined. In 1995 the company was selling rams to Russian sheep breeders, followed by Australian-made production technology to raw materials producers. Various Australian producers of dairy producing plants, abattoirs, dry cleaning plants and warehouses used Rangedale as a middleman, because the Russian market was too difficult and/or dangerous for them to pursue directly. Rangedale's extremely flexible approach has enabled the company to pick its way through the obstacle course constructed by the trade licensing authorities and the Russian Central Bank. 'As long as Russia is a risky place' said managing director Neil Kermeen, 'We stay in business.'[68]

NOTES

1 Michael J. Bradshaw and Nicholas J. Lynn (1996) *Resource-Based Development: what chance for the Russian Far East?* The University of Birmingham: Russian Regional Research Group, Working Paper Series No. 4, pp. 25–7.

2 A heavy blow was struck to Australia's food export prospects by the US donation on 16 November 1998 of 1.5 million tonnes of wheat and 100,000 tonnes of other food stuffs, together with a $US600 million loan to finance Russian purchases of meat, milk powder and other goods. Negotiations were also underway with the European union for a similar deal (*Business Review Weekly, 23 November 1998*).

3 Senate Standing Committee on Foreign Affairs, Defence and Trade, (1990) *Perestroika – Implications for Australia-USSR Relations*, Canberra, p. 83.

4 Ibid. p. 38.

5 Ibid. p. 83.

6 Ibid. p. 84.

7 Geoff Raby (1992) *Australia and North-East Asia in the 1990s: Accelerating Change*, Canberra, p. 9.

8 Ibid. p. 69–70.

9 Ibid. p. 22.

10 Paul Keating, '*The Perilous Moment: Indonesia, Australia and the Asian Crisis*'. Speech delivered at the University of New South Wales, 25 March 1998.

11 East Asian Analytical Unit, Department of Foreign Affairs and Trade (1996) *Pacific Russia: Risks and Rewards*, Canberra: EAAU, p. 1.

12 Ibid. p. 82, 83.

13 *New Europe*, 19–25 May 1996.

14 *New Europe*, 26 May–1 June 1996.

15 Department of Foreign Affairs and Trade, *In the National Interest*, Canberra, 1997, p. 10.

16 *New Europe*, 28 July–3 August 1996.

17 *ARNISBIC Newsletter*, 13 February 1998.

18 *New Europe*, 28 July–3 August 1996.

19 *Itar-Tass*, 29 August 1996.

20 *Business Review Weekly*, 12 August 1996.

21 *Business Review Weekly*, 7 September 1998.

22 Pavel A. Minakir and Gregory L. Freeze (eds) (1996) *The Russian Far East: an Economic Survey*, Khabarovsk: RIOTIP, pp. 234–43.

23 Vladimir Tikhomirov, (1997) 'Food Balance in the Russian Far East', *Polar Geography*, 21 (3), p. 178.

24 *Perestroika – Implications for Australia-USSR Relations*, p. 82.

25 *Risks and Rewards*, pp. 25–6; *New Europe*, 28 July–3 August 1996.

26 *New Europe*, 11–17 August 1996.

27 *Interfax Food and Agricultural Report*, 6 September 1996.

28 *Risks and Rewards*, p. 26; *DFAT Country Economic Brief: Russia April 1995*, p. 27.

29 Meat Research Corporation (195) *The Meat Market in the Russian Far East*, Project M.633, Melbourne.

30 *Risks and Rewards*, p. 26, 28, 30.

31 *Business Review Weekly*, 7 September, 28 September and 23 November 1998.

32 *DFAT Country Economic Brief*, p. 27.

33 *Business Review Weekly*, 20 February 1995, p. 54.

34 *Risks and Rewards*, p. 27; *DFAT Country Economic Brief*, p. 27; *New Europe*, 2–8 June 1996.

35 *New Europe*, 2–8 June 1996.

36 *Risks and Rewards*, p. 26–7.

37 *Risks and Rewards*, p. 29.

38 *Interfax Business Report*, 1/9/97.

39 *Perestroika – Implications for Australia-USSR Relations*, p. 89.

40 *New Europe*, 23–29 June 1996.

41 *Interfax*, 17 May 1995.

42 *Russian Far East Update*, September 1995.

43 *Russian Far East Update*, January 1996.

44 *Open Media Research Institute Daily News Report (OMRI)*, 6 May 1996.
45 *Business Review Weekly*, 29 April 1996.
46 *Rossiiskiye vesti*, 1 May 1995.
47 *Interfax Mining Report*, 11 February 1994
48 *Rossiiskiye vesti*, 1 May 1995.
49 *New Europe*, 4–10 August 1996.
50 *Rossiiskiye vesti*, 1 May 1995.
51 *OMRI*, 9 July 1996; *ORT*, 8 July 1996.
52 *Interfax Business Report*, 27 February 1997 and 31 March 1997.
53 *Interfax Business Report*, 7 April 1997.
54 *Interfax Business Report*, 9 June 1997.
55 *Business Review Weekly*, 7 July 1997.
56 *Kommersant-Daily*, 19 March 1998.
57 *Kommersant-Daily*, 19 March 1998; *Business Review Weekly*, 24 November 1997.
58 *Kommersant-Daily*, 3 April 1998
59 *Business Review Weekly*, 16 November 1998.
60 *Risks and Rewards*, p. 28.
61 *New Europe*, 11–17 August 1996
62 *Russian Far East Update*, November 1996; *Business Review Weekly*, 29 May 1995.
63 *Interfax Business Report*, 27 August 1996; *New Europe*, 14–20 July 1996; *Risks and Rewards*, p. 29.
64 *Business Review Weekly*, 31 March 1997.
65 *Business Review Weekly*, 20 February 1995.
66 *Interfax Business Report*, 2 September 1997.
67 See *Australia/Russia/NIS Business Council Report*, 6 June 1997 on IFP's problems in this regard.
68 *Business Review Weekly*, 10 June 1996; *New Europe*, 23–29 June 1996.

Chapter 15

The Russian Far East: prospects for the new millennium

Michael J. Bradshaw

INTRODUCTION

This final chapter develops a number of scenarios to explore the possible future development of the Russian Far East. Mention has already been made of the Federal Programme for the Economic and Social Development of the Far East and the Transbaikal for 1996–2005. This document was a major policy statement about the future economic development strategy for the RFE. The period of 1996–2000 was identified as a period of stabilisation during which economic decline ends and the preconditions for recovery are created. That period has now passed by and the best that can said is that the economy of the region now shows signs of having 'bottomed out'. The period of 2000–2005 was seen as the time frame for economic recovery. The Programme presented a solid analysis of the problems facing the region, but failed to explain adequately how the funds would be found and how and by whom the plan should be implemented. For the purposes of the current analysis it is important to note that according to the Federal Programme economic recovery is to be based on two factors:

- The Russian Far East and the Transbaikal at the present time and in the future represents one of the largest remaining resource bases in Russia. That natural resource potential can be used to meet the needs of the economy and also to generate income from exports for both the federal and regional budgets.
- The 'economic geographic position', including the border-coastal location, is favourable for the development of economic relations with the countries of the Asia-Pacific region. This factor can compensate for the situation of the distancing of the region from the Russian market and increasing transportation costs.

278

KEY DETERMINANTS OF GROWTH

As the analyses presented in this book have shown, during the 1990s the region suffered a deep-seated recession and a retreat in the primary resource-producing sectors. Furthermore, the region's enterprises clearly lack the capital to modernise and reorient their production and foreign investors have met with little success when trying to assist in the process of economic restructuring. If the region's economic recovery is to be tied to the exploitation of its natural resources to satisfy external markets, what factors are critical to the success of such an export-based development strategy?

The national economic situation

Despite being distanced from the domestic market, the RFE is heavily dependent, and will remain dependent, upon support from the Federal Government. Only economic recovery in Russia more generally will enable the Federal Government to meet its financial obligations to the region and may even allow more substantial funds to be allocated to the development programme. Since the 1998 financial crisis the Russian economy has benefited from increased export revenues, due to high oil prices, and import-substituting industrial recovery, due to rouble devaluation making import too costly. However, the current 'economic recovery' is extremely fragile and until there is substantial new investment in the Russian economy it is premature to talk of the kind of sustainable economic recovery needed to breath new life into regions such as the RFE. President Putin and his government will need to create the conditions necessary for investment to attract the billions of dollars of capital flight now sitting in offshore bank accounts.

The foreign trade regime

A more open economy and an improved environment for foreign investors is also critical to national economic recovery and to the prospects for the RFE. In large part it is the Federal Government and State Duma in Moscow that sets the legislative framework for foreign investors. But, as we have seen from our country case studies, the regional administrations in the RFE could do much more to attract foreign investment. The RFE is only just waking up to the fact that in the era of globalisation capital is footloose and no one will invest in the RFE unless they can gain a return on their investment (this is also true of private Russian investors).

International commodity and financial markets

As a resource-exporting region, the RFE is vulnerable to the boom and bust cycles of supply and demand. In international terms, the region is likely to be a 'high-cost' producer making it particularly susceptible to price fluctuations. Continued economic growth in Asia-Pacific is essential to provide a market for the RFE's resources, but the RFE will continue to face stiff competition from other suppliers. The supply of energy to China would seem to be one area where the RFE has potential advantages, but even here there is competition from East Siberia and Kazakhstan. Even then there is no guarantee of access to markets at prices that will return a profit. Cooperation with foreign MNCs, with exploration and development expertise and marketing experience, will make gaining a foothold in new markets much easier. Thus, the Sakhalin oil and gas projects and the Kovytka gas project not only need a resource that can be delivered and a market that can consume, they also need global partners, in the form of MNCs, banks and international lending agencies that can supply the necessary financing and access to technology.

Inter-regional cooperation

It is essential that the regions that comprise the RFE learn to work together to expand their economic relations with the APR. At one level they are in competition with one another; however, they are also dependent upon each other. In a context where the Federal Government has limited funds, local cooperation in the pursuit of an export-oriented development strategy will benefit the entire region. For example, the port cities are dependent upon freight generated in their hinterlands. At the same time, plans for industrial restructuring aim to reorient industry in the south to the needs of the resource industries in the north and offshore. Despite what their politicians may think, no region can go it alone.

Centre-periphery relations

At the same time as inter-regional cooperation is required, a clear demarcation of responsibilities and revenues between the Federal Government and the oblast-level administrative units is required. At present the local state cannot sustain the increased burden that has been placed upon it by the federal centre. The current asymmetries between the Republics and the rest are divisive and serve to undermine the federal system. In the run up to the 2000 elections, President Putin made clear his intentions to bring order to centre-region relations in Russia. If the regions of the RFE were to cooperate with one another and present a united front, they would surely strengthen their bargaining position vis-à-vis any newly empowered federal centre. Otherwise, Moscow will simply continue its strategy of 'divide and rule', rewarding regions who support the Moscow line and punishing those that don't. The fact that the electorate of the RFE and the region's elected representatives are not entirely pro-Putin does not bode well for a more beneficial relationship with Moscow.

Political relations with the APR

Given the importance attached to increased integration with the states of the APR, positive political relations are essential. Moscow needs to create a constructive environment within which local contacts can flourish. Neither the policy makers in Moscow, nor the local politicians in the RFE, can develop relations independent of one another. Russia's foreign policy in the region shapes what is possible at the local level, however, developments at the local level can serve to reinforce and promote good relations. Russia must accept that its involvement in the APR is likely to be judged by its economic performance and not the extent of its firepower, which is just as well given the current state of the Pacific Fleet!

SCENARIOS

Three scenarios are presented below in tabular form (see *Table 15.1*):

- *Boom* represents the successful pursuit of a resource-based export oriented development strategy and increased integration with the APR;
- *Muddling Through* represents a continuation of the present situation with the RFE failing to develop its export potential but managing to avoid further economic decline; and,
- *Bust* represents further economic decline, the collapse of the region's economy and increased isolation from the APR.

CONSEQUENCES

This section summarises the potential consequences for the RFE of the Boom and Bust scenarios presented above. This appraisal relates four dimensions of the future development of the RFE: the economy, the level of equality (within the region and in relation to Russia), the demographic situation and international relations.

Boom

Economy: Successful economic recovery based on the expansion of resource exports to the APR, together with substantial FDI and the development a resource processing industries. Thus, a greater amount of 'value added' is retained within the region, which increased the level of employment and thus the size and purchasing power of the local market. This leads to a further 'multiplier' in the economy as opportunities arise to supply and service the core resource sectors.

Table 15.1 Scenarios for the future development of the Russian Far East

Bust	*Muddling Through*	*Boom*
National Economic Situation		
Continued economic depression, prolonged payments problems, little effective restructuring, continued reliance upon resource exports and failing federal subsidies.	A 'bottoming out' of economic decline with selective economic recovery. Limited signs of new economic growth which is highly selective in terms of branches and regions of the economy.	Slow and steady economic recovery. Effective economic restructuring and the growth of new sectors and regions.
Foreign Trade Regime		
Closed economy, hostile to foreign investment (FI). Re-imposition of state control over foreign trade. Increased protectionism and import substitution. Failure to join WTO.	Ambivalent attitude towards FI, failure to create an attractive environment for FDI. FI restricted to a small number of large resource and manufacturing projects involving major MNCs. Protracted negotiations over WTO membership.	Open economy with a coherent and transparent foreign trade and investment regime that protects the right of investors. Domestic enterprises encouraged to participate in foreign trade. Membership of WTO etc.
International Commodity Markets		
Recession in the APR and increased competition squeezes the RFE out of resource markets. Depressed prices reduce profitability of exports. Little interest from MNCs in developing resource potential of RFE.	Selected opportunities remain as a supplier of 'unprocessed' raw materials. Limited FDI in new projects, but emphasis on production rather than processing.	Continued economic growth in the APR and the emergence of China as a new market creates new opportunities for resource exports from RFE. MNCs attracted to FDI in both resource production and primary processing.
Inter-regional Cooperation		
Increased conflict and rivalry between regions, no resolution of the non-payments problem, duplication of infrastructure problems with investors able to play one region off against another. The regional economic association collapses.	Continued reliance upon the federal centre to resolve non-payments problems. Limited cooperation on mega-projects, such as Sakhalin oil and gas. The regional economic association remains little more than a 'talking shop'.	Economic recovery provides a solution to the non-payments problems. Effective cooperation with joint development of infrastructure and agreement on inter-regional specialisation. The regional economic association presents a united front to Moscow and potential investors.

(Continued)

Bust	Muddling Through	Boom

Centre-periphery relations

Bust	Muddling Through	Boom
Increased conflict between the centre and the regions, non-payment of federal taxes causes fiscal crisis and the collapse of the federal system. Regions left to fend for themselves on the basis of the financial resources at hand. Federal Government abdicates responsibility for resolving regional problems and the Federal Program for RFE and Trans-Bakal is forgotten.	Continued lack of clarity between the centre and the regions. Individual regions continue to make special deal with the Federal Government. Crisis management response by the Federal Government to problems as and where they arise. The Federal Government fails to provide funds to implement the programme for the RFE and Trans-Bakal.	Clear demarcation of revenues and responsibilities between the centre and the region through a functioning federal system. Increased cooperation between the regions and the centre. The Federal Government shows a strong commitment, backed up by funds, to implement the programme for the RFE and Trans-Bakal.

Political relations with the APR

Bust	Muddling Through	Boom
Breakdown of discussion about the territorial dispute with Japan. Russian support for North Korea alienates South Korea. Increased illegal Chinese immigration in the RFE triggers border disputes. The US withdraws financial and technical support because of increasing nationalist policies and the failure of market reforms. The disengagement of the RFE from the APR.	No resolution of the territorial dispute with Japan, just an agreement to disagree. Financial problems sour relations with South Korea. Relations with China pay scant attention to events in the RFE as China rejects the idea of relying upon imported energy. The US judges economic support on purely financial grounds. The RFE fails to develop effective economic linkages with the APR.	Resolution of the territorial conflict results in substantial Japanese Government assistance and an influx of Japanese FDI in the RFE. Financial problems with South Korea are resolved and Russia supports unification. Energy supplies from the RFE play a major role in improved relations between China and Russia. Fearing a loss of opportunity, the US steps up support for US companies investing in the RFE. Substantial FDI and foreign trade with APR and increased integration of Northeast Asia.

Equality: Economic growth is concentrated in the southern border and coastal regions, but the closure of many northern settlements and the movement of people to the south reduce levels of inequality within the region. Socio-economic indicators in the south of the region are well above the national average, but the north requires substantial federal support to sustain its social infrastructure.

Demography: New employment opportunities and improving standards of living stabilise the population in the south and attract new workers to the region. The spatial redistribution of the population insures the effective occupation of those regions bordering China. A certain amount of migration from China is allowed to occupy certain segments of the labour market, thus compensating for the shortage of domestic labour in the economy. The emptying of the north is unavoidable, but creates major social and cultural problems for the indigenous populations that remain.

International relations: Economic recovery brings with it new linkages with neighbours in Northeast Asia and the Asia-Pacific region (APR) more generally. The RFE is widely accepted as part of Asia-Pacific and the growth of Vladivostok is symbolic of the region's new status.

Bust

Economy: Continued economic decline and depression results in the collapse of the region's economy, only isolated mining and forestry projects remain profitable, the manufacturing and food processing industries in the south cease to function and the energy system falls into disrepair. Foreign investors stay away and only the fishing industry is able to maintain foreign trade activity, but the proceeds from this are largely kept offshore.

Equality: Those regions that have resources are relatively prosperous, but the majority of the region is severely depressed; socio-economic indicators for the majority of the region are substantially below the Russian average and the entire region requires substantial Federal support.

Demography: The population of the RFE continues to decline, not just in the north, but also in the major cities of the south. The continued loss of younger and more able people aggravates the growing labour shortages and creates an increasingly elderly and dependent population. Increased immigration from China results and causes tensions.

International relations: The 'ineffective occupation' of the RFE causes problems for Moscow and influences its foreign policy towards the APR. Increased isolation and the development of a siege mentality (back to the garrison mentality) spark conflicts on the border with China and in territorial waters where foreign fishing boats encroach. Moscow is forced to strengthen its borders and finance the modernisation of its forces in the RFE. This time the emphasis is upon protecting territorial integrity rather power projection into the Pacific. The material and moral collapse of Vladivostok, despite increased military expenditure, is symbolic of Russia's failure to benefit from increased trade with the APR.

CONCLUSIONS

So where is the RFE now? I first conducted this scenario-building exercise in the autumn of 1997. At that time, I was persuaded to be optimistic in my assessment of the situation and concluded that the region was on the positive side of 'muddling through'. Not long after, four interrelated events forced me to become more pessimistic: the Asian crisis, the decline in energy prices, the Russian economic crisis and the seeming inability of the new Russian Government to come up with a strategy for dealing with the situation. Now, as I read through the economic dimensions of the bust scenario it all seems horribly familiar. With the Yeltsin era over and President Putin in power in the Kremlin, it remains to be seen is whether or not Russia will adopt a more introspective and/or combative foreign policy. It is possible that President Putin's vision of Russia's role in the world will be more 'eurocentric', less concerned with relations with Asia. If so, this will be bad news for the RFE. The analysis presented in this book suggests that President Yeltsin, and before him President Gorbachev, did much to build positive diplomatic relations between Russia and the APR. The fact that the improved geopolitical environment did not result in economic prosperity is down to the poor investment environment in the RFE, for which the region's political and new business elites are largely to blame, and the turbulence of the international economic environment in the 1990s. As we look back, in terms of the relationship between the RFE and the APR, the 1990s seem a lost decade. It started which much hype and ended in crisis and disappointment. As the Asian economies recover and resource demand picks up, there will be new opportunities to expand trade between the RFE and the APR. No doubt President Putin, like Yeltsin before him, will soon be visiting Tokyo and Seoul to promote investment opportunities in the RFE. However, those opportunities will only be realised if Russia gets its house in order. Politicians and business people in Moscow and in the RFE can do little to influence the international economic situation, but they can create a positive environment in which the region's resource potential can be developed in such a way that is sustainable and that improves living standards for all.

NOTE

This chapter is an updated version of the conclusions presented in Bradshaw, M.J. (1999) The Russian Far East: Prospects for the New Millennium, London: Russia and Eurasia Programme, The Royal Institute of International Affairs, Discussion Paper 80.

Index

For Product Safety Concerns and Information please contact our EU
representative GPSR@taylorandfrancis.com Taylor & Francis Verlag GmbH,
Kaufingerstraße 24, 80331 München, Germany

Printed and bound by CPI Group (UK) Ltd, Croydon, CR0 4YY
08/05/2025
01864399-0004